Armies of the Nineteenth Century:
The Americas

Armies of the Nineteenth Century:
The Americas

1: The Paraguayan War

Organisation, warfare, dress and weapons
252 figures, 60 illustrations, 16 maps

by Terry D. Hooker

Drawings by Ian Heath

A Foundry Books Publication

Series Editor: Ian Heath

First published in Great Britain in 2008
by Foundry Books
24–34 St. Mark's Street
Nottingham
NG3 1DE
United Kingdom
Tel 0115 8413000

Foundry Books is dedicated to furthering the study of all aspects of military history,
and is happy to consider suggestions for new books on
historical military subjects.
If you have an idea or project suitable for our list, please write to
Foundry Books Editorial Office
at the above address.

ISBN 1-901543-15-3

Typeset & digital scanning by Kevin Dallimore

Printed by C&C Offset Printing Co. Ltd.
+44 207 763 5771

Dedicated to my mother and father, Ivy and Ted Hooker

Other books by the same author:
The Armies of Bolivar and San Martin (Osprey 1991)

Published by the South & Central American Military Historians Society:
The Pacific War 1879–1884 (1993)
The Revolt in Texas leading to its Independence from Mexico 1835–36 (1994)
Buenos Aires 1807: A Personal Narrative, by an Officer of the 36th Foot (1995)
The Spanish American War: The Cuban Land Campaign, Order of Battle (1996)
Notes on the Mexican Army 1900–1920 (1997)
Notes on Haiti, 1793–1916 (1998)
Two 20th Century Wars from Latin America: The Leticia Conflict 1932–33 & The Soccer War 1969 (1999)
The Allied Occupation of Vera Cruz, Mexico 1861, from Official British Reports (2000)

Published by the Company of Military Historians:
New Spain & Mexico 1861–1868 (1) (with John R. Elting) (1999)
New Spain & Mexico 1861–1868 (2) (with John R. Elting) (2001)

PREFACE

This book should not be looked upon as a political or social history, although an understanding of these aspects would, I believe, give a clearer insight into why and how Argentina, Brazil, Uruguay, and Paraguay became embroiled in the largest war ever fought in South America. It is, rather, a work covering the military side of the events that took place between 1810–70, with a hint of the political undercurrents that motivated the various wars fought in the region during the same period. Hopefully it will encourage readers to become interested in Latin and Central American military history – a vast field of research largely neglected in both Britain and the United States.

Although I am listed as the author, I could not have contemplated such a project without the help and assistance of many friends, who, during the past three decades, have provided and exchanged information on Latin American military history. Those who I must thank for their co-operation and assistance in the research for this particular volume include José Balaguer, Charles A. Norman, Cristian Fernandez, Alberto del Pino Menck, David Prando, Jürg Meister, Dr Robert L. Scheina, Colonel R. Moreira de Miranda, Ian Sumner, Nick Dore, and Peter Wilson. Some of you will already be aware of the work of José Balaguer, Charles A. Norman, and Nick Dore, from their articles published in the journal *El Dorado*, some of which have been utilised in the writing of this book. I would also like to thank my son James and our friend Ben Young for their help solving various computer problems; Ian Heath for his efforts as illustrator, editor, and co-ordinator of this work; and Bryan Ansell for his faith and support.

Any mistakes in the following pages are my sole responsibility. As much as one would like to have written a perfect book, new information will continue to be unearthed – whether this week or in ten years time – shedding new light on this sadly overlooked era of South American history.

Terry Hooker
March 2008

CONTENTS

Appendices

Bibliography

The Paraguayan War

General area of hostilities 1816–70. *(After Charles J. Kolinski)*

Waged mainly within the triangle formed by the Paraná, Paraguay, and Plate rivers, the Paraguayan War, sometimes referred to as the Triple Alliance War, was more a war of attrition than a 'glamorous' colonial-period conflict – if you can call any war glamorous. Even so, every method of warfare available at the time was utilised, including torpedoes, railways, balloons, and rifled artillery, and experts with the appropriate knowledge were brought in from Europe and the US by both sides. The resultant carnage saw two-thirds of the Paraguayan male population killed or maimed and the remainder left as mere skeletons of their former selves. The Allied armies of Brazil, Argentina, and Uruguay suffered just as badly, but because their available manpower was far greater their casualties represented a much lower percentage of their respective male populations.

How and why could these countries go to war if the cost, not only in manpower but in financial terms, could be so great? Surely a short, sharp series of decisive battles in a period of one to two years should have been sufficient to bring the Paraguayan people to their senses? These are the most obvious questions likely to arise in the minds of people unfamiliar with these countries, the terrain, and South American military history. I hope to be able to offer some explanation of how this became the most sanguine war fought in South America, second only to the American Civil War in being the most bloody conflict ever fought in the Americas.

Although the Paraguayan War itself began in 1864, in order to understand how Paraguay managed to offend three of its neighbours to the extent that they all declared war on her we have to look back, albeit briefly, at the earlier history of this region, starting with the Argentine War of Independence in 1810.

THE BIRTH OF PARAGUAY

The Viceroyalty of Rio de la Plata (created in 1776 by the Spanish Crown from land formerly governed by the Viceroy of Peru) consisted in 1810 of the provinces that would eventually become the independent countries of Argentina, Uruguay, Bolivia, and Paraguay. However, on 25 May 1810 the *cabildo* (town council) of Buenos Aires renounced the Regency of Cadiz, which had, on the abduction of King Ferdinand VII by Napoleon, created a government that waged war against the French and retained control of relations with Europe and Spain's colonial empire. The *cabildo* declared that while it remained loyal to the captive king, it intended to govern its own national affairs rather than be dictated to by mainland Spain. It despatched notices calling for all the provinces to recognise the new government, or *junta*, based in Buenos Aires.

The politicians and citizens of Buenos Aires – sometimes called *Porteños* ('people of the port') – were referred to as 'Centralists' or 'Unitarists', because they wanted the country's power base to be controlled by their own politicians and merchants; while a rival political faction which sprang up at the same time, known as the 'Federalists', consisted of wealthy and/or powerful provincial landowners who considered that their own needs should take priority over those of the metropolis. This is an oversimplification of the situation, maybe, but one that fits. In what is now Argentina, these factions united to defeat the Spanish Royalist forces and thereby won the country's independence. Once that was secured, the power struggles really began.

In the province of Paraguay, Governor Bernardo de Velasco convened an assembly of notables to discuss how they would answer the Buenos Aires *junta*'s demand for recognition and control. Among those present was Dr José Gaspar Rodriguez de Francia. Through this assembly the Governor was able to ratify a united declaration which maintained both fidelity with the Regency of Cadiz and good relations with Buenos Aires. It also formed a *junta* of its own, to organise the defence of the province. The following year (1811) saw an Argentine army under the command of General Manuel Belgrano invade the province of Paraguay and march to within 35 miles (55 km) of Asunción, but on 19 January Belgrano's force of 1,000 men and six artillery pieces was confronted by Velasco with 4,600 men and 16 field-pieces at the Battle of Paraguarí and was forced to retreat. Receiving replacements for his losses, Belgrano regrouped and advanced back to the River Tacuarí, where on 9 March another battle was fought. This time Belgrano's force consisted of 550 infantry, 400 cavalry, and six guns, while the Paraguayans under the command of colonels Manuel Atanacio Cavanas and Juan Manuel Gamarra had 1,680. Belgrano was defeated again, following which the *junta* of Buenos Aires decided that, for the foreseeable future, actions against Royalist strongholds would be limited to the Viceroyalty of Peru and the Banda Oriental (the east bank of the River Uruguay, later to become the Republic of Uruguay), as these two regions maintained offensive forces strong enough to reconquer the newly formed Argentine republic.

After Paraguay's victories over the invading republican army, Governor Velasco – who was also a member of the ruling *junta* – entered into secret correspondence with Portuguese agents in Rio Grande do Sul, believing that the Paraguayan army's Creole[1] officer corps had acted in too friendly a fashion in the terms it granted to the defeated General Belgrano. At the same time a number of plots were unearthed which involved Creole officers communicating with agents from Buenos Aires. The Captain-General of Rio Grande do Sul therefore offered to send a sizeable army to support Velasco, the price for this aid being recognition of the claim of King Ferdinand VII's sister, Carlota Joaquina, to the Spanish throne. When they discovered this plot the Creoles mounted a *coup d'état* and deposed Velasco on 14 May 1811. The old *junta* was then replaced with a more liberal one that proclaimed independence from Spain but refrained from uniting with Buenos Aires. This revolution was directed by Dr Francia, who became a founding member of the new *junta*. Except for just one year, Dr Francia remained in control of the government thereafter right up until his death, becoming first 'Consul', then 'Temporary Dictator', and finally 'Perpetual Dictator', guiding the destiny of Paraguay for the next 29 years. Born in Asunción in 1766, he had obtained his degree as master of philosophy and doctor of sacred theology in 1785 at the University of Cordoba, there being only two 'doctors' in Paraguay at the time. He also owned Paraguay's largest library, containing 250–300 books. In 1806 he had become attorney-general for the province.

When the defeated republican army under General Belgrano retreated, Governor Velasco had ordered the occupation of part of the province of Corrientes on Paraguay's southern border, but within two weeks of Velasco's overthrow Francia and the new *junta* ordered its evacuation, declaring to the Buenos Aires *junta* that Paraguay desired 'nothing more than that her liberty be respected ... She does not meddle and will never meddle in the internal affairs of other provinces'. The only time during Francia's rule when external hostilities could have arisen was in 1832, when the Governor of Corrientes took exception to the presence of Paraguayan troops in the Misiones region, which Corrientes claimed. Francia stood his ground, maintaining Paraguayan sovereignty there.

Francia had also wished to increase trade with Great Britain, which had the naval resources to keep the River Plate open to commerce between the two nations, rather than allowing the warring factions of Argentina, Brazil, and Uruguay to hamper the passage of Paraguayan shipping by means of blockades (mainly of the sealanes around Montevideo). But in 1817 Buenos Aires formally prohibited the importation of tobacco from Paraguay until 'the incorporation of that province with the remaining provinces of the nation'. As a result of this Paraguay lost what had once been an extensive market. Francia therefore ordered that Paraguay's tobacco farmers switch to growing cotton (which until then had to be imported), and in 1820 closed the country's borders to all commerce, whether import or export.

When Brazilian independence was declared from Portugal on 6 August 1822 (though the dramatic declaration by Dom Pedro at Ipiranga on 7 September is better remembered), Francia opened the port of Itapua as a place for trade and diplomatic contact between the two countries. The relationship that developed with Brazil subsequently became so close that the United Provinces of La Plata (as the government of Argentina now called itself) feared that Paraguay might take Brazil's side in the Argentine-Brazilian War (1825–28) raging in the Banda Oriental. However, when Brazilian troops encroached upon Paraguayan territory the port of Itapua was closed.

The friendship between Brazil and Paraguay had resulted from Francia's deep distrust of the United Provinces' foreign policy towards his country, which, although isolated, had maintained internal peace and order, unlike its neighbours. A purely defensive standing army of 5,000 men, with a reserve of 20,000, had been organised to guard its borders, but militarism had no place in Paraguay. To prevent officers from thinking too highly of themselves none were given a rank higher than that of captain; even the commander of a fort was only given the title of 'commandant of a detachment'.

ARTIGAS AND THE BANDA ORIENTAL

Argentina, meanwhile, had decided to leave the province of Paraguay largely to its own devices in the hope that a coup by disgruntled citizens might eventually topple Dr Francia. It was far more concerned with Imperial Spain and, later, Brazil. Ousting the Spanish was achieved with the defeat of General Olañeta at Tumusla in Upper Peru on 1 April 1825 and the surrender of the Peruvian port of Callao on 22 January 1826, through the endeavours of such men as General José de San Martin and General Martin Miguel de Güemes. Argentine troops fought in Chile, Peru, and Alto Peru (Bolivia), while the naval war against Spain was led by an Irishman in Argentine service, Admiral William Brown.

With the Spanish threat removed, Argentina could shift its attention to the Banda Oriental (Uruguay), a region in which both Spain and Portugal had previously jostled for dominance. The Portuguese had founded Colonia in 1682, while the Spanish had founded Montevideo in 1724. For the next 50 years there had been nearly constant friction between the two colonial powers, but in 1777 the Portuguese were finally expelled as one of the conditions of the Treaty of San Ildefonso (signed in 1774), and the province came under Spanish control. However, a strong spirit of local patriotism and self-reliance had developed within its population during the years of unrest, and there was also resentment of the favouritism shown towards Buenos Aires over Montevideo, which had its own port facilities. Consequently when the *junta* of Buenos Aires rebelled against the Spanish Regency of Cadiz the citizens of Montevideo and the surrounding region remained loyal to the crown – whether as a result of the large Spanish garrison stationed there or distrust of the *junta*'s leadership, or both, is open to conjecture. In January 1811 Francisco Xavier de Elío, recently Captain-General, returned to Montevideo from Spain with a Viceroy's commission from the Regency of Cadiz. His authority was rejected by the *junta* in Buenos Aires and Elío therefore issued a formal declaration of war against it on 13 February.

At this time one José Gervasio Artigas was an officer in the *Blandengues* (a mounted corps of frontier guards). Born into one of Montevideo's leading families in 1764, he had fought against the Portuguese and smugglers while also managing his father's *estancia* or ranch at Casupa, thereby gaining the trust and friendship of the local gauchos or ranch-hands. With the return of Viceroy Elío to Montevideo and his preparations for war against the *junta*, Artigas went to join the rebels in Buenos Aires, leaving messages for his friends and fellow ranch owners that he would be back soon, and that they should organise themselves as a fighting force in readiness for his return. On his arrival in Buenos Aires he was given command of two companies that were to become the nucleus of the Oriental army that he was expected to raise. This small force was sent by water to the Banda Oriental while a much larger force was despatched by the slower land route.

The volunteer forces that now joined Artigas had started gathering as soon as word reached them of his joining the rebel cause, and within a month of his return all but Montevideo and its immediate vicinity were in rebel hands. On 11 May, Artigas, with 1,100 men and three cannon, defeated a force of 1,200 troops commanded by *Capitán de Fragata*[2] José de Posadas at the Battle of Las Piedras, and by the end of the month Montevideo was in a state of siege. The Buenos Aires land forces under General Rondeau had meanwhile also arrived to reinforce the besiegers.

Without any sign of relief arriving from Spain, Viceroy Elío sought assistance from the Portuguese court established in Rio de Janeiro (to which it had been evacuated from Lisbon by the British in 1808), urging Ferdinand VII's sister, Princess Regent Carlota Joaquina,

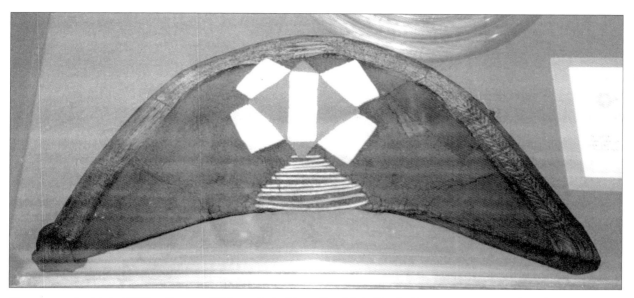

Bicorne worn by Admiral William Brown, c.1828, now in the Museo Naval de la Nación, Tigre, Argentina. Note the style of the cockade, which is white and light blue. (Author's collection)

to retrieve her brother's lost dominions. Consequently in July 4,000 Portuguese troops poured across the border and forced an armistice to be made. Called the October Treaty, this obliged the rebel forces to quit the Banda Oriental and left Viceroy Elío in control, while the Portuguese remained in the province with no clear date set on their departure. The Portuguese finally agreed to leave on 26 May 1812 only after very strong pressure from the British minister in Rio de Janeiro, Lord Strangford, who had been instructed by British Foreign Secretary Lord Castlereagh that he required 'the unconditional evacuation of all the Spanish American possessions' by the Portuguese.

The Portuguese evacuation and a successful coup on 7 October 1812 in Buenos Aires led to the dissolution of the old *junta* and the creation of a new one, this time led by radicals from the Lautaro Masonic Lodge. José de San Martin was one of these, and had assisted in the coup with the mounted grenadier regiment of which he was colonel.

The change of *junta* and the departure of the Portuguese prompted the United Provinces of La Plata (Argentina) to make plans for a second invasion of the Banda Oriental. Meanwhile the troops under General Rondeau had been quickly evacuated via the small port of Colonia within a few days of the October Treaty, leaving Artigas with his followers the choice of either disbanding and returning to their homes – already being harassed by Portuguese troops, both regular and irregular – or retreating to the province of Entre Ríos on the western bank of the River Uruguay as per the treaty. Almost to a man the rural population began to pack up their belongings and families for the exodus to the River Uruguay. Some 13,000 men, women, and children, plus 3,000 soldiers and 400 faithful Charrua Indians, armed with bolas and spears, made this trek, which is commonly referred to as the 'Exodus to Ayui' (the Ayui was a small river along the Uruguay where many refugees camped). So complete was the exodus that, on his entry into the city of Paysandú six months later, the Portuguese commander Souza found it deserted except for two aged Indians.

The October Treaty resulted in a break between Artigas and the *junta* in Buenos Aires, Artigas believing that he and his countrymen had been abandoned to their enemies. While the new *junta* still maintained its Centralist viewpoint, Artigas now began to believe that a Federalist system was the only way forward for both countries. In 1812 the treaty was broken with the *junta* of Buenos Aires, and on 12 April the latter appointed General Manuel de Sarratea 'General in Chief of the army operating in the Banda Oriental'. At this time the Montevideo garrison comprised 3,000 troops, 2,000 militia, and 335 guns, while the coastline was defended by a Brazilian squadron of 14 warships mounting 210 guns (the United Provinces had nothing with which to oppose this squadron).

On his march into the Banda Oriental, Sarratea camped near Artigas' headquarters, expecting Artigas to join forces with him as an element of the United Provinces army. Artigas, however, considered himself commander of an army *allied* with that of Buenos Aires, and in no sense subordinate. This issue remained unresolved, even though both forces united to renew the siege of Montevideo. Finally, in February 1813, Artigas demanded General Sarratea's retirement, and General Rondeau took command of the Buenos Aires troops.

A general assembly met in Buenos Aires on 31 January 1813. This demanded that the Banda Oriental formally recognise its authority and instructed General Rondeau to convoke a provincial assembly for that purpose. Artigas called his own assembly to choose six deputies to represent it in Buenos Aires and issued them with a set of instructions, amongst which were: a demand for absolute independence; a refusal to accept any other system of government than confederation; the division of governmental powers among three distinct branches (legislative, executive, and judicial); full civil and religious liberty; that each province in the Union was to have its own government with full economic autonomy and the power to raise its own armies; and that the capital of the confederation was to be somewhere other than Buenos Aires. It also named Artigas as military governor and president of the Banda Oriental. Unsurprisingly, the *junta* would not allow these demands to be read at the assembly and the six deputies were ejected on the grounds that their election had been irregular. This, of course, was just a legal nicety which enabled the *junta* to extricate itself from an awkward situation that questioned its right to be the centralised governmental body, and would have reduced the United Provinces to an agglomeration of mini-states ruled by petty *caudillos*.[3]

Although still at odds with the *junta* in Buenos Aires, Artigas and his followers remained with the besiegers of Montevideo until the night of 20 January 1814, when he silently withdrew his entire command from the siege rather than come to blows with General Rondeau's troops. All he could hope was that by quitting the siege a very heated situation might have time to cool off, thereby facilitating a satisfactory resolution of the questions at issue. However, once Montevideo was finally captured by General Rondeau, Artigas was forced to start fighting against the United Provinces army in order to liberate the Banda Oriental from outside dominance. His forces were only capable of mounting a guerrilla campaign, but with the defeat of Colonel Manuel Dorrego at the Battle of Guayabos on 10 January 1815 by Artigas' chief lieutenant, Fructuoso Rivera, the backbone of Buenos Aires' control was broken and Artigas was able to take the offensive. Shortly afterwards Montevideo was occupied and the evacuation of the United Provinces' troops began on 25 February.

With Artigas now in control in the Banda Oriental other provinces proclaimed their allegiance to his Federalist form of government; these were Corrientes and Entre Ríos, while Santa Fe and Cordoba also voiced their support. The *junta* of Buenos Aires, now with a new Director, Carlos de Alvear, despatched a force under the command of Ignacio Alvarez Thomas to subdue the province of Santa Fe, but Alvarez Thomas and his command rebelled (the Mutiny of Fontezuelas) and gave their support to the Artigas cause, bringing about the fall of Alvear and his replacement as provisional Supreme Director by Alvarez Thomas. Artigas by this time could look for support from the provinces of Corrientes, Entre Ríos, Santa Fe, Cordoba, Misiones, and Salta, where General Güemes strongly favoured the Federalist political system, being a *caudillo* himself. Artigas' zone of influence therefore stretched from Cordoba to the sea and encompassed an area of some 350,000 square miles (900,000 square kilometres).

1816 was an eventful year. Firstly, the United Provinces finally proclaimed their Declaration of Independence at the Congress of Tucuman on 9 July. Also, following the conclusion of the Napoleonic Wars the preceding year, 15,000 veterans were despatched to Brazil from Portugal to overawe any attempt at revolution, and to be on hand for any future developments that might arise south of the border.

During Alvear's rule in Buenos Aires, prior to the Congress of Tucuman, ways in which a Spanish colonial take-over could be averted had been discussed, and one suggestion had been to allow the entire United Provinces to be handed over to the Portuguese Crown. This was subsequently discussed at Tucuman, but under the *junta*'s new Supreme Director, Pueyrredon, a better plan was envisaged. Rather than the whole of the United Provinces being given to Portugal, maybe the surrender of a small part would suffice to buy immunity for the rest of the provinces. This would allow the main threat from Spain to be given the attention that it deserved. San Martin had established himself at Mendoza in late 1814 and with his friend Pueyrredon (both were Masons) had realised that the only way to defeat the Spanish forces stationed in Peru was by liberating Chile and then mounting a seaborne invasion, rather than by waging a constant guerrilla war in Alto Peru and Salta. The obvious choice of which portion should be given up to Portugal was the Banda Oriental, since the unrest stirred up from there by Artigas' Federalist ideals was a serious threat to the stability of any United Provinces government that wanted to eliminate the threat of Spanish reconquest.

The subsequent Portuguese invasion of the Banda Oriental began in August 1816, while a smaller force was sent into the Misiones province (this was later withdrawn). Artigas' army was no match for the well-equipped and seasoned Portuguese veterans and suffered a series of defeats. Appeals for aid to Pueyrredon prompted offers of assistance, but only on terms which involved absolute surrender to the authority of the United Provinces. On 20 February 1817 Montevideo capitulated to the Portuguese, and yet more defeats followed. Undaunted, Artigas recruited privateers, authorising them to attack any Portuguese or Spanish vessel that they wished. These caused tremendous damage to Portuguese commerce, some prizes even being taken within sight of Lisbon. It is doubtful whether Artigas' exchequer profited financially, but he was only too pleased that somebody was hurting the enemy. In January 1818 the port of Colonia was taken by the Portuguese and by the end of the year only Artigas and Rivera still commanded any forces of consequence. In a desperate bid to hurt the enemy, Artigas invaded Brazil in December 1819 but was forced back to the creek of Tacuarembo, where on 22 January 1820 he made his last stand with less than 2,000 men against a Portuguese force commanded by the Count of Figueira. Heavily defeated, he fled the field with just 300 men, having suffered 800 killed, 150 wounded, and 490 captured.

Leaving the Banda Oriental for the last time, Artigas hoped that his old allies in Corrientes and Entre Ríos would help him in his hour of need, but he received no aid and was hunted down by the *caudillo* of Entre Ríos, Ramirez. Finally seeking asylum from Dr Francia in Paraguay, he crossed the River Paraná on 23 September 1820. He remained in Paraguay thereafter until his death on 23 September 1850, 30 years to the day after crossing the river. Fructuoso Rivera, meanwhile, had finally surrendered to the Portuguese in 1820 and taken service under them.

On 18 July 1821 the Banda Oriental del Uruguay was incorporated into the Portuguese Empire as the Cisplatine Province. With Brazil's declaration of independence from Portugal in 1822 – Dom Pedro I being proclaimed first Emperor of Brazil on 12 October and crowned so on 1 December – the Cisplatine Province became part of the Brazilian Empire.

THE RISE AND FALL OF ROSAS

The United Provinces remained the official name of Argentina until Juan Manuel de Rosas changed it to the Argentine Confederation, which title remained in use until October 1862, when Bartolomé Mitre was elected Constitutional President of an undivided Argentine Republic. However, rather than confuse the reader with these various national titles I will henceforward refer to the country by its more familiar name of Argentina.

Having managed to eliminate the dominance of the Spanish Crown in Latin America with the united forces of Gran Colombia, Peru, and Chile, Argentina now found itself involved with internal power struggles which revolved around the debate regarding Central or Federal systems of government.

Among refugees from the old Banda Oriental residing in Buenos Aires at the time was Juan Antonio Lavalleja, who on 19 April 1825 crossed the River Plate with 32 companions and, landing near the city of Colonia, set about activating the latent resistance movement in the interior. Receiving backing from Argentine politicians and merchants, Lavalleja convened an Assembly that proclaimed union between the Banda Oriental and the Argentine Republic, and, in consequence, by December 1825 Argentina and Brazil were at war for possession of the Banda Oriental. Known as the Argentine-Brazilian War or Cisplatine War, this conflict lasted until 1828. Its most celebrated events were the Battle of Ituzaingo on 20 February 1827 and the many naval deeds accomplished by both the Brazilian Navy and by Argentina's Admiral William Brown, most notably the defeat of a Brazilian river-based fleet at the Battle of Juncal on 9 February 1827. Finally, with both countries facing financial ruin and internal unrest, a British proposal of an independent republic in the Banda Oriental (first mooted in 1826) was accepted in a peace settlement agreed on 27 August 1828. Although the definitive peace treaty was not concluded until 1859, when Uruguay was party to it, the validity of the convention agreed in 1828 was never disputed, although neither party strictly observed it.

With the close of this conflict Argentina became embroiled in a full blown civil war. The returning soldiery under the leadership of General Juan Lavalle, a distinguished officer in both the Liberation War in Peru and the latest Brazilian War, was proclaimed Governor of Buenos Aires on 1 December 1828. His troops stopped the ousted Governor Manuel Dorrego on his way to unite with Rosas and summarily executed him on 13 December. Lavalle then began a campaign against the provinces, whose troops were led by Estanisloa López. Rosas at the same time began to systematically cut off the food supply to Buenos Aires from the interior, thereby compelling Lavalle and his army to evacuate the city. The campaign which followed saw the defeat of Lavalle at Puente de Marquez on 26 April 1829, the destruction of his army (1,900 troops with four cannon against 2,000 troops under López and Rosas), and his enforced exile.

The stage was now set for the rise of Juan Manuel de Rosas, the ablest and strongest of the *caudillos*, who managed to get himself elected Governor of the Province of Buenos Aires and Captain-General, in which offices he was inaugurated on 8 December 1829, at the age of 33. Large numbers of Centralists then emigrated rather than be killed or imprisoned, many going to Montevideo where they formed the nucleus of future opposition to Rosas. The Argentine Army, renamed the *Ejército de la Confederación* (the Army of the Confederation) by Rosas, was composed of three battalions of infantry, four

Argentine General Lucio Mansilla, 1827, a painting by Juan Felipe Goulu in the Museo Histórico Nacional, Buenos Aires. He is wearing fashionable Mameluke-style scarlet overalls, and a dark blue coat with dark blue collar and cuffs, gold lace/bullion epaulettes, aiguillettes, and lace, and gilt metal buttons. His gilt waistbelt buckle bears a design of two shaking hands.

regiments of cavalry, a squadron stationed in Buenos Aires city, and the Militia, composed of a battalion of artillery, a regiment of infantry, and five regiments of cavalry.

By the end of Rosas' third year in office the Centralists had been defeated in all attempts at resistance, and the less dynamic Juan Ramon Balcarce was elected to replace Rosas, who in 1833 began his famous expedition against the southern Indians, during which more than 6,000 natives were killed or enslaved. However, following his return to Buenos Aires in March 1835 Rosas was re-elected as Governor on 13 April, this time with dictatorial powers and for a term of years as long as he considered necessary to restore peace and order. This appointment was confirmed by plebiscite at his own request.

Rosas would reign supreme in Argentina thereafter until the Battle of Caseros in 1852, creating a secret police force named the *Mazorca* which punished disloyalty by means of state terrorism. Its most notorious acts were committed during the months of April and May 1842, when, if contemporary accounts are true, the streets of the capital were awash with blood when Arana, acting as governor in the absence of Rosas, instituted a reign of terror.

The first of two events which helped in the downfall of this famous dictator occurred in September 1845, when French and British fleets blockaded the ports

Juan Manuel de Rosas in the full dress of a brigadier-general, 1845: dark blue tunic with dark blue collar, lapels, and epaulette boards, gold lace/bullion, gilt buttons, and red piping to the lapels and collar. Order sash over the right shoulder is red. Neck order is in gold with pearls. Note the red ribbon attached to his jacket, just visible behind and to the right of the neck order and sash. (Museo Histórico Nacional, Buenos Aires)

prisoners kneel down in a line and while they prayed he would walk behind them, hold their forehead, and, tilting the head backwards slightly, cut their throat from side to side as he would cattle, whispering soothingly as he did so 'A woman suffers more in childbirth'. The reader will therefore understand that during the civil wars of the Rosas period becoming a prisoner was not a viable option. Life was cheap, and a dead enemy was better than a live one. The wounded, of both sides, stood little chance of recovery.

A number of provinces had openly revolted against Rosas, among them Corrientes, which had made alliances against him with Paraguay in 1841 and 1845. Urquiza now united his force with that of Colonel Don Cesar Dias of Uruguay and some of the 12,000 Brazilian troops stationed in Uruguay under the command of Luiz Alves de Lima e Silva, Count (later Marquis and eventually Duke) of Caxias, and marched first towards Oribe at Montevideo, forcing him to raise the siege, and then returned to Argentina. Here his command was increased to 10,670 men from Entre Ríos, 5,260 from Corrientes, 4,240 from the province of Buenos Aires, 3,000 men and six field-guns from Uruguay, and 3,000 infantry, one cavalry regiment, and two batteries of artillery from Brazil (the Brazilian troops being under the command of Brigadier Márquez de Souza). This made a total force of 27,210 infantry, 16,679 cavalry, and 45 pieces of field artillery. These were engaged by Rosas at the Battle of

Argentine General José Felix Aldao in full dress, c.1845, a painting by Fernando García del Molino in the Museo Histórico Nacional, Buenos Aires. Tunic and trousers are dark blue, the jacket collar, cuffs, lapels, turnbacks, and epaulette boards also being dark blue, with the collar, cuffs, lapels, and turnbacks piped in red. Note the design of the trouser gold lace under his left elbow; the epaulette board design; and the red chest ribbon with a lengthy legend inscribed on it. (Museo Histórico Nacional, Buenos Aires)

of the Argentine Confederation and gave aid to the besieged city of Montevideo (of which more will be said later). The French and British squadrons captured the Argentine fleet commanded by Admiral William Brown, who was ordered by Rosas on 2 August 1845 not to aggravate the situation but to give in without firing a shot; this fleet was handed back in 1849. The British ended their blockade in July 1847, the French in June 1848, although the latter continued to blockade ports in Uruguay that supported General Oribe.

Without the plentiful revenues that would normally have accrued from the custom houses of these ports, the Argentine Treasury became so reduced that money to aid the provinces, and therefore to buy their support for Rosas' suzerainty, was not forthcoming. This created unrest in the provinces, which united under Justo José de Urquiza, from Entre Ríos, who until 25 May 1851 had been a leading general under Rosas and had defeated the Corrientes army under General Paz in 1846 and the Uruguayan army under Rivera at the Battle of India Muerta on 27 March 1845. After this battle Urquiza had ordered his 500 Uruguayan prisoners to be beheaded in time to the music of his units' massed bands (possibly only fifes, drums, and bugles). This sort of behaviour towards prisoners of war was not uncommon at the time. In the armies of Rosas and Oribe one NCO in each battalion, called the *degollador*, was employed solely for such work. Armed with a sharp knife, he would have the

Caseros on 3 February 1852, where his own army of 10,000 infantry, 12,000 cavalry, and 56 guns was routed. Rosas then fled to England aboard a British ship, leaving the victorious Urquiza in control of Argentina. He died of pneumonia on his small farm just outside Southampton on 13 March 1877.

Table 1: Orders of battle for the campaign that concluded with the Battle of Caseros, 3 February 1852

(From 'Memorias do Grande Exercito Aliado Liberador do Sul da America 1851–1852', *Biblioteca do Exercito* 151–152, 1950)

Commander-in-chief: Brigadier-General Justo José de Urquiza, Governor of the Province of Entre Ríos.
Major-General: General Benjamin Virasoro, Governor of the Province of Corrientes.

ARMY CORPS

ENTRE RÍOS
Artillery

Horse Artillery, Colonel Piran	230
Light Horse Artillery, Colonel González	200

Infantry

Battalion Entrerriano, Lieutenant-Colonel Lista	250
Battalion Urquiza, Colonel Baravilbaso	600

Cavalry

1st Division, Colonel Urdinarrain	1,300
2nd Division, Colonel Galarza	1,500
3rd Division, Colonel Palavecino	1,100
4th Division, Colonel Dominguez (Pacheco)	600
(Hernando)	700
5th Division, Colonel Salazar	500
6th Division, Colonel Almada	900
7th Division, Lieutenant-Colonel Paso	600
8th Division, Major López Jordan	650
9th Division, Lieutenant-Colonel González	500
San José Division, Lieutenant-Colonel Baron du Grati	300
General's Escort, Colonel Aquilar	250
General's Escort, Colonel Carballo	270
Guardia, Lieutenant-Colonel Reyes	200

BRAZIL
Divisional commander: Brigadier Manoel Márquez de Souza
Adjutant General: Lieutenant-Colonel Joaquim Procopie Pinto Chichorro
Commander, 1st Brigade: Colonel Francisco Felix da Fonseca Pereira Pinto
Commander, 2nd Brigade: Colonel Feliciano Antonio Falcao
Artillery

1st Regimente de Artilharia Volante (Light Artillery), including a battery of Congreve rockets, Major Joaquim José Goncalvos Fontes	360

Infantry
(Formed into two brigades)

No.5 Battalion, Major Manuel Lopez Pecegueiro	510
No.6 Battalion, Lieutenant-Colonel Luis José Ferreira	600
No.7, Battalion, Lieutenant-Colonel José Guilherme Bruce	490
No.8 Battalion, Major Carlos Resin (later commanded by Major Graduado Antonio Vaz do Almeida following Major Resin's promotion)	549
No.11 Battalion, Lieutenant-Colonel Francisco Vitor do Melo Albuquerque	529
No.13 Battalion, Lieutenant-Colonel Martinho Batista Ferreira Tamarindo	452

Cavalry

2nd Regiment, Lieutenant-Colonel Manuel Luiz Osõrio	550

URUGUAY
Divisional commander: Colonel Don Cesar Dias
Infantry and artillery

Light Artillery squadron (six 6-pdrs), Lieutenant-Colonel Mariano Vedia	188
Battalion 'Resistencia', Colonel Juan Lezica	404
Battalion 'Voltijeros', Lieutenant-Colonel Leon de Palleja	406
Battalion 'Guardia Oriental', Colonel José M. Salzona	397
Battalion 'Orden', Major Eugenio Abella	235
Staff Corps, Medical, and Escort	41

CORRIENTES
Artillery

Horse Artillery squadron, Lieutenant-Colonel Gonzáles	130

Infantry

Battalion 'Defensor', Major Martínez	350
Battalion 'Patricios', Major Acevedo	360

Cavalry

General's Escort, Colonel Caetano Virasoro	750
1st Regiment, Colonel Ocampo	680
2nd Regiment, Colonel López	500
3rd Regiment, Colonel Paiba	540
4th Regiment, Colonel Cáceres	600
5th Regiment, Lieutenant-Colonel Bajarano	650
6th Regiment, Colonel Ricardes	700

BUENOS AIRES
Divisional commander: Colonel Don José Miguel Galan
Artillery

Light Artillery squadron, Lieutenant-Colonel Bernardes Castro	110
Light Artillery squadron, Colonel Mitre	100

Infantry

1st Line Battalion 'Federación', Major Rodríquez	430
2nd Line Battalion 'Constitution', Lieutenant-Colonel Toledo	430
3rd Line Battalion 'San Martin', Lieutenant-Colonel Echenaguica	430
4th Line Battalion 'Buenos Aires', Lieutenant-Colonel Tijerina	430

Cavalry

1st Division, Colonel Burgoa	430
2nd Division, Colonel Hornos	600
3rd Division, Colonel Pedro do Aquino (later assassinated)	514
4th Division, Colonel Susbiela	450
5th Division, Colonel Gonzáles	325

Train, remounts, artillery park, invalids, etc	2,000

Grand total	*27,635*

THE ARMY OF GENERAL ROSAS

Division of the North

Coroada, General Echaque	1,000
San Lorenso, Colonel Santa Coloma	1,400
Rosario, Colonel Serrano*	1,600
Ramallo, General Mancilla	2,800
San Pedro, General Mancilla	400
Sarate, General Mancilla	300
Centre Division**	
Rojas, Colonel Cortina	1,000
Guardia de Lujan, General Pacheco	4,200
Barranca Sosa, Colonel Aguilera	600
Southern Division	
Laguna de los Padre, Comandante Cornet	700
Tuyu, Comandante Pedro Rosas	1,200
Salado, Comandante Pedro Rosas	600
Ensenada, Comandante Pedro Rosas	300
Palermo	
Veteranos	6,500
Santos Lugares	
Veteranos	6,200
Cidade	
Convalescencia, Comandante Sancher	500
Recoleta, Comandante Biedma	600
Rancheria (Colegio), Comandante Luis Fentana	400
Serenos e Comissarios Ativos, Comandante Larrazabal	700
Veteranos e Ativos, Comandante Aguilar	800
Veteranos e Ativos, Comandante Ramon Rodrigo	800
Veteranos e Ativos, Comandante Pedro Ximeno	1,100
Restauradores Veteranos, Comandante Rovelo	400
Iluminadores (Policia), Comandante Romero	400
Lieutenants Alcaides (Policia), Comandante Herrera	900
Vigilantes (Policia), Comandante Moreno	200
Passivos do distrito da Cidad	4,000
Passivos do distrito da Fronteira e Campanha	7,000
Grand total	*46,500*

*300 men from this brigade deserted and joined the army of Urquiza; they helped form the 5th Division under the command of Gonzáles.
**This entire division joined Urquiza's forces.

Urquiza was henceforth to become the dominant figure in the Argentine provinces, both during his own presidency and that of his successor Santiago Derqui, even after his defeat at the Battle of Pavon on 17 September 1861, where his army numbered 5,000 infantry, 11,000 cavalry, and 42 pieces of field artillery (compared to General Mitre's 8,550 infantry, 6,000 cavalry, and 35 guns). After the overthrow of Derqui's provincial government, and the resultant ascendancy of Buenos Aires under General Mitre (who had been elected governor of Buenos Aires in 1860), Urquiza continued to be a factor to be reckoned with, retiring to his ranch and from there exercising his functions as governor of Entre Ríos. To help you gauge the scale of his wealth and prominence in Entre Ríos, his ranch in that province had half a million cattle and 20,000 horses. There were other *caudillos* in Argentina who owned ranches on nearly the same scale, and these sustained the political rivalry

Argentine Colonel Santa Coloma, c.1840, a painting by Carlos Revol in the Museo Histórico Nacional, Buenos Aires. His top hat is in buff felt, with a red sweatband. The jacket is red with black lapels, pocket piping, and cuff piping, and gilt buttons. The tan cloth chiripá or apron, with a red floral design along its border, is worn over a white lace undergarment. The shabraque is black with a red border and gold lace embroidery, and there is a red-and-white cover over the saddle. The sword scabbard is steel, the hilt brass with a gold lace sword knot. A red ribbon is tied on his horse's tail. Note the artillerymen just below the horse: they are dressed all in red with white trousers, rather like Figure 51, but without the crossbelts. (Museo Histórico Nacional, Buenos Aires)

between Buenos Aires and the provinces that would still be felt during the Paraguayan War.

URUGUAY TO 1854

Now let us return to Uruguay and the internal conflict which can be traced back to Lavalleja and his 'expedition of the Thirty-Three', as it was called. We have seen that Fructuoso Rivera, Artigas' right-hand man, had taken service with the Portuguese following Artigas' retirement to Paraguay. Declaring to his troops that 'The revolution promises us a paradise and gives us a hell', he had negotiated favourable terms for himself and his men and surrendered to the Portuguese rather than permit the Banda Oriental to be consumed in an inferno. Receiving for himself a brigadier-general's commission and a title of nobility (Baron of Tacuarembo), this permitted the restoration of relative peace to his country – until Lavalleja's expedition.

Just before the commencement of this expedition, Rivera was visited by the then unknown Colonel Juan Manuel de Rosas, who was sent to seek his assistance for Lavalleja. Rivera promised that upon the proper occasion he would put himself in accord with Lavalleja. With this

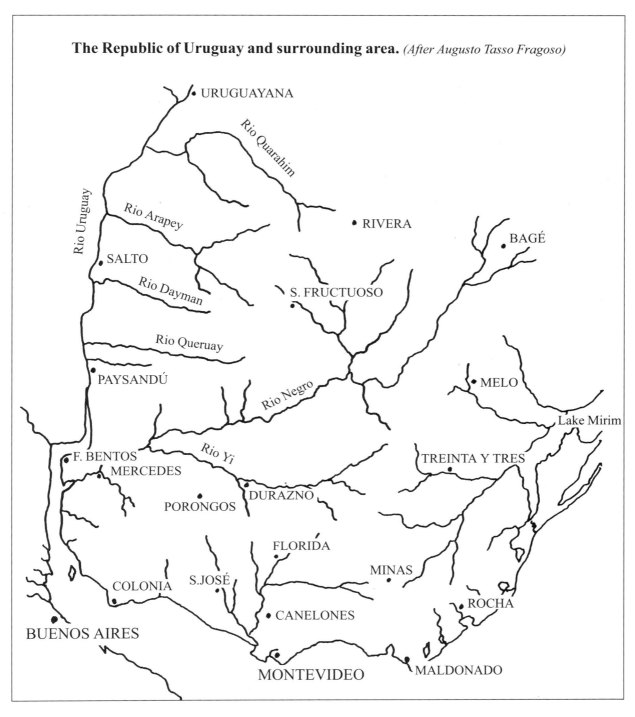

The Republic of Uruguay and surrounding area. *(After Augusto Tasso Fragoso)*

promise, the Thirty-Three were despatched to initiate the war for independence from Brazil. Rivera hastened to the landing area, ostensibly to suppress the rising but actually to join it. Almost immediately the rivalry between Rivera, the future 'Colorado' who wanted total independence, and Lavalleja, the later 'Blanco' wanting unification with Argentina, began to manifest itself. In later years the Colorado party would become socialist in its thinking, while the views of the Blanco party became more conservative.

After Uruguay achieved its independence in 1828 General José Rondeau was selected to become governor of the new state the following year, pending the organisation of a permanent government. He appointed Rivera as Chief of Staff and, later the same year, Minister of War. In 1830 the national assembly met and, deposing Rondeau, named Lavalleja governor in his place. One of his first acts was to remove Rivera from office. Rather than create unrest, Rivera waited for the election of the first legislative body in which was vested the right to elect a president. When this new assembly met in October Rivera was overwhelmingly elected first constitutional president of the republic and was formally inducted into office on 6 November 1830 to serve for a term of four years.

During the relative peace of those four years the

Federalist cavalrymen 1840, from a contemporary print. Note the absence of footwear. (Museo Histórico Nacional, Buenos Aires)

undercurrent of discord between Lavalleja and Rivera remained, with a failed assassination attempt on Rivera's life in June 1832. A planned revolt by followers of Lavalleja, intended to coincide with the assassination, took two months to suppress and compelled Lavalleja to take refuge in Brazil. Rivera had also allowed the many Unitarist or Centralist exiles escaping from the wrath of Rosas to settle in Uruguay. The succeeding president, who took office on 1 March 1835, was Manuel Oribe, a man whom Rivera thought would continue governing in a liberal and progressive democratic style like himself. Alas, Oribe was a follower of Lavalleja, and therefore believed in a conservative and authoritarian system of government. He initiated a commission to investigate the affairs of the preceding government. The financial accounts of Rivera's regime were scrutinised, and his commandant-generalship of the army and sword of honour were both taken from him.

Infuriated by these events, on 17 July 1836 Rivera initiated a new revolution. For identification purposes Oribe decreed that all government soldiers and public employees were to wear a white ribbon or emblem bearing the legend *Defensores de las leyes* ('Defenders of the laws')[4] – whence the term 'Blanco'. The followers of Rivera initially used a pale blue ribbon, but this was found to fade after exposure to the weather, causing it, too, to become a whitish colour. To avoid confusion a red ribbon was quickly adopted in its place, thereby creating the 'Colorado' political party.

The eventual outcome of this revolt was the defeat of Rivera at the Battle of Carpinteria in September 1836. This forced him to flee into Brazil, where he was allowed to regroup and rearm his troops, even though he was involved with some of the revolutionary movements that were then sweeping through the southern province of Rio Grande do Sul (where Garibaldi was fighting before moving to Uruguay). On Rivera's return to Uruguay another battle took place, at Palmar on 15 June 1838, but this time Rivera defeated Oribe and forced him to flee to Argentina to seek aid and assistance from Rosas, who was already angered by the refuge which Rivera had given to his Centralist opponents.

Seeking to again defeat Oribe, who was now in command of an Argentine Confederation army (made up of Rosas supporters fighting against the Northern Coalition of Argentine Provinces and Uruguay), Rivera invaded the Argentine province of Entre Ríos in 1842. Here, at the Battle of Arroyo Grande on 3 December, his allied force of 2,000 infantry, 5,500 cavalry, and 16 guns was defeated by Oribe's 2,500 infantry, 6,500 cavalry, and 18 guns, with a loss to Rivera of 1,600 men killed and 1,400 captured. Oribe's troops suffered only 300 killed and wounded. Following this victory General Oribe, aided by Rosas, entered Uruguay on 12 December. This was the campaign that brought about the nine-year siege of Montevideo, which began on 16 February 1843 and saw British and French fleets aid the besieged city.

Montevideo was defended initially by 5,397 infantry, 140 cavalry, and 600 artillerymen with 23 cannon, but by the end of March the number of guns had been increased to 170 of all calibres. General Oribe's besieging army consisted of 3,500 infantry, 9,000 cavalry, and 500 artillerymen with 30 field-pieces. The city's population at the beginning of the siege numbered some 42,000. Of these 21,854 were immigrants, of whom 10,200 were French, 6,376 Italian, 3,200 Spanish, and 500 British, the remainder being mostly from the Argentine provinces. By October 1843 the city's population had declined to 31,189, only 11,431 of them native Uruguayans, and during 1844 it dropped to 20,000. 'Foreign Legions' of volunteers were created among Montevideo's French, Italian, and Spanish communities, the French Legion – commanded by Colonel Thiebaut – comprising 3,000 men, who had to obtain Uruguayan citizenship in 1844 to appease the French Government. As a result, in April 1844 the French Legion was given the title of the 2nd Battalion of the National Guard. The Italian Legion was commanded by Colonel Garibaldi, who was also given command of a small flotilla of ships, while the Basque Legion of 700 men was commanded by Colonel Brie.

1845 saw the defeat of Rivera's forces at the Battle of India Muerta by the allied troops of Rosas and Oribe commanded by General Urquiza (we have already seen what befell the prisoners taken there), and Rivera was once again forced to flee into Brazil, leaving Montevideo under siege. While he was there the government in Montevideo formally deprived Rivera of his command and forbade him to return to the republic without the express permission of the minister of war, Pacheco y Obes. The Brazilian government then arrested him on the pretext that he had been connected with the earlier revolution in Rio Grande do Sul, although this could have been Brazil's way of excluding him from the diplomatic manoeuvrings then under way between itself and Rosas.

Luckily for Rivera this state of affairs between the two countries did not last very long and he was released in 1846 to journey on to Paraguay. En route, his ship stopped at Montevideo, which was still under siege, and a revolt in his favour broke out against the rule of Pacheco y Obes. This was successful, obliging Obes to leave Montevideo aboard one of the French ships. Again at the head of an army that had managed to gain access to the countryside, Rivera was defeated at the Battle of Paysandú and had to retire with his forces to the city of Maldonado, where he was quickly besieged by General Oribe.

Rather than fighting against this new siege, Rivera thought that he could negotiate peace with Oribe, but as soon as the government of defence in Montevideo learned of his actions it once again, in October 1847, decreed his banishment to Brazil. There he was imprisoned at the behest of the Uruguayan legation in Rio de Janeiro in February 1851, and remained under arrest even when an alliance was formed between General Urquiza, Uruguay, and Brazil. It was only after the defeat of Rosas that he was set free, leaving Brazil to become a member of a governing triumvirate that had been agreed by a convention of leading citizens of Uruguay (called for by Venancio Flores and Pacheco y Obes) to be the most satisfactory method of government for the country. The other members of the triumvirate were Flores and Rivera's old antagonist Lavalleja. Two of the three did not manage to live long enough to participate, Lavalleja dying in October 1853 and Rivera on 13 January 1854 during his voyage to Montevideo, which left Venancio Flores to govern Uruguay.

PARAGUAY AFTER FRANCIA

Dr Francia had died on 20 September 1840, his 29-year rule having created an independent country that, militarily, had limited itself to the defence of its own frontiers. His eventual successor was Carlos António López, who had taken office in March 1841 as one of two consuls, the other being Mariano Roque Alonso. Three years later a presidential system was established to run for a term of five years, and López was elected as Paraguay's first President, a position that he held, by being re-elected at regular intervals, until his death in 1862.

Under López the army and navy came in for extensive development and reorganisation, and a conscription system was introduced whereby in each district a quota of men between the ages of 18 and 30 was chosen by lot under direction of the local magistrate. New

Carlo Antonio López, President of Paraguay 1844–62. (Courtesy of the Arquivo Historico do Exercito, Rio de Janeiro)

This and the next four engravings come from La Plata, the Argentine Confederation and Paraguay *by Thomas J. Page (1859), which describes the exploits of the USS* Water Witch *during its visit to Paraguay in 1853–54, at a time of heightened tension between that country and the United States. This engraving shows five ships of the Paraguayan Navy and the guard outpost at Tres Bocas on the River Paraguay. The* Water Witch *is in the foreground. Note that none of the Paraguayan vessels depicted are steam powered.*

forts were built, especially along the River Apa, to the north of the republic, and in the Gran Chaco region; an arsenal was established with a factory for the manufacture of arms and munitions, plus the Ibicuy foundry where cannon were later produced; and shipbuilding was modernised. A railway from Asunción to Paraguarí was started in 1859 and finished in 1862, while roads began to be widened or new ones built following the erection of bridges. Where bridges were not practicable, ferries were established. All these improvements to the country's internal communication network would be of great assistance in the future war.

Diplomatic relations with both Argentina and Brazil were meanwhile tested to the limit, with Paraguay signing a treaty with the Argentine province of Corrientes, which by implication recognised it as a sovereign state. This was due to Rosas refusing to recognise Paraguay as an independent country. In 1847 a force of 5,000 Paraguayans under the command of the President's eldest son Francisco Solano López (who had been given command of the entire Paraguayan army at the age of 19), was sent into Corrientes, but the army of the latter was defeated at the Battle of Vences by General Urquiza, who at this time was Rosas' right-hand man. Luckily the Paraguayans were not present at the battle and managed to return home, leaving Corrientes to be occupied by the pro-Rosas forces. Strained relations with Brazil, meanwhile, resulted from its attempts to establish two forts on disputed Paraguayan land at Fecho de Morros and Pan de Azucar, but on both occasions they were forcibly ejected. It was only after the defeat of Rosas at the Battle of Caseros in 1852 that Paraguay was able to obtain general recognition of its independence.

With the death of Carlos António López on 10 September 1862 his son Francisco Solano was named as his successor, to serve as provisional president until a general congress could elect a new executive. His subsequent selection by this congress was a foregone conclusion, although an abortive attempt was made to revise the constitution so that the executive's powers could be curbed. However, this failed, allowing Francisco López to rule Paraguay for eight eventful years.

Francisco López had been sent to Europe for two years in 1853 as his country's representative, and here he purchased arms, munitions, and other supplies, and hired a number of foreign experts in various fields of engineering, both commercial and military. It was also on this trip that he met and befriended Elisa Lynch, who would become his wife in all but name, who deserves a book of her own to do justice to her influence on the future Dictator of Paraguay. She remained with him all through the forthcoming war, helping with political and military decisions while also maintaining his morale and fighting spirit during Paraguay's darkest days. López also continued with the domestic improvements begun by his father, which included the first working South American telegraph service and strengthening the fort at Humaitá.

Unlike the two previous rulers of Paraguay, Francisco López looked at the regions beyond his borders as potential zones of influence. With inflated ideas of his prowess as a diplomat, statesman, and general, and with a more modern army than those of either Brazil or Argentina, the possibilities of future advancement for both Francisco and Paraguay appeared particularly good after his successful mediation between the warring

The Paraguayan steamer Pilcomayo, *moored near an outpost on the River Vermejo in June 1854. This ship was built in Asunción, and was used as an exploring auxiliary alongside the USS* Water Witch.

fractions of Buenos Aires and the Argentine Confederation following the Battle of Cepeda. This had been fought on 23 October 1859 between a Confederation army of 10,000 cavalry, 3,000 infantry, and 33 guns commanded by President Justo Urquiza, and the army of Buenos Aires under General Mitre made up of 4,000 cavalry, 4,700 infantry, and 24 guns. Urquiza had won the day, capturing 2,000 prisoners and 20 guns. The Buenos Aires newspaper *El Nacional* declared 'Perhaps General López is destined by Providence to preside over a great nation composed of all the river provinces of the Paraná, Paraguay and Uruguay and guarding the equilibrium with the empire of Brazil.' Maybe López assumed this rhetoric was a prophecy of the future and a green light to unite these provinces in the way that José Artigas had done many years earlier.

The USS Water Witch *steaming past Fort Bourbon (later known as Olimpo) on the River Paraguay, 22 November 1853.*

THE PARAGUAYAN WAR

THE COUNTDOWN TO WAR

Having completed a very basic outline of regional events prior to the Paraguayan War, we have now to unravel how Francisco López mismanaged affairs so comprehensively that three countries dedicated their armies to ending his rule. Although Brazil had border disputes with Paraguay that were still unsettled, the main concerns of the court at Rio de Janeiro were Uruguay and the southern province of Rio Grande do Sul. The latter province was expected to revolt at any time under the control of the separatist General Felipe Netto, a cattle magnate who had made a huge fortune by supplying General Oribe with cattle during the nine-year siege of Montevideo.

In Uruguay, meanwhile, the Colorado presidency of Venancio Flores had been overthrown in August 1855. Manuel P. Bustamante had been elected as the Blanco provisional president, but a civil war had ensued that saw only short intervals of peace. In 1860 Bernardo P. Berro became the next Blanco president. Venancio Flores had, by now, taken refuge in Argentina, where he received support from his old comrade in arms General Mitre, now President, and on 19 April 1863 he returned to Uruguay at the head of an army, in an invasion known as the *Cruzada Libertadora* ('Crusade of the Liberator'). Without the assistance of the Argentine government it is doubtful whether this invasion would have succeeded. Any help that the Blanco party may have hoped to receive from its own Argentine confederalist allies was not forthcoming, memories of having been let down at the Battle of Pavon being still too fresh. On 6 September Francisco López sent a demand to the Argentine government asking it to explain its policy towards Uruguay and its assistance of Flores' invading forces, which could not be looked upon as an act of neutrality. This demand inaugurated the abandonment of Paraguay's old policy of isolation from the Rio de la Plata republics. However, President Mitre ignored these and subsequent demands and instead drew attention to the still unsettled question of the boundary between Paraguay and Argentina. Consequently in February 1864 López ordered a general conscription, which by August had produced an additional 64,000 troops for the army.

In 1864 the Brazilian Emperor Dom Pedro II conceded to the wishes of the representatives from Rio Grande do Sul for intervention in Uruguay and despatched José Antonio Saraiva, backed up by a Brazilian naval squadron, to obtain reparation for injuries suffered by Brazilian subjects. Also at this time Rufino de Elizalde, representing President Mitre, and Edward Thornton, the British Minister in Buenos Aires, proceeded to Montevideo for further discussions with the Blanco government of Anastasio Cruz Aguirre, which was co-operating with Saraiva. At the Conference of Puntas del Rosario on 18 June a peaceful settlement was nearly reached, but at the last minute President Aguirre – having been pressed into a corner by extremist elements of the Blanco party – allowed the peace plan to collapse. After the failure of another attempt to mediate, this time by the Italian Minister in Montevideo (the offers of Francisco López to mediate were declined by both Argentina and Brazil), Saraiva was ordered to present an ultimatum to President Aguirre that was backed up by a Brazilian army on the borders of Uruguay and a Brazilian naval squadron of three men-of-war (under the command of Admiral Tamandaré) stationed on the River Uruguay. This was delivered on 4 August. News of the Brazilian ultimatum resulted in a formal note from the Paraguayan Foreign Minister to the Brazilian Minister in Asunción on 30 August deploring this act of aggression and disclaiming any responsibility on the part of Paraguay for the consequences that might ensue. This boosted the Uruguayan Blanco party's belief that Paraguay would intervene if Brazil invaded.

The Brazilians had hoped to mount a joint intervention with the aid of Argentina, but, with the still powerful General Urquiza being known to favour the Blanco party and being quite capable of moving against President Mitre's government, this did not materialise. However, it was during meetings to discuss this possibility that a secret alliance between Brazil and Argentina, and later Uruguay, was first mooted. Both wished to clip Francisco López's wings and maintain the status quo.

On 12 October 1864 General João Propício Mena Barreto crossed the Uruguayan frontier with two divisions of Brazilian troops, the 1st Division under General Manuel Luiz Osório (1st Cavalry Brigade and 2nd and 3rd Infantry Brigades), the 2nd Division under General José Luís Mena Barreto (2nd and 3rd Cavalry Brigades and 1st Horse Artillery Regiment), a total of 6,000 men. These quickly occupied the capital of the Department of Cerro Largo, Villa de Mello, without a declaration of war being issued. Alas for the Blancos in Uruguay, no Paraguayan troops were forthcoming. The Uruguayan warship *Villa del Saíto* encountered the Brazilian squadron, which opened fire, forcing her to seek shelter at Concordia in Argentine waters. She afterwards attempted to dash past the Brazilian squadron and make for the port of Paysandú, on the River Uruguay, but when in danger of being captured her commander set fire to the ship. When news of this incident reached President Aguirre he broke off diplomatic relations with the Brazilian Consuls, while all treaties between the two governments were burned in public. Brazil reacted by ordering the army under João Propício Mena Barreto already in northern Uruguay to join forces with General Flores against President Aguirre, and to attack both Montevideo and Paysandú. Admiral Tamandaré, with a squadron of one frigate and four gunboats, was instructed to aid in the operations against Paysandú.

When the Brazilian steamer *Marquês de Olinda* docked at Asunción on 11 November it carried a special letter from Francisco López's chief spy in Montevideo, Juan Soto, which contained information about the cargo and passengers it was carrying. This steamer regularly did the trip from Rio de Janeiro to the Brazilian state of Mato Grosso – a journey which at this time was far quicker by boat than overland – but on this occasion its passengers included Colonel Federico Carneiro de Campos, the new Governor of Mato Grosso, while its cargo consisted of new supplies of arms and ammunition for the depleted garrison stationed there. Francisco López was at Cerro León in the north of Paraguay at the time, where a letter

The USS Water Witch *passing the Brazilian fort at Coimbra on the River Paraguay on 27 November 1853; and heading towards the Brazilian outpost of Curumba on the left bank of the river three days later. This was the highest point she reached during her cruise up the Paraguay.*

containing these details reached him by a special train. His instructions to seize the *Marquês de Olinda* were sent back by another special train, but did not arrive quickly enough, for the Brazilian ship had already left harbour that morning. The Paraguayan war-steamer *Tacuarí* was despatched to bring her back to Asunción, and the *Marquês de Olinda* was forced to heave-to on 12 November. Her passengers were taken prisoner and the cargo quickly taken off so that the vessel could be converted into a gunboat for the Paraguayan Navy.

This same day saw the Brazilian Minister in Asunción receive a letter, dated the previous day, that as Brazilian troops had invaded Uruguay, Paraguay would now implement the measures it had hinted at in its letter of 30 August: diplomatic relations between the two countries were severed, and the rivers Paraná and Paraguay were closed to Brazilian shipping. One could say that this is where the Paraguayan War had its beginnings.

President López immediately began to organise a division under the command of Colonel Vicente Barrios from the troops stationed at Cerro León. These were to advance into the Brazilian Province of Mato Grosso. At 12:00 noon on 14 December 1864, this expedition of 3,248 men (the 6th, 7th, 10th, and 13th Infantry Battalions, the 6th being commanded by Major Luis González; a regiment of artillery with three batteries; a battery of 24 Congreve rockets; two squadrons of cavalry; and two companies of sappers), boarded transports at Asunción, which were accompanied by a naval squadron under the command of *Capitán de Fragata* Pedro Ignacio Meza. This comprised the *Igurei*, *Tacuarí*, *Paraguarí*, and *Rio Blanco* (all with five cannon), the schooners *Independencia* (eight cannon) and *Aquidaban* (eight cannon), and two flat-bottomed gunboats each armed with an 8-inch gun, the *Humaitá* and the *Cerro León*. Four other ships joined the squadron later, these being the *Jequi*, *Rio Apa*, *Salto Oriental*, and *Marquês de Olinda*.

This task force journeyed up the River Paraguay to the town of Concepción, where Colonel Francisco Isidoro Resquín was stationed with the North Division of 4,650 men, made up of six cavalry regiments (the 6th, 7th, 8th, 9th, 12th, and one not known), two infantry battalions, and a battery of six guns. From here Colonel Resquín, with a brigade of 1,500 troops made up of two cavalry regiments, an infantry battalion, and an artillery battery, began an overland advance into Mato Grosso. An additional infantry battalion (the 27th) was later despatched to reinforce both advancing columns. Colonel Barrios, meanwhile, continued further upriver with his division. López hoped that the Bolivian President Melgarejo would assist the Paraguayan invasion by despatching a force of his own into Mato Grosso, for at the time this boundary was disputed between Brazil and Bolivia, but no such support materialised.

A fortnight later Colonel Barrios arrived off Nueva Coimbra, an old Portuguese fort situated in the extreme south of Mato Grosso. It was built of stone, with scarps some 14 ft (4.3 m) high, and was sited on high ground about 40 ft (12.2 m) above the River Paraguay, giving it a commanding view of the waterway and rendering it

Painting of President Francisco Solano López c.1864, dressed in a Paraguayan marshal's gala dress uniform: very Napoleon III.

assailable from only one side. A garrison of 142 men with 12 officers was stationed there. After a demand for its surrender was refused, the Paraguayans began a bombardment of the fort on the 27th, while the infantry were landed and set to work cutting a road to the fort through the dense undergrowth of cactuses, bromelias, and other thorny plants that surrounded it. While the besiegers were engaged in this work, the Brazilian armed steamer *Anhambahí* (a British-built vessel mounting six guns), which was moored beyond the fort, managed to gain the range of the working parties and took a heavy toll of them. At 4:00 p.m. on 30 December an assault against the fort was mounted by the 6th and 7th Infantry Battalions, but they received such a heavy fire from musketry and hand grenades as they reached the walls that they had to retreat at 7:00 p.m. after suffering 250 killed and wounded. Later that night the Brazilian Commander, Lieutenant-Colonel Hermenegildo Porto-carrero, decided that further resistance was futile and embarked his troops onto the *Anhambahí* and escaped. On occupying the fort the Paraguayans found that all of its guns – six 12-pdrs and two 32-pdrs – had been left un-spiked and still mounted, and that its store of powder, ammunition, and military equipment had also been abandoned intact.

With the capture of Nueva Coimbra the expedition advanced upriver, meeting with no resistance while capturing the towns of Albuquerque, Tagé, Miranda, Dourado, and Corumbá (the chief commercial town of the province, where an additional 23 brass cannon were captured), so that by the middle of January the southern portion of Mato Grosso was under Paraguayan control.

After the capture of Corumbá, Colonel Barrios despatched two of his steamers – one of them the newly-arrived *Iporá* (or *Yporá*; the name is found spelt both ways) – to follow Brazilian ships fleeing along the San Lorenzo river. The commander of these Paraguayan steamers was Lieutenant Herreros, who was stationed aboard the *Iporá*, this being the faster of them. It soon sighted the *Anhambahí*, which was commanded by Captain Barker, an Englishman, who manned and fired its 32-pdr rear gun without any assistance from his Brazilian crew (or so Thompson states in his *The War in Paraguay*). The Brazilian steamer was eventually boarded, at which Barker and most of the crew jumped into the river and, swimming to the bank, managed to escape despite being shot at from the steamers. Those Brazilians unlucky enough to be captured were killed and their ears cut off and strung together along the shrouds of the *Iporá*, although these were quickly removed by supreme order of the President when the ship docked at Asunción.

The column of Colonel Resquín was meanwhile continuing its advance into Mato Grosso, handicapped by the countryside which at this time of year was flooded by the various rivers and streams. This slowed all movement, and eventually the Paraguayan advance ground to a halt, leaving the capital Cuiabá still under Brazilian control as a result of the waterways leading to it being too shallow for the Paraguayan ships. A number of Paraguayan garrisons were left behind, amounting to some 1,000 men in all, but by the middle of 1865 the bulk of the invasion force had returned home with all of the captured arms and equipment, a large amount of booty and cattle, and 500 prisoners. It is not known how many

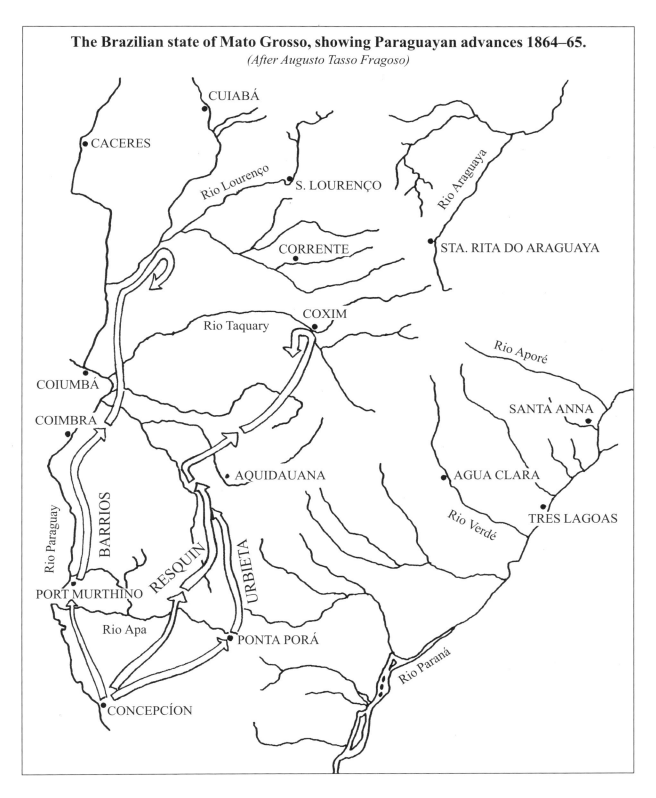

The Brazilian state of Mato Grosso, showing Paraguayan advances 1864–65.

(After Augusto Tasso Fragoso)

diamonds or how much gold was captured, but the flow of these items to the Brazilian capital was depleted through to 1869. Indeed, the importance of capturing the Mato Grosso mines could help to explain why this expedition was given greater importance by President López than the expedition to Rio Grande do Sul via the Argentine province of Misiones, or the formation of an alliance with the Argentine *caudillo* General Urquiza in

the province of Entre Ríos – both of which should have taken place in early December 1864, rather than being left until too late in April 1865.

The small Paraguayan garrisons remained in Mato Grosso until April 1868. Whether the Paraguayan troops mistreated the civilian population is a grey area. If the Paraguayans were ordered by López to seize as much gold and diamonds from the mine owners and their

Paraguayan General Vicente Barrios in frock coat. (Courtesy of the Arquivo Historico do Exercito, Rio de Janeiro).

families as they could, then one can see how acts of torture may have been committed and why owners were arrested. One, the Baron de Villa Maria, managed to escape with a bottle of diamonds in his pocket and, making a cross-country journey to Rio de Janeiro in the record time of 47 days, brought the first news of the Paraguayan invasion to the capital's notice. His two sons were executed when they too tried to escape, while 80,000 cattle and the entire contents of his mansion were taken by the Paraguayans. By contemporary Latin American standards the behaviour of the Paraguayans was neither as good nor as bad as it might have been, but the newspapers of the Triple Alliance soon painted a picture of an army that was despicable, quietly ignoring their own domestic and foreign military excesses over the past 40 years.

Now let us return to events occurring in Uruguay at the same time. The port of Paysandú had a Blanco Uruguayan garrison of 1,200 men and 15 cannon under the command of Colonel Leandro Gomez (his title was Commander General North of the River Negro, which is why he is sometimes referred to as General). Hoping that help from President López would arrive in time, Gomez undertook to defend Paysandú at all costs, even though it had no defences. The attacking forces were under the command of General Flores, with a Brazilian force of

1,200 men under the command of General Netto and a Brazilian naval squadron (made up of the *Araguari*, *Parnaíba*, and *Ivaí*) under the command of Admiral Tamandaré. A small 400-man naval brigade was also organised and landed from these ships. The attack on Paysandú commenced on 6 December 1864, eight days before the Paraguayan embarkation at Asunción that would begin the advance into Mato Grosso. The bombardment and assault lasted throughout the day. Hostilities were suspended the following day at the request of the commanders of several foreign warships (French, British, Italian, and Spanish) in order to convey as many women, children, and non-combatants as possible to a place of safety. When the loading of the ships was completed the bombardment resumed.

On 9 December news of a Blanco relief column commanded by General Juan Sáa reached General Flores, who with the approval of the Brazilian commanders halted the assault (but not the bombardment) and tried to intercept it. No battle ensued, however, as President Aguirre ordered General Sáa to return to Montevideo to assist in the defence of that city. Some ammunition and provisions nevertheless managed to get through to the defenders of Paysandú, although whether from the relief column or a friendly 'neutral' ship is not known; but whatever the source, these supplies helped to maintain the defence. With the return of General Flores the fighting recommenced on 31 December.

By now the city had been reduced to rubble by constant bombardment from land and sea – the 35 guns of the Brazilian 1st Horse Artillery Regiment, for instance, fired 4,000 rounds during the siege. Brazilian reinforcements arrived on 1 January 1865, and on the 2nd the city was carried by assault, forcing Colonel Gomez and what remained of the defenders to surrender.

Atrocities had been committed by both sides during the 35-day siege. One that may well have sealed the fate of Colonel Gomez involved the decapitation of 15 captured Brazilians, whose heads were placed above the defenders' trenches as a gesture of total defiance towards the besiegers. Following their surrender Gomez and another officer, Major Braga, were handed over to Colorado Uruguayan troops under the command of Major Gregorio Suárez (General Flores' third-in-command), who took them into a small garden and promptly shot them in cold blood. It is stated that this act was instigated without the prior knowledge of General Flores. The other survivors of the garrison would have been executed too, but an Argentine colonel managed to intervene on their behalf and saved their lives, though they were all forcibly enlisted into the Colorado army of Flores. The actions of the Brazilian forces on this occasion found few admirers in the other countries of South America, the one notable exception being Argentina, and even here it was only in the province of Buenos Aires that they were regarded favourably (President Mitre was a personal friend of Flores and had extended a large measure of protection to the latter during his exile in Buenos Aires). Although President López of Paraguay retained the sympathy of countries such as Peru, Chile, and Bolivia, which were all opposed to the Brazilian presence in the River Plate region, he could not convert these feelings into material support.

After the fall of Paysandú, the forces under the

command of General Flores and the 1st and 2nd Brazilian divisions under Generals José Luís Mena Barreto and Osõrio united to attack Montevideo, while the squadron under Admiral Tamandaré transported the sick and wounded to Buenos Aires. Having discharged its passengers, the squadron took up positions outside Montevideo. To deter an immediate advance upon the city President Aguirre sent an expedition of 1,500 men under General Basílio Muñoz, with its vanguard commanded by Colonel Timoteo Aparicio, to the eastern section of the Brazilian province of Rio Grande do Sul, a move that took into account the promised Paraguayan invasion of its western section, which never materialised. The Uruguayan expedition crossed the Brazilian frontier near Lake Mirim on 27 January 1865, occupying the town of Yaguarón, but its continued presence in this district could not be maintained and Colonel Muñoz was obliged to retreat after a defeat by a Brazilian force commanded by Colonel Fidelis.

This incursion by General Muñoz did not have the desired effect upon General Flores and his Brazilian allies, for they invested Montevideo with some 14,000 men in February. What it did help do was bring about in Brazil and Rio Grande do Sul the realisation that Paraguay might well decide to invade this southern province, as it had Mato Grosso in December. The

authorities in Rio Grande do Sul therefore called out their 29 battalions of National Guard to help protect the southern border.

President Aguirre, along with all the principal members of the Blanco party and the senior officials of his regime, was forced to flee Uruguay and seek refuge in Buenos Aires.[5] With his departure active resistance ceased. Dr Villalba, President of the Senate, opened peace negotiations with General Flores on 20 February 1865, and on the 22nd Flores entered the capital. Shortly afterwards he was proclaimed President of the Republic – a dictator in all but name – and the Brazilian forces withdrew.

Fears that the Brazilian province of Rio Grande do Sul was threatened were justified, for in early January both Brazil and Paraguay had asked Argentina for permission to cross the province of Misiones rather than use a much longer route around its northern border. President Mitre replied to both requests that the rivers Paraná and Uruguay were open to both parties in the conflict, but that no license could be granted to the belligerents to traverse Argentine territory. A force of some 20,000 Paraguayans was already stationed at Candelaría (situated in a disputed part of Misiones where both Paraguay and Argentina claimed sovereignty) under the command of General Wenceslao Robles, from which

---

Table 2: Brazilian Army in Uruguay 1 February to 1 March 1865

On 1 February the Imperial Brazilian Army stationed in the Republic of Uruguay (Banda Oriental) is recorded thus:

Special Corps	28
Artillery	823
Line Cavalry	998
National Guard Cavalry	2,160
Infantry	2,838
Transport Corps	21
Total	*6,868*

By 1 March the Imperial Brazilian Army stationed at Montevideo and in the surrounding districts had

increased to the following strength:

Special Corps

Generals	2
Staff Corps (1st and 2nd Class)	3
Clergy	7
Medical Corps	17
Superior commanders (temporary brevet brigadiers)	3

Artillery

2 batteries of the 1st Regiment of Horse Artillery	188
1 battalion of Foot Artillery	634
Battalion of Engineers (2 companies)	148

Cavalry

2nd Regiment of Line Cavalry	267

3rd Regiment of Line Cavalry	312
4th Regiment of Line Cavalry	211
5th Regiment of Line Cavalry	215
1st National Guard Cavalry Regiment (*Corpo Provisorio*)	303
4th National Guard Cavalry Regiment (*Corpo Provisorio*)	252
5th National Guard Cavalry Regiment (*Corpo Provisorio*)	369
6th National Guard Cavalry Regiment (*Corpo Provisorio*)	274
7th National Guard Cavalry Regiment (*Corpo Provisorio*)	358
8th National Guard Cavalry Regiment (*Corpo Provisorio*)	266
9th National Guard Cavalry Regiment *Corpo Provisorio*)	306

Infantry

1st Line Infantry Battalion	510
3rd Line Infantry Battalion	335
4th Line Infantry Battalion	526
6th Line Infantry Battalion	411
7th Line Infantry Battalion	431
8th Line Infantry Battalion	430
9th Line Infantry Battalion	501
12th Line Infantry Battalion	427
13th Line Infantry Battalion	362
Garrison corps from Espírito Santo	131
Caçadores of Bahia battalion	424
Police corps from Rio de Janeiro	389
Police corps from Bahia	368
Transport corps	55
	9,465

it was set to invade the Brazilian province, but this would have meant crossing Argentine territory. On 14 January, President López sent another letter to President Mitre, this time requesting permission for his army to transit through the eastern section of Corrientes province. This request was received on 6 February, and Mitre's refusal was sent on the 9th.

What made President López decide to abandon his initial plan and expand it to include the invasion of Corrientes, which would begin in April 1865? Could the initial plan always have been to mount a two-pronged offensive into Corrientes and Misiones – and not, as most Argentine, Brazilian, and foreign diplomats expected, to march through Misiones alone – so as to reach Rio Grande do Sul in early January and therefore be able to help the Blancos in Montevideo and Paysandú? We know that López was in correspondence with a number of influential Argentine *caudillos*, who favoured the Blanco party and regarded any thought of Brazilian interference in their republic as anathema. These were mainly from the provinces of Entre Ríos and Corrientes, among them being General Urquiza, who had earlier suggested to President Mitre that permission be granted for the belligerents to cross Misiones. It could well be that he knew that if this request was refused by Mitre the Paraguayan Army would advance into Corrientes, capture this province – where public opinion was still unhappy about Brazilian involvement in Uruguay and the recent bloody siege at Paysandú – and maybe even cause open revolt in Entre Ríos against Mitre, who had supported General Flores and his Brazilian allies against Paraguay.

Meanwhile, on 28 January General Flores had signed a formal alliance instigated by the astute Brazilian diplomat José Maria da Silva Paranhos, which concluded: 'Finally the undersigned assures the Government of His Majesty the Emperor of Brazil that the Uruguayan Republic from this moment, and with much more reason when it is completely liberated from its present oppressors, will afford to the Empire all the co-operation in its power, regarding as a sacred task its alliance with Brazil in the war treacherously declared by the Paraguayan Government, whose interference in the internal affairs of the Uruguayan Republic is a bold and unjustifiable pretension' (which sounds like the pot calling the kettle black).

If the current scenario led President López to believe that by using the two rivers that ran through Corrientes (the Paraná and Uruguay) he could at one stroke cause a general uprising against General Mitre – whose main backing was based in Buenos Aires province and city – while the River Uruguay advance might generate renewed Blanco support against Flores and his Brazilian allies (as well as providing a base from which to despatch expeditions into the Rio Grande do Sul), why did he leave it so long before ordering these advances? The only reason I can find is that a shipment of arms from Europe to Paraguay was being carried up the River Paraná in the *Esmeralda* and was expected in the city of Corrientes on 3 April. In addition he was trying to raise loans of £200,000 on the international money markets in Buenos Aires, London, and Frankfurt in early February for Paraguay to purchase war-supplies and vessels from Europe. Was it really necessary to send troops into Corrientes city and down the Paraná at this time? It

caused Argentina to unite behind President Mitre – not for long, but long enough to declare war and ally with Brazil and Uruguay.

There had been no threat from Brazilian forces along the River Paraná, as President Mitre had announced his intention to refuse his consent to the Brazilian blockade at Tres Bocas (where the rivers Paraguay and Paraná met), and to insist that the treaty of 1856 be observed. By the terms of this treaty the Brazilians were only permitted to blockade the ports on the Paraguay, and could not impede the navigation of the river. They could therefore only blockade the river as far as the Paraguayan flag was concerned. The British Minister in Buenos Aires reported that four Brazilian gunboats (the *Jequitinhonha*, *Araguri*, *Iguatemi*, and *Ipiranga*) and a brig loaded with coal left Buenos Aires on 5 April. It was supposed that they were going up the Paraná to establish a blockade at Tres Bocas, but they merely sailed to Colonia and anchored there. It would appear that they were waiting for President López to show his hand. Although President Mitre did not wish to see Brazilian ships on the Paraná, he sent the *25 de Mayo* and, later, the *Gualeguay* (initially delayed because it was undergoing repairs) to the city of Corrientes, to watch over events and reassure the Governor of Corrientes, Manuel I. Lagraña, that everything was under control. On 13 April a Paraguayan squadron of five steamers attacked these two ships and then bombarded the city, the Argentine ships being quickly boarded and 49 prisoners taken. The ships were then taken back to Asunción to be repaired and made serviceable for the Paraguayan Navy.[6]

After a small initial bombardment that was aimed at the fleeing seamen, the city of Corrientes surrendered. The Paraguayan steamer *Igurei* was despatched to meet the *Esmeralda*, but she had already been arrested by the Argentine authorities, who had been informed of what had occurred in Corrientes city by Governor Lagraña, who had managed to flee just in time. The *Esmeralda* was sent back to Buenos Aires. If the attack on Corrientes had been delayed by just one day this shipment of arms and munitions might have been in Paraguayan hands.

The day after Corrientes' capture General Wenceslao Robles began to disembark his 3,000 men into the city. Later the same day 800 cavalry arrived, having crossed the Paraná at Paso la Patria. Most of the future correspondence between the army in Corrientes and Paraguay would go via this route. Each day brought fresh reinforcements from Paraguay, allowing General Robles to leave a force of 1,500 men (the 3rd and 24th Infantry Battalions) and two small guns under Major Martínez to garrison the city, while he advanced slowly southward along the eastern bank with the bulk of his force.

THE WAR BEGINS

President López had wanted to delay the delivery of his actual declaration of war to President Mitre until 3 May 1865. In fact the Argentine President heard about it on 17 April, the day after he learnt about the surprise attack on Corrientes. A call for men to serve in Argentina's newly raised National Guard battalions was urgently issued, while a Paraguayan Legion under the command of Colonel Iturburu and Colonel Decoud was formed from dissidents living in Buenos Aires. News of the Paraguayan advances also forced General Urquiza's hand, and he now gave his full support to a united Argentine offensive against the Paraguayans, with a promise to raise an army among his followers in Entre Ríos. If we believe Thompson's memoirs, the first Argentine battalions left Buenos Aires on 24 April heading for Corrientes, which is a very quick response, so one has to suppose that they were regular units rather than National Guard. The formal Argentine declaration of war was approved by decree on 9 May.

The famous Treaty of the Triple Alliance was signed on 1 May 1865, with ratifications exchanged on 12 and 13 June. Although the terms were to have been kept secret, the British Minister in Montevideo, H.G. Lettsom, obtained a copy and transmitted it to London, where it was published in a parliamentary Blue Book early in 1866, so that its contents would be publicly known. It is worth reading, although I will not include it here due to the dictates of available space. News of the treaty and what it would mean to Paraguay, and not just to its ruler, if the Allies should win united the population behind López, for some 60,000 square miles (150,000 square km) of what was regarded as national territory would be taken by Argentina and Brazil. It therefore appeared to Paraguayans to be a war not against López, but rather an expansionist war against the Paraguayan nation.

By 11 May General Robles had reached the River Riachuelo, but here he was opposed by 2,000 Argentineans from the 1st, 2nd, and 3rd Line Battalions, the *Legión Militar*, and the 2nd Squadron of the 1st Horse Artillery Regiment (100 men and six guns), under the command of General Wenceslao Paunero. On receiving this news President López ordered the Paraguayan troops to feign a withdrawal, while at the same time sending a cavalry division to outflank the Argentine force. To avoid being caught in this trap, but with six Brazilian and two Argentine steamers under the command of the Brazilian Admiral Francisco Manoel Barroso da Silva close at hand, on 19 May General Paunero embarked his troops and proceeded up the Paraná until opposite the city of Corrientes. Realising that its garrison had been drastically reduced, it was decided to seize the city. A force of 800 men was initially landed, composed of the *Legión Militar* with two line companies and the light company of the Argentine 2nd Infantry Battalion, three companies of the Brazilian 9th Line Battalion, and 39 artillerymen from the 1st Artillery with two 6-pdr guns. These units were commanded by Colonel Charlone, assisted by Colonel Rivas and Colonel Rosetti.

On 25 May the positions outside the city were assailed under cover of a naval bombardment, and before nightfall it had been captured, but not without severe fighting that involved pushing the defending Paraguayan troops back 1,000 yds (900 m) to a stone bridge of one round arch that led into the city. This was defended at great cost, with the bridge being riddled by shot from the Allied ships' guns. The loss to the Paraguayans was 400 killed and wounded, besides 80 prisoners, one flag, three cannon, and a quantity of arms and equipment. The Allies' losses were three officers and 69 men killed and 19 officers and 160 men wounded. The following day outposts reported that a large Paraguayan force was approaching the city. This was composed of the 37th and 42nd Infantry Battalions and the 9th and 31st Cavalry Regiments. General Paunero then re-embarked his troops plus any civilians that wished to escape and steamed

Officers and men of Argentina's Legión Militar *battalion photographed c.1865. They still wear their unit's fashionable berets, which were replaced by kepis later in the war.* (Courtesy of the Archivo General de la Nacion, Buenos Aires)

downriver to a section of the province not invested by the Paraguayans. The Paraguayan commander at Corrientes, Major Martínez, was later shot at Paso la Patria on the orders of López, for allowing the city to be recaptured by the Allies.

After this raid by General Paunero, President López issued a proclamation on 2 June that he was assuming personal command of Paraguay's forces in the field. He began with a plan to destroy the Allied fleet. This called for the co-operation of the Paraguayan Navy, under the command of Captain Meza, and a small land-based force under the command of Lieutenant-Colonel José Maria Bruguéz which included a battery of rifled 12-pdrs. The latter contingent would establish itself some distance below the anchorage of the Brazilian fleet, to hinder its expected fight with the Paraguayan fleet. Although the smaller and less well-equipped Paraguayan fleet did attack, the tactics that López had ordered his Navy to use enabled the Brazilians to capitalise on the flawed Paraguayan plan once the initial panic had subsided. Ordered to attack at daybreak, or as near to it as possible, the Paraguayans were to pass their anchored enemy guns blazing, and then turn back to either capture the Brazilian vessels (by pairing off ship to ship for an all-out boarding attack) or drive them further up the river. This gallant but bizarre plan resulted from López's unwillingness to allow any of the enemy ships to escape. His fleet was therefore not allowed to drive the Brazilian ships downstream into the sights of the waiting artillery battery in case they should slip past. The chance of running some of them aground while still preserving the majority of the Paraguayan Navy for future operations was therefore lost.

THE BATTLE OF RIACHUELO

On the morning of 11 June 1865 the Paraguayan fleet of eight river steamers and seven *chatas* began its descent towards the Brazilian fleet. These *chatas* were a kind of double-prowed punt, strengthened with sundry layers of two-inch (50 mm) planking, undecked, drawing a few inches of water and standing hardly a foot and a half (0.45 m) above the surface. They were 18 ft (5.5 m) in length, with just room enough for men to serve a single gun, either a 68-pdr or an 80-pdr 8-inch cannon. This was placed in the centre of the vessel on a circular brass swivel set in a depression a foot (0.3 m) in depth that allowed the cannon to be turned to any point of the compass. A *chata* could thread the shallow streams either by poling or under tow and was able to inflict considerable damage upon an ironclad, but was itself hard to hit as only the gun muzzle appeared above the surface of the water. Later on individual *chatas* often singly engaged the whole Allied fleet. A Brazilian Admiral would subsequently call them *monitores de madeira* or 'wooden monitors'.

One Paraguayan gunboat, the *Iporá*, broke down before sighting the enemy, the resultant delay causing the remaining ships to reach the Brazilian fleet – anchored in line on a curve in the river – shortly before 9:30 a.m. The river at this point was nine miles (14.5 km) wide overall, but was divided into several channels which flowed past eight substantial islands. The distance between the opposing fleets was some 1,800 yards (1,650 m). Moving with difficulty as a result of having to tow the *chatas* into a 4-knot current that increased the fleet's speed to 12 knots, the Paraguayans' preliminary manoeuvre was nevertheless carried out without too much damage being sustained, the Brazilians being thrown into panic by the enemy's sudden appearance. However, they quickly recovered, not least because the vast majority of the Paraguayans' opening round of fire fell short, and the Brazilians' return fire became organised and accurate.

Their panic turned to amazement at the steadiness with which the Paraguayans steamed past under fire.

The *Jequi* was put out of action during this first engagement, while the tow cable of one of the *chatas* was severed, leaving it to drift. On board the Paraguayan flagship, Captain Meza reviewed the plan of attack in open water as ordered by President López, and decided instead to remain in the narrow channel where Lieutenant-Colonel Bruguéz's artillery column was situated, and wait for the Brazilians to attack. He therefore stationed his vessels below Bruguéz's batteries and positioned the remaining *chatas* in the gaps between the ships. Another plan of attack, suggested by Mr Watts, the chief engineer of the *Salto Oriental*, was waved aside. This had proposed sinking two of the smaller Paraguayan vessels below the fleet and then attacking the enemy with the heavy guns aboard the *chatas* until there was time for the land-based guns to be moved to a position overlooking the Brazilian ships.

It was now discovered that grappling irons for boarding the enemy ships had been forgotten or mislaid, but Captain Meza did not consider this to be significant, as his direct orders were to capture enemy shipping 'with or without grappling irons'. There was no specific plan of action for the ensuing engagement other than to fire at each Brazilian ship as it came through the narrow channel towards the Paraguayan positions. The first ship to come through was the *Belmonte*, which was soon holed below the waterline and was run aground to save her from sinking. The next to appear was the *Jequitinhonha*. Trying to turn and engage the land-based batteries this too ran aground on a sandbank after its pilot was killed.[7] At the same time the *Parnaíba* came through the channel, followed by the Brazilian flagship, the *Amazonas*, and the remainder of the fleet.

Three Paraguayan ships attacked the *Parnaíba*, for it was seen to have steering difficulties. These were the *Tacuarí*, followed by the *Marquês de Olinda* and *Salto Oriental*, which arrived in time to see the *Tacuarí* come alongside the *Parnaíba* with a boarding party of some 12 men standing atop its paddle-box, which was on the same level as the Brazilian warship's deck rail (this gives a good idea of the physical differences between the ships of the opposing fleets). However, all of the Brazilian ships

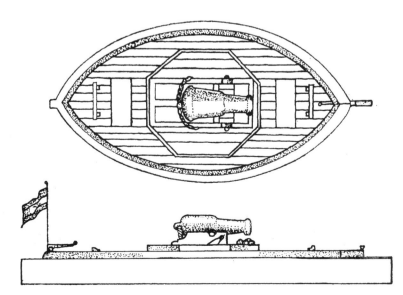

A Paraguayan chata or flat-bottomed gunboat as drawn by Sergeant Mario of the Brazilian Engineers, from the first edition of General Augusto Tasso Fragoso's História da Guerra entre a Trílplíçe Aliança e o Paraguai.

Table 3: Orders of Battle, Riachuelo (11 June 1865)

Brazil

2nd Naval Division
Commander: Francisco Manoel Barroso

Amazonas (flagship): wooden paddleship 'frigate'; armament 1 x 70-pdr Whitworth, 1 x 68-pdr (muzzle-loading), 4 x 68-pdrs (breech-loading); tonnage 1,050; engine 300 hp. Commander: *Capitão de Fragata* (Commander) Teotonio Raimundo de Brito. Complement: 15 naval officers, 134 sailors, 10 army officers, 303 soldiers.

Iguatemi: wooden gunboat; armament 3 x 68-pdrs (muzzle-loading), 2 x 32-pdrs (breech-loading); tonnage 406; engine 80 hp. Commander: *Primeiro-tenente* (First-Lieutenant) Justino José de Macedo Coimbra. Complement: 6 naval officers, 90 sailors, 7 army officers, 110 soldiers.

Parnaíba: wooden corvette, constructed 1860; armament 1 x 70-pdr Whitworth, 2 x 68-pdrs (muzzle-loading), 4 x 32-pdrs (breech-loading); tonnage 602; engine 120 hp. Commander: *Capitão-tenente* (Lieutenant) Aurello Garcindo Fernandes de Sá. Complement: 9 naval officers, 132 sailors, 8 army officers, 114 soldiers.

Araguari: wooden gunboat; armament 2 x 68-pdrs (muzzle-loading), 2 x 32-pdrs (breech-loading); tonnage 415; engine 80 hp. Commander: First-Lieutenant Antonio Luiz von Hoonholtz. Complement: 8 naval officers, 81 sailors, 6 army officers, 77 soldiers.

Mearim: wooden gunboat; armament 3 x 68-pdrs (muzzle-loading), 4 x 32-pdrs (breech-loading); tonnage 415; engine 100 hp. Commander: First-Lieutenant Elisiario José Barbosa. Complement: 7 naval officers, 118 sailors, 4 army officers, 63 soldiers.

Ivaí: wooden gunboat; armament 2 x 68-pdrs (muzzle-loading), 4 x 32-pdrs (breech-loading); tonnage 415; engine 100 hp. Commander: First-Lieutenant Guilherme José Pereira dos Santos. Complement: 7 naval officers, 118 sailors, 4 army officers, 63 soldiers. (Although forming part of this Naval Division and sometimes listed as having participated in the battle, the *Ivaí* had actually been despatched to a different part of the river and was not present.)

3rd Naval Division
Commander: *Capitão de Mar e Guerra* (Captain) José Segundino de Gomensoro

Jequitinhonha: wooden paddleship 'corvette', constructed 1853; armament 2 x 68-pdrs (breech-loading), 6 x 32-pdrs (breech-loading); tonnage 647; engine 130 hp. Commander: Lieutenant Joaquim José Pinto. Complement: 11 naval officers, 109 sailors, 6 army officers, 160 soldiers.

Beberibe: wooden paddleship 'corvette', constructed 1853; armament 1 x 68-pdr (muzzle-loading), 6 x 32-pdrs (breech-loading); tonnage 637; engine 130 hp.

Commander: Lieutenant Joaquim Bonifacio de Santana. Complement: 9 naval officers, 169 sailors, 8 army officers, 138 soldiers.

Belmonte: wooden paddleship 'light corvette', constructed 1860; armament 1 x 70-pdr Whitworth, 3 x 68-pdrs (muzzle-loading), 4 x 22-pdrs (breech-loading); tonnage 602; engine 120 hp. Commander: First-Lieutenant Luíz Maria Piquet. Complement: 7 naval officers, 102 sailors, 3 army officers, 92 soldiers.

Ipiranga: wooden paddleship; armament 1 x 30-pdr (muzzle-loading), 6 x 30-pdrs (breech-loading); tonnage 325; engine 70 hp. Commander: First Lieutenant Alvaro Augusto de Carvalho. Complement: 8 naval officers, 98 sailors, 4 army officers, 61 soldiers.

Itajai: wooden gunboat; armament 2 x 68-pdrs (muzzle-loading), 2 x 32-pdrs (breech-loading); tonnage 415; engine 80 hp. Commander: First-Lieutenant Tomaz Pedro de Bittencourt Cotrim. Complement: 6 naval officers, 90 sailors, 4 army officers, 100 soldiers. (Although forming part of this Naval Division and sometimes listed as having participated in the battle, the *Itajai* had actually been despatched to a different part of the river and was not present.)

Paraguay

Commander: *Capitão de Fragata* (Commander) Pedro Ignacio Meza

Tacuarí: ironclad paddleship 'corvette', constructed in England 1855, two funnels; armament 2 x 68-pdrs, 6 x 32-pdrs; tonnage 448; engine 120 hp. Commander: *Capitão de Fragata* Pedro Ignacio Meza.

Paraguarí: wooden paddleship 'corvette', constructed in England; armament 2 x 68-pdrs, 6 x 32-pdrs; tonnage 730; engine 130 hp. Commander: *Teniente de Marina* (Second-Lieutenant) José M. Alonso.

Igurei (*Ygurey*): wooden paddleship, launched 15 May 1862, two funnels; armament 3 x 68-pdrs, 4 x 32-pdrs; tonnage 650; engine 130 hp. Commander: *Capitán de Corbeta* (Lieutenant-Commander) Remigio Cabral.

Iporá (*Yporá*): wooden paddleship, launched 1856; armament 4 x 14-pdrs; tonnage 300; engine 80 hp. Commander: *Teniente de Marina* (Second-Lieutenant) Martínez.

Marquês de Olinda: wooden ex-Brazilian paddleship; armament 4 x 18-pdrs; tonnage 300; engine 80 hp. Commander: *Teniente de Navío* (First-Lieutenant) Ezequiel Robles.

Jequi (*Jejuy*): wooden paddleship, launched 1859; armament 2 x 18-pdrs; tonnage 200; engine 60 hp. Commander: *Teniente de Marina* (Second-Lieutenant) Aniceto López.

Salto Oriental (*Salto del Guaira*): wooden screw-driven vessel, launched 1857; armament 4 x 18-pdrs; tonnage

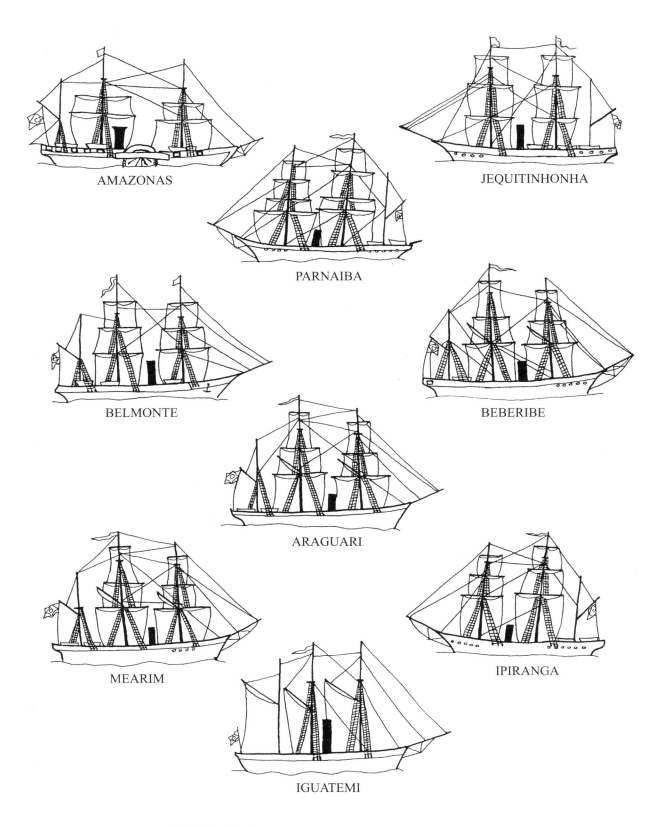

AMAZONAS

JEQUITINHONHA

PARNAIBA

BELMONTE

BEBERIBE

ARAGUARI

MEARIM

IPIRANGA

IGUATEMI

SHIPS FROM THE NAVAL SQUADRON OF
ADMIRAL FRANCISCO M. BARROSO, JUNE 1865

Drawings of ships from the squadron of Admiral Francisco M. Barroso by the author, after a print published in A Marinha em Revista *188, June 1965, special issue on the Paraguayan War.*

SHIPS OF THE PARAGUAYAN NAVY 1865

Ships of the Paraguayan Navy, by the author, based on a contemporary print of a review of 10 June 1865. Key: 1 Rio Apa; 2 Jequi (Jejuy); 3 Aabui; 4 Ipora (Ypora); 5 Rio Blanca; 6 Tacuarí; 7 Paraguarí; 8 Olimpo; 9 Pirabebé; 10 Igurei (Ygurey); 11 not known; 12 Marquês do Olinda; 13 Paraná; 14 Yberá; 15 Salto Oriental (Salto del Guaira). Ships not shown are the Aquidaban *and* Independencia, *plus the captured Argentine ships* Gualeguay *and* 25 de Mayo, *and the captured Brazilian* Anhambany, *renamed the* Amambay. *Note that throughout this book I have adhered to the Paraguayan versions of their ships' names; however, some sources render these names in Argentine Spanish, and since this might otherwise cause confusion I have included both versions when necessary.*

300; engine 70 hp. Commander: *Alférez de Marina* (Sub-Lieutenant) Vicente Alcaraz.

Pirabebe: wooden screw-driven vessel; armament 1 x18-pdr; tonnage 150; 60 hp. Commander: *Teniente de Marina* (Second-Lieutenant) Toribio Pereira.

Two *chatas* (wooden gun batteries) officered by artillery lieutenants; armament 1 x 80-pdr in each; tonnage 40.

Five *chatas* (wooden gun batteries) officered by artillery lieutenants; armament 1 x 68-pdr in each; tonnage 35.

2nd Paraguayan Horse Artillery Regiment (based on the riverbank to give additional fire support): 22 x 12-pdrs. Commander: Colonel Bruguéz.

6th Infantry Battalion: 500 men, placed aboard the Paraguayan ships to provide boarding parties.

---

had their anti-boarding netting fitted, and the only two Paraguayans who managed to gain a foothold were obliged to jump back aboard their own ship. At the same moment the *Salto Oriental* managed to gain hold of the *Parnaíba*'s port side and got 30 men aboard her, who hacked through the anti-boarding netting with their sharp knives.

Leaping down on the deck, they saw the officers and crew hurrying down the various hatches without waiting to see how many boarders there were. If the Paraguayans had immediately secured the hatches the outcome might have been different, but they didn't. They did, however, cut away the steering wheel, thereby impairing her movement for the remainder of the battle. The Brazilian flagship *Amazonas* now came to the boarded vessel's assistance, and, with the *Beberibe*, fired grape into the occupied portion of the *Parnaíba*, killing and wounding over half of the boarders. A few minutes later a force of Brazilian marines rushed back on deck through the *Parnaíba*'s hatches with fixed bayonets and drove the remaining Paraguayans overboard, while the *Salto Oriental* and *Marquês de Olinda* made their escape, the latter having attached itself to the *Parnaíba*'s stern. The *Amazonas* ceased firing and, steaming full ahead, rammed both the light Paraguayan vessels.

After four-and-a-half hours of fighting the surviving Paraguayan ships made their escape amid the confusion, having suffered severe losses. The *Marquês de Olinda* had been grounded, a worthless wreck. The *Salto Oriental* had sunk immediately on being rammed, but in water so shallow that part of her deck remained above it. Both had also had their boilers shot through, as these were converted merchant vessels with their unprotected engine areas situated above the waterline. The *Paraguarí* also grounded in shallow water and caught fire after being rammed by the *Amazonas*, leaving only her hull and machinery intact, while the *Jequi* was completely smashed by gunnery. The *Tacuarí* had the packing around one of its boilers ripped off by gunfire from the *Ipiranga*, but the boiler itself remained uninjured. In addition two

of the *chatas* were sunk. Casualties were admitted as being 750 men, with two British engineers killed and Captain Meza mortally wounded (he died at Humaitá).

By comparison losses to the Brazilian Navy were minimal. The grounded *Belmonte*, although riddled with shot, was refloated the following day, while the *Jequitinhonha*, grounded on a sandbank near the shore and peppered by the Paraguayan land batteries, eventually had to be abandoned. (Bruguéz later managed to salvage several guns from her – two 68-pdrs, four 32-pdrs, two brass 5-inch howitzers, and a rifled Whitworth 40-pdr.) The official cost in men was 104 killed, 123 wounded, and 20 missing.

The Brazilian Admiral failed to follow up his success by pursuing the retreating Paraguayan ships, two of which – the *Tacuarí* and *Igurei* – were badly damaged. Instead, fears that the river level was falling resulted in the Brazilians retiring farther down the Paraná. Lieutenant-Colonel Bruguéz, having received reinforcements (three battalions of infantry under the command of Major Aquino), advanced downstream in early August to Bella Vista, just past the Brazilian fleet, and established his batteries and troops on 50-foot (15 m) cliffs overlooking the river. Not wanting to be cut off from its supply base the Brazilian fleet, along with two Argentine steamers, was forced to run this gauntlet on 11 August, but they kept their infantry on deck and in the rigging to act as snipers. However, by placing their men in the open in this way the Allies tempted fate, and the Paraguayan artillery and infantry marksmen had a field day as the ships steamed by, the artillery firing canister and grapeshot at these easy targets rather than shooting at the ships' hulls.

The Allied fleet managed to steam a further six miles (9.6 km) downstream before stopping for the night to tend to the wounded. Little did they know that Bruguéz had broken camp and was following them, pushing on during the evening and night to be ready in position below the fleet again the next day, this time at Cuevas. Having learnt from the previous day's lesson, this time the ships steamed past with nobody visible on deck, the only exception being the Argentine steamer *Guardia Nacional*, which returned fire as it passed. The Allied fleet was not seen or heard of again in these parts for another eight months.

THE BATTLE OF YATAÍ

Meanwhile the second Paraguayan advance, that of Colonel António de la Cruz Estigarribia, had crossed the River Paraná at Itapua and headed towards San Carlos in the Paraguayan-claimed part of Misiones. Estigarribia's force consisted of 12,000 men, composed of ten infantry battalions, the 8th, 14th (Captain Mereles), 15th (Captain Campurno), 16th (Lieutenant Matino), 17th (Captain Diogo Alvarenga), 28th (Lieutenant Zorilla), 31st (Captain Ibanez), 32nd (Captain Avalos), 33rd (Captain Joel Rozario Tellez), and 41st; and six cavalry regiments, the 24th (Lieutenant Cabrero), 26th (Major Pedro Duarte), 27th (Major López), 28th (Captain Centurion), and 33rd (Captain Manuel Coronel); plus six cannon under the command of Lieutenant Ignacio Tereiro. Estigarribia also took with him 30 carts carrying a total of 20 boats, each with a capacity to carry 25 men. These were to be used to cross the River Uruguay. There were

'The Naval Battle of Riachuelo' by Vítor Meireles, who visited the site of the action and took notes before starting on this painting. The picture was actually painted twice, the first painting being so damaged by humidity after being shown in the Brazilian Pavilion at the International Exhibition of Philadelphia in 1876, that, on its return, Emperor Pedro II requested the artist to produce another copy. This second copy now hangs in the Museu Historico Nacional, Rio de Janeiro. (Courtesy of Museu Historico Nacional)

also 4,000 horses and 800 oxen, six oxen or mules being used to haul each cannon while a further six were required for each of their caissons.[8]

In early June 1865 this division began its advance through the northern section of Corrientes province that bordered Misiones, and on 10 June it was confronted at San Borja, a town situated on the banks of the River Uruguay, by Lieutenant-Colonel Araújo Nobrega. His small force consisted of 230 men of the 22nd Provincial National Guard Cavalry and 100 men from the 3rd Battalion National Guard of Rio Grande do Sul, with a reserve of 50 men, while 600 men of the 1st Battalion of *Voluntários da Pátria* were camped two leagues outside the town.

Estigarribia was forced to lay siege to the town, for it was here that he had planned to cross the river, but it took two days to force the garrison out. During the fighting the Brazilian 1st Battalion of *Voluntários da Pátria* nearly lost its standard, which was saved by the courageous action of Sub-Lieutenant Paulino Gomes Jardim. After the Paraguayans had captured and sacked the town it was decided that the vanguard needed to stay on the right bank while Colonel Estigarribia crossed with the remainder of the division. The vanguard under Major Pedro Duarte, consisting of 2,500 men (the 16th and 28th Infantry Battalions and 24th and 26th Cavalry Regiments) therefore proceeded along the right bank, the two columns keeping in touch with each other by means of the 20 canoes.

On 6 August the Brazilian town of Uruguayana was captured by Colonel Estigarribia's division. It had been defended by the Brazilian General David Canabarro, who had begun fortification of the site but had decided to retreat on the 4th, leaving behind two cannon. He was later court-martialled for this and for not making contact with the Paraguayans while they had been attempting to cross the river at San Borja, despite having nearly 8,000 men under his command. It would appear that only Colonel Payba with a force of 2,000 men harried the main Paraguayan advance, while the 4th Brigade under the command of Lieutenant-Colonel Sezefredo de Mesquita attacked and defeated a column of Paraguayan cavalry, inflicting 116 killed and 120 wounded and capturing two flags; the Brazilian loss was 29 killed and 86 wounded. This was at Botui on 26 June. Baron de Jacui was also in the area with another 15,000 troops in three brigades, but he was rather inactive, having had to travel from his base at Bagé, in Uruguay.

On 20 July the Brazilian Government named General Baron de Pôrto Alegre as commander-in-chief of the army of operations in the province of Rio Grande do Sul. He would take over from Lieutenant-General João Frederico Caldwell, who was recalled to Rio de Janeiro to report on events. He had been trying to contain the Paraguayan forces with only one division, the 2nd Division having at that point not yet arrived from Bagé. General Pôrto Alegre would take over command on 21 August, when he arrived outside Uruguayana.

Meanwhile a unit from the Brazilian *Zuavos Bahianos* ('Zouaves of Bahia'), commanded by Lieutenant Floriano Peixoto, had been despatched along the River Uruguay in two small armed vessels to disrupt the supply and communication lines between Colonel Estigarribia, Major Duarte, and their outposts along the

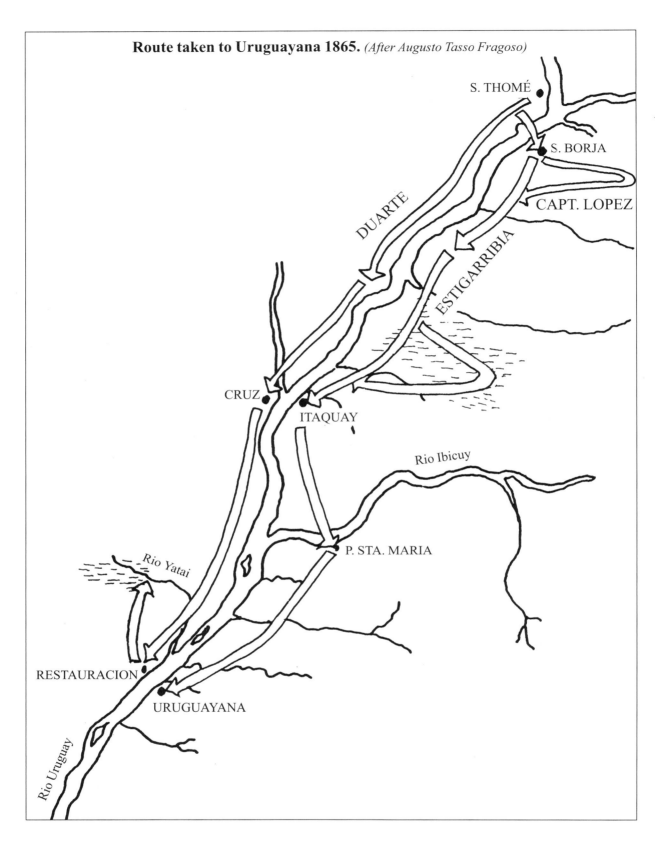

Route taken to Uruguayana 1865. *(After Augusto Tasso Fragoso)*

river. The Conde d'Eu, the Brazilian Emperor's son-in-law (who was to be commander-in-chief of the Allied Army in 1869–70), wrote that this unit was composed of blacks[9] – no whites, Indians, or mulattos were allowed – and that their uniform consisted of red trousers, green vest, blue jacket, and a red fez. By this time the Allies had organised a force of 13,000 men, made up of 16 infantry battalions (5,200 men), numerous cavalry units (5,000 men), and 32 cannon. With its vanguard division under the command of General Flores, this was heading for

Uruguayana, which it reached on 17 August.

By 14 August 1865, Major Duarte's column – now increased to 3,200 men by the addition of the *Batallón Provisorio* infantry battalion – was encamped on the opposite bank at a place called Yataí, where it was attacked on the 17th by General Flores' vanguard. When offered the chance to surrender Duarte refused, ordering his troops to take up defensive positions in and behind a small row of houses, with their rear protected by the river. In the ensuing battle the Allies' superiority in numbers soon made itself felt: 1,700 Paraguayans were killed and 300 wounded, the remaining 1,200 being taken prisoner, Major Duarte among them. Allied losses are quoted as 320 killed and 220 wounded, most of these being Uruguayans. A captured Paraguayan lieutenant was later used to carry messages between the Allies and Colonel Estigarribia in September.

The following description of the battle was written by a Uruguayan participant, Colonel Leon de Palleja: 'The troops were paraded at an early hour and quickly marched off in parallel columns. The General-in-Chief gave me command of four regiments of the Uruguayan Brigade. Moving in the formation mentioned we arrived in sight of the town. The irregular cavalry of the enemy were concentrated near some farms at a distance of half a league from Restauracion [Yataí]. The General ordered a halt and summoned a council of war to determine how the action should be fought. My brigade was ordered to deploy by Battalions, covering the advance with a line of skirmishers, and to attack the enemy's front. The Brazilian [Kelly] and Argentine [Arredondo] columns followed in the rear, inclining towards the left to outflank the enemy. The Paraguayans occupied a slope which fell away until lost in a swamp about a league in extent formed by the Uruguay and another stream. The Paraguayan skirmishers and sharpshooters were posted in trenches near the ridge of the hill. The effective strength of the force under Major Duarte comprised 3,000 men [Thompson says 2,500] consisting of three regiments [battalions] of infantry and two of cavalry.

'My brigade deployed, the 24th Regiment ["24 de Abril") in the centre, the "Florida" Regiment on the right, and the "Voluntários Garabaldinos" on the left. The "Libertad" Regiment acted as skirmishers in front of the line. The band played the national hymn and we moved forward to the attack. The enemy's sharpshooters in the trenches received us with a heavy fire, but did not check us. We succeeded in occupying the first line of the Paraguayan defence, inflicting severe loss on the defenders.

'The "Florida" Regiment cut off the retreat of a detachment of the enemy. When this first line was driven in we discovered the main body of the Paraguayans in strong positions, and were exposed to a storm of musketry fire. My men charged and drove the Paraguayans back to their encampment. Here the enemy attempted to re-form, but were prevented by another bayonet charge and by the attack of our cavalry on both flanks, with the result that they fell back to the edge of the swamp.

'At this period of the fight several Argentine regiments came up on the left in support of the 24th Regiment and the "Voluntários Garabaldinos". The "Florida" Regiment now broke through the Paraguayan line and made prisoners of a section of infantry and

cavalry. The remainder of the enemy dashed into the swamp and attempted to wade or swim to a place of safety on the other side, but unsuccessfully. About a hundred of the enemy swam out into the Uruguay and succeeded in reaching an island mid-stream. At 2:30 p.m. the fight was over.

'Some 250 Paraguayans were left dead on the field, the majority of the remainder taken prisoners. Our losses were one officer killed, ten wounded and 250 men killed or wounded. The wounded were numerous on the part of the enemy, and special care was taken by General Flores to see that they were given proper attention.'

Palleja gives Allied losses as 19 Brazilians killed and 34 wounded, 13 Argentines killed and 86 wounded, and 51 Uruguayans killed and 137 wounded. It is interesting to note that, after receiving a new issue of clothing (their original Paraguayan issue being completely worn out), the Paraguayan 'other rank' prisoners were drafted into the Allied forces. The Uruguayan regiments, incidentally, should really be classed as battalions.

THE ALLIED ATTACK ON URUGUAYANA

Though a defeat, the battle at Yataí had at least given Colonel Estigarribia's 8,000 men time to make good the fortifications at Uruguayana, including the addition of an abattis all round. By September the Allies had assembled 18,584 men and 42 pieces of artillery before the city, grouped into three corps. The 1st Corps 'Oriental' comprised four battalions of Uruguayan infantry (1,347 men), one cavalry regiment (300 men), the 12th Brazilian Brigade (1,107 men), and a squadron of Uruguayan horse artillery (8 guns and 132 men). The 2nd Corps 'Argentine' was made up of ten infantry battalions (3,060 men) and a brigade of artillery (24 guns and 365 men), some of these Argentine troops having been transferred from the River Paraná side of Corrientes. The 3rd Corps 'Brazilian' consisted of four infantry divisions (4,150 men), dismounted cavalry (2,123 men), and cavalry (6,000 men), plus eight field-pieces, two howitzers, and four Congreve rocket stands. The Brazilian Navy also had a presence on the river, with the steamers *Taquary*, *Tramandahy*, *Onze de Junho*, *Iniciador*, *Uruguay*, and *Uniáo*.

The Emperor of Brazil and his son-in-law the Conde d'Eu had also travelled to join the Brazilian troops two days after hearing news of the invasion, setting out on 10 July. It is recorded that on entering the church of Carmo during his journey, to attend mass, the Emperor and his entourage were taken by the congregation to be Paraguayans. As the Emperor wrote, 'it required much trouble to maintain order in the church'!

President Mitre too arrived at Uruguayana in late August 1865, having departed Buenos Aires in June after leaving the administration of the government to Vice President Marcos Paz. At Concordia, which was the main grouping area for the Allied armies, Mitre was to meet General Urquiza, who had assembled an army of 10,000 from Entre Ríos at Basualdo on the frontier. But while General Urquiza was en route to his meeting with Mitre a messenger caught up with him with news that almost his whole army had dispersed. Giving the remainder a month's leave of absence, he wrote to Mitre that the following month he would come with an army of 12,000 men instead. However, this promise was never fulfilled, since after three months he had only succeeded in raising a few thousand men, and once again the majority of these dispersed before the army had even left the province.

After these two episodes no more was heard of General Urquiza. Probably he really had initially wanted President López to come and help his old friends in Uruguay, doing so via the short-cut of Misiones as he had advised. That way the Paraguayans could have relied on the backing of his old *caudillo* companions in the provinces (except maybe Buenos Aires), and wait for President Mitre to make a mistake in handling events, which would allow him to be overthrown by Urquiza's supporters. But as the months passed it had become clear that López lacked a clear idea of how to utilise his resources – by uniting Argentine and Uruguayan federalists against Brazil and creating a confederation of these two countries with Paraguay to dominate the Rio Plata basin – while Urquiza's realisation that López was an autocrat who did not like to take advice, and was not as level-headed as he had once assumed, must have made Urquiza have second thoughts about their friendship. In addition President Mitre's realisation that he had to tread carefully on all fronts led to him placing Urquiza in a position of personal trust and honour, which paid off when López attacked Corrientes against Urquiza's advice. The people looked towards Urquiza for their direction, and when he offered President Mitre his allegiance and sword the country became united – or so it seemed for a few months, until his army mutinied. But was that by design?

A call for Uruguayana to surrender on 4 September was rejected, but on the 18th, with nearly all of his supplies exhausted other than lump sugar, General Estigarribia accepted the terms offered by the Emperor and President Mitre. Only 5,545 of his men had survived, including 59 officers, the rest having died of hunger and sickness. Emílio C. Jourdan, in his work *Historia das campanhas do Uruguaï, Mato Grosso e Paraguaï* (1893), lists the Paraguayan prisoners as:

Infantry battalions	14th	700
	15th	610
	17th	754
	31st	440
	32nd	680
	33rd	676
Cavalry regiments	27th	440
	28th	475
	33rd	485
Artillery		115
Train		80
Staff Corps		20
Boatmen		70

The rank and file were to be treated as prisoners of war, but the officers were allowed to take up residence in any place that they might choose, with the exception of Paraguay. General Estigarribia went to Buenos Aires and from there to Rio de Janeiro. Again the practice of drafting the Paraguayan other ranks into the Allied armies was adopted, with each Allied nation taking a third of the prisoners. The Brazilian contingent was assigned to road construction projects in the interior provinces, while many of the Argentine and Uruguayan share of prisoners were drafted into infantry battalions, although a couple of hundred who were too ill were sent to hospital camps. However, when the Allies advanced into Paraguay many of the prisoners managed to escape and eventually rejoined the Paraguayan army, some of them accompanied by the rifles issued to them by the Allies.

Among the Paraguayan equipment captured at Uruguayana were 540 swords, 850 lances, 34 carbines, 110 pistols, and 3,630 muskets, all of the muskets being old flintlocks (the same was true of the muskets captured at the Battle of Yataí). Seven standards and eight cannon were also captured. The Conde d'Eu reported of these cannon that 'one had been cast at Douai in 1790, another at Barcelona in 1788, and a third at Seville in 1679.' (The 1788 and 1790 cannon were possibly the two left behind by General Canabarro in August.)

Other unusual sights which caught the Conde d'Eu's eye included the Rio Grande cavalry actually entering Uruguayana before the surrender had been completed and fraternising almost immediately with the Paraguayans. He was particularly astonished to observe many of the cavalrymen madly galloping about, each with an ex-enemy soldier seated behind! Elsewhere he noted that the Paraguayan infantry took all the loot they could carry with them – every man he saw carried pointed iron bars ripped from fences and windows, with which they could prepare *churrasco* (barbecued beef). He also noted that the enemy prisoners could be distinguished from Argentines and Uruguayans by their manner of walking and the nature of their dress. The Paraguayans he saw wore two *mantas* or blankets: the *bichará*, a *manta* wrapped around the body, and the *chiripá*, a blanket or leather apron wrapped around the lower body including both legs and not around each leg individually as in the case of the gauchos from Rio Grande do Sul, Argentina, and Uruguay.

Following the fall of Uruguayana the remaining small Paraguayan garrisons that had been left along the route of advance now retreated as best they could, some being harried by two Allied columns commanded by Colonel Castro, with 2,000 men, and Colonel Reguerra, with 700. These columns had been despatched from the Allied army before the Battle of Yataí specifically to cut off this route back to Paraguay.

THE FIGHT AT CORRALES

With the defeats at Uruguayana and Yataí, following that of the ill fated Battle of Riachuelo, President López ordered the total evacuation of Corrientes province and announced that Paraguay's frontier fortifications would be defended against the Allied armies. General Resquín began the evacuation after being recalled from Mato Grosso, where he had been second-in-command to General Robles, who had been relieved of his command by President López on 23 July. He placed the Paraguayan artillery onto steamers at Cuevas, while extending his troops to form an arc with which he could sweep the country clean of horses, cattle, and every kind of livestock as he retired. He finally reached and crossed the River Paraguay at Paso de la Patria, taking with him many thousand head of cattle (Thompson says 100,000), which were forced to swim across. The entire crossing, which began on 31 October and took until 3 November to

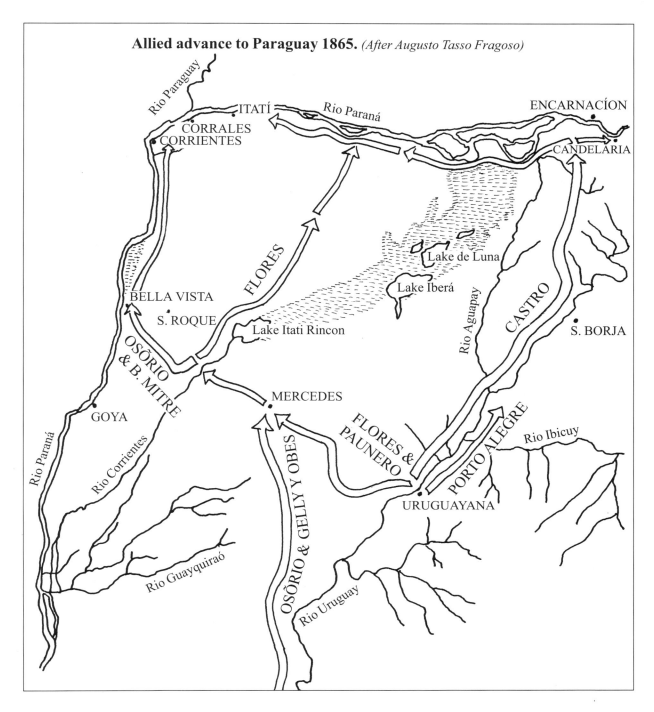

Allied advance to Paraguay 1865. *(After Augusto Tasso Fragoso)*

complete, was carried out within sight of the Brazilian ironclads, whose commanders, believing that there were concealed shore batteries, did not dare approach any closer.

As it turned out the cattle brought from Corrientes were of very little use to the Paraguayans, as they almost all died, either of fatigue, starvation (there being very little pasturage near Paso la Patria), or from eating a poisonous herb called *mio-mio* which abounds in the south of Paraguay and which only animals reared in the district have the instinct to avoid. The number of decaying animals on the ground about Itapirú and a few leagues beyond it was terrible over the next few months. (One wonders how the Allied livestock managed in this

environment once it had crossed the River Paraná into southern Paraguay.)

General Resquín had brought back 19,000 men. Of these some 5,000 were sick, though many of these had become ill earlier in the Corrientes campaign and were already back in Paraguay by mid-August. Thompson says that during the campaign there had been 8,500 deaths in this division, so if we take the two figures (19,000 living and 8,500 dead) as accurate then the division had seen 27,500 men go through it from 13 April to 3 November, of whom nearly 50% had become casualties in one form or another – a pretty high percentage. Thompson also states that up to this time Paraguay had suffered 40,000 deaths in all since the

Argentine officer (left) with a captured Paraguayan officer. (Courtesy of the Arquivo Historico do Exercito, Rio de Janeiro)

beginning of the recruitment drive the previous year. Add this figure to the men captured with Colonel Estigarribia's division and the picture is not too rosy. Most of these deaths were the result of disease. There had been epidemics of measles and smallpox in both Paraguay and Corrientes, while the change from a cereal and/or vegetable-based diet to one containing a large amount of meat (beef or horse) created havoc, with diarrhoea and dysentery cutting swathes through the raw recruits.

After the withdrawal of the Paraguayan forces from Argentine territory it was widely considered that Argentine national honour had been satisfied and that any further sacrifice of blood and expense to the nation was unnecessary. Urquiza was of this viewpoint, and was in favour of immediate peace negotiations. Another reason for seeking an early settlement was that Indian raiders were again on the rampage on the southern frontier, killing, robbing, and destroying to within 120 miles (200 km) of the city of Rosario. In Uruguay too the Blanco party agitated for a suspension of hostilities. Other countries which considered that action against Paraguay had gone far enough included Chile, Peru, Great Britain, France, and the USA. But it was Brazil that would decide what policy was to be followed, and Dom Pedro II

declared that as the Paraguayans were still in the Brazilian province of Mato Grosso he felt it necessary to continue the campaign, and that if Argentina and Uruguay decided to make peace then he would abdicate in favour of his daughter in protest. Such strong words carried the day and the war continued.

The Allies now began to move as many troops as were available to the town of Corrales on the River Paraná, just past the city and port of Corrientes and opposite the village of Paso de la Patria. Troops under the command of Osõrio and Emilio Mitre took the route via Mercedes to Bella Vista and up along the River Paraná to Corrientes. General Flores took the central route via Mercedes, past Lake Itati Rincon to Ita Ibate, uniting here with General Castro's command, which had come via San Borja and Candelaría on the River Paraná. From there they continued along the Paraná from the opposite direction to that of Osõrio and Emilio Mitre, to reach the main campsite outside Corrales.

During December 1865, López, who had now taken overall command of all Paraguay's armed forces, created a base opposite the only ford across the Paraná, at Paso de la Patria. This village stood 30–40 ft (9–12 m) above the surrounding impassable *carrizal*, which was land intersected by deep lagoons and deep mud, with between the lagoons either impassable jungle or equally impenetrable intertwined grass standing 9 ft (2.75 m) high. He had with him the major part of his army (30,000 men). The encampment itself, which mounted 30 guns, was noted as being a fine work, with a trench 11 ft (3.4 m) wide and 6 ft (1.8 m) deep that followed the general form of the crest of the bank, having various small redans and curtains. Its flanks rested on two lagoons (the Sirena and Panambi), while the ground to its front was open for a mile (1.6 km).

López began to send small raiding parties of 100–200 men across the river at various points nearly every day to attack any Allied posts that they found. This carried on for three months. Among the most notable of these raids was that carried out on 13 January 1866, in which a force of 109 Paraguayans attacked a unit of nine Argentine guns. On the 16th a force of 200 men from the 12th Infantry Battalion under the command of Major Viveros attacked a force of Correntine National Guard Cavalry, while the 17th saw a bigger raiding party of 600 men and a Congreve rocket launcher attacking an element of the cavalry force under General Manuel Hornos, commander of the National Guard Cavalry units that made up the 2nd Cavalry Division of Correntine that was stationed in this particular region. In this action the Argentine cavalry was forced to fight dismounted. The 19th and 25th saw raiding parties of 200 and 400 men respectively again attacking elements of General Hornos' cavalry.

The main Allied camp was in the riverside village of Corrales, sometimes called Correntine Paso de la Patria. On 29 January 1866 a number of Paraguayan raiding parties of about 400 men crossed the Paraná, assailed the Argentine pickets round the village, and drove out its defenders, the Argentine 6th Correntine National Guard Cavalry, forcing the latter to retire to the riverbank of San Juan, some 650 yds (600 m) away. News of this attack having reached General Mitre, the following day he despatched the 2nd Division, Buenos Aires, to reinforce the command of General Hernos and recapture

Table 4: Allied Order of Battle from Leon de Palleja's *Diario de la Campana de las Fuerzas Aliadas contra el Paraguay* **(1865–66)**

Commander-in-chief: President Bartolomé Mitre (Argentina)

ALLIED ARMY OF OPERATIONS IN CORRIENTES (15 NOVEMBER 1865)

ARMY OF THE VANGUARD
General-in-Chief: General Venancio Flores

	Generals	Field officers	Officers	Other ranks
Staff Corps 1	12	15	7	
General C. Suárez (HQ)	1	1	6	32
Lieutenant-Colonel M. Mendieta, Presidential Escort Regiment	–	2	18	274
Colonel N. Garcia, Regiment San Martin	–	5	33	403
Artillery (6 pieces) Commander: Major I. Yance 2nd Battery Light Regiment	–	1	11	210
Cavalry *Division Castro* Lieutenant-Colonel T. Albin, 1st Regiment Uruguayan National Guard Lieutenant-Colonel N. Ramirez, 2nd Regiment Uruguayan National Guard Lieutenant-Colonel A. Castro (Brevet Colonel), 3rd Regiment Uruguayan National Guard				
Divisional total	1	6	83	613
Division Reguera Colonel N. Reguera, Corrientes Cavalry Militia	–	3	27	600
Infantry *1st Brigade* Colonel L. de Palleja, Battalion 'Florida'	–	1	27	592
Major M. González, Battalion '24 de Abril'	–	1	20	486
2nd Brigade Lieutenant-Colonel C. Bustannente, Battalion 'Voluntários de la Libertad'	–	1	29	486
Lieutenant-Colonel F. Elias, Battalion 'Independencia'	–	1	16	332
Lieutenant-Colonel N. Galvão, 3rd Battalion *Voluntários da Pátria*	–	2	31	357
Medical Corps	–	3	6	–
12th Brigade of Infantry (Brazilian) Commander: Lieutenant-Colonel D.N. Netto Kelly Major N. Cemison, 5th Infantry	–	1	19	296
Major N. Silva Pedra, 7th Infantry	–	1	16	329
Major N. Gruppi, 16th Battalion *Voluntários da Pátria*	–	1	20	311
Train (Uruguayan)	–	–	1	24
Total, Army of the Vanguard	*3*	*42*	*378*	*5,160*

ARMY OF THE REPUBLIC OF ARGENTINA

FIRST CORPS
Commander: General Wenceslao Paunero

	Generals	Field officers	Officers	Other ranks
Staff Corps	1	5	5	54

INFANTRY
1st Division
Commander: Colonel I. Rivas

Table 4: Allied Order of Battle from Leon de Palleja's *Diario de la Campana de las Fuerzas Aliadas contra el Paraguay* **(1865–66) (continued)**

	Generals	Field officers	Officers	Other ranks
1st Brigade				
Lieutenant-Colonel M. Rosetti, 1st Line Battalion	–	2	21	319
Lieutenant-Colonel I. Boerr, Battalion 'San Nicolas'	–	1	34	460
2nd Brigade				
Commander: Lieutenant-Colonel S. Charlone				
Lieutenant-Colonel L. Pagola, 3rd Line Battalion	–	1	11	262
Lieutenant-Colonel S. Charlone, *Legión Militar*	–	2	23	383
2nd Division				
Commander: Colonel I. Arrendondo				
3rd Brigade				
Lieutenant-Colonel M. Fraga, 4th Line Battalion	–	2	21	244
Major L. Campos, 6th Line Battalion	–	1	18	287
4th Brigade				
Colonel A. Orma, 2nd Line Battalion	–	2	25	313
Major I. Giriboni, 1st Legion of Volunteers	–	1	18	319
5th Brigade				
Commander: Colonel Rivero				
Major D. Sosa, Battalion 1st de Corrientes	–	1	17	246
Colonel I. M. Avalos, Battalion 1st de Santa Fe	–	2	31	441
Colonel T. lturburu, Paraguayan Legion	–	1	20	145
CAVALRY BRIGADE				
Commander: Colonel J.M. Fernández				
Capt D.R. Acosta, 1st Squadron Presidential Escort	–	–	7	69
Lieutenant-Colonel D.I. Segovia, 1st Cavalry Regiment	–	2	12	293
Colonel J.M. Fernández, Volunteers of Santa Fe	–	2	24	274
Major A. Díaz, Company of Engineers	–	1	15	113
Medical Corps	–	4	9	59
Lieutenant-Colonel C.G. Videla, Train	–	1	3	90
ARTILLERY BRIGADE				
Commander: Lieutenant-Colonel L. Nelson				
Major I. Viejo Bueno, 2nd Battery of Light Artillery	–	1	9	137
Major E. Maldones, 3rd Battery of Light Artillery	–	1	10	147
Lieutenant-Colonel L. Nelson, 4th Battery of Light Artillery	–	1	8	146
SECOND CORPS				
Commander: General J.A. Gelly y Obes				
INFANTRY				
1st Division				
Commander: Colonel E Conesa				
Colonel N. Arenas, 2nd Battalion of National Guard				
Major J.M. Serrano, 3rd Battalion of National Guard				
Lieutenant-Colonel N. Obligado, 4th Battalion of National Guard				
Divisional total	–	6	70	1,377
2nd Division				
Commander: Colonel J.M. Bustillos				
Lieutenant-Colonel J. Cobos, 1st Battalion National Guard of Buenos Aires				
Lieutenant-Colonel J. Urien, 2nd Battalion National Guard of Buenos Aires				
Lieutenant-Colonel J. Morales, 2nd Battalion 3rd Regiment of Buenos Aires				

Table 4: Allied Order of Battle from Leon de Palleja's *Diario de la Campana de las Fuerzas Aliadas contra el Paraguay* **(1865–66) (continued)**

	Generals	Field officers	Officers	Other ranks
Lieutenant-Colonel L. Amadeo, 4th Battalion 3rd Regiment of Buenos Aires				
Divisional total	–	9	112	1,400
3rd Division				
Commander: Colonel J. Vedia				
Lieutenant-Colonel B. Calveti, 9th Line Battalion				
Lieutenant-Colonel J. Martínez, 1st Battalion 3rd Regiment of Buenos Aires				
Colonel N. Susini, 2nd Legion of Volunteers				
Colonel N. Esquivel, Battalion 'Libertad' National Guard				
Divisional total	–	9	108	1,500
CAVALRY DIVISION				
Commander: Colonel M. Oryazabal				
Colonel N. Arnramburu, 1st Regiment of National Guard Cavalry				
Lieutenant-Colonel P. Sotelo, 2nd Regiment of National Guard Cavalry				
Lieutenant-Colonel S. Albarinos, 3rd Regiment of National Guard Cavalry				
Divisional total	–	6	45	450
ARTILLERY				
Colonel Frederico Mitre, 2nd Regiment of Light Artillery	–	2	20	250
THIRD CORPS				
Commander: General Emilio Mitre				
INFANTRY				
1st Brigade				
Commander: Colonel J. Ayala				
Colonel J. Ayala, 12th Line Battalion, Light Infantry				
Lieutenant-Colonel C. Keen, 5th Battalion of National Guard				
Divisional total	–	4	54	650
2nd Brigade				
Commander: Colonel C. Dominguez				
Colonel C. Dominguez, Battalion 'Cordoba'				
Lieutenant-Colonel J. Suffra, Battalion 'San Juan'				
Divisional total	–	4	50	550
3rd Brigade				
Commander: Lieutenant-Colonel J. Cabot				
Lieutenant-Colonel J. Cabot, Battalion 'Pringles'				
Major N. Morillo, Battalion 'Mendoza'				
Divisional total	–	4	50	500
CAVALRY BRIGADE				
Lieutenant-Colonel F. Vidal, 3rd Line Cavalry Regiment	–	4	25	250
ARGENTINE ARMY IN ENTRE RÍOS				
Commander: General Justo José de Urguiza				
(Individual units not listed)	3	75	450	5,000
ARGENTINE ARMY IN CORRIENTES				
General Caceres' division				
(Individual units not listed)	1	20	100	2,000

Table 4: Allied Order of Battle from Leon de Palleja's *Diario de la Campana de las Fuerzas Aliadas contra el Paraguay* **(1865–66) (continued)**

	Generals	Field officers	Officers	Other ranks
General Hornos' division				
(Individual units not listed)	1	10	50	1,000
Colonel Paiva's division				
(Individual units not listed)	–	6	40	500
RESUMÉ OF THE ARGENTINE ARMY				
1st Corps	1	35	348	4,554
2nd Corps	1	32	355	4,977
3rd Corps	1	16	179	1,950
Army of Entre Ríos	3	75	450	5,000
Army of Corrientes	2	36	190	3,500
IMPERIAL BRAZILIAN ARMY				
Commander: Brigadier-General Manuel Luiz Osõrio				
Staff Corps and Headquarters	1	18	20	50
INFANTRY				
2nd Brigade				
14th Battalion Provincial Infantry	–	2	21	530
15th Battalion *Voluntários da Pátria*	–	2	30	310
20th Battalion *Voluntários da Pátria*	–	2	38	353
5th Brigade				
4th Line Battalion	–	2	20	488
6th Line Battalion	–	2	37	490
12th Line Battalion	–	2	7	495
4th Battalion *Voluntários da Pátria*	–	2	24	381
7th Brigade				
1st Line Battalion	–	2	27	479
13th Line Battalion	–	2	31	430
6th Battalion *Voluntários da Pátria*	–	2	40	530
3rd Battalion *Voluntários da Pátria*	–	2	41	504
8th Brigade				
8th Line Battalion	–	2	18	334
16th Line Battalion	–	2	29	374
10th Battalion *Voluntários da Pátria*	–	2	19	358
10th Brigade				
3rd Line Battalion	–	2	18	409
2nd Battalion *Voluntários da Pátria*	–	2	25	377
26th Battalion *Voluntários da Pátria*	–	2	37	441
11th Brigade				
2nd Line Battalion	–	2	16	369
10th Line Battalion	–	2	27	508
1st Battalion *Voluntários da Pátria*	–	2	16	398
Transport/Train	–	2	8	249
ARTILLERY BRIGADE				
Engineer Battalion	–	2	20	259
1st Regiment of Horse Artillery	–	2	18	233
1st Battery of Foot Artillery	–	2	33	488

Table 4: Allied Order of Battle from Leon de Palleja's *Diario de la Campana de las Fuerzas Aliadas contra el Paraguay* **(1865–66) (continued)**

	Generals	Field officers	Officers	Other ranks
3rd Battery of Foot Artillery	–	2	30	333
CAVALRY				
1st Brigade				
2nd Light Cavalry Regiment	–	2	31	255
3rd Light Cavalry Regiment	–	2	35	337
3rd Brigade				
5th Provincial Corps of National Guard	–	2	12	131
6th Provincial Corps of National Guard	–	2	16	133
7th Provincial Corps of National Guard	–	2	13	66
6th Brigade				
1st Provincial Corps of National Guard	–	2	25	199
2 Provincial Corps of National Guard	–	2	16	150
8th Provincial Corps of National Guard	–	2	20	140
Light Cavalry Brigade				
1st Corps of Volunteer Cavalry	–	2	19	277
2nd Corps of Volunteer Cavalry	–	2	20	270
3rd Corps of Volunteer Cavalry	–	2	23	231
4th Corps of Volunteer Cavalry	–	2	23	184
5th Corps of Volunteer Cavalry	–	1	9	63
ON THE BORDER WITH ARGENTINA				
9th Infantry Brigade				
14th Line Battalion (2 companies)	–	–	7	52
Various units in transit	–	–	10	216
9th Line Battalion	–	2	7	305
12th Line Battalion	–	2	20	359
Zuavos Bahia (2 companies)	–	–	6	118
Colonel Jontis' Infantry Brigade				
4 battalions	–	9	100	1,800
Colonel Valenza's Cavalry Brigade				
4 regiments	–	11	75	900

Corrales. Commanded by Colonel Conesa, this division comprised four battalions of National Guard from Buenos Aires – a total of 128 officers and 1,751 men – plus two 6-pdr guns from the 2nd Corps.

Early on the morning of the 31st López sent another raiding party to reinforce the first one, this time made up of 1,200 men with two Congreve rocket launchers under the command of Lieutenant-Colonel José Eduviges Díaz. This force was divided into three sections. The first, of 300 men and the rocket unit, commanded by Lieutenant Celestino Prieto, was to go directly to the village of Corrales. The second section, of 200 men commanded by Lieutenant Saturnino Viveros, drawn from the fort of Itapirú,[10] was to join with the first section in the village. The third section, of 700 men, was to be the reserve and would be stationed at Itapirú. There was some Paraguayan artillery positioned on the small Isle of Carayá, in the middle of the Paraná, which was to give covering fire if required.

Lieutenant Prieto's section, having landed safely, advanced towards the Argentine positions with one rocket launcher, reaching the bank of the Pehuajó river. Seeing this, General Hornos despatched the newly arrived 2nd Division under Colonel Conesa, situated along the bank of the San Juan some 275 yds (250 m) from the Paraguayan positions, to assail Prieto's force as it was digging in along the Pehuajó. The Argentine 4th Battalion, commanded by Major Manuel Obligado, was to attack the Paraguayan centre assisted by artillery (commanded by Captain Cascobo); the 2nd and 3rd Battalions, commanded by Major Miguel Martínez de Hoz, were to attack on the right flank; and the 5th Battalion, commanded by Major Keen, was to attack on the left flank (the 2nd and 5th Battalions made up the 4th Brigade, commanded by Colonel Pedro José Aguero). Both flank attacks would be assisted by squadrons of the

6th Correntine National Guard Cavalry.

After hard hand-to-hand fighting the Paraguayan position was taken, despite Keen's battalion having come under fire from the artillery stationed on the Isle of Carayá. The Paraguayans left behind 30 dead, and four corporals were taken prisoner. Continuing his attack, Colonel Conesa followed the Paraguayans into Corrales village, where Lieutenant Viveros' 200 men had now landed. These reinforced Prieto's force, while Colonel Conesa now came under fire from the two Paraguayan

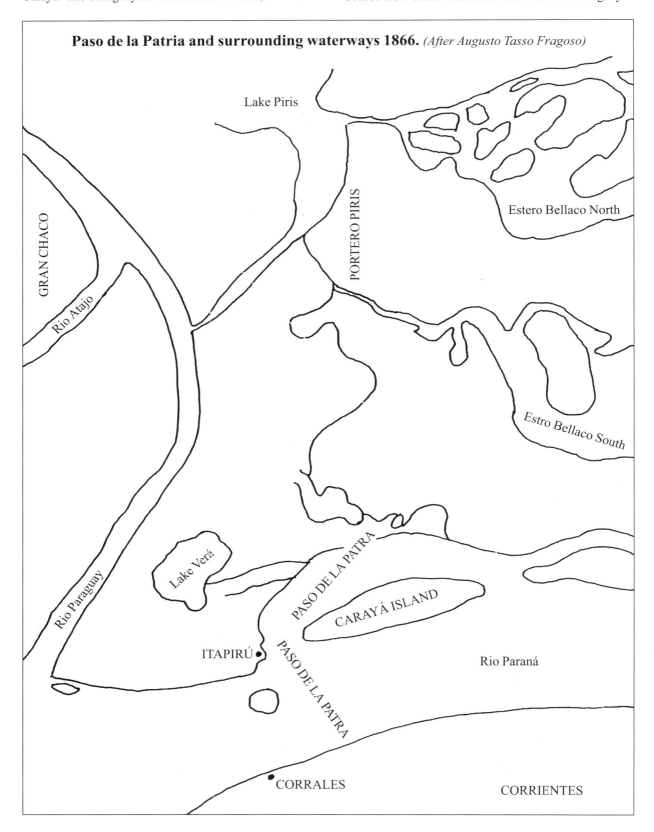

Paso de la Patria and surrounding waterways 1866. *(After Augusto Tasso Fragoso)*

Lake Piris

GRAN CHACO

Rio Atajo

PORTERO PIRIS

Estero Bellaco North

Estro Bellaco South

Rio Paraguay

Lake Verá

PASO DE LA PATRA

CARAYÁ ISLAND

ITAPIRÚ

PASO DE LA PATRA

Rio Paraná

CORRALES

CORRIENTES

Table 5: Brazilian reinforcements to the Allied Army, 1 January 1866

On 1 January 1866 the Brazilians received an additional 13,000 men – 4,000 infantry, 8,000 cavalry, and 1,000 for the various specialist corps (artillery, transport, and pontoniers) – under the command of Baron de Pôrto Alegre, Manoel Márquez de Souza. According to General Augusto Tasso Fragoso's *História da Guerra entre a Tríplice Aliança e o Paraguai*, at the time of their arrival they were organised as follows:

1st Division
Commander: General José Gomes Portinho

1st Brigade
Commander: Camelo Junior
1st Corps of National Guard Provincial Cavalry
2nd Corps of National Guard Provincial Cavalry
3rd Corps of National Guard Provincial Cavalry
4th Corps of National Guard Provincial Cavalry
5th Corps of National Guard Provincial Cavalry

2nd Brigade
Commander: Dinis Dias
6th Corps of National Guard Provincial Cavalry
7th Corps of National Guard Provincial Cavalry
8th Corps of National Guard Provincial Cavalry
9th Corps of National Guard Provincial Cavalry

2nd Division
Commander: General Goncalves Fontes

3rd Brigade
Commander: Higino Coelho
2nd National Guard Battalion
8th Battalion *Voluntários da Pátria**
29th Battalion *Voluntários da Pátria*
34th Battalion *Voluntários da Pátria*

4th Brigade
Commander: José Maria Barreto
18th Battalion *Voluntários da Pátria*
32nd Battalion *Voluntários da Pátria*
35th Battalion *Voluntários da Pátria*
36th Battalion *Voluntários da Pátria*

5th Brigade
Commander: Nicolau Feguerstein
5th Battalion *Voluntários da Pátria*
11th Battalion 'Corps of Zouaves' (temporary line unit)

3rd Division
Commander: Colonel Silva Ouriques

6th Brigade
Commander: Lucas de Lima
10th Provisional Corps (*Corpo Provisorio*)
11th Provisional Corps (*Corpo Provisorio*)
12th Provisional Corps (*Corpo Provisorio*)

13th Provisional Corps (*Corpo Provisorio*)
14th Provisional Corps (*Corpo Provisorio*)

7th Brigade
Commander: Figueiredo Neves
15th Provisional Corps (*Corpo Provisorio*)
16th Provisional Corps (*Corpo Provisorio*)
17th Provisional Corps (*Corpo Provisorio*)
18th Provisional Corps (*Corpo Provisorio*)
19th Provisional Corps (*Corpo Provisorio*)

Light Division
Commander: Barao de Jacui (Baron of Jacui)

8th Brigade
Commander: Pereira Machado
20th Provisional Corps (*Corpo Provisorio*)
21st Provisional Corps (*Corpo Provisorio*)

9th Brigade
Commander: Astrogildo Pereira
22nd Provisional Corps (*Corpo Provisorio*)
33rd Provisional Corps (*Corpo Provisorio*)

Two independent brigades

10th Brigade
Commander: Tristao Nobrega
3rd Infantry Battalion (Line)
24th Provisional Corps (*Corpo Provisorio*)
25th Provisional Corps (*Corpo Provisorio*)
26th Provisional Corps (*Corpo Provisorio*)

11th Brigade
Commander: Apolinario Trindade
27th Provisional Corps (*Corpo Provisorio*)
28th Provisional Corps (*Corpo Provisorio*)
29th Provisional Corps (*Corpo Provisorio*)
30th Provisional Corps (*Corpo Provisorio*)
1 squadron (mounted) of *Voluntários da Pátria*
1 company of National Guard Reserve (based at Alegrete)
1 company of National Guard Reserve (based at Sant' Ana do Livramento)

Independent units

4th Foot Artillery Battalion
Provisional Corps of Artillery (*Provisorio Corpo de Artilharia*)**
Corps of Pontoniers
Corps of Transport
3rd Line Cavalry Regiment

*In Tasso Fragoso's list this and the other *Voluntários da Pátria* units are called *Corpo de Voluntários da Pátria*. For clarity I have named them battalions, this being a more accurate term regarding their strength than the British equivalent 'corps'.
**The Artillery consisted of six smoothbores, six rifled guns, and eight 'Paixan cannon' (light carronades), the last being taken from Brazilian ships stationed at Montevideo.

guns on the island. The Argentines then made an attempt to retake the village at bayonet point, the infantry having used up their ammunition, but at 18:30 Conesa gave the command for an orderly withdrawal, possibly to regroup and obtain a fresh supply of ammunition. During the night of 1 February the Paraguayans embarked on their boats and returned to Itapirú.

Losses to the Argentines in this action were 88 killed and 314 wounded, while the Paraguayans lost 200 killed, 400 wounded, and nine taken prisoner. The engagement had special interest in Buenos Aires, as most of the National Guard troops of the 2nd Division had originated from here, and many of the casualties were from well-known families in the city. The irregularity of the Argentines' ammunition supply led to the creation of a factory for the manufacture of small arms ammunition at Corrientes, under the direction of Lieutenant Americo de Vasconcelos, which by 10 January 1867 had produced 138,000 line infantry cartridges, 178,000 light infantry cartridges, 410,000 cavalry carbine cartridges, 300,000 pistol cartridges, and 1,041,000 percussion caps. This factory would continue production throughout the war.

THE FIGHTING ROUND ITAPIRÚ

In February 1866 three Paraguayan steamers – the *Igurei*, *Gualeguay*, and *25 de Mayo* (the latter two being the Argentine ships captured at Corrientes the previous year) – left Humaitá and steamed to Paso de la Patria. Here, on the 20th, they took aboard a force of 1,000 men made up of two infantry battalions, two cannon, and two rocket launchers, under the command of Lieutenant-Colonel José Díaz, and steamed toward the Allied town of Itatí, further along the Paraná, where the Allied vanguard division was stationed. General Flores was absent at this moment and had left General Gregorio Suárez in command, who had received orders from General Mitre to avoid any engagement with the enemy. Following these orders, he therefore ordered a withdrawal to San Cosmé some eight miles (13 km) away. The Paraguayans did not follow him, but simply looted and destroyed the town and campsite. The *Igurei* and *25 de Mayo* then returned to Humaitá while the *Gualeguay* remained on the Paraná.

The following month it was the turn of the Allied fleet, under the command of Admiral Tamandaré, to assist its land forces. On 21 March, Tamandaré set out with his fleet from the mouth of the River Paraguay towards the town of Corrales. With him were 18 steam gunboats of six to eight guns each, three casemate ironclads (the *Tamandaré*, *Brasil*, and *Barroso*), plus the monitor *Bahia*, which had two 150-pdr Whitworth guns in a revolving turret. The fort of Itapirú would be their first obstacle, or so they thought. The River Paraná was deep everywhere, except opposite the island of Carayá in the northern channel, where there was only 12 ft (3.6 m) of water. López had sunk two large canoes filled with stones here in order to block the inner channel, in which he placed two of his flat-bottomed gunboats or *chatas*, each armed with an 8-inch smoothbore cannon firing 68 lb shot. In addition the steamer *Gualeguay*, under the command of Lieutenant López, was stationed close by.

On the 22nd the *Gualeguay* towed one of the *chatas* to a position half a mile (0.8 km) below Itapirú, close to the shore, from where it opened fire on the assembled Allied fleet. Its fire was instantly returned, with shot and shell falling everywhere except in the neighbourhood of the gunboat. The three Allied ironclads surrounded the gunboat, keeping up an incessant fire, and as the distance between the opposing vessels closed to only 100 yds (90 m) the *chata*'s crew leaped off and swam to the riverbank. The Brazilians then sent three small boats to take the abandoned gunboat, but as they reached it a company of Paraguayan infantry stationed in woods along the bank opened fire, forcing the enemy to retire empty-handed. The ironclads then resumed their fire on the gunboat until a lucky shot hit its powder magazine. Though this rendered the boat useless, its cannon was not harmed and was recovered by the Paraguayans to be used again.

The 27th saw the second *chata* towed down to the same place to fire on the Allied fleet, although this time its cartridges were kept on the river bank to prevent them blowing up, and a man was continually employed carrying them to the boat. Again the three Allied ironclads were sent to deal with the gunboat, until one of its massive balls struck the *Tamandaré* on a port-sill, entered the turret, hit the opposite wall and bounced back, disabling its 68-pdr gun and splintering into fragments that killed 20 crewmen and wounded a further 15. (Among the dead was the *Tamandaré*'s commander Mariz e Barros, who died while having both legs amputated without chloroform.) Though this forced her to retire the other two ironclads continued firing, at the gunboat, at the infantry on the riverbank, and at the fort of Itapirú – which was now only armed with a rifled 12-pdr, its other cannon having been taken elsewhere. The following day the Allies sent the three ironclads, the *Bahia*, and four wooden steamers to destroy the *chata*, and this time the ironclad *Barroso* received four holes through her plates while one of her Whitworths was shot in two. But the *chata* was not so lucky today, as her cannon was also struck and put out of action.

Now it was the turn of the *Gualeguay*, with its two 12-pdr guns, to defy the Allied fleet, which it did in the same fashion as the two gunboats had, to the amusement of President López, who used to watch the proceedings from his base at Paso de la Patria using his telescope. The *Gualeguay* was hit only once during the three weeks that it held this position, and that was in its funnel. Each day it would retire at dusk and return in the morning. The Allied ships meanwhile continued to fire at Itapirú as well as at the *Gualeguay*. Twelve rifled 12-pdr cannons and four 13-inch mortars were also placed in Corrales by the Allies, to fire at Itapirú.

The *Gualeguay* would later be sunk by the Paraguayans as they retired from the Paso de la Patria, so that she would not fall into the hands of the Allies. However. The latter raised her and she was returned to the Argentine Navy.

On 5 April 1866 a Brazilian detachment of 900 infantry, commanded by Lieutenant-Colonel João Carlos de Willagran Cabrite of the Engineers, seized the Banco de Itapirú or Cerrito – a sandbank in the middle of the Paraná some 1,650 yds (1,500 m) from the fort of Itapirú – and fortified it, running up the Brazilian flag. Cabrite's force comprised the 7th *Voluntários da Pátria* commanded by Lieutenant-Colonel Pinto Pacca and the 14th Line Battalion commanded by Major José Martins, with two batteries of four cannon each, four 22-inch mortars, two 12-inch La Hitte cannon, two light horse-artillery pieces, 100 Engineers, and a rocket battery. President López then ordered the fort of Itapirú to bombard the sandbank, and on the night of the 10th he sent 600 men from the 3rd Battalion and 186 dismounted cavalry armed with only their sabres to retake it. This force was commanded by Lieutenant-Colonel José Díaz, who directed the attack from Itapirú fort, while a further 480 men of the 9th Battalion, commanded by Major Vázquez, were held in reserve.

The attacking force was divided into two divisions of about 400 men each. The first, commanded by Captain N. Romero (who was captured in the attack), was transported to the island in 32 canoes and captured the first line of enemy trenches. Reinforced by the second division, commanded by Major Luis González, the fighting then centred around the Allied artillery, which responded by firing grape. When the attack was called off at dawn only 300 Paraguayans managed to get back, and many of these were wounded. In addition the Paraguayans lost 30 canoes and 700 muskets. Brazilian losses were four officers and 48 men killed and six officers and 96 men wounded. The afternoon of the same day saw the death of Lieutenant-Colonel Cabrite and his ADC, killed by a shell from the fort of Itapirú. (During Carlos López's presidency Cabrite had been sent to Paraguay as an instructor to the army, and while there had become a friend of José Maria Bruguéz, who was in command of the artillery that killed him.) The island of Cerrito was later reinforced and made into an Argentine garrison.

THE ALLIES INVADE

Initially it was proposed that a landing opposite the town of Itatí would be the Allies' best invasion plan, but this idea was later rejected. Instead, they organised their naval units into three divisions: the first was to bombard the fort of Itapirú, the second was to steam up the River Paraguay and bombard Paso de la Patria from its flank, and the third was to protect the transports that would be used to carry the Allied troops across the Paraguay. A force of 14,365 men was organised, made up of 9,465 Brazilians (the 1st and 3rd Infantry Divisions from the 1st Brazilian Corps, with a battery of artillery) under the command of General Osório, plus 4,000 Argentines and 900 Uruguayans commanded by General Flores. The Argentine troops were infantry drawn from the 2nd Corps under the command of General Paunero. These would be transported in two waves by eight steamships and four gunboats towing 12 canoes, the Brazilians landing first and the Argentine and Uruguayan troops forming the second wave.

At 7:30 a.m. on 16 April 1866 the naval units began their bombardment of Itapirú and Paso de la Patria, while the Brazilian troops under General Osório landed a mile and a quarter (2 km) upriver, transported in the steamers *Wiper*, towing the barge *Rio Grande*, with a total of 1,300 men; *Whiteinch*, towing the barge *Cearense*, with another 1,300 men; and *Suzan Bearne*, with the barge *Pernambucana* carrying a total of 1,460 men. These troops were from the Brazilian 3rd Infantry Division under General Sampaio. The first wave, landed from the *Whiteinch*, comprised 100 sappers, who cleared the bank and began to dig trenches, and 500 infantry consisting of

two companies of the 2nd Line Battalion, two companies of the 2nd Battalion of Volunteers, and one company of the 11th Battalion of Volunteers. With them was General Osório with his aides and eight escorts. Gradually the remainder of the Brazilian troops were landed, including the artillery battery of four cannon under Lieutenant-Colonel Emílio Luís Mallet. By 1400 hours this vanguard force had managed to advance three miles (5 km) towards the fort of Itapirú.

The second wave had to land at night because of a storm during the day. This was transported aboard the *Marcílio Dias* (1,300 men), *Presidente* (914 men), *Riachuelo* (1,400 men), *Duque de Saxe* (260 men), and *Berenice* (540 men) and entrenched itself immediately in readiness for the expected Paraguayan counter-attack. The following day 200 Paraguayans with two cannon under the command of Captain Benegas reconnoitred the Allied force and immediately attacked it, Benegas also sending word to his superior Lieutenant-Colonel Basílio Benítez to bring his 1,400 men to assist in pushing back the invaders. However, force of numbers prevailed and Benítez was forced to harass the Allies rather than attempt a full attack. Realising the fort of Itapirú could soon be surrounded, López ordered the withdrawal of its garrison, while sending 1,800 additional troops to Benítez with orders to attack again. These reinforcements were composed of the 7th, 8th, 12th, and 18th Infantry Battalions and the 20th and 29th Cavalry Regiments, the latter of whom were to fight both as dismounted and mounted troops. But General Osório had time to despatch the 1st and 13th Line Battalions under Colonel Jacinto Machado to outflank the attacking Paraguayans, this manoeuvre capturing two cannon and inflicting losses of 400 killed and 100 captured. Brazilian losses were given as 65 killed, 288 wounded, and four missing.

After keeping the fort of Itapirú under constant bombardment, General Osório sent the Brazilian 6th Infantry Battalion to capture it, not knowing that it had been evacuated the day before. Lieutenant-Colonel Díaz's garrison, composed of the 20th, 27th, 39th, and 40th Infantry Battalions, half of the 7th Infantry Battalion, the 21st Cavalry Regiment, and half of the 20th Cavalry Regiment, had withdrawn successfully, taking the fort's two 68-pdr guns with it. Why López did not order this force to join that of Lieutenant-Colonel Benítez to assist in opposing the Allied advance is not known. The Brazilian occupation of the fort meant that the invasion could now proceed without this noteworthy thorn in its side.

The Allied vanguard pressed on to Paso de la Patria, before which their fleet arrived on the 19th without opposition and made preparations for the bombardment of the Paraguayan encampment the following day. On seeing the ships take up their positions López departed, leaving General Resquín in command. Resquín ordered a general evacuation of the 24,000 men encamped there, only retaining a garrison sufficient to cover the trenches. The artillery of this holding force was under the command of Lieutenant-Colonel Bruguéz, while the infantry were commanded by Lieutenant-Colonel Hilario Marcó. By daybreak of the 20th most of the other troops and the army's camp-followers had managed to escape, and the small garrison was left to defend the parapets as best it could. However, after two days of bombardment the entrenchments were also

Colonel Hilario Marcó, Paraguay's Chief of Police. (Courtesy of the Arquivo Historico do Exercito, Rio de Janeiro)

evacuated, the garrison being ordered to burn everything left behind as it retired to regroup with the main army. This withdrawal was completed early in the morning on the 23rd. If the position had been defended as Thompson suggests in his memoirs, rather than being evacuated, López would have lost all of the artillery and maybe most of the garrison. One presumes that López had expected the Allies to use the same route that his forces had to cross the Paraná, and his flanks were consequently protected by no more than the marshy terrain. However, by taking advantage of local knowledge his next line of defences would be more of a problem for the Allies.

The Allied army took two more weeks to be transported into Paraguay from the town of Corrales. In all this force consisted of 42,000 infantry and 15,000 cavalry, composed of 81 infantry battalions (29 of them regular line units), six regiments of regular cavalry, 40 additional units of volunteer/militia cavalry, a battalion of engineers, and 87 pieces of artillery, plus supplies to feed, clothe, and shelter the whole army. In April 1866, the Brazilians had 32,868 men in their 1st Corps, while the 2nd Corps of 15,660 men was on the march from San Borja to unite with the 1st Corps on the Paraná. Colonel Beverina writes that at this date the Argentine forces

mustered against Paraguay numbered 25,000 men, made up of 12,600 infantry, 700 artillery (in four squadrons with a total of 33 field-pieces), a battalion of sappers, and 25 units of cavalry including four line cavalry regiments, the Squadron of Guides, the Paraguayan Legion, and the Piquete Correntino. The Uruguayan troops amounted to 2,857 men, including four infantry battalions, the 1st, 2nd, and 4th National Guard Cavalry regiments, the General's Escort, and a squadron of light artillery.

The Paraguayans had meanwhile retired behind the great marsh of the Estero Bellaco, which had the River Paraguay on one side and the River Paraná 100 miles (160 km) to the east on the other. This formed a natural barrier with few causeways across it. Two parallel streams ran through it that were generally about three miles (5 km) apart, these helping to create the marshlands. This was the country of both the yatai palm and the pirí rush, the latter growing in 3–6 ft (0.9–1.8 m) of water and standing to a height of 5–9 ft (1.5–2.75 m) above the surface, while the palm trees reach 30–100 ft (9–30 m). Causeways were created where the rushes had been pulled out and replaced by sand, although these too were often under water. López despatched 50 marksmen from his Rifle Guard to conceal themselves in these marshes and pick off any enemy officers that might come within range.

The vanguard of the Allied forces under the command of General Flores was encamped near the southern edge of the marsh. This consisted of four Uruguayan infantry battalions ('Florida', '24 de Abril', 'Libertad', and 'Independencia') totalling 1,300 men; a Uruguayan artillery battery of six guns commanded by Major Yance; the Mounted Escort to General Flores (200 men); six Brazilian infantry battalions from the 6th Division (the 5th and 7th Line Infantry, and the 3rd, 16th, 21st, and 38th *Voluntários da Pátria*); the Brazilian 5th Artillery Battery; and the Brazilian 4th Cavalry Regiment. Further behind on the right flank were camped three companies of the Argentine Infantry Battalion of Rosario and the 1st Cavalry Regiment, while the main body of the Allied army was camped a mile (1.6 km) north of the Paso la Patria and busily building trenches.

On 2 May 1866 a force of 4,500 Paraguayan infantry, 1,000 cavalry, and a mixed battery of 4-pdrs and 8-pdrs (commanded by Lieutenant-Colonel Bruguéz), under the command of Lieutenant-Colonel José Díaz, was sent to surprise the Allied vanguard. Its main column – consisting of the 13th, 24th, 36th, and 40th Infantry Battalions, with artillery under the command of Major Giménez – used the Paso Sidra; a column under the command of Lieutenant-Colonel Francisco Fidel Valiente, made up of the 4th and 21st Cavalry Regiments, advanced along the Paso Pires; and Lieutenant-Colonel Benítez, commanding the 7th and 13th Cavalry Regiments, made his way via the Paso Carreta. The reserve, under the command of Major Avelino Cabral, was made up of the 1st, 19th, and 42nd Infantry Battalions with the 10th Cavalry Regiment.

The surprise, at 11:00 a.m., was complete, the Allied artillery having only enough time to fire one salvo before being captured. The Brazilian 7th Line Infantry was the first unit to be set upon. They fell back onto the positions of the 21st and 38th Volunteer Battalions, which were also forced back under a lively fire from the Paraguayan artillery. This gave the Uruguayan brigade enough time to take up arms, but it only managed to check the assault as it reached the encampment of the main body. The '24 de Abril' Battalion advanced to assist the Brazilian 21st Volunteers but both units were pushed back. To save the situation Colonel Palleja ordered his 'Florida' Battalion to fix bayonets and charge, but the attack received no support and the battalion was surrounded for an hour until the main Allied body came into action and repulsed the Paraguayans.

The Paraguayan column under Lieutenant-Colonel Benítez targeted the encampment of the Argentine 1st Cavalry Regiment, which had the support of three companies from the Volunteer Battalion of Rosario commanded by Major Racedo. The commander of the 1st Cavalry, Lieutenant-Colonel Segovia, ordered his 250 men to mount up and meet the oncoming Paraguayans, who after a hard fight were forced to retreat.

Of the Uruguayan troops involved in this action the 'Florida' Battalion had only eight effective officers remaining by the time it was over, having lost 19 officers and 100 men; the '24 de Abril' Battalion lost four officers and 80 men; and the 'Libertad' lost three officers and 33 men. The three leading Brazilian battalions received 300 casualties. In all Allied losses comprised: Brazilians, 15 officers and 236 men killed, 67 officers and 776 men wounded, and one officer and seven men taken prisoner; Uruguayans, 400 killed and wounded; and Argentines, 61 killed and wounded, all from the 1st Cavalry Regiment. While the fighting was still going on, four 9-pdr rifled brass La Hitte guns complete with their ammunition wagons, and three Allied standards, were sent back to López. The guns were subsequently called the 'Flores guns' by the Paraguayans, who would use them for the rest of the war. Several other guns were also captured, but had to be abandoned when, instead of retiring from the field with them and making good his escape, Lieutenant-Colonel Díaz chose to confront the oncoming Allied troops under Generals Osõrio and Mitre, who outflanked him and forced him to retreat.

Paraguayan casualties in this battle – which would become known as the Battle of Estero Bellaco – totalled 2,300 killed and wounded, including 330 men wounded and taken prisoner. Lieutenant-Colonel Benítez was among the dead. A number of Paraguayans (a figure of 700 has been quoted) who had been previously captured at Uruguayana and pressed into service for the Allies took the opportunity to desert and rejoin their old comrades during the fighting.

After the battle General Flores wrote to his wife: 'Yesterday the vanguard, under my orders, sustained a considerable defeat, the Oriental Division being almost completely lost ... In future my vanguard will be composed of Argentines.'

THE FIRST BATTLE OF TUYUTI

On 20 May 1866 the Allied army of 32,000 men began to move through the Estero Bellaco in three columns, encamping on the low ground just south of the northern point of the marshes, where they occupied a front of about 4,200 yds (3,800 m) in the shape of a horseshoe. Here they constructed two redoubts, one in the centre and the other on the left flank, and emplaced their 150 field-pieces, most of which were rifled. At the same time López removed his headquarters to Paso Pucú, where he

was to remain based for two years, while trenches were dug in all the passes from Gomez to Rojas. In front of these trenches were the marshes, ranging in depth up to 6 ft (1.8 m), while between the passes were *carrizal* of impenetrable jungle. His intention was to await the Allied advance, and by using a secret pass send in a flanking movement of 10,000 men against the Allied rear. One can only imagine the confusion that this would have caused.

When, on 23 May, news reached López that the Allies intended to advance against these positions on the 25th, he changed his plan and decided that his troops would attack the enemy the following day in what would be called the First Battle of Tuyuti. General Vicente Barrios, with 8,000 infantry (six battalions), 1,000 cavalry (two regiments), and ten artillery pieces, was to attack the Allied left flank; General Isidoro Resquín, with 7,000 cavalry (eight regiments), 3,000 infantry (two battalions), and four Congreve rocket launchers, was to go for the right flank; while Colonel José Díaz, with 6,000 infantry (nine battalions), 1,000 cavalry (four regiments), and four howitzers, was to attack the centre. Díaz's command was divided into two columns, the second, made up of four battalions of infantry and two regiments of cavalry, being commanded by Colonel Hilario Marcó. The reserve, of 7,000 men and 48 field-pieces commanded by Lieutenant-Colonel José Maria Bruguéz, was positioned along the Paraguayan entrenchments of Estero Rojas.

As General Barrios had the hardest journey to make through *carrizal* before he would arrive at Paso Gomez near the Piris Potrero clearing and lake, he left camp at four in the morning on 24 May. His cavalry was

Photograph of President Francisco Solano López, in dress uniform, taken c.1866. (Courtesy of the Arquivo Historico do Exercito, Rio de Janeiro)

obliged to dismount and the column had to proceed in single file. The column's expected time of arrival was 9:00 a.m., but it didn't arrive until 11:00, and deploying it took another hour. Finally, at 11:55, a Congreve rocket was fired as the signal for the general advance. The plan was for the infantry on the flanks to push back the defenders so that the two columns of cavalry could sweep forward and head for the stores and ammunition stockpiled at the rear of the Allied camp.

Luckily for the Allies, at the time of the attack General Mitre was in the process of organising a reconnaissance in force ready for the following day's main attack on the Paraguayan positions, which was intended to provide a victory to coincide with Argentina's Independence Day, the 25th. Consequently within just a few minutes of the Paraguayan advance commencing, a skirmisher of the Brazilian 4th Infantry Battalion is recorded to have informed his commanding officer that 'The woods are full of red-shirted Paraguayans!' Following this, the noise of musketry fire soon became a continuous din, with sporadic cannon fire along the whole front. General Barrios' forces pushed back the Brazilian troops under the command of General Osõrio, but the latter rallied and forced the Paraguayans back in turn; this happened three times. The Brazilian artillery under the command of Colonel Emílio Luís Mallet, comprising 28 Whitworth and La Hitte guns, created havoc amongst Barrios' men. The Allied position here had been prepared with a hidden ditch in front of the emplacements, known as the *Fosso de Mallet*, and Colonel Mallet's famous call to his men of '*Por aqui nao entram!*' ('They shall not enter here!') is now part of Brazilian military legend. General Barrios states that Mallet's guns fired shrapnel with fuses cut to six seconds, and because of their high rate of fire the Allied troops nicknamed them *artilharia de revolver* ('revolver artillery'). Meanwhile the Paraguayan cavalry on this flank also played a key part in the attack, with some managing to manoeuvre around the first defences only to come up against another Brazilian position and be caught in a withering fire.

In the centre Colonel Díaz, with the column commanded by Colonel Marcó on his left, was up against the Vanguard Division of General Flores. In front of him was a long stretch of marshland, across which he had to advance before reaching the enemy artillery positions, which contained 34 guns. Many of Díaz's troops were newly recruited and as such often became bunched up and made easy targets for the Allied artillery, which had only been allocated two charges of grape per gun, the remainder of their ammunition consisting of shells. One Paraguayan battalion that had a particularly large influx of new recruits was the 25th, and they found themselves bogged down before the Allied gun emplacements. When General Flores called out to them to surrender or face certain death, their reply was that they had no order to surrender from their President, so they were raked with artillery fire until this section of the battlefield was literally filled with their dead.

Further along the line the Paraguayan infantry did manage to charge home against the Allied positions and engaged in furious hand-to-hand fighting. On the left flank units from both Barrios' and Díaz's commands came up against the Brazilian 3rd Division, supported by the artillery batteries of Colonel Mallet. This division was under the command of General Antonio Sampaio. The

Paraguayans were forced to retreat, but only after General Sampaio had been mortally wounded by three bullets (he would die on 8 June). The 3rd Division was to suffer 1,033 casualties during the fighting. One of its units, the 4th Infantry Battalion, started the day with 490 men, but by 4:30 p.m. only 200 remained unwounded, having lost seven officers, seven cadets and sergeants, and over 100 men. Its commander continued to shout '*Fogo, Batalhão!*' ('Fire, Battalion!') even when seriously wounded, before being carried off the field and his place on the firing line taken by General Sampaio. Following this battle the 3rd Division became known as the *Divisão Encouracada* or 'Armoured Division'.

The Paraguayan cavalry under General Resquín managed to charge and put to flight the Correntino cavalry under the command of Generals Caceres and Hornos, before pushing on to attack the artillery on their right, taking 20 guns. However, Resquín's cavalry were not supported quickly enough, and the Argentine 1st Line Infantry Battalion and the *Legión Militar* Infantry Battalion, both from General Wenceslao Paunero's division, managed to counter-attack and save the guns while decimating the remaining Paraguayan cavalry. By the time that General Resquín's infantry arrived the recaptured field-pieces were in action again, supported by the Argentine 1st Infantry and *Legión Militar*. With the arrival of Brazilian reinforcements from General Osõrio's divisions, the destruction of this Paraguayan force soon began. However, all was not yet lost, as Resquín's reserve cavalry managed to skirt the right flank to unite with the cavalry under General Barrios. Though the four Argentine battalions from the National Guard of the Buenos Aires Division quickly formed a defensive line and laid down a deadly fire on them, the Paraguayan 9th Cavalry, under the command of Major Olabarrieta, was still able to force its way through, but without support from the cavalry of General Barrios it had to fight its way right through the Allied camp, and only a few men returned with the badly wounded Olabarrieta to reach the Paraguayan lines.

By 4:30 p.m. the battle was over. The Paraguayans left behind 6,000 dead (the Allies counted 4,200 bodies on the battlefield), while 370 were captured, many of them wounded. A further 7,000 wounded managed to make it back to the Paraguayan lines. Of the Allies, four Argentine field officers were killed (Matias Rivero, Roja, Lindolfo Pagola, and Benjamin Basabilbaso), and overall casualties are stated to have been 4,000. The official report of 27 May gives these figures: Argentines, 126 killed including four field and seven other officers, and 480 wounded including two field and 35 other officers; Brazilians, 489 killed and 2,522 wounded, including one general, ten field and 203 other officers; Uruguayans, 133 killed including 12 officers, and 163 wounded including 17 officers. Another list, drawn up ten days later, gives the Brazilian dead as 718 including 61 officers and one General, so it would appear that a number of the wounded had died in the interim.

Following the battle the Allied forces stayed at their encampment until September, despite General Mitre being told, in a letter from Vice-President Marcos Paz, that a major victory was needed to offset the adverse publicity provided by the heavy casualties suffered at Tuyuti. There are a number of factors which might explain this lack of determination. The most obvious are

Table 6: Orders of Battle, First Battle of Tuyuti (25 May 1866)

PARAGUAY

1st Column
Commander: General Barrios
6 infantry battalions
2 cavalry regiments
4 rocket launchers and light artillery
Total: 3,500

2nd Column
Commander: Brigadier-General Resquín
2 infantry battalions
8 cavalry regiments
2 rocket launchers
Total: 6,300

3rd Column
Commander: Colonel José E. Díaz
5 infantry battalions
2 cavalry regiments
4 light howitzers
Total: 5,030

4th Column
Commander: Colonel Hilario Marcó
4 infantry battalions
2 cavalry regiments
Total: 4,200

Reserve units
Commander: Colonel José M. Bruguéz
These included 2 horse artillery regiments
Total: 7,000

From Jürg Meister's *Francisco Solano López: Nationalheld order Kriegsverbrecher?* (1987) and Adolfo I. Baez's *Tuyuty* (1929), we know that the Paraguayan units involved were: the Rifles Battalion, the 1st, 4th, 6th, 7th, 9th, 11th, 12th, 19th, 20th, 21st, 30th, 37th, 40th, 41st, and 42nd Infantry Battalions, the Dragoon Regiment No.11, and the 1st, 10th, 13th, 15th, 17th, 19th, 21st, 26th, and 34th Cavalry Regiments. However, neither author records which units were in what column.

ALLIES

ARGENTINA
Commander-in-Chief: Brigadier-General Bartolomé Mitre

1st ARMY CORPS
Commander: General Wenceslao Paunero

I Division
Commander: Colonel Rivas

1st Brigade
Commander: Lieutenant-Colonel Rozetti
1st Line Infantry Battalion
5th Line Infantry Battalion

2nd Brigade
Commander: Lieutenant-Colonel Charlone
Legión Militar (later to become the 3rd Infantry Battalion)

II Division
Commander: Colonel Arredondo

3rd Brigade
Commander: Lieutenant-Colonel Fraga
4th Line Infantry Battalion
6th Line Infantry Battalion

4th Brigade
Commander: Lieutenant-Colonel Orms
2nd Line Infantry Battalion
1st Volunteer Infantry Battalion

5th Brigade
Commander: Colonel Riveros
1st National Guard of Corrientes
1st National Guard of Santa Fe
Paraguayan Legion (Colonel Iturburu with 167 men)

Brigade of Artillery
Commander: Lieutenant-Colonel Nelson
2nd Horse Artillery (light)
3rd Horse Artillery (light)
4th Horse Artillery (light)

Brigade of Cavalry
Commander: Colonel Fernandes
Commander's Escort
1st Line Cavalry Regiment
Volunteer Cavalry Regiment of Santa Fe

Auxiliary troops
Medical Corps and Quartermaster Corps (total of 295 men)

2nd ARMY CORPS
Commander: General Gelly y Obes

(I believe the battalions I have marked with an asterisk to be the 2nd battalions of their respective units.)

I Division
Commander: Colonel Coneza
2nd National Guard Battalion of Buenos Aires
3rd National Guard Battalion of Buenos Aires
4th National Guard Battalion of Buenos Aires

II Division
Commander: Colonel Bustillos
1st National Guard Battalion of Buenos Aires
5th National Guard Battalion of Buenos Aires
2nd National Guard Battalion of Buenos Aires*
4th National Guard Battalion of Buenos Aires*

Table 6: Orders of Battle, First Battle of Tuyuti (25 May 1866) (continued)

III Division
Commander: Colonel Vedia
9th Line Infantry Battalion
1st National Guard Battalion of Buenos Aires*
2nd Legion of Volunteers

Cavalry Division
Commander: Colonel Oryazabal
1st National Guard Cavalry Regiment
3rd National Guard Cavalry Regiment
(Total cavalry: 501 men)

Artillery
Commander: Colonel Frederico Mitre
2nd Regiment (total of 272 combatants)

URUGUAY
Commander-in-Chief: General Venancio Flores

Staff Corps (69 men)
Cavalry Escort, Lieutenant-Colonel Fortunato Flores
    (265 men)

I Division
Cavalry Brigade
Commander: Henrique de Castro
1st National Guard Cavalry Regiment
2nd National Guard Cavalry Regiment
4th National Guard Cavalry Regiment
(Total 776 men)

1st Infantry Brigade
Commander: Colonel Leon Palleja
Infantry Battalion 'Florida'
Infantry Battalion '24 de Abril'
(Total 924 men)

2nd Infantry Brigade
Commander: Lieutenant-Colonel Marcelino
Infantry Battalion 'Libertad'
Infantry Battalion 'Independencia'
(Total 564 men)

Artillery Brigade
(Total 249 men)

(235 battalion and regimental officers need to be added to the total of troops in this division.)

BRAZIL
Commander-in-Chief: General Osōrio

1st Division
Commander: General Argollo

8th Brigade
Commander: Colonel D. José
8th Infantry Battalion (Major Azevedo)
16th Infantry Battalion (Major Fagundes)
10th Infantry Battalion (Volunteers) (Lieutenant-Colonel Mauricio)

46th Infantry Battalion (Volunteers) (Lieutenant-Colonel D'Araujo)

10th Brigade
Commander: Colonel Resin
2nd Infantry Battalion (Major W. Lins)
13th Infantry Battalion (Major A. Cezar)
22nd Infantry Battalion (Volunteers) (Lieutenant-Colonel Albuquerque)
26th Infantry Battalion (Volunteers) (Major F. de Mello)
40th Infantry Battalion (Volunteers) (Lieutenant-Colonel F. Pocha)

3rd Division
Commander: General Sampaio

5th Brigade
Commander: Colonel Belo
3rd Infantry Battalion (Lieutenant-Colonel Mesquita)
4th Infantry Battalion (Lieutenant-Colonel de Carvalho)
6th Infantry Battalion (Lieutenant-Colonel Paranhos)
4th Infantry Battalion (Volunteers) (Lieutenant-Colonel Guimarães)

7th Brigade
Commander: Colonel J. Machado
1st Infantry Battalion (Major G. Peixoto)
6th Infantry Battalion (Volunteers) (Major S. Valente)
9th Infantry Battalion (Volunteers) (Lieutenant-Colonel J. Bueno)
11th Infantry Battalion (Volunteers) (Major I. Cavalcante)

4th Division
Commander: General de Souza

11th Brigade
Commander: Colonel Auto
10th Infantry Battalion (Major Tavora)
14th Infantry Battalion (Major A. de Oliveira)
20th Infantry Battalion (Volunteers) (Lieutenant-Colonel C. de Castro)
31st Infantry Battalion (Volunteers) (Colonel Machado)

13th Brigade
Commander: Lieutenant-Colonel C. Pereira
12th Infantry Battalion (Major J. Nepomuceno)
1st Infantry Battalion (Volunteers) (Major Araujo e Mello)
19th Infantry Battalion (Volunteers) (Lieutenant-Colonel Cavalcante Bello)
24th Infantry Battalion (Volunteers) (Captain Valporto)

6th Division
Commander: General Monteiro

12th Brigade
Commander: Colonel Kelly
5th Infantry Battalion (Major B.J. Goncalves)

Table 6: Orders of Battle, First Battle of Tuyuti (25 May 1866) (continued)

7th Infantry Battalion (Lieutenant-Colonel Pedra)
3rd Infantry Battalion (Volunteers) (Lieutenant-Colonel Rocha Galvão)
16th Infantry Battalion (Volunteers) (Major do Corpo)

14th Brigade
Commander: Lieutenant-Colonel Salustiano
2nd Infantry Battalion (Major Wanderley Lins)
14th Infantry Battalion (Volunteers)
21st Infantry Battalion (Volunteers) (Major G. Olympio)
30th Infantry Battalion (Volunteers) (Lieutenant-Colonel Apolionio)

18th Brigade
Commander: Colonel E. Silva
38th Infantry Battalion (Volunteers) (Lieutenant-Colonel Freire de Carvaiho)
41st Infantry Battalion (Volunteers) (Major Souza Guedes)
51st Infantry Battalion (Volunteers) (Lieutenant-Colonel F. Villar)

2nd Cavalry Division
Commander: General José Luís Mena Barreto

1st Brigade
Commander: Lieutenant-Colonel Bastos
2nd Line Cavalry Regiment (Captain Wenceslao)
3rd Line Cavalry Regiment (Captain da Rocha)
1st Corps of National Guard Cavalry (Major Silva)

4th Brigade
Commander: Lieutenant-Colonel M. de Oliveira Bueno
2nd Corps of National Guard Cavalry
5th Corps of National Guard Cavalry (Lieutenant-Colonel Leirina)

7th Corps of National Guard Cavalry (Lieutenant-Colonel Niéderauer)

5th Cavalry Division
Commander: Colonel T. Pinho

3rd Brigade
Commander: Lieutenant-Colonel Mesquita
4th Corps of National Guard Cavalry (Major Ferrador)
6th Corps of National Guard Cavalry (Lieutenant-Colonel Jardim)
11th Corps of National Guard Cavalry

15th Brigade
Commander: Colonel Demetro Ribeiro
3rd Corps of National Guard Cavalry
9th Corps of National Guard Cavalry
10th Corps of National Guard Cavalry

Independent Volunteer Cavalry
Commander: Brigadier-General Neto
1st Volunteer Cavalry Corps (Major Rozado)
2nd Volunteer Cavalry Corps
3rd Volunteer Cavalry Corps
4th Volunteer Cavalry Corps

Artillery Train
Commander: General Andrea

17th Brigade
Commander: Colonel Gurjao
1st Mounted Artillery Regiment (Lieutenant-Colonel Mallet)
1st Foot Artillery Battalion (Major Valente)
3rd Foot Artillery Battalion (Major Hermes)

19th Brigade
Commander: Colonel Freitas
Engineer Battalion (Major Conrad Bittancourt)
7th Infantry Battalion (Volunteers) (Lieutenant-Colonel Carolino)
42nd Infantry Battalion (Volunteers) (Major Caldas)

---

that it was the winter season and that provisions were consequently in short supply. In a letter by General Flores to his wife dated 3 May, he says: 'Some of the corps have had nothing to eat for three days. I don't know what will become of us, and if to the critical situation we are in, you add the constant apathy of General Mitre... There are no horses or mules for the trains, and no oxen to eat. If we remain here a month longer, we shall have to repass the Paraná and go into winter-quarters at Corrientes.' The food situation for the Paraguayans, by contrast, was assisted by López sending out raiding and reconnoitring parties daily to steal lightly guarded oxen and horses left out to graze, though the number of horses available for both sides was nearly non-existent.

The Paraguayans had used up the best of their horses at Tuyuti, after which their stamina and physique went downhill; as Thompson states, 'Aides-de-camp and commanders of corps were mounted on jades with nothing but skin and bone, and which could not possibly go beyond a poor walk ... Those horses which had the least strength left had been kept for the event of a battle, [and] had been used on May 24.' The Allies could obtain fresh horses (some 14,000 were sent from the Brazilian province of Rio Grande), but provisions and pasture to feed them were in short supply and the horses were soon past their best. The Argentine Government decreed that all horses in the Argentine Confederation were contraband of war, and then bought up the greater part of the carriage, cart, and pack-horses found in the country's various towns and cities so that they could be sent to the front for use by the army.

Sickness, largely brought on by exhaustion, also played its part in delaying the Allied advance after Tuyuti. Sir Richard Burton states that the diseases found in the Allied camp included cholera, smallpox, fever, and diarrhoea, some 10,000 men becoming victims. Commander Kennedy reports that 'The new, and very young recruits, which, by the great efforts of the Brazilian

Brazilian officers in camp at Tuyutí, showing a variety of daily uniforms, including one man in civilian dress. The photograph was taken by Javier López, who worked for Bate & Co of Montevideo. (Courtesy of SODRE, Montevideo)

government, were being continually raised and hurried off to the front, died almost as soon as they joined their regiments ... This fatal epidemic affected the animals also to such a degree that the cavalry and artillery were nearly unhorsed.' In addition the winter rains turned the marshland rivers into swollen torrents which overflowed into the Allied camp, drowning many men and sweeping away large numbers of horses and cattle.

BATTLES BEFORE THE ALLIED CAMP

During the first few days after the 24th, as wounded stragglers continued to make their way back to the Paraguayan lines, López expected the Allies to make their forward thrust, but, as we have seen, the Allied high command had other things to worry about. In addition to the problems in their camp, the Allied Navy was not clearing the left bank of the River Paraguay as quickly as needed; nor was General Baron de Pôrto Alegre making good speed from the Brazilian province of Rio Grande with reinforcements consisting of 14,000 men and 50 field-pieces.

The breathing space provided by this delay was not wasted by López. A site for a sunken battery was constructed along the cliffs at Curupaytí some 30 ft (9 m) above the River Paraguay, where field artillery and infantry were stationed to impede Allied naval operations and prevent a landing. A small gabion battery armed with an 8-inch gun and two 32-pdrs was placed 3,000 yds (2,750 m) further downriver at a position named Curuzú, where 14 small calibre guns were also placed in reserve. In addition the 10th Infantry Battalion was brought down from recently captured Corumbá in the Brazilian

province of Mato Grosso to garrison Curuzú. Both of these batteries were commanded by Major Sayas. Raiding parties were organised to surprise and harass the Allied outposts, which were ordered to maintain an incessant fire throughout the night as a means of keeping the guards awake.

Due to its losses the Paraguayan army had to be reorganised, and many battalions were amalgamated. All males aged from 12–60 were ordered into the army, and 6,000 black slaves were drafted into its ranks. A group of 200 Payaguá Indians also volunteered for service, and were placed in the heavy artillery units. More trenches were constructed along the defensive lines of Rojas, while additional artillery was manhandled from Asunción and Humaitá, many of these guns being emplaced between the Paso Gomez and Paso Fernández. This short stretch had 37 field-pieces of every imaginable shape and size. In the middle of June there began an almost daily bombardment of the Allied camp, though only the vanguard troops of General Flores were within range. Two Naval officers, sub-lieutenants José Maria Fariña and José Maria Mazó, showed particular skill in the handling of their respective guns, their 8-inch shells reaching whatever point they aimed at.

Both sides now began to erect lookout towers called *mangrullos*, from 50–60 ft (15–18 m) in height, to detect enemy movements and to serve as artillery observation posts. They were made from four straight tree trunks, one being set up at each corner of a square with crossbars that formed landings and provided stability. Though they often looked rather unstable, being lashed together with rawhide straps, they worked, and were quick and easy to make. Telegraph lines were also extended to the Paraguayan front line and to other headquarters such as Humaitá, Curupaytí, and Sauce. All his commanders were obliged to report back to López, who appointed an officer whose sole responsibility was to bring him their despatches. By the end of June 1866 the Paraguayan army on this front had reached 20,000 men and boys, including men recovering from wounds and the walking wounded.

Impatient for the Allies to attack his defensive works, López now strove to entice them to leave their encampment, but was disappointed when a small attacking party failed to persuade them. Not to be diverted from this strategy, on 10 July he despatched two battalions of infantry, the 8th and 30th, under the command of Colonel Elizardo Aquino, to make a feigned attack on a new position taken up just outside the camp perimeter by two companies of the Argentine Infantry Battalion Catamarcqueño, commanded by Major Matoso. This position was quickly reinforced by the Battalion Corrientes, commander Colonel Ignacio Rivas, who, after some skirmishing, followed the retreating Paraguayans, but only for a short distance.

The following afternoon a Paraguayan force of 2,500 men made up from four infantry battalions (the 8th, 13th, 20th, and 30th), the 10th Cavalry Regiment (which was to act as a reserve), and two Congreve rocket launchers was sent forward under the command of the recently promoted General José E. Díaz. This force was divided into two columns. The first, consisting of the 8th and 30th Battalions under Díaz, was to attack the left flank, while the other, made up of the 13th and 20th Battalions and the 10th Cavalry, commanded by Colonel Aquino, was to attack the right flank. This time the Argentines had artillery, commanded by Colonel Vedia, and three infantry battalions (the Battalion Corrientes, the 1st Line Infantry, and the Battalion San Nicolás) under Colonel Ignacio Rivas, with Colonel Arredondo in command of the reserve battalions. After a great deal of firing both parties were forced to leave the field at dusk due to the rockets having set the long grass alight, which impeded further fighting.

When the fire eventually subsided Colonel Rivas advanced with two infantry battalions (the 3rd Line Infantry and *Legión Militar*) to occupy the field, colonels Esquivel and Susini also coming up with four battalions (the 1st, 4th, and 6th Line Infantry and the 1st Legion of Volunteers) when Rivas' force was attacked. The fighting finally stopped at 9:00 p.m., a heavy cannonade having been kept up by both sides throughout the battle, and the Paraguayans retired after having sustained some 400 casualties, including Captain Casimiro Báez (commander of the 8th Battalion) killed and 30 wounded men captured. The Argentines suffered 30 men killed, 177 wounded, and 51 missing. Among the dead were Lieutenant-Colonel Aldecoa of the 3rd Line, Major Fernando Etchegaray of the 1st Line, and Major Valerga, commander of the *Legión Militar*. This engagement was called the Battle of Yataiti-Corá.

Another plan devised by López involved two trenches being dug close to the Brazilian left flank of the Allied position during the night of the 13th, from which snipers and artillery could fire into the camp. The 6th and 7th Infantry Battalions were detailed to dig these trenches, possibly having been selected for the task because they had made such good and fast work of both

the emplacements at Humaitá and the earthworks constructed for the railway. Seven hundred picks and shovels – all that were to be had in the Paraguayan army – were handed out to these men and they were sent off through the two passes that allowed access to Potrero Sauce. A hundred men were also sent out to act as skirmishers 20 yds (18 m) ahead of the trench as a protection against possible attack. The first trench, the southern one, was to be dug a yard wide and a yard deep with the soil being thrown up on the side facing the Allied camp, initially to afford quick protection. This trench was 900 yds (825 m) long. The second entrenchment, at Punta Ñaró, defended the northern entrance to Potrero Sauce on the Allies' right flank. This was made of two trenches, in front of which were placed four small cannon that could easily be removed. Both entrenched positions were placed on the only dry land available, being surrounded by flooded marshland or dense woods.

Somehow this work was carried out without being discovered by the Allied sentries, who should have heard the noise made by Paraguayan sappers. Only at daylight were the entrenchments noticed. The Allied artillery then opened fire on them but with little effect, and no movement against them occurred for two days, the delay in responding possibly being explained by the fact that

Argentine lookout post or mangrullo *in Paraguay, commanded by Captain José 'Pipo' Giribone. Note the crooked lengths of wood used in its construction.* (Courtesy of the Archivo General de la Nacion, Buenos Aires)

General Osório had been taken ill and was only relieved of his command by Lieutenant-General Polidoro da Fonseca Quintanilha Jordao on the 15th. But at 5:00 a.m. on 16 July the Brazilian General Guilherme Souza, with 3,000 men (the 4th Brazilian Division of eight infantry battalions, six horse-artillery guns, and 50 engineers), was ordered to advance to within striking distance of the southern trench. A second attack was to be made by Colonel Oliveira Belo with the 5th Brigade, 3rd Division (four infantry battalions), while Colonel José da Silveira with his 8th Brigade, 1st Division, was to act as reserve. An Argentine force from the 2nd Corps, 1st Division National Guard of Buenos Aires, consisting of the 2nd, 3rd, and 4th Battalions under Colonel Emilio Conesa, was sent to be an additional reserve for the Brazilian troops.

A fierce fight with the Paraguayan defenders ensued, the latter consisting of the 6th, 7th, and 9th Infantry Battalions under Colonel Elizardo Aquino. These eventually retired into the woods situated at the rear of the clearing and from there began a heavy and constant fire of musketry, artillery, and rockets into the Brazilian troops who now occupied the trench at quite close range, and a number of counter-attacks were made using a reinforcement of a further three Paraguayan battalions. In one of these attacks Colonel Aquino was mortally wounded and was replaced by Major António Giménez.[11] At the same time as the initial Brazilian attack on the trench had begun, three Brazilian cavalry regiments attempted to make a left flank attack via the pass into the Potrero Piris to fall on the rear of the Paraguayan position, but the terrain in this sector had deteriorated and become impassable.

After 16 hours of fighting and four counter-attacks the Paraguayans, having done as much damage as possible to the enemy troops who had occupied the trench all day, retired off the field. The Brazilians had suffered losses of 282 men killed including 26 officers, 1,579 wounded including 127 officers, and 38 men missing. The Argentines lost three men killed and 52 wounded, while the Paraguayans had 2,000 killed and wounded, their losses being caused mainly by the many counter-attacks they threw against the Brazilians. This action was called the Battle of Boquerón.

The 17th was taken up by the Allies deciding on their next plan of action, while the two northern trenches were subjected to heavy bombardment. The following day saw a general Brazilian attack on these trenches. The southern trench to Potrero Sauce captured on the 16th received a constant artillery barrage, maintained by General Bruguéz against the advancing Allied columns – made up of the 1st Brigade 2nd Division, 8th Brigade 1st Division, and the 4th Brigade – under the Brazilian General José Luís Mena Barreto, which had begun a flanking movement. This just left a frontal attack to be mounted on the trenches at Punta Ñaró, which was ordered by General Flores. The first wave would consist of the Brazilian 6th Division under the command of General Victorino J.C. Monteiro, while the second wave would be made up of the Argentine 3rd Division of Colonel Cesareo Dominguez (the 2nd Entre Ríos, Mendoza-San Luis, San Juan, and Cordoba Battalions) and two Uruguayan battalions ('Florida' and 'Independencia'). The reserve was made up from the 4th Brazilian Division commanded by General Guilherme

Souza. The Paraguayan defenders, under General Díaz, consisted of the 6th, 7th, 12th, 13th, 36th, and 40th Infantry Battalions and the 21st Cavalry Regiment, supported by four guns and a rocket battery situated further to the rear.

The Allied column nearly reached the Paraguayan trench before being forced to retreat by the withering fire of its defenders. General Flores managed to rally his troops, and, replacing the wounded General Monteiro with General Souza, he ordered one last attack. By this time half of the Paraguayan cannon had come loose from their mountings and could not be fired, but a heavy fire was nevertheless directed against the advancing Allied troops, whose route of attack involved coming along a narrow causeway through the marshland; but this time they overran the trench and planted the Argentine flag on its parapet. At the same moment a reinforcement of 200 dismounted Paraguayan cavalry from the 21st Regiment appeared at the edge of the woods and, armed with nothing but their drawn swords, these charged the Allied troops in the trench and managed to drive them from it. Retaking the cannon, which had been spiked, they soon had the support of the Paraguayans in the second trench.

While the fight for the trench was in progress, López had sent a cavalry force supported by rockets to attack the right flank of the Allied camp, which was occupied by Argentine troops. The section actually attacked was held by the 12th Line Battalion (a light infantry unit, despite its name), commanded by Major Lucio V. Mansilla, which succeeded in repulsing the charge.

Among the Allies killed during this day's action – known as the Battle of Sauce – were Colonels Palleja, Aguero, and Martínez, while the Brazilian General Monteiro was wounded. Brazilian casualties were 630 killed including 50 officers, 2,938 wounded including 210 officers, and one officer and 53 men missing. Argentine losses were 201 killed including 15 officers and 421 wounded including 32 officers. Uruguayan losses were 250 killed and wounded. The Paraguayans lost 2,500 men killed and wounded.

THE BATTLE OF CURUZÚ

At an Allied council of war held on 30 June 1866 it had been agreed that the Navy, under the command of Admiral Tamandaré, should bombard and capture the Paraguayan battery situated at Curupaytí which blocked the passage for further advance up the River Paraguay. This battery had meanwhile been increased to 25 guns, of which three were 8-inch guns and six were 32-pdrs and 24-pdrs, the remainder being of mixed calibre. It was thought that the Paraguayan trenches facing the Allied camp were too difficult to attack, so the river seemed the easiest option, with less risk to the troops involved. On 16 July the Allied Navy steamed to Curupaytí but did not attempt to bombard it. This was the same day as the Battle of Boquerón was being fought, and one can guess what was said to the Navy after the casualties of 16 and 18 July became known.

A landing of Allied troops was thought necessary further down the river, on the left flank of the batteries at Curupaytí. These would then be able to attack the rear of the batteries facing the river, and by so doing would also outflank the Paraguayan forces facing the Allied camp.

López and his staff also saw the risk, and a new line of entrenchments was created, using the battery and infantry positions at Curuzú on the River Paraguay as its starting point and extending it through to Lake Chichi, on the left-hand side. This area of land thereby became a virtual island, enclosed not only by the lake and river to either side, but by marshes and lagoons in front and behind. The only way to the batteries at Curupaytí was by a narrow road that ran along the riverbank. The number of troops here was increased to 2,500 men (the 4th, 10th, and 27th Infantry Battalions, with a dismounted cavalry regiment commanded by Major Blas Montiel), while 13 guns were added to the defensive line, probably from the reserve mentioned earlier.

The task of constructing and commanding this defensive line was given to Colonel Manuel António Giménez, who was based at Curupaytí. Major Sayas was placed in command at Curuzú, while the three batteries there were commanded by naval captains Pedro V. Gill and Domingo A. Ortiz, and Major Ceferino Lugo. In front of the trench was an open space of some 400 square yds (335 square m) of firm ground. Beyond that was a marsh with a jungle of canes, through which a pathway had been made by the Paraguayans. This path was the only way to attack the trench. A naval bombardment would not have helped its Allied attackers, as the trench was concealed from the warships on the river by woods along the riverbank.

On 1 September the five Brazilian ironclads from the Allied fleet (the *Bahia*, *Brasil*, *Barroso*, *Rio de Janeiro*, and *Lima Barros*) began a bombardment of the riverside battery at Curuzú. The battery responded but neither side had much effect on the other. This bombardment continued the following day, and this time it was furious, with the *Rio de Janeiro* steaming closer than the other ironclads. Her 4-inch iron plating was twice perforated by 68 lb shot, while a hole was blown into her bottom by two static torpedoes.[12] This sank her almost immediately with the loss of 50 crewmen and four officers, including her captain, *Primeiro-tenente* Americo Brazil Silvado. The *Ivaí* – which had only joined the attacking squadron that day – also had one of her boilers shot through, killing four men, and many of the other vessels received hits but suffered little damage. On the other side the Paraguayan battery had one of its 8-inch guns dismounted.

While this was happening the 8,391 men (4,500 infantry and 3,800 dismounted cavalry) of the Brazilian 2nd Corps, under the command of General Baron de Pôrto Alegre, were being embarked aboard 11 ships for transport from Itapirú, and at 11:00 a.m. they landed along the River Paraguay near Las Palmas. They then marched towards Curuzú. The vanguard suffered 12 killed and 60 wounded from Paraguayan sharpshooters, who, as they retired, also set fire to the surrounding jungle through which the advancing Brazilians had to pass. When the latter finally emerged into a clearing it was only to find the new Paraguayan defensive work confronting them. Until now they had been ignorant of this, as they had expected to attack the rear of the battery on the riverbank. The Brazilians also found that the draught animals pulling their artillery refused to wade through the floating red-hot ashes and burning tree stumps of the still smouldering jungle, and the field-pieces had to be manhandled to their designated places.

3 September saw both the renewal of the naval bombardment and the commencement of the Brazilian 2nd Corps' attack against the Paraguayan trench, in what would be called the Battle of Curuzú. Pôrto Alegre's attack, which began at 6:00 a.m., was in two columns. The first was under the command of General Fontes, who was to lead his 6,000 men against the weakest part of the defences, found to be the section on the northern or lake flank. Fontes' troops were therefore sent through the lake, wading in at least 4 ft (1.2 m) of water, to outflank the defenders and get into their rear, this movement being hidden from view by the forest. The Brazilian artillery meanwhile proceeded to bombard the Paraguayan defences until the first column began its attack, at which point General Albino de Carvalho with the remainder of the infantry attacked along the whole southern front of the Paraguayan position.

The lake flank was held by a single Paraguayan cannon and the 10th Infantry Battalion. These troops, who had never been in action before, began to flee the field after their commander was killed, and the flank crumbled. The Brazilian columns then united and attacked the river batteries in three columns, forcing the Paraguayan defenders to retreat to Curupaytí leaving behind all their field-pieces. Fontes' column of 1,200 men followed but was ordered to return to Curuzú by General Pôrto Alegre. If this order had been delayed by just half an hour this column might have carried the next battery and Curupaytí, 3,000 yds (2,750 m) down the road, before it reached them. As it was, Pôrto Alegre's decision would prove costly later. Thompson certainly believed that the battery could have easily been taken that day, giving the Brazilians an open route to attack the main Paraguayan force, only six miles (10 km) away, from the rear, which if planned in conjunction with an assault by the troops under General Mitre could have brought the war to a close.

The Paraguayans lost 700 killed, 1,800 wounded, and 32 taken prisoner in this battle, but this was not the end of their casualties, for López ordered the 10th Infantry Battalion to be decimated. Consequently on 10 September 1866 this unit was paraded in front of the whole division and every tenth man was shot, a total of 61 men. The officers of the battalion then drew lots for which of them would be executed , two of the ten officers being shot. The surviving officers were then reduced to the ranks and the battalion was broken up and divided up among the other battalions of the division, which was now under the command of General Díaz. The Brazilians had suffered 11 officers and 148 men killed and 52 officers and 577 men wounded.

THE BATTLE OF CURUPAYTÍ

The strength of the batteries at Curupaytí was quickly increased to 5,000 men, composed of seven infantry battalions – the 4th (Captain António Insaurralde), 7th (Lieutenant-Colonel Luis González), 9th (Major Bernardo Olmedo), 27th (Major Juan González), 36th (Major Juan Fernández), 38th (Major José Azcurra), and 40th (Major José Duarte); and four dismounted cavalry regiments – the 6th (Captain Gregorio Escobar), 8th (Captain Bernardino Caballero), 9th (Captain Francisco Peralta), and 36th (Captain Pedro Avalos). In addition defences that would prove so formidable to the Allies were begun on 8 September under the direction of Colonel Wisner de Morgenstein and Lieutenant-Colonels Thompson and Luis Leopoldo Myzkonski, the men working day and night. Complete silence was enforced, and as little noise as possible was made with spades and shovels. Trees and shrubbery were removed, and the clay soil – so hard that it could hardly be broken with pickaxes – began to be transformed into defence works. The Brazilian camp some 3,000 yds away never had the least suspicion of these labours, as no orders were issued for outposts or reconnoitring parties to be sent into the swamps.

On 12 September 1866 a meeting took place between López and Generals Mitre and Flores at Yataiti-Corá. Instigated by López as a peace conference, it turned into a heated argument between López and Flores, with both sides unable to come to an agreement that required López to retire to Europe and leave Paraguay for 'a few years'. It is often said that this meeting was a ploy by López to gain more time for the defensive works at Curupaytí to be completed. Maybe this is true, although López also knew that there was unrest against the war in the various provinces of Argentina. It was reliably reported from Argentina that whenever a government conscription decree was posted in a town its entire male population would melt away into the mountains or the pampas. The contingent sent from Taboadas deserted to a man once it was clear of the province; in La Rioja troops murdered their officers to escape being sent to the war zone; and popular support for the war in Uruguay and Brazil was not as high as in the previous year.

By 13 September the 1st and 2nd Argentine divisions had disembarked at Curuzú in preparation for the big push to take Curupaytí. The defences of this place now consisted of a line of entrenchments for the battery about 550 yds (500 m) from the fort. The right wing of these fortifications rested on the bank of the River Paraguay, which was here covered with almost impenetrable thickets; the left wing touched Lake López. The work had several projecting angles, was 2,000 yds (1,800 m) in length, and consisted of an earth wall 9 ft (2.75 m) wide and 7 ft (2.1 m) high, with a defensive ditch. It was so arranged that it could not be observed by the Allied fleet. At the battery fort two additional parallel trenches were dug, each 18 ft (5.5 m) wide and 15 ft (4.6 m) deep, and beyond the farthest ditch was an abattis of branches 30 ft (9.1 m) wide. The fort had 49 cannon, 12 of them 68-pdrs, and two Congreve rocket stands. Thirteen guns from this total faced the river, including four 68-pdrs. The artillery was under the command of Naval Captain Domingo A. Ortiz and Major Sayas, who a court martial had cleared of responsibility for the disaster at Curuzú. Very few trials in Paraguay during the war ended this way.

Overall command at Curupaytí was given to General Díaz. His infantry, commanded by Colonel Luis González, was positioned on the right flank, while the dismounted cavalry units, commanded by Captain Bernardino Caballero, were on the left flank. The artillery was positioned as follows: four batteries of 12 field-pieces were mounted on the entrenchments to the front, among which were the remaining four 68-pdrs; a battery of two guns under the command of Ortiz covered the narrow strip of solid ground which ran along the riverbank to the south-west; four cannons commanded by Naval Captain Pedro B. Gil swept the front; two others commanded by Captain Adolfo Saguier covered the lake; and the remaining four guns, commanded by Major

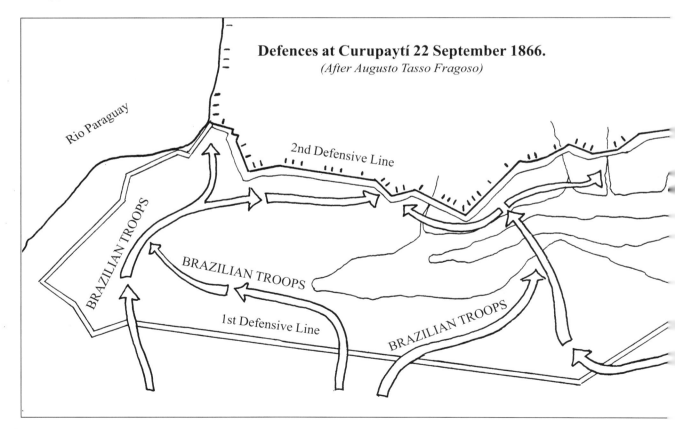

Defences at Curupaytí 22 September 1866.
(After Augusto Tasso Fragoso)

Rio Paraguay

2nd Defensive Line

BRAZILIAN TROOPS

BRAZILIAN TROOPS

1st Defensive Line

BRAZILIAN TROOPS

Photographs of the Brazilian monitors Tamandaré *and* Brasil *taken after the bombardment of Curupaytí on 22 September 1866.* (Courtesy of the Arquivo Historico do Exercito, Rio de Janeiro)

Pedro Hermosa, were placed on the extreme left wing but pointed to the front. Actual flank attacks were not expected on account of the natural obstacles of the ground.

The planned Allied attack was set for 17 September but was postponed until the 20th. When heavy rain started that morning and continued for two days, the attack was further delayed until the 22nd. At 7:00 that morning Admiral Tamandaré began a spirited bombardment of Curupaytí, using the ships *Brasil*, *Barroso*, *Tamandaré*, *Ipiranga*, *Belmonte*, *Parnaíba*, *Pedro Affonso*, and *Forte de Coimbra*, and gunboats Numbers 1, 2, and 3. This lasted until noon, with little

Lake Lopez

ARGENTINE TROOPS

effect on the fort or defenders except for one shot which struck and dismounted one of the Paraguayan 8-inch guns in the river battery, cutting off the muzzle halfway up the chase. The same shot also killed Major Sayas. The damaged gun was later placed in the trenches, from where it could fire grape at the enemy troops.

The land attack was to begin at noon with 18,000 men in four columns. The right wing was in two columns composed of Argentine troops under the command of Generals Emilio Mitre (brother of the commander-in-chief) and Wenceslao Paunero; these were to wade through the northern part of the lake to a small peninsula and proceed to the attack from there. The reserve column, of Brazilian troops, formed the centre and was to attack after the others. This was commanded by Colonel Lucas de Lima, though it was originally intended to be commanded by General Pôrto Alegre. The other two columns, of Brazilian troops commanded by General Albino de Carvalho and Colonel Augusto Caldas, were to attack the left wing. All the attacks were to have the support of field artillery. At the same time the Brazilian General Polidoro with 20,000 men was to attack the main Paraguayan defences at Paso Gomez and along the Estero Rojas 'at an opportune moment', while General Flores with a cavalry force was to attack in a wide flanking movement on the Allied right to fall upon any Paraguayans retreating from General Polidoro's attack. The Allied troops were given fascines, made from rushes and canes, to fill up the trench, and 15 ft (4.5 m) scaling ladders were also issued. Saucepans found among the Allied dead following their attack indicate that the Allies had expected to eat in the captured fort that night.

All five Allied attacks were made against a hailstorm of canister, grape, and musket fire, from guns that were supposed to have been silenced by the powerful naval bombardment, and the soft spongy soil rendered it exceedingly difficult for the Allies to bring up their own guns to provide covering fire. Nevertheless, the two ditches were crossed and the wall was scaled without meeting any stubborn resistance. But when the attackers reached the top of the wall they found, to their surprise, a broad expanse of water before them, caused by the previous week's heavy rainfall, and their intended target – the fort of Curupaytí – lay beyond this. The Paraguayan

63

A detail from 'The Trenches of Curupaytí' by Candido López. Note the abatis beyond the trench. (Courtesy of the Museo Nacional de Bellas Artes, Buenos Aires)

artillery and infantry which had been defending the wall were quickly withdrawing on submerged causeways known only to themselves, General Díaz having ordered that as soon as the Allies had possession of the ditches the defenders should retreat to the fort.

As the Allied troops began to crowd on to the ridge of the wall the Paraguayan batteries opened up on them with grape, canister, and shell, killing and wounding hundreds. At this point General Bartolomé Mitre ordered a general assault on the distant fort, and the Allies' field-guns were advanced to the wall, soil from which was used to create ramps to haul them over the two ditches. However, these batteries were soon silenced by the heavier guns of the fort. The assault itself, made through the water, was subjected to a murderous fire from the artillery and, when close enough, the muskets of the Paraguayan infantry, and was virtually halted by the formidable abattis. Only 60 men succeeded in crossing this and scaling the wall of the fort, and all of these were killed as they reached the summit. At 2:00 p.m. the Argentine attack was abandoned and a little while later the Allied army began its retreat to Curuzú, which it finally reached at 5:00 p.m.

As the Allies retreated the Paraguayan 12th Battalion was sent out onto the battlefield to gather up arms and equipment and kill any wounded unable to get back to their own camp. Only six were taken prisoner, of whom two, being Paraguayans captured at Uruguayana, were immediately hung by General Díaz. Among the captured equipment were 3,400 firearms, including some 300 Liège Enfield rifles, plus enough uniforms to help clothe several Paraguayan units.

During the battle the Allied Navy had fired nearly 5,000 bombs and shells while the Paraguayan artillery had fired nearly 7,000 rounds. The assault had been costly for the Allies. Argentine losses alone totalled 162 officers and 2,063 other ranks killed, wounded, and missing, the commander of each of the Argentines' 17 battalions being wounded or killed; Lilia Zenequelli (1997) gives their casualties as 983 killed, 2,002 wounded, 272 walking wounded, and 294 missing, with which I am inclined to agree. Charles Kolinski (1965) wrote that 'if the flower of the Spanish race in Paraguay was said to have been obliterated at First Tuyuti, the same might nearly have been said of the finest of Buenos Aires' aristocracy at Curupaytí.' The Brazilians suffered 442 killed, 51 of them officers, and 1,560 wounded including 150 officers. Paraguayan losses were a mere 54 men killed and 38 wounded, though I think that the walking wounded were not counted, as General Resquín gives the figure as 250 killed and wounded. Among the Paraguayan dead were Lieutenants Lescano and Urdapilleta.

The expected assault by General Polidoro on the main Paraguayan defences had not materialised. His troops were lined up and gave the impression that they were about to attack but they didn't, though this still tied down the Paraguayan units facing them. The flanking cavalry attack by General Flores' force of 2,500 Brazilians and 500 Argentines and Uruguayans nearly reached Tuyucué, a town on the Allied right flank. Although some descriptions of Flores' outflanking movement say it was intended to link up with the forces of General Mitre attacking Curupaytí by means of a route on the Allied left, this would have brought him up against defended positions, whereas the right flank was open but marshy. An attack using the right flank would have surprised the Paraguayans and created an Allied offensive on three sides, but Flores retreated when news of the failed attack on Curupaytí reached him. Maybe if his initial attack had succeeded then both of these assaults would have been pressed with more vigour.

A PAUSE IN THE FIGHTING

The defeat at Curupaytí ended the Allied offensive for ten months, until July 1867. Between December 1864 and 20 February 1866 the Allies had suffered the following casualties: Brazil 228 officers and 2,486 men killed, 744 officers and 8,772 men wounded, 13 officers and 202 men missing; Argentina 79 officers and 1,206 men killed, 305 officers and 2,991 men wounded, six officers and 231 men missing; Uruguay 1,160 officers and men killed and wounded. In the same period the Paraguayans had suffered 13,110 killed, 17,190 wounded, and 7,853 taken prisoner (data from Augusto Tasso Fragoso, 1934). Add to this the subsequent battle casualties up to and including the Battle of Curupaytí and it will give a good idea of the magnitude of the losses being suffered by both sides.

In addition there was the sickness factor, which was usually much higher than actual combat losses. The first case of cholera was reported in the Allied camp at Itapirú on 26 March 1866, brought in by Brazilian troops that had arrived on the transport *Goya* from Rio de Janeiro. In late 1866 at the Brazilian hospital situated at Corrientes, 33 men died per week from diarrhoea alone; by January 1867 the rate had risen to 16 deaths per day for this hospital. Beriberi was also causing fatalities. An additional two Allied hospitals were established – one on the island of Cerrito the other at Itapirú – to try and cope with the increasing number of patients. A malaria epidemic also hit the Allied camp during the humid summer months, causing some 280 men per day to report sick. Thompson writes that at Curuzú 4,000 Brazilians became ill with cholera of whom 2,400 died, including 87 officers, while 50 men were kept busy each day just digging graves, but the Argentine troops on this flank had luckily been withdrawn before the epidemic struck. At the main Allied camp 13,000 men were in hospital. The Navy was also affected: during a period of 32 days after 7 April 377 sailors were struck down with cholera, of whom 240 died.

The cholera epidemic also found its way amongst the Paraguayan forces, with two cases being reported on 18 April at Paso Gomez, and by May it had begun to spread through the whole army. Two large hospitals were established to treat the sick, and the average of daily deaths for a long time was 50. López prohibited his doctors from telling the troops what the illness was, and they began to call it *chain*. The epidemic would eventually spread through the whole country, killing many thousands of civilians.

Another cholera epidemic hit the area in September 1867. Although the casualty rate was not as high as during the first, it still killed and incapacitated many, and both epidemics spread to the civilian population as far away as Buenos Aires, Montevideo, Rosario, Santa Fe, and Córdoba, as well as into Paraguay.

These casualty figures led to strong public opposition in Argentina to continuation of the war. On 9 November 1866 disturbances were reported around government buildings, which quickly spread to include Salta and Jujuy in the north, Cuyo in the west, and Cordoba and Corrientes. By January 1867 open revolt was reported. On the 5th a detachment of government forces was defeated at Pocitos, and other rebellious acts were reported in San Juan, La Rioja, and Catamarca. This situation caused General Mitre, who, it will be remembered, was also President of Argentina, to despatch General Wenceslao Paunero with 4,000 men – nearly half the Argentine contingent in Paraguay – to quell the revolts, this force being given the title 'The Army of Pacification'. Mitre wrote to his vice-president: 'Who doesn't know that by declaring war upon us, the traitors have given new heart to Paraguay?' April saw the battles of San Ignacio on the 1st and Pozo de Vargas on the 10th, both of them victories over the rebels. The first involved the defeat of 4,000 rebels under General Juan Saá by Colonel Arredondo, General Paunero's second-in-command, while the second saw the defeat of another 4,000 under Felipe Varela by 2,100 government troops commanded by General Antonino Taboada. One of the rebel units was named the 'Batallón Urquiza', while a captured flag bore the legend '*Federación o muerte. Viva la unión americana. Viva el ilustre Capitán General Urquiza. Abajo los negreros brasileños!*' ('Federation or Death. Long Live the American Union. Long Live the illustrious Captain General Urquiza. Down with the Brazilian Negroes!').[13]

Another domestic problem caused by the war was the increase in Indian raids along Argentina's southern frontier as a result of troops being withdrawn for use elsewhere. Some of these raids came within 120 miles (200 km) of the city of Rosario, twice forcing General Mitre to leave the Allied camp, the first time in February 1867 (when he appointed General Juan A. Gelly y Obes commander of the Argentine contingent and placed Field Marshal the Marquis of Caxias in overall command of the Allied forces).

In Uruguay, civil disturbances stirred up by the Blanco party caused General Flores to be recalled to Montevideo on 26 September 1866. He left General Enrique de Castro in command of the Uruguayan troops, who now amounted to only 700 men including an artillery battery, 250 men having gone with Flores as his escort. He would be assassinated while driving his carriage in Montevideo on 19 February 1868.

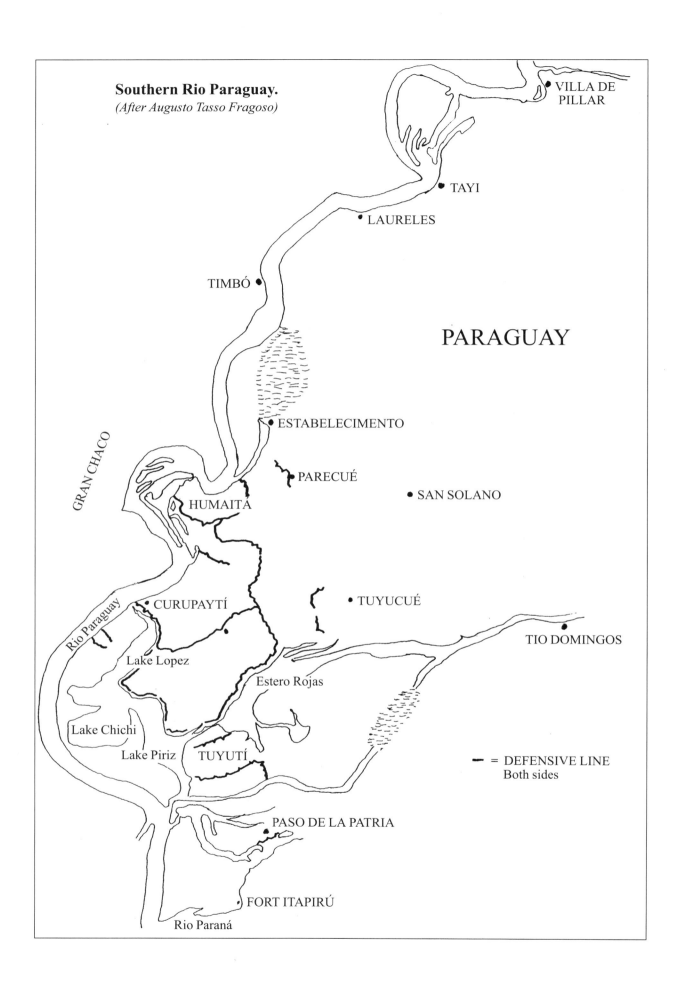

Southern Rio Paraguay.
(After Augusto Tasso Fragoso)

VILLA DE PILLAR

TAYI

LAURELES

TIMBÓ

PARAGUAY

ESTABELECIMENTO

PARECUÉ

SAN SOLANO

GRAN CHACO

HUMAITÁ

Rio Paraguay

CURUPAYTÍ

TUYUCUÉ

TIO DOMINGOS

Lake Lopez

Estero Rojas

Lake Chichi

Lake Piriz

TUYUTÍ

━ = DEFENSIVE LINE
Both sides

PASO DE LA PATRIA

FORT ITAPIRÚ

Rio Paraná

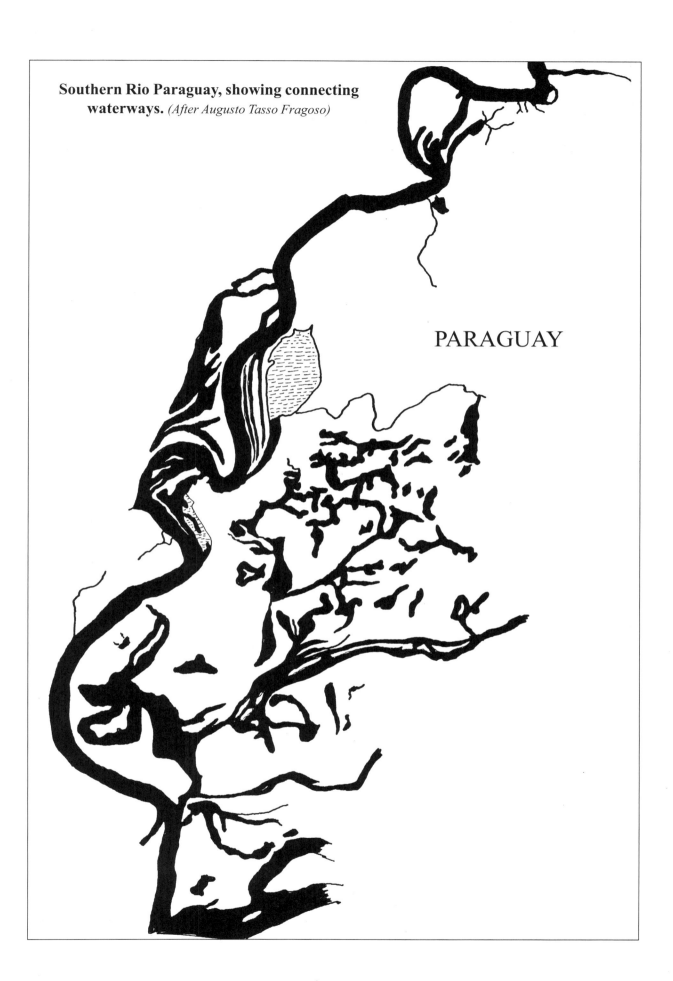

Southern Rio Paraguay, showing connecting waterways. *(After Augusto Tasso Fragoso)*

PARAGUAY

The Duke (earlier the Marquis) de Caxias, painted after his return to Brazil. (Courtesy of Museu Nacional de Belas Artes, Rio de Janeiro)

In early November 1866 Field Marshal the Marquis of Caxias landed at Corrientes and on the 18th assumed command of the Brazilian Army. General Polidoro was relieved of his command of the 1st Corps and replaced by General Alexandre Gomes de Argollo. General Pôrto Alegre, who had been ill since the Battle of Curuzú, relinquished command of the 2nd Corps and went back to Brazil, but returned and resumed command on 1 March 1867. General Osôrio had already been sent to Rio Grande do Sul to build the 3rd Corps. Finally, on 21 December Admiral Tamandaré was replaced by Admiral José Joaquim Ignacio.

Late in 1866 the Brazilians began to receive supplies of the new German needle rifle and several infantry units were equipped with them, while some cavalry units were issued with Spencer repeating carbines. Other weapons seen in Brazilian units included Liège Enfield and Minié rifles. Brazil's artillery was also improved, with more Whitworths, La Hittes, and even some Krupp guns finding their way to the front. The navy began to replace its older wooden ships with new armoured monitors, and in 1867 a Balloon Corps was created to assist in Allied observation of enemy gun emplacements and trenches.

The Brazilian Balloon Corps won high praise from the Allied General Staff. Initially a French balloonist had been employed by the Brazilian Government, but his balloon caught fire and he was court-martialled (it being mistakenly believed that he was attempting to set fire to a nearby powder magazine) and sentenced to death, though the sentence was not carried out. Then in March 1867 James and Ezra Allen from the USA were offered positions in the Brazilian Army to form and command the Balloon Corps, both having served with the Federal Army's balloon corps under Professor Thaddeus S.C. Lowe during the American Civil War. They were given the ranks of Engineer Captain (James) and Assistant Aeronaut (Ezra), and were equipped with two balloons made in the US by their former commander, Professor Lowe. The larger measured 40 ft (12.2 m) in diameter, with a capacity of 37,000 cu ft (1,047 cu m), and could carry six to eight people; the smaller was 28 ft (8.5 m) in diameter with a capacity of 17,000 cu ft (481 cu m) and could carry only two people. They were connected to the ground by two ropes held by troops, who could walk the balloon in any direction needed, although the larger balloon could use four ropes. The first ascent, using the smaller balloon,[14] was made on 24 June, reaching a height of 270 ft (82 m), when James Allen was accompanied by Major Robert A. Chodasiewicz of the Argentine Engineer Corps. The second ascent, this time using the larger balloon, was made on 8 July, when Lieutenant Céspedes, a Paraguayan acting as chief of guides to the Argentine Army, was also included. On this occasion the three men stayed aloft for three hours, with Céspedes looking for trails through the marshes and thickets while Chodasiewicz drew a map of the previously unknown area on the Paraguayan left flank. There were frequent subsequent ascents thereafter to note details of Paraguayan artillery positions, trenches, and terrain.

In a letter to Professor Lowe, Ezra Allen states that 'we have kept the balloon up in front of the enemy all the time possible and the General in Command, the Marques de Caxies [Caxias], is more than pleased. James is now at work preparing the basket and everything to take him – General Marques de Caxies – up.' It is not recorded

A Brazilian balloon taking off. Note the drums to manufacture the hydrogen gas, and the manhandled tow ropes. (Courtesy of the Arquivo Historico do Exercito, Rio de Janeiro)

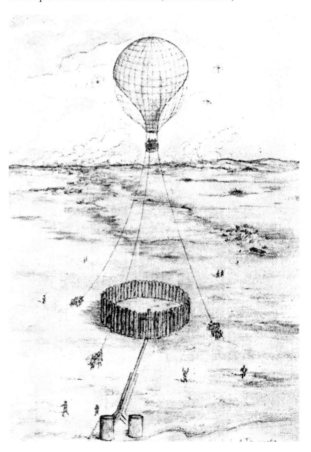

whether the Marquis ever did take to ballooning, although one of his ADCs, Dr Francisco Pinheiro Guimarães, did. Other Brazilians recorded to have been taken aloft were Captain Francisco Cesar da Silva Amaral of the Staff Corps, First Lieutenant Cursino do Amarante of the Engineer Corps, and Captains Conrado and Madureira (units not recorded). The Paraguayans tried to counter these near daily ascents by setting fire to the bush to create smoke screens in order to hide their emplacements, but to no avail.

One of the Marquis of Caxias' other first acts on taking command was to issue an order prohibiting Brazilian officers from wearing any device whatever which might distinguish them from the common soldiers, excepting only their swords. Their kepis were to be covered with white cloth like those of their troops. These measures were taken because Paraguayan snipers and artillery would invariably fire at any group of officers that they saw, while groups of other ranks were not fired upon so often.

In early January 1867 a common daily occurrence was the Brazilian naval bombardment of the Paraguayan defences. In a show of defiance General Díaz would often be seen riding about the camp at Curupaytí during these bombardments to help morale. On one such occasion, on the 26th, he and some aides had set out at nine o'clock to fish from a small canoe in sight of the Brazilian fleet, when, unluckily for the Paraguayan cause, a 13-inch shell exploded overhead, capsizing the canoe, and a piece of shrapnel nearly cut off one of Díaz's legs. His aides swam to the shore with him and took him to his hut, and a telegraph message was quickly despatched to López informing him of the disaster. Dr Skinner was sent by López to help as best he could. The leg was amputated and General Díaz was brought back to headquarters so that López could visit him each day, but he died on 7 February. His death at this point in the war was inopportune to say the least. Colonel Paulino Além succeeded to the command of Curupaytí.

A Brazilian column that had originally left Rio de Janeiro on 1 April 1865 arrived on the northern frontier of Paraguay in April 1867, having taken almost two years to march 1,311 miles (2,112 km) to reach Vila de Miranda in Mato Grosso. It had started out 3,000 strong under the command of Colonel Manoel Drago, who was later replaced by Colonel Galvão. Upon Galvão's death near the Rio Negro on 1 January 1867 Colonel Carlos de Morais Camisão took command. A third of the column's original strength was lost through sickness and desertion during the march, so that by April 1867 it had been reduced to 1,907 men. It was composed of the 20th (Captain Joaquim Ferreira de Paiva) and 21st (Major José T. Gonçalves) Line Infantry Battalions, the 17th *Voluntários da Pátria* (Lieutenant-Colonel Antonio E.G. Galvão), the Provincial Corps of Artillery (Major João T. de Cantuária) with four La Hitte rifled cannon pulled by oxen, and the 1st Corps of Mounted *Caçadores* (Captain Pedro J. Rufino).

In late April the column finally crossed the River Apa and advanced into Paraguay, as information suggested that there were no troops defending the northern part of the country and that the river port of Concepción could be taken, allowing the Brazilian artillery to close the River Paraguay to internal traffic. On hearing of this expedition, López despatched the 21st

A cartoon published in the Paraguayan newspaper El Centinela *of 8 August 1867, showing the Paraguayan troops' response to Brazilian balloon reconnaissance.* (Author's collection)

Cavalry Regiment (Lieutenant-Colonel Blas Montiel) and two companies of the 12th Infantry Battalion (Major Medina) by steamer to Concepción, where they were reinforced by a further 200 cavalry and a battery of light artillery stationed there under the command of Major Martín Urbieta. With these troops Montiel marched north to meet the Brazilians, who had set out from Vila de Miranda with only a minimum of food and ammunition.

In the absence of a significant cavalry contingent no advance knowledge of terrain or Paraguayan troop dispositions could be gained, though Paraguayan cavalry units were often seen scouting on the horizon. The lack of supplies began to be felt when intelligence that cattle could be found en route proved false, and this lack of food forced Colonel Camisão to head for a ranch called 'Laguna', reported to be owned by President López, where there were said to be large herds of cattle. But on reaching 'Laguna' on 1 May they found only a burning hut and a provocative message left by the Paraguayans. On the 8th was fought the Battle of Baiende, which, though a Brazilian victory, persuaded Colonel Camisão to withdraw into Brazilian territory, as his supplies were fast running out. There followed a 35-day retreat, during which starvation, cholera, and the skirmishing tactics of the Paraguayan cavalry (commanded by Major Urbieta) reduced Camisão's force to 578 men. (One of the tactics employed by the Paraguayans was to set fire to the brush ahead of the Brazilian vanguard.) The Brazilian force

Photograph of the Paraguayan General José Díaz. (Courtesy of the Arquivo Historico do Exercito, Rio de Janeiro)

reached the port of Canuto on 11 June, having dragged back their four La Hitte cannon while still retaining their battalion flags. Colonel Camisão and his second-in-command Lieutenant-Colonel Juvencio Manuel Cabrál de Menezes were among those who died of cholera during the retreat.

In June 1867 another Brazilian force stationed in Mato Grosso, consisting of 800 men commanded by Lieutenant-Colonel Antonio Maria Coelho, embarked on two steamers at Cuyabá and headed for the port of Corumbá, held by a Paraguayan garrison of 313 men with six pieces of light artillery commanded by Lieutenant-Colonel Hermógenes Cabral. In addition 500 Brazilian prisoners of war were encamped there. The port was captured on the 13th with a loss to the Paraguayans of 50 killed and 150 prisoners, their commander and Major Fleitas being among the dead. The Brazilians re-embarked on the 24th and headed back to Cuyabá when a

new Paraguayan force was sighted supported by the gunboats *Salta de Guairá*, *Río Apa*, and *Amambaí* (the ex-Brazilian *Anhambahí*), this Paraguayan squadron being under the command of Captain Romualdo Núñez.

On 11 July a further expedition was organised to capture Corumbá again, this time commanded by Lieutenant-Colonel Antonio José da Costa and embarked on six transports escorted by the gunboats *Jaurú* and *Antonio João*, under the command of *Capitão de Fragata* Balduino José Ferreira de Aguiar. This time Captain Núñez was waiting for them with the *Salta de Guairá*, *Río Apa*, and *Iberá*, and he was able to attack the two enemy ships, capturing the *Jaurú*, though in the process he and a good number of his men were wounded by rifle fire from the massed Brazilian infantry on board. The *Jaurú* was later left behind because of its damaged engines and was scuttled by the Brazilian navy.

THE PARAGUAYANS STRENGTHEN THEIR DEFENCES

During this relatively quiet period peace proposals were presented by representatives of the French (Viscount Beaumont), American (Charles A. Washburn), and British (G.Z. Gould) governments; all were rejected. Meanwhile a general improvement to the Paraguayan emplacements was implemented following the lessons learned from the defence of Curupaytí, and a system of trenches and strongpoints was constantly improved upon, establishing a defensive line around the Paraguayan camp. In the north was the emplacement of Humaitá, often called the first line of defence. From there entrenchments followed the River Paraguay down to Curupaytí; through the marshes and *carrizal* on the banks of lakes Chuki and Piriz to the Paso de Gomez; and along the marshes on the edge of the Estero Rojas, heading gradually northward past the Paso de Angulo, Espinillo, Tanymbú, and Benites, back to Humaitá. This outer line of defences is often called the third line, and was nearly 18 miles (30 km) in length. A second line of defence was also built that ran from Paso Espinillo across to the top of Lake Chuki just below Curupaytí. This line passed López's headquarters at Paso Pucú. Dams were also included in these works, one at the Paso de Gomez allowing the water to rise to 6 ft (1.8 m) – making this place almost unassailable by the Allies – and another at Potrero Sauce with a 6 ft sluice-gate that could be opened from the new trench to release a terrible flood of water.

An account of these defences was prepared by the secretary of the British Legation in the River Plate, G.Z. Gould, who visited the Paraguayan lines during September 1867: 'The riverside batteries of Humaitá at present mount only 46 guns, namely one 80-pounder, four 68-pounders, eight 32-pounders; the rest are of different calibres. The battery of Curupaytí towards the river mounts thirty 32-pounders, the centre is defended by about a hundred guns. On the left are 117 guns, including four 68-pounders, one 40-pounder rifled Whitworth [recovered from the wreck of the Brazilian gunboat *Jequitinhonha* after the Battle of Riachuelo], one 13-inch mortar, fourteen 32-pounders, and many rifled 12-pounders.' The centre and left lines would be, I believe, the trench that continued the Paraguayan defences up again to Humaitá from the River Paraguay. Gould continues: 'Humaitá, on the land side, is protected by three lines of earthworks, on the innermost of which 87 guns are mounted. Total on the left, 204 guns. The grand total is therefore, 380 guns ... The garrison of Humaitá consists of five battalions, of which three are composed of old soldiers, one of boys and convalescents, and one of wounded men returned to duty; in all about 3,000 men. 6,000 are stationed along the left from Humaitá to the Angulo, and 5,000 from hence to Curupaytí. The reserves, consisting of three battalions of infantry and four or five weak dismounted cavalry regiments numbering altogether from 2,000 to 2,500 men are stationed at Paso Pucú, the most central position in the camp, and the headquarters of President López.'

When Sir Richard Burton visited Humaitá after its capture he noted the following details: 'The batteries are eight in number, and again we will begin with them up-stream. After a scatter of detached guns, some in the open, others slightly parapeted, we find the Bateria Cadenas, or chain battery of thirteen guns, backed by the Artillery Barracks. The chain, which consisted of seven twisted together, passed diagonally through a kind of brick tunnel. On this side it was made fast to a windlass supported by a house about 100 yards from the bank. Nearer the battery stood a large capstan: the latter, however, wanted force to haul taut the chain. Thrown over the stream where it narrowed to 800 metres, it was a twist composed of one large [1.75 in] and six smaller diameters [1.25 in], and it rested upon three *chatas* [barges], which were soon sunk by the Brazilian guns. The heavy obstacle then sunk below the surface with a deep sag, and as there was no donkey-engine to tighten it, the Monitors might have passed safely over the bend. But it lay at a point where all the battery-fires converged, and no attempt was made either to blow up the chain house, to remove it with gunpowder, or to cut the obstacle ... Crossing by one of the three dwarf bridges the little nullah Arroyo Humaitá somewhat below the Presidential "palace" we come upon the Bateria Londres, that Prince of Humbugs ... The walls were twenty-seven feet thick, of brick [not stone and lime]. It was supposed to be rendered bomb-proof by layers of earth heaped upon brick arches, and there were embrasures for sixteen [not 25] guns. Of these ports eight were walled up and converted into workshops, because the artillerymen were in hourly dread of their caving in and crumbling down. The third battery is the Tacuary of three guns. Then comes the Coimbra mounting eight bouches à feu, and directed by the Commandante Hermosa. The three next are the Octava or Madame Lynch, with three guns en barbette; the Pesada, five guns, and the Itapirú, seven guns – all partly revetted with brick. Being the westernmost and the least exposed to fire they have suffered but little. Lastly, at the Punta de las Piedars [Piedias] stands the Humaitá redoubt, armed with a single eight-inch gun.' This gives a total of 56 possible emplacements for field-pieces; if the eight ports bricked up are not counted then the figure is 48, which is close to the figure that Gould states he saw earlier, when the fort was still occupied by the Paraguayans. It should be noted that all of these batteries faced the River Paraguay on the horseshoe bend.

Burton continues: 'Beyond this point begins the entrenched line running south-south-west along the Laguna Concha, alias Ambericaia, and then sweeping round to the east with a gap where the water rendered an attack impossible. The profile is good simply because [it is] defended by impenetrable bush. The guns stand in pairs, with a Paiol or magazine to every two, and they had been provided with 200 round of grape, shell, and case. The wet ditch is still black with English gunpowder; some fine, mostly coarse ... The Londres work, besides being in a state of decay, was an exposed mass of masonry which ought to have shared the fate of the forts from Sumpter to Pulaski, and when granite fails, bricks cannot hope to succeed. Had the guns been mounted in Monitor towers, or even protected by sand-bags, the ironclads would have suffered much more than they did in running past them ... In 1868 the river batteries had 58 cannons, 11 magazines ... The whole line of Humaitá mounted 36 brass and 144 iron guns: these 180 were increased to 195 by including the one eight-inch gun and the fourteen 32-pounders found in the Gran Chaco. The serviceable weapons did not however exceed sixty.'

A few days later Burton was allowed to ride along the entrenchments, often called the 'Quadrilateral'. Starting off at Humaitá, he followed the defences along the Paraguayan left flank, which he describes thus: 'The only outworks were the usual lose abattis of branches and brushwood defending a sloping trench nowhere five feet deep, with at the most eleven inches of water. There were no inner defences but a shallow drain eighteen inches deep and four feet wide: the earthwork parapet barely four feet high, and not more than nine feet thick, was propped up by palm trunks and provided with a banquette.' He also visited Paso Pucú to see the remains of López's headquarters.

Next he went with an Argentine guide to visit the Paraguayan battery at the Paso de Angulo. He wrote: 'Passing out of the second line at Paso Espinillo, we found the approaches strongly guarded; there were "bocas de lobo" even under water. At this point the enemy had been more than usually active: the parapet and covered way were often built over swamps for many yards, and plank bridges had been carefully laid down.' At Angulo, he writes, 'the works were composed of two bastions en flèche to the front, and of a curtain with a smaller bastion closing the gorge. Outside is a shallow trench, and a deep ditch requiring ladders. The garrison numbered 200 men, who worked only two of their sixteen guns ... Leaving the redan we rode along the outer line of entrenchments. Here we saw the same kind of work, trenches 18 feet wide and deep; and platforms for guns, 14 feet 6 inches square, and 3 feet 6 inches high; magazines at every 36 to 42 feet, traverses, sod-revetted parapets 6 feet tall and equally thick.'

George Thompson also wrote about the Paraguayan earthworks that he helped design and construct: 'With the exception of some of the old batteries of Humaitá, which were revetted with brickwork, all of our defences consisted of earthworks, with sod or hurdle revetments ... The ground was in general so irregular, that no definite form could be given to the works; but redans were placed to flank approaches, which were accessible only through the passes, opposite to which re-entering angles were always placed. Small salient angles were made for guns, in order that they might project beyond the line of trench where the infantry was placed, and which they could consequently flank. The guns were all mounted "en barbette," to give them the widest possible field of action, by means of raised platforms. The Paraguayans had not many infantry, and they relied most on their artillery in case of an attack.

'The profile was almost the same in all the works, the ditch being made generally twelve feet wide and six feet deep, with a slope of 3/1. No berm was ever made, but the exterior slope of the parapet and the scarp formed one, the earth being generally strong enough to admit of this. The exterior slope was revetted with sod-work; being in one slope with the scarp, it was much more difficult to be scaled than if it had had a berm. A banquette was made generally about twelve to eighteen inches high and three feet wide, being formed entirely of sods. In places exposed to be bombarded, the parapets were gradually made higher, and further protection given to the men, by digging a small ditch to the rear of the banquette, in which they could sit. At Curupaytí the bombardment was so continual that hide-sheds had to be made over this ditch and banquette.

'The turf in Paraguay is much more solid than in England, and the thicker the sods were cut the better revetments they appeared to make; the best revetment we had was made of hurdle-work. At the batteries of Fortin, at the Tebicuary, I revetted some traverses twelve feet high, with hurdle-work, of which the pickets were the whole height of the traverse, with a very light slope, and were interwoven with a creeper called "Üsüpó," which grows to a length of many yards and is about 3/8 inch thick. Three or four of these were twisted together into a sort of rope, which formed the basket-work, and was also carried across in many places between the stakes, to act as ties. This creeper has the property of not rotting under the earth, and was very useful. It made a very neat and good revetment, which, being frequently struck by 150 pounder Whitworth shells, received no damage beyond that of the basket-work being cut just where the shell entered, which left hardly any trace of its passage. The sod-work, on the contrary, when struck by a shot, would be considerably disarranged. At Angostura, as none of this creeper was to be obtained, the works had to be revetted with hurdles made of flexible rods. This was not nearly so good, but was still much superior to the sod-work.'

THE ALLIED OFFENSIVE RESUMES

During this lull in the fighting the pressure was kept up on the Paraguayans largely by artillery barrages delivered from the river and from the main Allied forward camp at Tuyuti. On 8 February 1867, for instance, Brazilian ironclads bombarded Curupaytí, Captain Delphim of the *Bahia* steaming past the batteries to come within three miles (5 km) of Humaitá before turning back. However, two assaults by the Brazilians were also mounted during this period. The first, on 19 January, was an attack by General Jacinto Machado de Bittencourt against the Paraguayan positions on Lake Piris; while the second, on 6 May, led by Major Tomas Goncalves, was against Paraguayan troops at the Arroyo Primero.

As much as, at this time, the Allied army was trying to cope with the ravages of disease and the training of replacement troops, replacements were a luxury that López did not have. Instead, he had been obliged to fall back on enrolling black slaves between the ages of 12 and 60 to fill the ranks. Slave owners who voluntarily released their 'property' were to be reimbursed by the treasury; whether they ever received payment is another matter. According to John Hoyt Williams (1979) the number of slaves and *libertos* (free blacks) recruited in this manner was probably about 1,700 for the nation, with many of these being sent to Humaitá to help build the defences. López had also ordered, in April, that all male children from the ages of 12 to 15 were to be enlisted, with no exceptions, and that crippled and mutilated veterans should be mobilised and sent to man telegraph offices, railroad facilities, and other vital establishments, thereby freeing healthier men for active service. All towns and villages were cleared of soldiers convalescing from wounds or illnesses, so that, for instance, the strategically important frontier town of Villa del Salvador was left unprotected by May 1867, its only defence force being the military band that was left there. Even prisoners from the jails at Asunción and Villeta were assigned to war work, being sent to labour in the foundries of Ibicuy.

When information was received by López that the Brazilian 3rd Corps under General Osõrio was not going to cross the River Paraná at Encarnación as had been expected, the Paraguayan defenders there, under the command of Major José Maria Núñez, were recalled to form the basis of a reserve force based at Paso Pucú. Núñez brought with him two infantry battalions, a cavalry regiment, and six cannon, while a small garrison was left behind to act as an observation post. He was also promoted to lieutenant-colonel and became second-in-command to General Barrios. The complete reserve brigade consisted of seven infantry battalions, two cavalry regiments, and 30 field-pieces, mostly rifled. These troops would be sent to any point of the defences that came under attack. General Osõrio, meanwhile, had been delayed from leaving Candelaría in Rio Grande do Sul province by an outbreak of cholera, but he arrived at Tuyuti with 5,451 men on 13 July.

An Allied Army report of 20 July 1867 states that its overall strength now stood at 35,831 men ready for action, with a further 4,118 men acting as clerks and supply train personnel (*empragados*) and 10,557 men in hospital. Similar figures are quoted by the British diplomat G.Z. Gould, who wrote that 'the Allied forces now amount to 48,000 men in the field, and from 5,000 to 6,000 men in hospital. Of these 45,000 are Brazilians, 7,000 to 8,000 Argentines and 1,000 Orientales [Uruguayans]. Since my last visit, in April, the Brazilian Army has been rejoined by the 2nd Corps, which held Curuzú, and the 3rd under General Osõrio, which was at that time somewhere in the Misiones. Moreover, large reinforcements have arrived direct from Brazil, and the Imperial Government has engaged to send out 2,000 men per month to keep up the army to its present strength. President Mitre has also returned with a part of the forces lately employed in quelling the insurrection in the Argentine Provinces ... The Paraguayan forces amount altogether to about 20,000 men, of these 10,000 or 12,000 at most are good troops, the rest mere boys from twelve to fourteen years of age, old men and cripples, besides 2,000 to 3,000 sick and wounded ... The [Paraguayans'] horses have nearly all died off, and the few hundreds which yet remain are so weak and emaciated they can scarcely carry their riders, the last 800 or 900 mares in the whole country have, however, just been brought in ... Many of the soldiers are in a state bordering on nudity, having only a piece of tanned leather round their loins, a ragged shirt, and a poncho made of vegetable fibre. They all wear clumsy-looking leather caps. A great part of them are still armed with flint guns, though in the course of the war many Minié rifles have been captured from the Allies.'

On the morning of 22 July 1867 Marshal Caxias advanced in a flanking movement. With a force of 28,521 men and 48 cannon drawn from the Brazilian 1st and 3rd Corps, he marched – or, rather, waded – eastward across swamps to the village of Tuyucué, which he reached on the 29th, having to go via the village of Tio Domingos to find a suitable crossing of the Estero Bellaco. This area had been cleared of its population by López only two days before, the people being moved to the northern bank of the River Tebicuary, where many died over the following months. On the 30th a unit of Paraguayan cavalry commanded by Majors Crescencio Medina and Benito Rolón skirmished with the Brazilian Vanguard Division at the Paso Gaona, and next day were attacked by General Osõrio with the 39th and 55th Volunteer Battalions supported by artillery, while flanking moves were undertaken by the cavalry divisions of Generals José Joaquim de Andrade Neves, Barão do Triunfo, and José Luís Mena Barreto. The Paraguayans lost 102 men killed or captured in this action, while the loss to the Brazilian force was 31 killed and wounded. The Marquis of Caxias had left General Pôrto Alegre's 2nd Corps at the base camp and defensive line at Tuyuti, and also kept open the Allies' lines of communication and supply to the newly built harbour at Itapirú.

The 6,016 Argentine troops with 13 cannon, and the 600 Uruguayan troops with eight cannon, were incorporated into the Vanguard Division and sent to demonstrate against the Paraguayan lines, to prevent scouts being sent out to spy on the movements of the 1st and 3rd Corps. By the 27th the Uruguayans were with the Brazilians at Tio Domingos.

It was also on the 27th that General Mitre arrived back in the Allied camp and resumed his post as commander-in-chief, although acknowledging the greater military skill of Caxias. On the 29th a force of 1,500 men, made up of units of the Vanguard Division that included the Argentine cavalry regiment of San Martin, reached the village of San Solano, from which could be seen the shattered remains of the church at Humaitá. By the 31st they had cut the telegraph wire from Humaitá to Asunción that ran along the main road only about three miles (5 km) distant from San Solano, so a new means of communication between these two positions had to be devised. Thompson says that in fact López had already organised another telegraph line to go through the *carrizal* and along the riverbank to Villa del Pilar and then on to Asunción, but always had the line along the road repaired in order to make the Allies believe it was his only route for telegraph messages. In addition, on 22 July López had sent Lieutenant-Colonel Núñez with two cavalry regiments (dismounted due to lack of horses), an infantry battalion, and six cannon to construct defences and a road from Timbó to Monte Lindo about six miles (10 km) above the mouth of the River Tebicuary, while also laying another telegraph line to Asunción. This road would be 54 miles (87 km) long, going through deep mud and crossing five streams and the River Bermejo. It should be noted that Timbó was on the Chaco side of the River Paraguay and away from the Allied troop movements.

Another skirmish occurred between Major Benito Rolón's Paraguayan troops and the cavalry of General Andrade Neves on 3 August in the Arroyo Hondo, the Paraguayans losing 154 killed and 34 taken prisoner, plus 600 cattle and 360 horses, two carts of ammunition, and 400 carbines and lances. It was from information provided by the prisoners that Marshal Caxias began planning his next movements, as it was learnt that there were up to 20,000 Paraguayans at Humaitá, who had little contact with the interior. A siege designed to starve the defenders was therefore decided upon. With Allied ships closing all the river routes and the army controlling access by land, in time the defenders must surrender.

With the Brazilian 1st and 3rd Corps located where they were their own supply lines had also become somewhat extended, and supply columns had to be sent every other day. On 11 August one such column with a guard of 80 cavalrymen was attacked by 300 Paraguayan troops under Captain José González, who was quickly counterattacked by Colonel Antonio da Silva Paranhos with three cavalry units and two infantry battalions. The supply column was recaptured but only after the Brazilians had lost 50 men killed and wounded. The Paraguayans lost 15 men, three of them officers.

Before any further land actions should be undertaken, President Mitre insisted upon a naval operation being mounted to get a flotilla past the Paraguayan defences at Curupaytí and Humaitá. Consequently at 7:30 a.m. on 15 August, Admiral Ignacio passed the batteries at Curupaytí with ten ships. These were in two divisions, one of wooden vessels the other of ironclads. The 1st Division, that of wooden-hulled ships, consisted of the *Cabral*, *Barroso*, *Herval*, *Silvado*, and *Lima Barros*; while the ironclads of the 3rd Division comprised the *Brasil*, *Mariz e Barros*, *Tamandaré*, *Colombo*, and *Bahia*. There were two channels opposite Curupaytí. That nearest to the batteries was narrow and winding but was the shortest route and was therefore the one that was chosen. Later, when the area was in Allied hands, the other channel was found to contain numerous torpedoes lying in wait for the Brazilian ships.

The 1st Division led the way, and although it fired on the Paraguayan positions no response was forthcoming. Only when the ironclads appeared did the batteries open fire. The *Tamandaré* was hit in the engine room and stopped, but was taken in tow by the *Silvado*. The *Colombo* was also hit in the engine room. Being close astern to the *Tamandaré* she had to stop all engines to avoid ramming her, and the current brought her close under the Paraguayan batteries, which concentrated their fire on her and managed to cause serious damage before she could be backed out of danger. Meanwhile the *Lima Barros* provided covering fire while the damaged ships limped downstream. The Brazilian Navy had fired 665 shot and shell during this action and its ships had been hit 256 times. The five wooden ships were then stationed between Humaitá and Curupaytí, while the ironclad division proceeded to Humaitá, where it arrived at 2:00 p.m.

The channel at Humaitá was again narrow, and would subject each passing ship to concentrated fire from the land batteries. If the Brazilian attempt at forcing the passage failed there would be no room to turn and the ships would run onto the banks and possibly be captured. In addition the level of the river above Humaitá was beginning to fall, and would continue to do so until the following February, when autumn rains would increase the water volume of the river system. So if the Brazilian ships did manage to get past the batteries they could well become stranded, with little or no fuel and possibly no supporting Allied troops on the banks as promised. It was therefore decided that the best plan of action was to moor behind a small island beyond the range of the fort's batteries and await the arrival of shallow-draft monitors, which, it was believed, could resist the Paraguayan batteries and cope with the shallowness of the river downstream. In anticipation of this, López ordered most of his heavy guns from Curupaytí to Humaitá, placing Colonel Além in command of Humaitá, while leaving Captain Gil to command at Curupaytí. The advanced Brazilian ironclad division, meanwhile, was kept supplied by a road constructed along the Chaco side of the river, which was defended by a Brazilian Naval Battalion.

THE ACTION AT TATAYÍBÁ AND THE FALL OF TAYÍ

Returns for the Brazilian Army at the end of August 1867 give the following figures:

	Fit	Admin	Sick
1st Corps	10,734	924	3,477
2nd Corps	10,331	1,351	4,208
3rd Corps	8,852	971	2,749
Battalion of Engineers	506	72	136
Corps of Transport	52	788	7
Special Corps	125	–	–
Totals	*30,600*	*4,106*	*10,577*

Note: Admin = Administrative and logistical staff, transport drivers, cooks, personnel assigned to look after livestock, and so on.

On 20 September 1867 a force under the command of General Andrade Neves captured the village of Villa del Pilar situated on the River Neembucú, which was defended by 260 Paraguayan infantry under the command of Captains Simón António Villamayor and Isidoro Ayala. A large proportion of the defenders were amputees and convalescent wounded. During the fighting, Paraguayan reinforcements consisting of a company of infantry and some sailors had arrived on the steamer *Pirabebé*, but even with these additional troops the Paraguayans could not mount a counterattack in sufficient numbers and the river port was captured on the 24th with a loss to the Paraguayans of 100 killed and 74 captured. The Brazilians lost 31 men killed and wounded.

24 September also saw a Paraguayan task force attack a Brazilian supply convoy marching from Tuyuti to Tuyucué. The Paraguayan force, under the overall command of Lieutenant-Colonel Núñez, consisted of six infantry battalions (the 18th, 19th, 21st, 24th, 27th, and 29th), under Majors José Tomás Viveros and Sebastián Bullo, and five squadrons of cavalry commanded by Major Valois Rivarola, plus one field-piece and four rocket launchers. The Brazilian convoy was escorted by Lieutenant-Colonel Augusto Caldas' infantry brigade,

made up of four Volunteer Battalions (the 29th, 41st, 43rd, and 49th) and the Cavalry Brigade of Colonel Vasco Alves, composed of two National Guard units and the 12th and 5th Mounted *Caçadores*, a total of 1,600 infantry and 704 cavalry. These were under the command of General Albino de Carvalho.

The Paraguayan attack would be made using only the cavalry regiment. This was to retire back to the waiting infantry and artillery, hopefully drawing the bulk of the Brazilian escort troops in pursuit. The infantry were to be divided into three sections: the 18th and 27th were to form the reserve, the 19th and 29th were to be the troops to which the cavalry would retire, and the 21st and 24th with the artillery would form the defensive line. The attack went well. The Brazilian troops became disorganised, but soon recovered, and when the attacking cavalry retreated it was pursued by the Brazilian cavalry while reinforcements of 1,500 infantrymen from the 36th, 47th, and 56th Volunteers under the personal command of General Pôrto Alegre was quickly on the battlefield. The Paraguayan cavalry, having completed their task, fell back behind their assigned infantry while the 21st and 24th infantry and artillery confronted the charging Brazilian cavalry. These were repulsed by musket fire and canister at 150 yds (140 m), with the rockets causing confusion and panic amongst the horses. The Brazilian infantry did not advance against the Paraguayan line, and the engagement came to an end. It had cost the Brazilians 38 men killed, 283 wounded, and 140 missing, the Paraguayans losing only 80 men killed.

On 3 October 1867 a Paraguayan cavalry force of 2,000 men under Major Bernardino Caballero, composed of the 8th, 13th, and 30th Regiments and two squadrons each from the 7th, 15th, and 31st Regiments (a total of 18 squadrons), was sent to reconnoitre the area between San Solano and Parecué, 7.5 miles (12 km) north of Humaitá – a daily event in this section of the defences. A Brazilian cavalry force of 400 men from the 6th Cavalry Division under the command of Colonel Fernández Lima engaged this column but was beaten back. A further Brazilian force under the command of General Andrade Neves, consisting of 1,000 men from the 2nd Cavalry Division, and General José Luís Mena Barreto, with 800 men from the 1st Division (the 50th Volunteer Battalion), then arrived, General Mena Barreto taking overall command when these forces united. Another cavalry clash ensued, the fighting lasting for only 45 minutes before the Brazilian cavalry was forced to retire to a defensive line held by the 50th Volunteer Battalion under the command of Lieutenant-Colonel Albuquerque Belo, which managed to force the Paraguayan cavalry back. Seeing this, the regrouped Brazilian cavalry charged once more but were again repulsed, leaving Major Caballero in control of the field. The casualties for the Paraguayans were 300 killed and wounded, while the Brazilians lost 500. It would be interesting to know the condition of the Paraguayan horses or mules fielded here, since, as we have seen, most reports say that the Paraguayans' horses were in a poor state, while the quantity involved in the action must indicate that new mounts had been acquired from outside Humaitá, either in raids on Allied stock or found during one final scouring of Paraguay.

These daily sorties by the Paraguayan cavalry under the command of the newly promoted Lieutenant-Colonel Caballero had to be stopped, so on 21 October

5,000 Allied cavalry were dispersed behind the many woods along the plain that was often used by the Paraguayans, and a Brazilian cavalry regiment, the 5th Line, was used as a decoy to lure the latter into a trap. The plan worked. A force of 1,500 Paraguayans under Caballero, composed of the 7th, 8th, 13th, 23rd, 30th, and 31st Cavalry Regiments, gave chase for three miles (5 km) to a place called Tatayíbá, where they found themselves suddenly surrounded by the awaiting Brazilians. Somehow the Paraguayans managed to fight their way back to Humaitá, but only after losing 583 men killed and 173 captured. The Brazilians lost just ten men killed and 113 wounded, including 24 officers. For his bravery in this engagement Caballero was promoted to full colonel and a medal was ordered to be given to all survivors of the action at Tatayíbá. The medal was struck the following February, but since only 200 were issued it would seem that 550 of the survivors didn't stay alive long enough to receive it.

On 27 October, the Brazilian General José Luís Mena Barreto was sent with 5,000 men from Villa del Pillar to capture the small town of Tayí, on the banks of the River Paraguay about 15 miles (25 km) north of Humaitá, and the entrenchments situated at Potrero Ovello. The Brazilian force was composed of the 1st and 2nd Cavalry Divisions, seven infantry battalions from the 1st Infantry Division, four artillery pieces, and 50 sappers, while the entrenchments were defended by Captain José González with 300 men. If Tayí could be captured a blockade of the river against supplies destined for the Paraguayan garrison could be achieved. The outer defences at Potrero Ovello were captured on the 28th with a loss to the Paraguayans of 143 killed and wounded and 56 captured, the Brazilians suffering 85 killed and 310 wounded among the six battalions that attacked (the 2nd, 7th, 8th, and 9th Line and the 24th and 33rd Volunteers), the 1st Line Battalion being kept in reserve. The Paraguayan survivors made their way back to Humaitá.

Tayí itself was captured on 2 November, losses to the Paraguayans here being 240 men killed, 68 severely wounded and taken prisoner, and three cannon. The defenders had been commanded by Major Toribio Villamayor, who had received 400 reinforcements under Captain Gervasio Ríos from the 9th Battalion just the previous day. Most of the survivors reached the village of Laurel, where they regrouped. The Brazilians lost 33 killed and 93 wounded. In addition the Paraguayan ship *Olimpo* was sunk by Brazilian artillery fire; the *Veinticinco de Mayo* (or *25 de Mayo*) was set ablaze by gunfire and burnt down to the waterline; and the *Yporá* was damaged but managed to escape. This area had been used by López to pasture the small stock of cattle that his army needed to survive. Following its capture General Berreto began construction of entrenchments around Tayí and had fourteen 32-pdr Whitworth guns mounted along the cliff by the riverbank. He also had a heavy chain laid onto pontoon boats and stretched across the river.

With the loss of the Tayí, the road built earlier that year connecting Humaitá to Timbó and on to Monte Lindo was now the only route along which supplies could be brought to the besieged Paraguayan camp. The terrain traversed by this road was part of the Gran Chaco, a region deemed unfit for the operation of armies, being a wilderness of impenetrable woods and impassable swamps and marshes, and therefore an escape and supply route that the Allies would not have thought possible. The road that the Allies had constructed to supply their own vanguard of warships had proven to them how difficult it was to work in this terrain. Yet the Paraguayans brought supplies and droves of oxen down to Timbó by means of this route, and then transferred them to flatboats, barges, and rafts to finish the last leg of the journey by river. The fort at Timbó, now defended by 30 cannon, was situated on the other side of the River Paraguay, about four miles (6 km) above Humaitá and below the town of Tayí, and was on that part of the river not controlled by the Allies. In command of the road and supplies was Lieutenant-Colonel Núñez, with the 45th Infantry Battalion and two squadrons of cavalry.

At the beginning of November 1867 the Allies had 5,000 men under General José Luís Mena Barreto stationed at Tayí, while a Brazilian division commanded by General Andrade Neves was encamped at the Estancia San Solano which lay between Tayí and Tuyucué. At the latter were 25,000 troops under the command of Marshal Caxias, and at Tuyuti there were 16,000 men under General Pôrto Alegre. The Navy had 18 steamers armed with 75 guns moored at Curuzú, and five ironclads with 34 guns anchored almost opposite Humaitá. The only Paraguayan outpost not yet taken was the fort at Timbó, and that was on the other bank of the River Paraguay. The Brazilian report on its personnel for the end of October provides the following strengths for its various corps:

Special Corps	146
1st Artillery Corps	717
1st Cavalry Corps	2,908
1st Infantry Corps	10,934
2nd Artillery Corps	2,108
2nd Cavalry Corps	2,991
2nd Infantry Corps	9,653
3rd Artillery Corps	248
3rd Cavalry Corps	3,589
3rd Infantry Corps	8,015
Engineer Battalion	701
Transport Corps	863
Total	*42,873*

Of these, 10,708 are listed as being sick but figures are not given for individual corps. Also no figures are given for the Argentine and Uruguayan contingents.

THE SECOND BATTLE OF TUYUTI

One would have thought that by now López would have decided to cut his losses and fall back before becoming totally surrounded, but no, his reaction was to see what effect it would have on the Allied forces to be at such a distance from their main supply depots at Tuyuti and the port of Itapirú on the River Paraná. And he reasoned that if one or both of these could be captured and destroyed it might yet save the day. At the very least it would put the Allies under pressure to either attack his defended lines or withdraw back to Tuyuti, or agree to end the war because of their straitened supply position. Certainly there was no food to be obtained locally, for this had been removed by the orders of López when the Allies first began their advance on the right flank in July.

With this in mind, López ordered Major Thompson to draw up detailed plans of the Allied camp, using the watchtowers and information gleaned from interviewing prisoners. On the night of 2 November 1867 López ordered the field officers of units assigned to the operation to be at his headquarters at Paso Pucú the following morning to receive their instructions for the coming battle; this was not the norm, as López usually instructed each officer individually. He appointed Brigadier-General Vicente Barrios to command the attacking force of 9,000 men, made up of the 1st, 3rd, 6th, 8th, 9th, 11th, 13th, 18th, 19th, 20th, 27th, 30th, 34th, 37th, 38th, and 40th Infantry Battalions, the 2nd, 8th, 9th, 10th, 11th, and 20th Cavalry Regiments, and three squadrons of artillery. These were organised into two infantry divisions commanded by Colonels Giménez and González, each division having two brigades of four battalions, a total of 16 battalions. Colonel Ximenez was to command the Vanguard Division. The infantry brigades were commanded by: 1st Brigade, Colonel Manuel António Giménez, second-in-command Major Sabastián Bullo; 2nd Brigade, Lieutenant-Colonel Eugeno Lezcano, second-in-command Major Martin Villolba; 3rd Brigade, Colonel António Luis González, second-in-command Major José Duarte; 4th Brigade, Major Juan Fernández, second-in-command Major Bernardo Olmedo. The Cavalry Division was commanded by Colonel Caballero, being made up of two brigades with two regiments in each.[15] The 1st Brigade was under Colonel Caballero, second-in-command Major José Manuel Montiel, the 2nd Brigade under Major Rivarola, second-in-command Major Benito Rolón. The artillery squadrons were commanded by Captain Cándido Mendoza.

The Paraguayan attack was to be made from the east using only the infantry, while the cavalry, by making a wide sweep, would charge into the Allied camp and press forward as far as the port of Itapirú, cutting down everything in their path. On arriving there, they would wheel about and charge the enemy's rear. All buildings, barracks, and corrals were to be burnt, while the soldiers were to loot the Allied camp and destroy such stores as could not be carried away. All captured field-pieces were to be sent back to the Paraguayan camp as soon as they were taken. The troops were to be moved that night through the Paso Yataiti-Corá, and would camp there ready for the surprise attack, which was planned for 4:30 a.m., just before dawn.

It so happened that a Brazilian supply column commanded by Colonel Antonio da Silva Paranhos was sent out that day for Tuyucué, with 1,600 men from the 41st, 42nd, 46th, and 54th Volunteer Battalions as escort. These men were stationed on the flank that was to be attacked and would become a useful reserve when the Allies needed them most. If the Paraguayan attack had taken place the following day these troops would have been camped at Tuyucué and could not have assisted in what would be known as the Second Battle of Tuyuti.

The Paraguayan infantry were formed into three columns with one in reserve. They encountered two Argentine picket units, which opened fire on them, but these were bypassed rather than attacked, so as not to begin the battle prematurely. The outer Allied entrenchments were quickly scaled by the Paraguayan 1st Column, surprising the 300 men of the 41st Volunteer Battalion defending this part of the defences. The Argentine artillery placed at the San Martin redoubt was

taken by the 2nd Column, having time to fire only two guns before being overwhelmed. The Argentine Infantry Battalion of Corrientes and the Paraguayan Legion were also attacked and forced back. The Paraguayan 3rd Column attacked the redoubt containing the Brazilian 4th Battalion of Artillery and the 48th Volunteer Battalion, and this was also captured. The Paraguayan infantry then stormed forward to attack the second line of entrenchments, leaving detachments to set fire to the captured barracks, corrals, and powder magazines.

The second Allied line was made up of five Brazilian infantry battalions (the 6th, 11th, 29th, 47th, and 54th Volunteers), but these were pushed back into the supply camp, where 2,000 private sutlers and merchants had set up shop to sell their wares to the Allied troops alongside the normal army quartermasters. The attack resulted in utter confusion among the fleeing civilians, but an artillery redoubt had luckily been sited close to the camp in a central position. This the Paraguayans had no knowledge of, and, following their orders, the troops of the 1st and 2nd Columns set about pillaging the camp, with many becoming drunk. However, their celebrations were abruptly ended when a salvo of canister and shrapnel came screaming at them from the redoubt, where General Pôrto Alegre had said to his gathered artillerymen, 'A vitória depende hoja dos senhores; a glória é da artilharia.' ('Men, victory this hour depends on you; for glory and the artillery.')

By now it was daylight, and the dismayed Paraguayans could make out the unexpected artillery redoubt, with its 14 guns from the 2nd Artillery Battalion, reinforced by the 36th, 41st, and 42nd Volunteer Battalions – a total of 1,800 men under the command of General Pôrto Alegre, who was to be wounded in the ensuing battle and have two horses shot from under him. General Barrios ordered his officers to regroup their men and attack the redoubt, but seeing the futility of this course of action the assault was stopped and a retreat was begun. This was attacked by Pôrto Alegre's infantry, which now included the 37th and 43rd Volunteer Battalions from the 11th Brigade while the remnants of the 28th and 46th Volunteers remained with the artillery.

The Paraguayan cavalry under Colonel Caballero had meanwhile pushed southward, crossing the Estero Bellaco by the Paso de la Carretas, and had managed to reach as far as the Paso de la Patria, close to the port of Itapirú. Here they wheeled round and began to attack the fleeing civilians and retreating Allied troops, making their way to the westerly Paso Sidre to return to Tuyuti in order to attack the enemy in the rear. On the way they captured three artillery redoubts and managed to send back 257 prisoners, including six women, Major Cunha Mattos (commander of the Brazilian 4th Battalion of Artillery) and Major Aranda (Argentine), plus the captured field-pieces. But by the time Caballero's column reached the camp at Tuyuti the Paraguayan infantry had already begun its retreat. An Argentine cavalry brigade of 800 men, under the command of General Hornos, had managed to travel from Tuyucué to Tuyuti after the sounds of cannon had first been heard,[16] and these now attacked the Paraguayan cavalry, who were forced to retreat after a further hour of fighting. The battle ended at nine o'clock.

One of the 13 artillery guns that had been captured

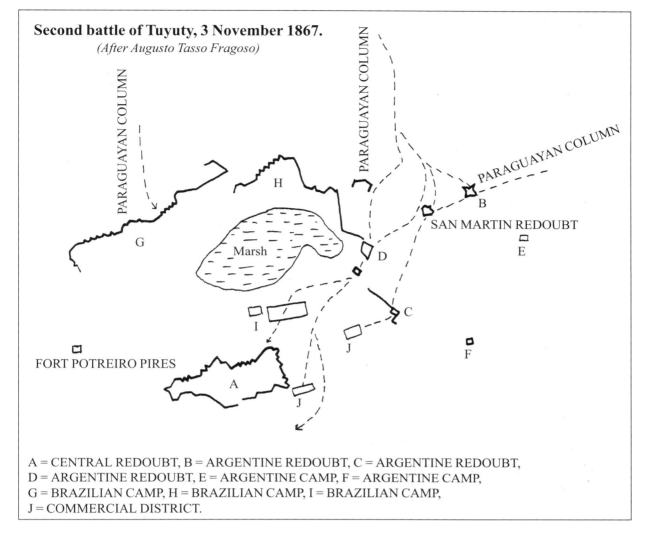

Second battle of Tuyuty, 3 November 1867.
(After Augusto Tasso Fragoso)

PARAGUAYAN COLUMN

PARAGUAYAN COLUMN

PARAGUAYAN COLUMN

H

G

Marsh

D

SAN MARTIN REDOUBT

B

E

I

J

C

F

FORT POTREIRO PIRES

A

J

A = CENTRAL REDOUBT, B = ARGENTINE REDOUBT, C = ARGENTINE REDOUBT,
D = ARGENTINE REDOUBT, E = ARGENTINE CAMP, F = ARGENTINE CAMP,
G = BRAZILIAN CAMP, H = BRAZILIAN CAMP, I = BRAZILIAN CAMP,
J = COMMERCIAL DISTRICT.

and were being hauled back to the Paraguayan lines became stuck up to its axles in the mud and, being within rifle-shot of the Allied lines, it was abandoned. This was a 32-pdr Whitworth. On being told of this López went into a rage, and General Bruguéz volunteered to retrieve the gun if he was given two infantry battalions to assist him. This sortie was quickly arranged, and provided with 12 oxen, spades, planks, ropes and so on, but by the time it reached the gun Allied troops were already endeavouring to haul it away with a team of cattle. A lively skirmish ensued, the Allied troops were forced to withdraw, and the gun was finally pulled out of the mud and presented to López, although Captain Cándido Mendoza of the artillery was killed during the skirmish.

In the battle itself the Paraguayans lost 1,200 men killed and 1,000 wounded. The 40th Battalion returned from the attack with only 100 men; the 20th Battalion started the day with 460 men but ended it with just 76; while the 3rd Battalion came back with only 100 men out of 400. Brazilian sources, however, state that they buried 2,734 enemy bodies and took 155 prisoners. Perhaps some of the buried Paraguayans were ex-prisoners of war who had been forced to join the Argentine Army after capture but had rejoined their old comrades when the opportunity arose. An Argentine source gives Paraguayan casualties as 78 officers and 1,441 other

ranks killed in the camp, with a further 830 bodies found in the marshes to its front. The Allies lost 294 killed (259 Brazilian, 35 Argentine), 1,316 wounded (1,163 Brazilian, 151 Argentine), and 435 captured, plus the 13 cannon, 12 of which were Argentine. Civilian losses are not recorded. Brigadier-General Barrios was promoted to the rank of General of Division, although he never wore the insignia of this rank, as López was the only other person to hold it.

What had saved the day for the Allies had been the artillery redoubt. If it had been noticed or known about and attacked as soon as the camp had been overrun, then the outcome of the battle could well have been very different. A British officer, Commander A.J. Kennedy, wrote: 'This action, in which a force of Paraguayans had been able to attack and completely rout a body of the Allies twice their number, capture their cannon, burn their camp, and destroy the reserve stores of the whole army, was viewed with the greatest astonishment.' J.J. Pakenham, secretary to the British Legation in Rio de Janeiro, wrote in his report to Lord Stanley: 'A curious incident connected with the recent engagement ... is, that the vanquished seized, and were able to carry off, several pieces of artillery belonging to the victors; a proceeding unusual, I believe, in modern military annals.'

The captured artillery pieces included a 7-inch

howitzer, a 9-pdr rifled gun, and a 12-pdr Krupp rifled steel breechloader that had been captured still loaded. Ammunition for this piece was subsequently made at Asunción, and the gun was taken to different parts of the defensive line for use against the Allies. The 32-pdr Whitworth retrieved by Bruguéz had to have a new vent-piece fitted. Its ammunition-wagon had also been captured, although hundreds of Allied shells fired into Humaitá that fitted it were re-used too. This gun was placed at Curupaytí and fired on the unsuspecting wooden warships that had anchored well within its range, hitting the Brazilian *Belmonte* and dismounting her 150-pdr Whitworth, killing its crew. After being hit 34 times by this gun in a single afternoon the Allied fleet was forced to move out of range. Nicknamed 'Phew' by the Paraguayans on account of the noise its shells made, this gun was later moved to Espinillo, facing the Allied camp at Tuyucué.

SKIRMISHES AND RIVER ACTIONS

Although it had come so near to success, the Paraguayan attack had failed to produce the effects on the Allied high command that López had hoped for. The Allied troops were not withdrawn from Tayí or Tuyucué, and the army's supplies had not been completely destroyed. López's next option was to reduce his perimeter defences so that his men would not be so thinly spread. A new trench was therefore begun, which would run from Lake López (Laguna López) on its right flank and follow the crest of the Paso Pucú through to a junction at Espinillo. Triangular redoubts constructed at Angle and at intervals along the trench to Humaitá were made to flank, as far as possible, the intervals between them. The old trench from Sauce to Angle was left with only guards, its 150 guns being removed. The heavier guns were emplaced at Humaitá while the lighter ones were positioned along the Paso Pucú trench. The trench from Espinillo through to Humaitá was well defended by artillery in the numerous redoubts. Captain Barrios was stationed at Sauce with 100 men and one gun; the old centre and left flank were commanded by Major J. Fernández with a regiment of dismounted cavalry; and General Bruguéz commanded the whole of the new entrenchment.

30 November 1867 saw fortifications at Timbó begun, a trench being dug near the edge of the river but masked by the surrounding wood. This was garrisoned by six infantry battalions, three cavalry regiments, and 30 cannon, under the command of Colonel Caballero, who was also given command of the communication line through the Chaco. His second-in-command was Major Manuel Montiel. Later, in February 1868, this garrison was increased to include six 8-inch and eight 32-pdr guns. These were situated by the river and placed 3 ft (0.9 m) above ground level so that they would not become flooded if the level of the river rose. Naval Captain Domingo António Ortiz was in command of this battery.

During December López offered the women of the camp a way of escape, saying they could go to Asunción via the road through the Chaco. Although this meant a walk of nearly 250 miles (400 km), many took the opportunity to leave.

During November and December 1867 the Allied Navy – or, rather, the Brazilian Navy, for there were no Uruguayan or Argentine warships with the advanced

squadrons – had maintained its harassment of the batteries and encampments of Curupaytí and Humaitá, the ironclad division keeping in touch with the remainder of the fleet via the road that had been cut through the Chaco. This period also saw the arrival of the first three monitors specially built in Rio de Janeiro for the operation against the batteries at Humaitá. These were the *Rio Grande*, armed with a 120-pdr Whitworth; the *Para*, armed with a 70-pdr Whitworth; and the *Alagoas*, also armed with a 70-pdr Whitworth (these Whitworths were all muzzle-loaders). The ships displaced about 340 tons and carried 36–39 men, four of whom worked the gun while another four operated the movement of the turret. Their wooden hulls were 18 ins (46 mm) thick, made from Brazilian sucupira and peroba trees that are harder than oak, and they had armour plate 4½–6 ins (114–152 mm) thick. The hulls of these monitors were raised only a foot (250 mm) out of the water, and their draught was 8 ft 10 ins (2.69 m). The revolving turret had a circular porthole for the gun, this being only slightly larger than the gun itself in order to lessen the risk of a shell breaching the armour. The turret itself was an oval shape, which according to the Brazilians was an improvement upon the more common circular design. Thompson says that the armour plating on the hull was 4 ins (102 mm) thick while the turret armour was 6 ins (152 mm), but in their book *Ironclads at War* (1989) Jack Greene and Alessandro Massignani say that the armour plating of the turret was backed by 10 ins (254 mm) of wood. These ships also had a funnel.

Commander A.J. Kennedy RN wrote of the Brazilian Navy at this period: 'Amongst the most efficient of the Iron-clads were the "Lima Barros" and the "Bahia". These vessels were built by Messrs Laird of Birkenhead, and fitted on Captain Coles principle, the former with two turrets, the latter with one, each turret being armed with two 150 pounders (Whitworths). The "Lima Barros" which left England under the name of "Bellona" is 1,340 tons burthen and draws twelve feet of water, she is a twin screw with engines of 300 horse power, and made 12 knots at the measured mile with all stores and armaments on board. Both ships are plated with 4½ inch plate. The "Bahia" is 1,000 tons and draws only eight feet of water, twin screw, 140 horsepower, and 10 knots a mile. The "Colombo" and "Cabral" were built by Messrs Rennie of Greenwich, they were sister ships designed especially for the Paraguayan War, length 160 feet, breadth 35 feet 6 inches, draught of water with stores and armaments on board 9 feet 6 inches, tonnage 930 tons, 200 horsepower, direct action horizontal driving twin screws. Each vessel was fitted with two batteries one at each end, the space between being occupied by the Officers cabins and accommodation for the crew. Their armament consisted of eight guns, 70 pounders, 4 in each battery with 4½ inch plating of iron. The hull gradually sloped from the base of the battery to within one foot of the water's edge. This slope was plated with 2½ inches of iron and allowed the guns in the battery above a clear range ahead or astern.'

Also in December 1867, Marshal Caxias listed the cannon given in Table 7 as available at the front in the service of Brazil. Brazilian Army returns for the same month show 883 artillery, 3,264 cavalry, and 11,952 infantry at Tuyucué and São Solano; 691 artillery, 2,455 cavalry, and 10,688 infantry at Tuyuti; 216 artillery,

1,422 cavalry, and 6,265 infantry at Tayí; 140 Special Corps, 859 Engineer Battalion, and 851 Transport Corps at Tuyucué, São Solano, and Tayí; 1,327 men in the Chaco; 2,278 men in the city of Corrientes; and 2,500 men at Aguapai (Province of Corrientes) – a total of 45,791 men in all. The sick for the Brazilian army at this time were: artillery 701 men, cavalry 1,246 men, and infantry 8,588 men, a total of 10,535 from the above figures. The Argentine army based on the Rio Blanco had a total of 6,000 men, while the Uruguayan troops amounted to some 500 men.

On 11 January 1868 news of the death by cholera of the Argentine vice-president Dr Marcos Paz reached the Allied camp. To mourn his passing, flags were flown at half-mast, a cannon was fired from the Argentine camp every half-hour followed by one from the Brazilian camp, and the Argentines held a full dress parade. To López, all this activity could mean only one thing: that President/General Mitre had died. He therefore published news to this effect in his different newspapers for the next few months, and captured prisoners were flogged until they said that Mitre was dead even though he was not – despite López having discovered the real truth after just a few days. Could this have been a morale-boosting exercise for his troops, or was it merely a whim?

General Mitre himself returned to Buenos Aires on the 13th, leaving General Gelly y Obes in command of the Argentine troops in Paraguay. It is interesting to read a message sent by the Brazilian Emperor to the Condessa de Barral just a week earlier, on 6 January: 'A revolution has occurred in the Argentine Province of Santa Fe along the Paraná. Even though it is only a brief time, I do not like such neighbours, for our recruits and our ammunition ships which travel up the Paraná bound for the army and the squadron.' Internal political problems were not Mitre's only worry. As we have already seen, a serious consequence of the removal of workers and soldiers from frontier areas – particularly in Santa Fe and Córdoba –

was that it rendered them susceptible to raids by marauding Indians. The first serious attack occurred in southern Córdoba in March 1866, and raids continued thereafter throughout the war, until President Sarmiento began to devote military forces to the problem in 1869. British minister G.Z. Gould reported to London in 1868 that 'the frontier districts are continually overrun by Indians who so seldom meet with any opposition in their raids that they now bring their women and children with them and boldly encamp for days together in the immediate vicinity of large settlements.' In April 1868 the Indian chief (or cacique) Calfucurá led 2,000 Indians in an attack on southern Córdoba and made off with 200 captives and 20,000 head of cattle. In a review of the situation in 1869 the British vice-consul, Gordon, wrote: 'The number of cattle, sheep and horses that have been swept off by the Indians from the frontier districts of Mendoza, San Luis, Córdoba and Santa Fe may be counted by the hundreds of thousand and the number of persons carried into captivity amounts to nearly four hundred.' No wonder the Argentine forces in Paraguay were not being maintained to their 1866 level, as the Brazilians might have hoped.

27 January saw General Pôrto Alegre return to Brazil. He was succeeded as commander of the Brazilian 2nd Corps by General Alexandre Gomes de Argollo Ferrão of the 1st Corps, which was henceforth commanded by General Victorino José Monteiro, Baron de San Borja.

All this time the Allies kept up a series of sorties against the Paraguayans, such as that of Major Sabastián Tamborim, commanding the Brazilian 26th Volunteers, on 2 December, who advanced along the riverbed of the Caimbocá towards the village of Laureles and was ambushed there, suffering 7 killed, 11 wounded, and 15 taken prisoner. Likewise, to maintain pressure on the Allied lines various raids were made by small units of Paraguayans, which often brought back cattle – one

Table 7: Artillery with the Brazilian Army, December 1867

Type	Tuyuti	Tuyucué	Tayí	Chaco
Whitworth calibre 2	–	–	–	4
Whitworth calibre 32	2	–	1	–
La Hitte 4	–	–	–	3
La Hitte 12	12	–	–	–
Cannon calibre 4 (Brazilian size)	6	8	4	–
Cannon calibre 4 (French size)	4	4	4	–
Cannon calibre 6 (French size)	19	–	–	–
Cannon calibre 12 (Brazilian size)	5	–	6	–
Cannon calibre 12 (French size)	–	5	2	–
Cannon calibre 4 (mountain artillery)	12	4	2	–
Howitzer 4½-pdr	12	8	–	5
Howitzer 5½-pdr–	–	–	4	
Mortar 15-inch	–	–	–	2
Austrian cannon calibre 24	–	2	–	–
Austrian cannon 2-pdr	1	–	–	–
Austrian cannon 2½-pdr	2	–	–	–
English cannon 2-pdr	–	2	–	–
English cannon 2½-pdr	2	2	–	–
Prussian cannon	4	–	–	–
Totals	*81*	*35*	*19*	*18*

brought back 800 head, another 1,800. One such raid was against the Brazilian encampment at Paso Poi on 25 December (occupied by the 30th Volunteers, commanded by Lieutenant-Colonel Apolonio Campelo). The raiding party, led by Captain Eduardo Vera, comprised 160 men from the 4th, 6th, 19th, and 21st Infantry Battalions, and the attack lasted 40 minutes. On another occasion a raiding party of 50 men under the command of Major Rivarola crossed the marsh naked and attacked the rear of a Brazilian battalion. The latter were reinforced by another battalion, which, coming up from behind the Paraguayans, prevented the defending Brazilians from firing in case they hit their own countrymen; the fighting was therefore a fierce hand-to-hand combat in the darkness. Another raid was made on 17 February, when two companies of Paraguayan infantry and a squadron of cavalry commanded by Captain Urbieta surprised an Argentine reconnaissance force of 80 infantry and 110 cavalry from Tuyucué, commanded by Colonel José Pipo Giribone. The Argentines lost 52 men killed in this engagement, including three officers (one of them Giribone), as well as 15 wounded (including another officer) and three taken prisoner or lost. The Paraguayans lost 30 killed and wounded, Captain Urbieta being wounded in the thigh.

It was during this period that López had the redoubt at Cierva constructed. Completed on 14 February 1868, this was situated 3,500 yds (3.2 km) to the north of Humaitá and was defended by nine field-pieces and 500 men under the command of Major António Olabarrieta. An Allied attack on this redoubt was mounted just a few days later, on 19 February, by a Brazilian force consisting of the 8th Cavalry Brigade commanded by Colonel Hipólito Ribeiro (the 4th Corps of Mounted Caçadores and the 20th Provincial Cavalry Corps), the 1st Infantry Brigade commanded by Colonel Barros Falcão (the 16th Infantry Battalion and the 30th Volunteer Battalion), the 5th Infantry Brigade commanded by Colonel Dr Pinheiro Guimarães (the 1st and 18th Infantry Battalions), and the 6th Provincial Corps of Cavalry commanded by Major Isidoro Fernandes. The majority of the infantry were equipped with the new needle guns recently imported from Europe.

The first Brazilian attack was carried out by the 1st Infantry Brigade while the 8th Cavalry Brigade tried to outflank the Paraguayan position. Both of these assaults were met with brisk musketry and artillery fire, canister and grape being used effectively. When these attacks were repulsed the 5th Infantry Brigade was sent in, supported by the 6th Provincial Cavalry Corps and covering artillery fire, only to meet the same fate. Some of the attackers had nevertheless managed to reach the counterscarp, with many being hit in the ditch. By this time, however, the Paraguayan artillery was running out of ammunition, and when a gunner's call to his commander that their ammunition was used up was overheard by the Brazilians they made ready for a final assault. The delay in organising this assault allowed the defenders to embark on the war-steamers *Tacuarí* and *Ygureí*, which had been firing in support of the redoubt. The Paraguayans left behind their nine field-pieces and suffered 300 men killed and wounded. The Brazilians lost 120 killed and 456 wounded, but had succeeded in capturing the redoubt after three hours of fighting.

With the return of General Mitre to Buenos Aires,

Vice-Admiral Baron de Inhauma (Admiral Ignacio had recently been awarded this title by the Brazilian Emperor) could finally begin to draw up plans with Marshal Caxias to which they could both agree. (One assumes that General Mitre had wanted the Brazilian Navy to carry out impossible missions without question, in order to help the beleaguered land forces, even at the risk of substantial naval losses.) In February the rivers began to increase in depth, making it possible for ships to pass Humaitá without the risk of becoming stuck on unseen sandbanks or hitting the mines and torpedoes anchored in the river. The fleet was therefore assembled on the night of 19 February in readiness to run the gauntlet, the three monitors having passed the batteries at Curupaytí on the 13th and joined the three warships stationed below Humaitá. It started toward Humaitá at 2:20 a.m. in this order: the ironclad *Barroso* (Captain Lieutenant Silveira da Motta) towed the monitor *Rio Grande* (First-Lieutenant Antonio Joaquim); the *Bahia* (*Capitão de Fragata* Guilherme dos Santos) – the divisional leader, commanded by Commodore Delphim Carlos de Carvalho – towed the *Alagoas* (First-Lieutenant Joaquim Maurity); and the *Tamandaré* (Captain Lieutenant Pires de Miranda) towed the *Pará* (First-Lieutenant Custodio de Mello). The monitors had to be towed due to the strength of the current, it being felt that they would be unable to pass the batteries under their own power quick enough to avoid being damaged or sunk.

During the journey the *Bahia* suffered steering problems and ran into the bank on the Chaco side, but was quickly mended and, with the *Alagoas*, managed to get back in line. At 2:40 a.m. signal rockets were fired from both banks to forewarn the batteries at Humaitá of the movements of the Brazilian squadron. The 'London' battery (which had perhaps got its title from being constructed by British engineers) was the first to open fire, and fireballs were shot into the air to illuminate the river and shore.

The Paraguayan chain across the river being secured on two barges to keep it above water-level, the first thing the Brazilians needed to do was to sink these so that it would submerge to a depth sufficient to allow their ships passage. This was quickly accomplished. After 40 minutes the *Barroso*, with the *Rio Grande do Sul*, passed the last battery at Humaitá and fired off a rocket to announce the fact, each of the following ships doing the same as they passed the battery. However, a lucky shot from the 'London' battery cut the towing hawser of the *Alagoas* and she was swept downstream towards one of the batteries. Vice-Admiral Inhauma, in the supporting squadron, signalled the monitor to anchor, fearing that her 30 hp engines might not be powerful enough to compete against the current, but her commander ignored the signal and managed to get his vessel back under control, even though her engine would not start. This incident caused the *Tamandaré* and *Pará* to drop out of line, and they too became easy targets for the Paraguayan gunners.

Still without power, the *Alagoas* collided with the ironclad *Herval* (part of the supporting squadron) further downriver before her engine was finally repaired by her chief engineer (Etchburne, a Frenchman), but she was then able to steam over the chain, albeit well behind the rest of the squadron. As she was now alone and struggling

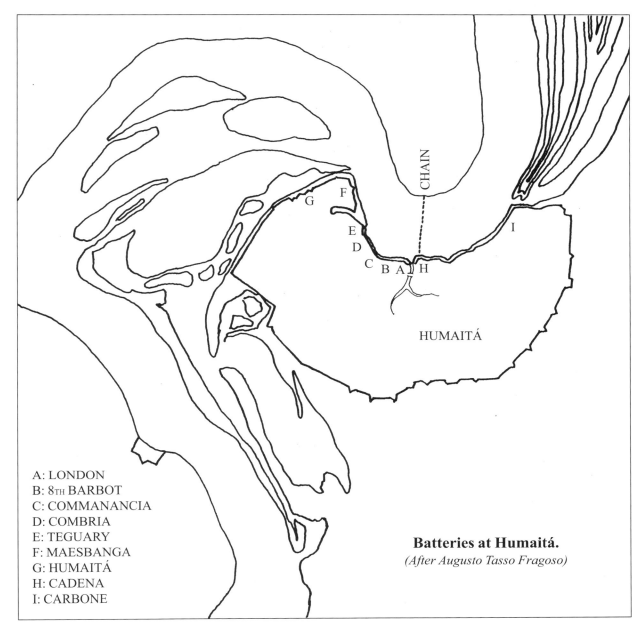

A: LONDON
B: 8TH BARBOT
C: COMMANANCIA
D: COMBRIA
E: TEGUARY
F: MAESBANGA
G: HUMAITÁ
H: CADENA
I: CARBONE

Batteries at Humaitá.
(After Augusto Tasso Fragoso)

against the flow of the river, the Paraguayan batteries were able to concentrate their fire on the *Alagoas*; but as Thompson states, though 'the fire of Humaitá was well sustained and true … the balls flew in pieces on the plates of the ironclads.' It nevertheless took an hour to pass the batteries, which contained 93 guns of heavy calibre. Following this, it now being full daylight, the *Alagoas* was set upon by 20 canoes from which Paraguayan troops tried to board her, but these were repulsed, as all the hatchways had been closed and the boarders were subjected to a withering fire from within the turret which cleared the deck in five minutes. The *Alagoas* then pursued the remaining canoes, crushing and sinking many, before finally rejoining the rest of the squadron at 5:00 a.m.

After getting past the batteries of Humaitá the Brazilian ships next ran into the batteries at Timbó. These caused much more damage than the guns at Humaitá, as they were lower and nearer the level of the river. By the

time the squadron reached and anchored at Tayí at midday the *Alagoas* had been hit 187 times, a violent shiver running through the whole vessel each time it was struck by a heavy projectile, and the *Tamandaré* 120 times, but just ten men had been wounded from all six ships. The *Alagoas*, *Tamandaré*, and *Pará* were so badly damaged that they required several weeks of repairs. Damage consisted chiefly of bent, crushed, and loosened armour plating, many of the bolts having been loosened. Burton states in his book that the *Alagoas*' armour plates 'were deeply pitted by the 68-pounders, like plum-pudding from which the "plums" had been picked out. In some cases they were dented and even pierced by the Blakely steel-tipped shot, of which Marshal-President López had but a small supply. Our naval officers have reported that the cast-iron projectiles impinging upon the armour, shivered into irregular fragments, which formed a hail of red-hot iron, and left the gun without a gunner to work it. The battery men always knew when a ball had struck the plates at night, by the bright flash which followed the shock.'

In recognition of the their achievement in passing the Paraguayan batteries, Commodore Delphim Carlos de Carvalho became Baron de Passegem, while First-Lieutenant Maurity of the *Alagoas* was promoted to Captain of Corvette and was decorated with the cross of a commander of the roses.

Supporting Carvalho's squadron had been the Brazilian warships *Lima Barros*, which put her bow into the bank during the night, and *Silvado*, which became entangled with trees on the riverbank and could not move until morning. Both of these events occurred on the Paraguayan side of the river. On the Chaco side were the *Cabral* and *Brazil* (flagship of the supporting squadron), both iron hulled, and the ironclads *Colombo* and *Herval*. All of these were to give support if required and maintain a bombardment of Curupaytí. They had begun their attack at 2:30 a.m. Further downriver was the ironclad *Mariz e Barros*, which was to guard the stores and hospital ships plus the gunboats and light craft that were anchored nearby. Some of the Brazilian gunboats went into Lake Piris to bombard positions along its bank. The artillery at Tuyucué also bombarded entrenchments at Espinillo. The Paraguayan ships *Tacuarí* and *Ygureí*, meanwhile, were sent into the Arroyo Hondo to be hidden from the Brazilian squadron.

On the 20th the ships *Bahia* and *Barroso* and the monitor *Rio Grande do Sul* steamed further upriver to bombard the city of Asunción, which they reached on the 24th. On the way they made a landing at Monte Lindo to burn storage sheds, and intercepted the Paraguayan warship *Pirabebé* towing the schooner *Angélica* towards Asunción; the *Pirabebé* managed to escape, but the schooner was sunk. Nearer to Asunción, at Tacambé, an entrenchment with two 68-pdrs, commanded by Lieutenant-Colonel Núñez, opened fire on them. This fire being returned, the battery was silenced after a two-hour engagement. By this time López had ordered Vice-President Francisco Sánchez to have every man capable of bearing arms leave the capital, and had sent Elisa Lynch to Asunción to remove his valuables to a place of safety. Both of these orders dated from 18 February, and were being carried out by the 22nd. By the 23rd a speedy evacuation of the city had also been implemented, with the transfer of the government to Luque, a village nine miles (15 km) down the railway line.

Commodore Delphim fired 68 shells into Asunción during a four-hour period, aimed at the Presidential Palace and the dockyard, where the sunken Paraguayan steamers *Paraguarí* and *Rio Blanco* were found; but with no signs of surrender, and with only 295 men in his three ships (an extra 100 infantrymen had been boarded at Tayí at the beginning of the voyage), a landing party to capture the city was out of the question – although it appeared to be deserted (except for the US, Italian, and French consulate buildings), his ships encountered small arms fire, and three rounds from the artillery piece called 'Criollo' that had been cast at the Asunción arsenal (all three missed their target). He therefore returned to Tayí, not wanting to be enticed into a trap within the city. Other Paraguayan field-pieces were sighted towards the river, but for some reason none of them were fired. López and others believed this to be the result of treachery.

It is often said that if Commodore Delphim had deployed two of his ships between Timbó and Humaitá then the defenders of the latter could not have made their escape, and the war might have ended sooner. But with only three serviceable vessels under his command this would have left his ships isolated and open to the risk of attack, the Paraguayans having shown in the past that they could and would attack individual vessels given the chance. If all six ships had passed the batteries with little damage then it would have become an option worth thinking about.

On 24 February Delphim and his three serviceable vessels steamed on and attacked the Paraguayan positions at Laurel, destroying the fortifications there. The Paraguayan defenders comprised three light cannon and 500 men under the command of Lieutenant-Colonel Franco, who had orders to retire into the interior if attacked by superior forces. He therefore abandoned Laurel on the 26th.

López, meanwhile, had decided that if his men could capture one of the enemy's ironclads then this could be used to halt the Brazilian fleet's advance: capturing just one vessel would put the Paraguayan navy on a near equal footing with the advance squadron's remaining three ships. He therefore assembled a handpicked force of 300 men who could swim and row, many of whom were sergeants and corporals. Commanded by Captain Ignacio Genes, a trusted ADC to López, these were divided into four companies of 77 men, each under a captain (Genes, José Tomás Céspedes, Eduardo Vera, and Manual Bernal). Groups of four canoes were then lashed together, two canoes on either side, with a rope about 20 yds (18 m) long strung between them that would catch across the bows of an enemy ship and bring the canoes alongside it. There were 24 canoes, each holding 12 men (according to Thompson) armed with sabres, pistols, hand-grenades, and rockets. The canoes were camouflaged with foliage and brush to make them look like *camalotes* (floating islands of debris from the flooded riverbank).

Genes' orders to his men were to let the groups of canoes drift downriver with the current, get alongside an ironclad, and board her, the Brazilian warships having no bulwarks and a low freeboard. The vessels actually selected for this daring Paraguayan attack were stationed between Humaitá and Curupaytí. Early on 2 March the force of canoes drifted towards the first four Brazilian ships under cover of an intensely dark night. The two foremost vessels had placed guard boats about a hundred feet (30 m) upstream to give warning of any approaching danger, and at about two o'clock in the morning José da Silva, a marine on the guard boat of the *Lima Barros*, sighted an unusually large number of *camalotes* drifting downstream towards the squadron. On closer inspection the quiet movement of oars could be discerned under the branches, and the guard boat rushed back to raise the alarm. Realising that they had been discovered, the Paraguayans discarded their camouflage and a race with the guard boat began. Consequently at the very moment that the guard boat reached the *Lima Barros* (commanded by Captain Aurello Garcindo Fernandes de Sá) 16 of the Paraguayan canoes under Genes also arrived, the other eight, under the command of Captain Manuel Bernal, making for the nearby *Cabral* (commanded by Captain Alves Nogueira).

The sentries on the *Lima Barros* were surprised and quickly overwhelmed, the officers on deck were surrounded, and Commodore Rodrigues da Costa, using this vessel as his flagship, was cut down, yelling down a hatch as he died for the crew to sweep the decks with small arms fire. Other crewmen made their escape into a gun turret, which also opened fire into the Paraguayans. On board the *Cabral* a similar action was taking place.

As the engagement commenced Captain-Lieutenant Jeronima Golcalvez of the *Silvado* despatched a boat to forewarn Vice-Admiral Baron de Inhauma of the danger confronting the squadron. Luckily the *Silvado* herself was able to steam in between the *Lima Barros* and *Cabral*, firing grape and canister across their decks to clear them of boarders, and was closely followed by the *Herval* (Captain Helvesio Pimentel), which executed the same manoeuvre. The Paraguayan boarders now tried desperately to open the hatches, throwing rockets and hand-grenades down the ventilation shafts and smoke stacks, causing some damage and wounding some crewmen, but could find no cover.

When the noise of the battle was heard on the flagship *Brasil*, Inhauma ordered full steam ahead towards the sound of the gunfire and instructed the *Mariz e Barros* and *Colombo* to follow him as soon as they could get up steam. Upon arriving at the scene of action he ordered the *Silvado* to board the *Cabral* while the *Brasil* and *Herval* boarded the *Lima Barros*.

At the close of the action not a single Paraguayan was left alive aboard the Brazilian ships, the bodies of 30 being found on the *Cabral* and 78 on the *Lima Barros*. Fifteen were taken prisoner (these were presumably picked up from the river), while many others were fired upon as they tried to swim to safety. Thompson says that the Paraguayans lost over 200 men killed in all. The Brazilians had suffered 10 killed and 73 wounded.

THE PARAGUAYANS WITHDRAW

With this defeat López was forced to acknowledge that if he wanted to avoid becoming completely surrounded then the time had come to begin evacuating his army. He began with his cannon. The artillery from all the trenches was taken to Humaitá, leaving just six guns at Curupaytí, one at Sauce, and 12 along the trench between Angle and Humaitá. In addition an infantry battalion was stationed at Espinillo and small units were despatched to guard other points of the trench. The Paraguayans' two remaining steamers were used to ferry military equipment (and, of course, the private belongings of López) out of Humaitá. The Whitworth 32-pdr and the Krupp 12-pdr were the first artillery pieces to be loaded and shipped across the River Paraguay. After these went eight 8-inch guns, and then anything else that could be useful and carried. On 3 March 1868 López himself crossed the river to the Chaco side, where he promoted officers who were to be left in command of Humaitá: Colonel Paulino Alén, his second-in-command Colonel Francisco Martínez (a favourite ADC to López), and the naval captains Cabral and Gill, both promoted to lieutenant-colonel and appointed third- and fourth-in-command respectively. A force of 3,000 men was left to garrison the 15,000-yard (almost 14 km) trench, with 200 cannon.

With the departure of the bulk of the Paraguayan army it was realised that the Allied prisoners who had accumulated at Humaitá, amounting to some 1,500 men, would be a liability if moved across the river, while to guard them with the limited troops now available at Humaitá was not feasible. George F. Masterman (1869) states that they were consequently all executed before the bulk of the army left.

López made a temporary headquarters at Seibo, about four miles (6.5 km) from Monte Lindo, were he placed some of his guns, although a few days later he directed them to be sited at the mouth of the River Tebicuary on the island of Fortín. These batteries were constructed within a week, the first being completed in three days. One battery was sited at the mouth of the Tebicuary and mounted seven 8-inch guns and two 32-pdrs; the second, with two 8-inch guns and three 32-pdrs, was sited 2,000 yds (1.8 km) higher up the River Paraguay but on the same island. A further battery of two 32-pdr rifled howitzers was emplaced facing the Tebicuary, in case a landing was attempted there. Three hundred men of the 18th Infantry Battalion were stationed on the island to support the batteries against attack.

On visiting this site Richard Burton wrote: 'At the angle where the Fortin fronts the Paraguay river, was an eleven-gun battery, in which the defenders had copied the invader. Here we saw gabions for the first time; there were traces of sod-revetted embrasures, not mere platforms "en barbette"; curtains were raised behind to traverse side shots, and épaulements prevented the works being raked from the south-west. Facing the Tebicuary, disposed at a right angle and connected with the former by rifle-pits, was a second battery of three field-pieces; whilst about 200 feet higher up the stream a ditch and a small earthen parapet defended the ford, where a landing might have been effected at low water. In the rear of each battery was a separate magazine, rough but useful ... Still further up the left bank of the Paraguay, and connected by rifle pits with the south-western work, was a third battery, built for six guns. The floor and platforms had been raised to keep them above the mean level of inundation. All was of the poorest and simplest tracing.'

With these batteries in place López moved his headquarters to San Fernando, four miles (6.5 km) north of the island of Fortín, and once drainage ditches had been dug in the low-lying ground, a campsite was quickly established for the 8,000 Paraguayan troops that had so far managed to reach this point.

Meanwhile an Allied general assault was made against the outer trenches of Humaitá by General Argollo on 21 March, his troops comprising the 11th Line Battalion, the 27th, 34th, 37th, 46th, and 48th Volunteer Battalions, and a company of pontoniers. A reserve brigade was also available if needed, commanded by Brigadier Hilario Maximiano Antunes de Gurjão. Argollo's force attacked Sauce, which was defended by 100 infantry drawn from two battalions under the command of Majors Olmedo and Medina, supported by two 4-pdr field-pieces, and after 2½ hours' fighting the trench was captured. The Paraguayans retreated to Paso Pucú, leaving behind 21 dead and one of their cannon, while General Argollo suffered 28 killed and 150 wounded. The attack on Angle by an Argentine force of six infantry battalions and 120 cavalrymen in two columns under General Emilio Mitre was not a success (though Allied losses here were just five killed and 13 wounded), and General Osõrio's attack against the positions at Espinillo was thrown back after 4½ hours' fighting, though some of his assaults came very close to the emplacements and reached the counterscarp. At just five killed and 49 wounded, Allied losses were light here too. The Paraguayan defenders of the latter positions, commanded by General Bruguéz, comprised six infantry battalions, three cavalry regiments, and 12 cannon.

The following day saw the evacuation of the old trench, including Curupaytí, by the Paraguayans, taking their remaining artillery pieces with them into the defensive works of Humaitá. In the afternoon an assault was made on Curupaytí after the Brazilian flag was seen flying above the river batteries, planted there by a landing force from the *Bereribe* (which had been sent with the *Magé* to observe any movement from the entrenchments). The Brazilians found the fort deserted, with dummy field-pieces constructed from tree trunks and defenders made from sacking and reeds.

Also on this day the *Barroso* and *Rio Grande do Sul* steamed past the batteries at Timbó and took up position between these and Laurel, making communication extremely difficult. The Paraguayan warship *Ygureí* was sighted in this part of the river and sunk by the Brazilian ships, while further downriver the *Tacuarí* unloaded her cargo under fire from the ironclads *Bahia* and *Pará* (now stationed to patrol from the River Tebicuary down to Humaitá) and was then scuttled by her commander. The six surviving Paraguayan warships, among them the *Iporá* and *Pirabebé*, were based further upriver. Later it was decided to lay them up at Ihu on the Rio Manduvira, and all their personnel, except one officer and 30 sailors who would remain aboard as skeleton crews, were incorporated into the army's Naval Battalion and several artillery batteries. These warships were finally set ablaze at their moorings on 18 August 1869 to prevent their capture by the Allies.

23 and 24 March saw the Brazilian warships *Bahia*, *Rio Grande*, and *Pará* bombard Humaitá. The night of the 23rd also saw Generals Barrios, Resquín, and Bruguéz, with other officers, manage to cross the river to the Chaco side. A large store of ammunition that had been collected near the riverbank at Humaitá ready for transportation exploded on 24 March, a heavy loss to López as powder was becoming scarce.

The Allies now drew up a plan to send an Argentine force of 1,500 men under General António Rivas to advance on the Chaco side of the river from the River de Oro, and unite with a Brazilian force composed of the 1st, 3rd, 7th, 8th, and 16th Infantry, 50 sappers, and four cannon – a total of 2,500 men – commanded by Colonel João do Rego Barros Falcão, which was to land below Timbó. This would create a line across the peninsula and cut off communications between López and Humaitá. The Brazilian force used three ironclads and two monitors to cross the river. General Rivas began his march on 30 April, having to cut his way through the dense *carrizal*. He was attacked on 2 May by Lieutenant Florentin Ovledo with 200 men of the 27th Infantry Battalion and six 4-pdr artillery pieces, sent from Humaitá by Colonel Além to see what was happening. The Paraguayans were repulsed, but noted the quantity of men being sent against them. The same day saw Major Santiago Florentin with men from the 7th Infantry Battalion from Timbó, reinforced by another company of

infantry under Captain Zoilo Escobar, attack the Brazilian force, inflicting 137 casualties on it. The next day the two Allied columns united, with General Rivas in command. A redoubt was then begun at a place called Andai on the banks of the Paraguay. Its right flank lay on the riverbank and its left upon a lake (Laguna Verá), so that it could only be assailed at the front and back, which were protected by abattis.

Meanwhile the Argentine Volunteer Legion, under the command of Lieutenant-Colonel Matoso, had been sent forward to reconnoitre. The defenders of a Paraguayan outpost – Lieutenant Ovledo with his 200 men and six 4-pdrs – fled as they approached, but on following them the Argentines found that they had been lured into a Paraguayan trap under the command of Major Vincent Ignacio Orzúza. Five hundred were killed or wounded and very few managed to get back to the Allied redoubt, those who did being later drafted into other Argentine battalions. The 4th saw the redoubt itself attacked by Colonel Caballero from Timbó, commanding four infantry battalions and two dismounted cavalry regiments. The attack started at 4:30 a.m. and was met by the Allied artillery and the Brazilian 8th and 16th Infantry Battalions, with the 7th acting as a reserve battalion. The *Bahia* and *Pará*, which lay within hearing distance, also helped in the defence, firing their Whitworths at the Paraguayans from the river. The attack was consequently driven back, the Paraguayans losing 356 men killed and wounded and seven taken prisoner, while the Allies lost six killed and 144 wounded.

On 5 May 1868 Brigadier Jacintho Machado Bittencourt replaced Colonel Barros Falcão as commander of the Brazilian troops on the Chaco side of the river. This force was now formed into two brigades. The 1st Brigade, commanded by Colonel Hermes da Fonseca, comprised the 1st, 8th, and 16th Infantry Battalions, while the 2nd, commanded by Lieutenant-Colonel Manuel José de Menezes, was made up of the 3rd, 7th, and 14th Infantry Battalions.

During this period the Allies had also been sending out cavalry reconnaissance units. The first, consisting of 3,000 men composed of the 13th, 14th, 15th, 23rd, and 24th National Guard Cavalry with four horse-artillery guns, was despatched towards the River Tebicuary on 4 June – Paraguayan cavalry units were reported to be based here, which had been sent on scouting missions towards Vila del Pillar. This Allied sortie reached the River Yacaré on the 8th, but was attacked while crossing the river by a force of 200 Paraguayan cavalry commanded by Major Rojas and was driven back. It had nevertheless confirmed the whereabouts of the Paraguayans.

After the repulse on 10 June of a Brazilian naval attack (by the *Bahia*, *Alagoas*, *Barroso*, and *Rio Grande do Sul*) on the new batteries placed along the River Tebicuary, López decided to mount another attempt at capturing an enemy ship, since at this time only two were stationed at Tayí. These were the *Barroso* and the *Rio Grande do Sul*, both anchored close to the shore batteries. A force of 240 volunteers was mustered for the attack, drawn mainly from the newly formed Paraguayan *Cuerpo de Bogabantes* (Canoe Paddlers Corps) but including naval officers and engineers to bring back any steamers that might be captured. Their commander was Major Francisco Cabriza, an adjutant to López. Divided

Brazilian monitors advancing against the Paraguayan batteries at Tebicuary, an engraving published in the French newspaper L'Illustration *in 1868.* (Author's collection)

into two groups, they set off downriver on the night of 9 July in 24 canoes disguised as floating plants and flotsam. The first group was beaten off the *Barroso* but quickly paddled to assist the second, which had managed to get aboard the *Rio Grande do Sul*. Although surprising the latter's few sentries, the boarders could not secure an open hatchway, and became targets for the batteries at Tayí and the guns of the *Barroso*, which raked the deck with grape. The Paraguayans were consequently driven off, losing their commander and many men – 42 bodies were found on the decks and 24 men were captured (four lieutenants, one sub-lieutenant, and 19 other ranks). The Brazilians lost just one man killed on the *Rio Grande do Sul* (her commander, First Lieutenant Antonio Joaquim) and 12 wounded on the *Barroso*. Although the attempt had failed the Brazilian navy had to maintain a higher level of security thereafter against the possibility of further such attacks.

At this time the Paraguayan garrison in Mato Grosso was reduced to a single squadron of cavalry stationed on the River Apa. The 400 cavalry (minus this squadron), 100 infantry, and four guns which had been based at Encarnación were withdrawn to reinforce the defences on the River Tebicuary.

THE BATTLE OF ACAYUAZÁ

After weeks of bombardment the defenders of Humaitá were coming to the end of their ability to withstand the Allied siege. Colonel Alèn, not wanting to advise López of the seriousness of the situation, attempted suicide with his revolver, but succeeded only in blinding himself. His second-in-command, Colonel Martínez, then took over. He devised a plan whereby on 14 July intense activity was seen on the riverbank, with canoes and boats full of men being ferried across. It looked as if Humaitá was being abandoned, but many of the men were actually wounded troops (Colonel Alèn among them), to be transported to San Fernando; the 3,000 able-bodied troops were staying behind. At the same time the fire from the Paraguayan sentries gradually slackened and then ceased, and on close inspection no movement of

troops could be seen at all. To the Allies, Humaitá seemed deserted, just as Curupaytí had been. The following day a bombardment by the Brazilian Navy and the Allied artillery commenced, lasting from sunrise to dusk, without a single musket or cannon shot being returned. Consequently on the 16th a general advance was made by the majority of the Allied army in three columns. After a while two of these were ordered to halt, and only the 6,000 troops of General Osŏrio's column continued to advance, flags flying and bands playing, towards a seemingly undefended position on the north-east side of Humaitá – where 46 concealed Paraguayan guns awaited them under the command of Colonel Pedro Hermosa. As Osŏrio approached, Martínez sent 2,000 men – two-thirds of his available troops – to defend this portion of the entrenchments.

The advancing Brazilians found a small redoubt about 200 yds (180 m) ahead of the main entrenchments, from which a few Paraguayans fired at the 1st Corps of Brazilian Provincial Cavalry (under Lieutenant-Colonel Vasco Antonio da Fontoura Chananeco) who formed the vanguard. However, these Paraguayans retreated before the redoubt was taken, and the advance of the Brazilian cavalry became a race for the entrenchments, which was brought to an abrupt halt by an abattis. This was being pulled apart to make an opening when suddenly there came a shout of '*Muerto á los cambas!*' and Hermosa's loaded cannon were run into the embrasures to fire a storm of canister and grape into the dismounted troops. Faced with such destruction, the Brazilian vanguard wavered and then retreated onto the advancing 7th Infantry Brigade under the command of Colonel Frederico Augusto de Mesquita. (This consisted of the 4th and 13th Infantry Battalions, a battalion of Engineers under the command of Lieutenant-Colonel Conrado Maria da Silva Bitencourt, and a Volunteer Artillery Brigade under the command of Colonel Emílio Luís Mallet.) Behind this was a reserve made up of the Brazilian 6th Infantry Brigade (Colonel Carlos Betbesé de Oliveira Nery), 8th Infantry Brigade (Colonel Herculano da Silva Pedra), and the 12th Infantry Brigade (Lieutenant-Colonel Wanderlei). The 4th and 13th

Battalions charged at the entrenchments in turn but were also struck down by the defenders' heavy fire as they tried to manoeuvre through the abattis. The 36th, 38th, and 39th Battalions then joined the attack, but to no avail. General Osõrio had three of his ADCs killed next to him and his horse under him, while his troops suffered losses of 279 killed, 754 wounded, and 100 taken prisoner. The Paraguayans lost just four officers and 85 men killed and ten officers and 94 men wounded.

Although General Osõrio requested additional troops from his Reserve Division to resume the attack and capture the trenches, Marshal Caxias would not permit it; it would appear that he did not want a repeat performance of Curupaytí to be blamed on him, and that he now believed his intelligence on the strength of the Paraguayan defences had been wrong. Thinly stretched as the Paraguayans were, however, it seems likely that if their whole line had been attacked by the Allies things might well have turned out differently.

To bring about a barrage on the camp of General Rivas at Andai, a Paraguayan redoubt was hastily constructed on the road between Andai and Timbó. Called the Corá redoubt, it was garrisoned with an infantry battalion, 200 dismounted cavalrymen, and two 32-pdrs. An attack on this emplacement was ordered by Rivas on 18 July, Colonel Miguel F. Martínez de Hoz being sent to take it at the head of a mixed brigade of Argentine and Brazilian infantry, made up of the Argentine *Cazadores* de la Rioja Battalion (250 men) under the command of Lieutenant-Colonel Gaspar Campos and the 3rd and 8th Brazilian Volunteers under the command of Lieutenant-Colonels A.P. de Oliveira and A.J. Bacellar respectively. This attack faltered upon reaching the Corá redoubt's abattis, and in an ambush led by Colonel Caballero and Lieutenant-Colonel José Manuel Montiel the two Argentine colonels were taken prisoner. Argentine losses were 90 killed, 87 wounded, and 35 captured, and the Brazilians lost 67 killed, 221 wounded, and two captured, the Paraguayans having suffered 120 casualties. The Paraguayan pursuit of the retreating Allies was itself brought to a halt by an assault led by General Rivas, which forced them to fall back to their redoubt.

A colour sergeant from one of the Argentine battalions, although mortally wounded, managed to save his colours by throwing them into the river, where they were picked up by the Brazilian monitor *Pará*, which was also able to pick up 12 Argentine survivors. The standard was not returned to the Argentines until a receipt had been exchanged for it. This action was to become known as the Battle of Acayuazá, with López granting a silver medal, in the style of a Maltese cross, to those who took part. In addition Bernardino Caballero was rewarded by promotion to brigadier-general and José Manuel Montiel to the rank of colonel.

On 19 July Colonel Martínez wrote to López to inform him that the vast majority of the cattle that were to have fed Humaitá's garrison had been killed during the Allied bombardment. The answer he received was that he was to hold out for another five days, and then retreat. The 21st saw the Brazilian ironclads *Cabral* and *Silvado* and the monitor *Piauhy* steam past the riverside defences to bolster the Vanguard Squadron. The Paraguayan withdrawal began three days later, using 30 river craft. The first wave, leaving on the night of the 24th, transported 1,200 men, the remainder of the army remaining in the camp during the 25th being ordered to play cheerful music in honour of the President's birthday. A salute of 21 guns was also fired off to mark this occasion. The music ceased towards midnight, and by 5:00 a.m. all of the remaining Paraguayan field guns had been spiked and all of the able-bodied defenders had crossed the river. The Allies only discovered that Humaitá was deserted ten hours later, when they quickly set about occupying it with the 5th Brazilian Cavalry Division. They found 144 iron and 37 bronze spiked field-pieces, plus eight other guns, 600 muskets, and 400 bayonets.

Meanwhile the unusually high river had flooded the route to San Fernando, which could only be reached with great difficulty by crossing Laguna Verá, a mile and a half (2.5 km) wide; the road itself was also blocked by the Allied camp of General Rivas at Andai. Among some 300 troops who were successfully ferried across the lake and reached San Fernando was the wounded Colonel Alèn, who would later be placed in irons as a traitor. However, the majority of the weaker and wounded troops, accompanied by some women and children, remained on the only large area of dry ground under the command of Colonel Martínez, awaiting their turn to be ferried across the lake. Here platforms were constructed to support the five brass 2-pdr and 4-pdr guns that they had with them, under the command of Lieutenant-Colonel Vallovera.

Argentine officers in camp, unit unknown, summer 1868. Note their long boots and mainly white shirts. (Courtesy of the Archivo General de la Nacion, Buenos Aires)

It did not take too long for this encampment to be discovered by a Brazilian scouting party sent out by General Rivas. He summoned the Paraguayans to surrender, but this was refused. Four Brazilian ironclads were then brought down to add weight to the demand to surrender, but still the Paraguayans refused. The ferryboats were then fired upon by 11 cannon and by 60 armed rowing boats patrolling the 1.5 square miles (4 square km) of the lake, so that henceforward the Paraguayans could only undertake crossings at night. When Colonel Martínez was offered surrender terms yet again he ordered some of his men to fire on the flag of truce. This provoked a two-day naval bombardment of his position that destroyed the few remaining craft that could have ferried them across the lake. Finally, on 5 August 1868, Colonel Martínez surrendered, having not eaten for four days and barely able to stand unsupported. With him were Captains Remigio Cabral and Pedro Gil, 96 other officers, and 1,228 troops, a third of whom were wounded. With the prisoners were the chaplain P. Ignacio Esmerat and Friar Abolla who had been sent by General Rivas the previous night to persuade Colonel Martínez to surrender. Eight hundred Paraguayans had died during the fighting here. The Paraguayan officers were allowed to retain their sidearms as a mark of respect, but four standards, 1,200 muskets, and all five guns were handed over. Allied losses were 156 men killed and 449 wounded. Thompson writes that 10,000 Allied shells had been fired against the retreating Paraguayans during a seven-day period. When news of the surrender reached López he declared that Martínez and his troops were traitors to their country. Some of the officers' innocent wives bore the brunt of his brutal vengeance in the place of their husbands, the wife of Colonel Martínez being among those murdered.

16 August 1868 saw the election of Domingo Faustino Sarmiento as the new President of Argentina. Replacing General Mitre in that office on 12 October, on the 14th he confirmed General Gelly y Obes as commander-in-chief of the Argentine Army of Operations in Paraguay.

FURTHER RIVER ACTIONS

The Brazilian naval captain Teodoro Fix gives the strength of the Brazilian fleet stationed in the Humaitá theatre of operations on the River Paraguay during late 1867 and early 1868 as 21 steamers with 139 guns, 348 officers, and 1,897 sailors and soldiers; nine ironclads with 47 guns, 178 officers, and 1,079 sailors and soldiers; three monitors with three guns, 24 officers, and 115 sailors and soldiers; two gunboats with six guns, 18 officers, and 77 sailors and soldiers; one transport with five officers and 28 sailors and soldiers; and five forward transports with two guns, 95 officers, and 412 sailors and soldiers, making a total of 41 ships with 197 guns, 668 officers, and 3,608 sailors and soldiers. Richard Burton gives figures for the Brazilian Navy at the same station on 26 August 1868 as:

Armed steamers
Taquary – 2 guns, 96 men.
Chuy – 2 guns, 73 men, 30 hp engine.
Tramandahy – 2 guns, 44 men.

Silvado – 8 guns (4 x 70-pdrs; not 8 guns), 130 men, 200 hp engine.

Ironclads
Brasil – 8 guns (4 x 68-pdrs, 4 x 7-inch), 145 men, 250 hp engine.
Tamandaré – 6 guns (2 x 68-pdrs, 2 x 70-pdrs), 120 men, 80 hp engine.
Barroso – 7 guns (2 x 68-pdrs, 2 x 32-pdrs, 2 x 7-inch), 149 men, 130 hp engine.
Bahia – 2 guns (2 x 7-inch [150-pdrs]), 147 men, 140 hp engine.
Herval – 2 guns (given as 4 x 7-inch), 134 men, 200 hp engine.
Lima Barros – 4 guns (4 x 8-inch [150-pdrs]), 171 men, 300 hp engine.
Colombo – 8 guns (4 x 68-pdrs, 4 x 70-pdrs), 132 men, 200 hp engine.
Mariz e Barros – 2 guns (2 x 68-pdrs), 124 men, 200 hp engine.
Cabral – 8 guns (4 x 68-pdrs, 4 x 70-pdrs), 130 men, 200 hp engine.
Belmonte – 8 guns, 129 men.
Paranáhyba – 8 guns, 141 men.
Maracaná – 8 guns, 89 men, 80 hp engine.
Mearim – 8 guns, 187 men, 100 hp engine.
Magé – 8 guns, 140 men, 120 hp engine.
Itajahy – 6 guns, 79 men, 80 hp engine.
Beberibe – 8 guns, 164 men, 130 hp engine.
Iguatemy – 5 guns, 120 men, 80 hp engine.
Araguary – 8 guns, 82 men, 100 hp engine.
Ivahy – 6 guns, 101 men, 100 hp engine.
Ipiranga – 8 guns, 79 men, 70 hp engine.

Monitors
Alagoas – 1 gun (70-pdr), 39 men.
Rio Grande – 1 gun (5.8-inch Whitworth), 60 men, 30 hp engine.
Pará – 1 gun (70-pdr), 60 men, 30 hp engine.
Piauhy – 1 gun, 60 men, 30 hp engine.
Ceará – 1 gun, 60 men.
Santa Catharina – 1 gun, 60 men.

Gunboats
Onze de Junho – 2 guns, 83 men, 40 hp engine.
Lindoya – 1 gun, 22 men.
Enrique Martins – 6 guns, 108 men, 40 hp engine.
Greenhalgh – 2 guns, 100 men, 40 hp engine.

Bomb-ketches
Pedro Affonso – 3 guns, 43 men.
Forte de Coimbra – 3 guns, 52 men.

Corvette
Bahiana – 22 guns, 166 men.

Schooner
Iguassú – 4 guns, 37 men (carried the Commodore).

Brig
Pipirí-assú – 1 gun, 33 men.

This makes a total of 39 ships, 192 guns, and 3,889 men. Note that though Burton lists the *Silvado* as a steamer, it should be an 'iron-hulled' armoured turret ship, while the transports *Apa*, *Marcilio Das*, *Izabel*, and *Princesa de Joinville* are not listed; perhaps they were further downriver during his visit. The additional data listed is from *Warship International* XIV, No.2 (1977); *A Marinha D'Outr'ora* by Visconde de Ouro Preto (1895); and *La Plata, Brazil and Paraguay during the Present War* by Commander A.J. Kennedy RN (1869).

A list of Argentine naval vessels at this same period is also of interest. Although these vessels remained outside the war zone once Corrientes was liberated, they did take part in the war as transports, etc. The list is compiled from Lilia Zenequelli's *Crónica de una Guerra la Triple Alianza* (1997):

Ironclads
25 de Mayo (ex *Primer Argentino*) – 75 men.
Gualeguay (ex *Rio Bermejo*) – 15 men.

Armed steamers
Guardia Nacional (ex HMS *Camila*) – 110 men and 25 marines.
Pavón (ex *Montevideo*) – 85 men.
Buenos Aires – 45 men.

Schooner
Argos (ex *General Alvear*) – 45 men.

Transport steamers
Iniciador – 12 men.
Espigador – 12 men.
Pampero (ex *Maurice*) – 35 men.
Esmeralda – 10 men.
Chacabuco – 72 men.

Prison ship
Vigilante – 15 men.

The *Guardia Nacional* was Admiral Muratori's flagship. Lieutenant-Colonel Beverina lists Argentine ships in 1865 as the steamers *25 de Mayo*, *Gualeguay*, *Guardia Nacional*, and *Pampero*; the schooner *Argos*; the coastguard schooner *Concordia*; the transports *Pavón*, *Buenos Aires*, *Hércules*, *Constitución*, *Salta*, and *Caaguazu*; the barge *Concepción*; the brigantine *Rio Bamba*; and the storeship *Córdoba*; while the steamers *Libertad*, *Menay*, and *General Pinto* were in dry dock for repairs. The commander of the Argentine squadron which assisted the Brazilians during 1865 was Colonel Murature.

On 16 August 1868 Vice Admiral Inhauma steamed from Humaitá with the ironclads *Brasil*, *Cabral*, *Tamandaré*, and *Colombo* with the wooden steamer *Princesa de Joinville* in tow, plus the transports *Guaicuru* and *Alice*, two lighters, and a small steamer, the *Dezeseis de Abril*. By 4:00 a.m. all but the *Colombo* (which had to return for repairs) had passed the shore batteries at Timbó. This force would later join up with the Vanguard Squadron at Tayí, and, using Villa del Pilar as its base, would co-operate with Allied land forces in future operations. The immediate effect of its arrival was the abandonment of the Paraguayan position at Timbó by Brigadier-General Caballero on 20 August (the Corá redoubt had been evacuated on the night of the 7th). 17 August saw the 2nd Cavalry Division under General Andrade Neves start to explore the northern territory above Humaitá and Villa del Pilar.

On 26 and 28 August the Naval squadron used its monitors to bombard the Paraguayan positions on the River Tebicuary, and as most of the Paraguayan artillery was being taken to its new positions at Angostura it was left to the small battery of three old 32-pdrs sited at Fortin with the 18th Infantry Battalion to return the monitors' fire. These units were under the overall command of Major Moreno, who when ordered to retire on the night of the 28th had to throw his three guns into the river before retreating. On the 29th the monitors *Pará*, *Rio Grande*, and *Piauhy* steamed past the abandoned Paraguayan positions.

THE ROAD TO ANGOSTURA

Meanwhile, on 26 August 1868, López had left San Fernando with the main part of the Paraguayan army heading for defensive lines at Angostura, which were reached in early September. The 26th also saw Marshal Caxias advance in a northerly direction from Villa del Pilar with 31,000 men, crossing the rivers Njembuca and Montuoso; General Osório commanded the Vanguard Division and General de Bittencourt the Rearguard Division. At the River Yacaré they encountered a small fort which formed the Paraguayan advance position, garrisoned by 200 cavalrymen under the command of Captain José Matias Bado. These put up a stiff resistance against the 800 cavalrymen of the Brazilian 6th Provincial Cavalry Corps under Colonel Juan Niéderauer, inflicting 80 casualties although themselves losing 76 men killed and five captured. The remainder retreated across the river to San Fernando to report the approach of the Allied force.

Marshal Caxias reached the River Tebicuary on 28 August, where, on the northern side, a redoubt with three field-pieces, under the command of Major Miguel Rojas, was found protecting the right flank of the Paraguayan defences. Flanking this were trenches defended by 400 troops under Captain Bado. These positions were attacked by the 2nd Cavalry Division forming the vanguard of the Allied Army. Made up of the 3rd and 8th Cavalry Brigades, the 5th and 6th Infantry Brigades, a battery of four guns, and a company of sappers, this division captured the Paraguayan positions with a loss of 22 men killed, 162 wounded, and three missing. The Paraguayan defenders lost 117 killed and 93 captured, including Major Rojas and Captain Bado.

A general assault on the positions at San Fernando was made on 1 September, the Allied attack being supported by an artillery and naval bombardment. The camp was taken with little resistance, as it had been evacuated during the previous night. It was at San Fernando that many executed bodies from a plot to overthrow López were found. Whether the plot was as widespread as appeared from the number of people questioned and tortured, or whether it was just used by the investigating judges as a good excuse to settle old scores, lies outside the remit of this book.

The Paraguayans had by now retreated to the small port of Angostura and the town of Villeta, and a new defensive line was established along the stream of Pikysyry. This was 10,000 yds (9.1 km) long, with 142 gun-platforms besides those at Angostura. At the mouth of the Pikysyry two dykes were built, so that the river

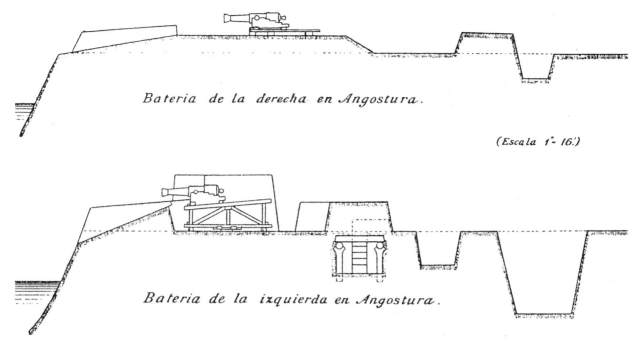

Cross-section of the two Paraguayan artillery emplacements at Angostura, by George Thompson. The top section depicts the 'right battery', the bottom the 'left battery'. Note the ammunition store and its entrance in the latter.

became 5 ft (1.5 m) deep in front of the defences. This line was further protected from attack by the swamps which surrounded it. Field-pieces brought down to Angostura from Asunción by steamer included the 150-pdr 'Criollo', and left the capital without any cannon at all. López established his headquarters first at the town of Villeta and then at Cumbarity, on a high ridge called Lomas Valentinas (Lomas de Itaibaté to the Allies) about four miles (6.5 km) from the River Paraguay. The town of Villeta was just 35 miles (56 km) south of Asunción and 125 miles (200 km) north of Humaitá. Protecting these camps were the fortified emplacements of Angostura, with similar characteristics to Humaitá, being on a narrow bend in the River Paraguay. Two batteries were placed on the riverbank 700 yds (640 m) apart, to protect the small port. The northern or right battery was armed with seven guns, the southern battery with eight guns including the 'Criollo'.

The illustration of both batteries at Angostura by Lieutenant-Colonel George Thompson, reproduced above, is helpful here. So too is his description: 'Two methods of mounting our 8 inch guns. The first figure is the old mounting, by which the garrison are necessarily exposed, when no embrasures are used. The defect becomes worse from the pivot being at the end instead of in the centre of the slide, as our guns had to be so mounted that they might fire in any direction, either to the front or to the rear. In the trench shown at the right battery, the few infantry of the garrison were to stand to defend it against a land attack, and the guns were to fire grape and cannister over their heads, which were protected by the parapet. The mode of mounting the guns in the left battery almost completely protected the garrison [crew] which worked the guns, while they were also much more easily traversed, being mounted on rollers. By the inclination given to the slide, the gun was run out with greater

facility, besides the advantage of not straining the breechings. The mound of earth over the powder-magazine served also as a parapet against the land side, and the garrison of each gun was thus protected on every side. In case of an attack by land, the guns would fire over the powder-magazines, the doors of which were on the opposite side to the guns, and the battery was itself protected by a deep ditch, enfiladed by a 32 pounder, placed at the re-entering angle. This 32 pounder, and also the left gun in the battery, were protected by epaulments from the fire of the fleet, as it was of the utmost importance that these two guns should not be dismounted in action. Every gun in the battery had a small deep embrasure to enable it to fire down on to the ironclads just below it, should they seek for protection by passing under the high bank of the river. Between the magazine and the ditch there was a smaller ditch, in which were kept spare carriages, tackle, etc.'

To the east of these positions was the ridge of hills known as the Lomas Valentinas. In front of Angostura and the Lomas Valentinas was the River Canabé, which created the extensive swamps. Through the eastern section ran the railway linking Asunción with Cerro León and Villa Rica. On the northern side was a series of small rivers and large swamps that also contributed to the area's defence. On the west flank was the River Paraguay, which at this point was 600 yds (550 m) wide.

López had 12,000 troops concentrated here. Angostura was under the command of Lieutenant-Colonel Thompson. On the right flank of the Pikysyry was Colonel Hermosa, on the left flank Colonel Valóis Rivarola, and at the centre Colonel Luis González. A reserve division of 3,000 men with 12 field-pieces was under the command of General Bernardino Caballero. Just over 100 guns were available to the Paraguayans. At Angostura were twelve 8-inch guns, one 150-pdr, two smoothbore 32-pdrs, and the Whitworth 32-pdr that had been captured at the Second Battle of Tuyuti. Thompson managed to get seven high traversing carriages made for these batteries, six of them for use by the 8-inch guns and the last by the 150-pdr. These raised the guns above the men's heads, and a high parapet was made so that, except for the man serving the vent, the crews of the guns were under cover. As large quantities of ammunition had been lost during the retreat from Tebicuary, the guns were supplied with less than 100 rounds each, with many having only 20 to 30. The infantry were similarly supplied with only 60 to 100 rounds instead of the 240 that they should have had. These were carried in two hide bags slung around the neck.

On 2 September the ironclads *Lima Barros*, *Silvado*, *Herval*, and *Mariz e Barros* went to reconnoitre these new Paraguayan positions to find out if the terrain and shallow water were likely to present any special problems. By this time all of the ships in the squadron required constant work to keep them serviceable, especially the hastily-built monitors; adequate repair facilities were needed badly.

7 September saw the *Silvado* (Commander José da Costa Azevedo) hit at the waterline by a 150 lb shell while reconnoitring the batteries at Angostura, causing considerable damage. As she was in a part of the river that was only about 80 yds (73 m) wide, her captain had decided to force his way past the position, the ship being within range of the two batteries for 45 minutes. She steamed on as far as Villeta, where three Paraguayan steamers were sighted, which managed to escape. The *Silvado* then started on her return journey past Angostura and rejoined the Brazilian squadron. From then on the Brazilian navy maintained an almost daily bombardment of the batteries at Angostura, mostly at long range.

López sent Colonel José Manuel Montiel and Lieutenant-Colonel Julián Roa with a company from the Rifles Battalion and 200 men of the 'Acaverá' Cavalry Regiment to ambush General Andrade Neves' vanguard, composed of the 2nd Infantry Division under the command of Colonel Herculano da Silva Pedra. The Brazilian column was surprised at the River Surubiy on 23 September, the 5th Infantry Battalion becoming disorganised and fleeing the field. However, two squadrons of the Brazilian 6th Cavalry Regiment under Major Isidoro Fernandes managed to charge the Paraguayan troops, forcing them to retreat and capturing a flag. The Brazilian vanguard suffered 12 officers and 78 men killed, 26 officers and 178 men wounded, and 11 men taken captive, as well as the loss of a standard (doubtless the 5th Battalion's). Paraguayan losses totalled 139 men, the greater part of them wounded. Following this skirmish the Brazilian 5th Infantry Battalion was disbanded, its officers and men being distributed to other battalions while its commanding officer, Major Joaquim José de Magalhães, was court-martialled. The 24th saw advance Allied cavalry units reach the new Paraguayan line along the Pikysyry.

Just before daybreak on 1 October the batteries of Angostura were passed by four Brazilian ironclads, the *Tamandaré*, *Bahia*, *Barroso*, and *Silvado*. Various ships slipped past the Paraguayan positions in this way over the next few weeks, using night as cover and assisted by the thickly wooded riverbank, which cast a shadow over half of the river. The warships, with all their lights

extinguished, would drift downstream with the current, only bringing their engines up to full speed when they were detected by the shore batteries.

THE BATTLE OF YTORORÓ

Marshal Caxias, seeing that the Paraguayans' southern defensive line could become yet another serious drain on time and manpower, decided to outflank López and attack from the rear. This project began with the sending of 1,122 men under the command of Lieutenant-Colonel Antonio Tiburcio to construct a road on the left flank, running northward towards Santa Helena through the Chaco side of the River Paraguay. From here the Paraguay could be crossed near the town of Villeta. This force was composed of six officers and 135 men of the Engineers, two officers of the *Corpos Especiais* or Special Corps (civil engineering specialists), the 4th Infantry Battalion (30 officers and 406 men), the 16th Infantry Battalion (36 officers and 397 men), a unit of 80 cavalry, and 30 artillerymen. These were landed on 11 October 1868. The road was constructed almost entirely of palm tree trunks laid transversely, side by side, on the ground, which was muddy and liable to become flooded whenever the level of the river rose. A number of bridges also had to be built over streams. To assist and speed the construction of the road, an additional 2,925 infantry, 327 pontoniers, 198 artillerymen, and 94 cavalry from General Argollo's Brazilian 2nd Corps were transported down from Humaitá and landed on the Chaco side of the river. Lieutenant-Colonel Rufino Galvão of the Engineers was given the task of overseeing construction of the road, reporting each day's progress to General Argollo. The completed road was 11,722 yds (10.7 km) long. On 27 November Marshal Caxias moved his headquarters to the Chaco side of the Paraguay.

López heard of this Allied plan during October, and despatched some small units to mount guerrilla attacks against the construction teams and engineers. However, these did not delay the progress of the road very much, and López was astonished when he was informed in early December that it had been completed as far as Santa Helena, and that 19,000 Allied troops would soon be concentrated there, ready to cross. Although San António, a small river port four miles (6.5 km) north of Villeta, was to be the landing site of the Brazilian troops, López thought that the town-cum-port of Villeta would be the Allies' first choice. This was therefore garrisoned with a small body of troops, which on 3 December was bombarded by the monitors *Pará* and *Alagoas*. The only Allied troops not with Marshal Caxias by this time were General Gelly y Obes with 4,354 Argentines, General Enrique de Castro with 800 Uruguayans, and Colonel Antonio da Silva Paranhos with his 6th Infantry Brigade, a regiment of artillery, and a company of pontoniers, making a total of 2,846 Brazilians. This force was to defend or attack the southern flank along the River Pikysyry. The cavalry units of Generals Andrade Neves and João Manuel Mena Barreto were left at Palmas.

On 26 November the *Brasil* steamed past Angostura but was hit by 31 balls, five of them 150-pdrs, wounding her commander and killing three officers, the pilot, and several crewmen. The 29th November saw the ironclads *Bahia* and *Tamandaré*, and the monitors *Alagoas* and *Rio Grande* steam up to Asunción and, at

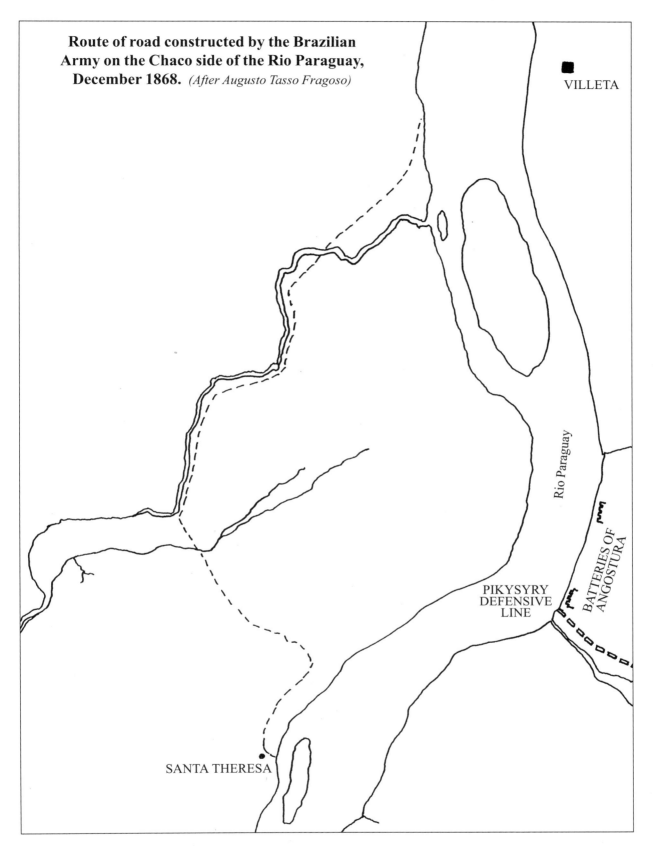

Route of road constructed by the Brazilian Army on the Chaco side of the Rio Paraguay, December 1868. *(After Augusto Tasso Fragoso)*

VILLETA

Rio Paraguay

PIKYSYRY DEFENSIVE LINE

BATTERIES OF ANGOSTURA

SANTA THERESA

11:00 a.m., begin a three-hour bombardment of the capital.

The Allied crossing of the River Paraguay started at 7:00 a.m. on 5 December 1868 aboard the Brazilian ironclads *Bahia* (capable of carrying 800 men), *Silvado* (1,000 men), *Lima Barros* (1,500 men), *Cabral* (1,000 men), *Brasil* (1,000 men), *Tamandaré* (600 men), and *Barroso* (800 men). By the end of the day 16,999

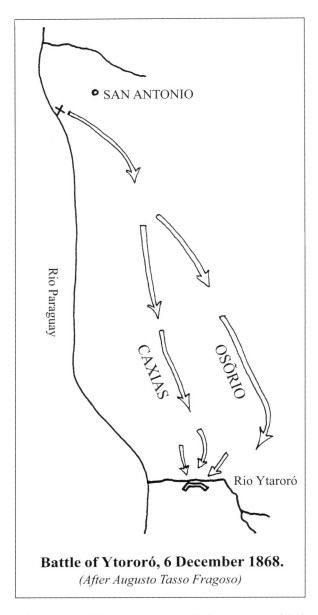

Battle of Ytororó, 6 December 1868.
(After Augusto Tasso Fragoso)

had a terrible disaster, we owe it to M. Caminos.' Sir Richard Burton's comment was that Luis Caminos was the 'Grouchy of the Paraguayan Waterloo'. Juan E. O'Leary states that 'Colonel Caminos left the capital on the 23rd by train, but by the 26th with news of the defeat at Lomas Valentinas he decided that his column would be of greater assistance to López at Cerro León'.

After landing on 5 December the Brazilian vanguard was sent along the road towards Villeta, but during the march from San António the River Ytororó had to be crossed. This was a deep and narrow river, the only bridge spanning it being made of wood and less than 10 ft (3 m) wide. It was lightly defended, but enough to force the Allies to halt their march until the following day. During the night López quickly sent reinforcements from his reserve force under the command of General Caballero, comprising 5,000 men (14 infantry battalions and four cavalry regiments) and 12 guns under the command of Major Moreno.[17] These were divided into five brigades. The 1st and 3rd Brigades were stationed on the right flank with five field-pieces placed in the centre; the 2nd and 4th Brigades were placed on the left flank with four field-pieces in their centre; and three more field-pieces were placed in the centre of the line. The 5th Brigade, consisting of the four cavalry regiments, formed the reserve. On the 6th the Allies mounted a general attack, Marshal Caxias advancing against the bridge across the Ytororó with the troops of General Argollo's 1st Corps, while General Osório made a wide flanking movement with the bulk of the cavalry but became lost and took no part in the battle. The only cavalry therefore available to Caxias were two squadrons – one from the 7th Cavalry Regiment, the other from the 20th Provincial Corps – under the command of Colonel Niéderauer. These charged and captured a battery of four Paraguayan field-pieces, but this was quickly recaptured by Lieutenant-Colonel Serrano, and the guns, having not been spiked by the retreating Brazilians, were soon back in action.

Colonel Fernando Machado's infantry brigade tried twice to capture the bridge but was repulsed by its Paraguayan defenders, and the bridge changed hands four times amidst repeated charges and counter-charges and bitter hand-to-hand fighting. It was finally captured, intact, by Brazilian volunteer battalions from the brigades of Generals Salustiano dos Reis and Hilario Maximiano Antunes de Gurjão, led personally by Marshal Caxias, who called out 'Follow me, those of you who are Brazilians!' Withstanding the withering Paraguayan fire, they charged home and captured the bridge and its defending entrenchments, while repulsing a Paraguayan cavalry charge. The Paraguayans then quit the field in disorder, leaving behind six guns and one standard. They had lost 330 men killed including 13 officers, and 1,116 wounded including 29 officers. Of the 300 men with which the 23rd Battalion, under Captain José Romero, had started the day only nine remained unwounded by nightfall. López promoted Valois Rivarola and Germán Serrano to the rank of full colonel for their bravery during this battle, Rivarola having acted as second-in-command to General Caballero.

The Brazilians lost 285 men and 45 officers killed and 1,474 men and 103 officers wounded, many of their casualties resulting from Paraguayan artillery fire against their dense attacking columns. Included among the

infantrymen, 926 cavalrymen and their mounts, and 742 artillerymen and pontoniers with equipment, had been ferried to the Paraguayan side of the river at San António. Why was this landing site left undefended? It appears that a flying column of 2,000 men with 18 light artillery pieces based in Asunción as its garrison, under the command of the Minister of War and Navy, Colonel Luis Caminos, had orders to attack any Allied troops that might land from the Chaco side of the Paraguay, López hoping to lure the Allies into landing troops that could be destroyed in their landing area and along the road by ambushes mounted from the surrounding bush by Caminos. This was not to be. Because of delays, Caminos was unable to field his column against the invaders until it was too late. By the time he was ready to move the only viable option open to him was to save his troops by retreating to Cerro León, ready to fight another day. What the outcome would have been if López's orders had been carried out promptly is open to conjecture, although Elisa Lynch commented to the French Consul after the flight from Lomas Valentinas on 27 December that 'We have wounded were General Argollo, hit in the neck and thigh, and General Gurjão, while Colonel Machado had been killed at the head of his troops.

THE BATTLE OF AVAY

Further advance from the Ytororó was stalled by heavy rain over the next few days, although this actually benefited the Allies, as it gave time for the cavalry units under Generals João Manuel Mena Barreto (900 men) and José Joaquim de Andrade Neves (2,500 men) to be transferred from Palmas through the Chaco and across the River Paraguay so that they were available to Marshal Caxias when he ordered another general assault on 11 December. By then Caxias had amassed 13,939 infantry, 4,100 cavalry, 428 artillery with 26 guns, and 496 engineers and pontoniers. The 3rd Corps (General Osõrio) was to be the vanguard, the 2nd Corps (General José Luís Mena Barreto) was to form the centre, and the 1st Corps (General Jacinto Machado Bittencourt), with the 600 men of the 1st Cavalry Division (General João Manuel Mena Barreto), was to act as rearguard.[18] Ahead of the 3rd Corps was the 5th Cavalry Division under the command of Colonel José António Corrêa da Câmara (1,000 men) and the 2nd and 3rd Cavalry Divisions under the overall command of General Andrade Neves (2,500 men), which were to attack when appropriate and try to get behind the Paraguayan defences.

The day was extremely hot and many of the Brazilian troops broke off branches from trees and bushes and tied these to their backs to give themselves some shade from the blistering heat of the sun. From a distance they gave the impression of a small forest on the move. The advance stopped at a point where the road ran alongside and then crossed a stream called the Avay, where the remnants of General Caballero's division were entrenched. With reinforcements of two infantry battalions and artillery this force had been brought up to a strength of nearly 5,000 men and 18 guns. Of the artillery, ten guns had been placed on a small elevated ridge in the centre of the line, and four pieces on each flank. The Brazilian 3rd Corps assailed the Paraguayan positions with its 3rd and 7th Infantry Brigades, but was repulsed. A second assault followed using the 2nd and 3rd Corps. Soon afterwards the cavalry divisions of Andrade Neves were despatched to hit the Paraguayan left flank, and the 1st Cavalry Division of João Manuel Mena Barreto was eventually directed to advance on the right flank, in an attempt to encircle the defenders.

The battle had begun at noon and lasted for five hours during a heavy rainstorm. Paraguayan counter-attacks by Colonel Serrano and General Caballero, although costly to the Brazilians, gradually eroded the manpower available to Caballero, forcing his troops to retire to a second ridge. The Brazilian 3rd Corps suffered high casualties too as it pressed home its attack. The initial advance of its 3rd Infantry Brigade in two columns, with the 3rd and 14th Battalions in one and the 9th and 15th Battalions in the other, were rescued from almost certain annihilation by a series of spirited cavalry charges under the command of Colonel Câmara, whose 5th Cavalry Division had been directed to act as the rearguard for this advance on the left flank. Most of the mounted Paraguayan cavalry were sent to counter-attack the 5th Cavalry, which allowed the full deployment of the 2nd and 3rd Cavalry Divisions on this flank to proceed. General Osõrio was wounded in the jaw during an assault by his corps, but he refused to leave the battlefield and was transported by cart among his troops so that they could still see he was alive and in command, though General José Auto Guimarães had to replace him towards the end of the battle.

Despite the wounding of General Osõrio the 1st Corps was brought up ready to go into action if and when required, and some of its units saw action on the right flank. But it was the flanking attacks by the 1st, 2nd, and 3rd Cavalry Divisions that really sealed the fate of so many Paraguayans, for when these units arrived on the battlefield and charged into the Paraguayan rear escape became next to impossible. With the total defeat of General Caballero's force Marshal Caxias reached the town of Villeta, capturing 12 field-pieces, 11 standards,

The battle of Avay (Avaí) on 11 December 1868, a massive painting by Pedro Américo (1843–1905) measuring 5 x 10 metres. (Courtesy of the Museu Nacional de Belas Artes, Rio de Janeiro)

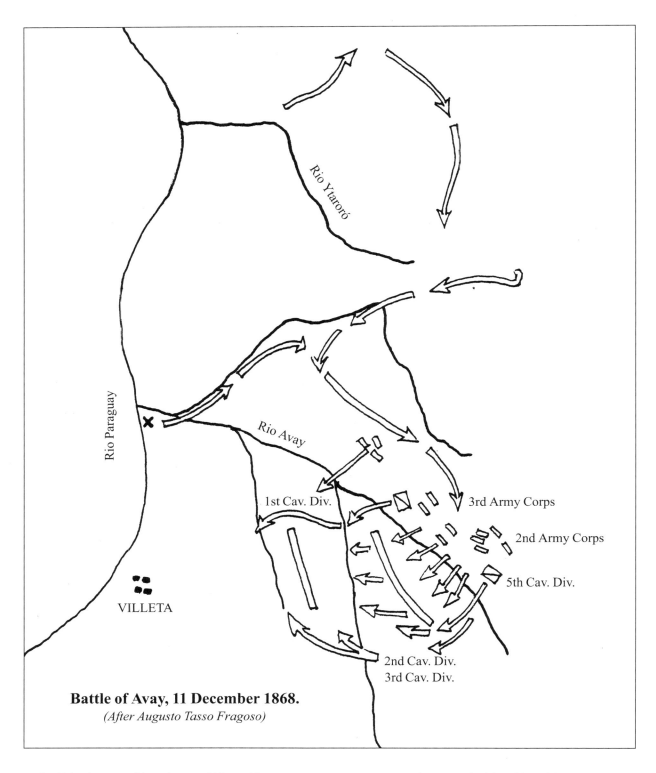

Rio Ytororó

Rio Paraguay

Rio Avay

✕

1st Cav. Div.

3rd Army Corps

2nd Army Corps

5th Cav. Div.

2nd Cav. Div.
3rd Cav. Div.

VILLETA

Battle of Avay, 11 December 1868.
(After Augusto Tasso Fragoso)

and 1,400 prisoners, although some 200 would manage to make their escape during the next few days. Three thousand Paraguayans had been killed and 600 wounded, the latter becoming prisoners; among these were Colonels González and Serrano. The Brazilians had 297 men killed including 31 officers, 1,366 wounded including 134 officers, and 60 missing. Colonel Niéderauer, commander of the 2nd Cavalry Division, had to have a leg amputated. This is considered to be the bloodiest battle fought in South America, in which no quarter was given or asked by either side. Less than 50 Paraguayans managed to escape from the battlefield. Among these were General Caballero and Colonel Valois Rivarola, who had been shot through the throat. As a result of the heavy casualties suffered at Ytororó and Avay, Marshal Caxias was forced to disband six volunteer infantry battalions on 12 December (the 26th, 28th, 42nd, 44th, 48th, and 55th), their men being incorporated into other units to maintain them at a reasonable strength. Again, heavy rain put any further advance out of the question until the 20th.

The Paraguayan survivors of the Battle of Avay headed towards the heights of Lomas Valentinas, where the defences had been completed. By 12 December 3,000 Paraguayan troops had been assembled there, with 2,000 men stationed along the defences of the Pikysyry and 700 men in the batteries of Angostura. López now began to send small columns of troops into forward positions to guard against surprise attacks on his headquarters.

On 17 December a brisk action was fought between the Brazilian 3rd Cavalry Division (composed of the 13th, 14th, 17th, and 18th National Guard cavalry) under the command of Colonel Vasco Alves, which was making a reconnaissance of the positions at Angostura, and a Paraguayan force under the command of Zanja Blanca, consisting of the 20th and 45th Cavalry Regiments. The Paraguayan cavalry were surprised and overwhelmed, suffering 140 killed and 54 taken prisoner while the Brazilians lost just seven men killed and four wounded, including an officer. The following day López ordered the evacuation of Asunción to the provisional capital based at the village of Piribebuy, giving Vice-President Sánchez the authority to take charge of this transfer of power and people.

THE BATTLE OF LOMAS VALENTINAS

The Allied plan to attack the heights of Lomas Valentinas anticipated a simultaneous attack on the front and rear positions, but to accomplish this manoeuvre the defensive lines along the Pikysyry had first to be captured. Frontal assaults on these defences by the troops of General Gelly y Obes during the early days of December had shown the difficulties entailed in such tactics, and they were quickly revised. This objective was achieved instead by sending a column under General João Manuel Mena Barreto on a flanking movement that

would attack the Paraguayan lines from the rear. This force was composed of 700 men from the 1st Cavalry Division; two brigades of infantry (the 7th and 11th) with 1,000 men in each, commanded by Colonels Frederico Augusto de Mesquita and Manuel de Oliveira Bueno respectively; and a battery of light artillery. The troops under the command of General Gelly y Obes were to make a simultaneous feint attack on the Paraguayan front, a grand total of 8,000 troops being involved in the operation. Mounted on 21 December, the attack was a complete surprise to the Paraguayans, whose artillery was facing the wrong way. The defenders lost 600 men killed and 200 men plus 34 guns captured, although 500 men managed to escape to Angostura and some 200 others found their way to Lomas Valentinas.

While this attack was going on, General Andrade Neves' 2nd and 3rd Cavalry Divisions were sent out to reconnoitre the area towards Potreiro Marmoré and guard against any flanking movement that might be attempted from this direction while the defences along the Pikysyry were assailed. At 3:00 in the morning they surprised and defeated a Paraguayan force that had encamped for the night, capturing four men and killing two, one being their commanding officer, Lieutenant-Colonel Julián Roa. Later in the morning General Andrade Neves was ordered to take the 2nd Cavalry Division and 9th Cavalry Brigade and regroup with General Bittencourt at Loma Cumbarity, leaving Colonel Vasco Alves Pereira with 700 men of the 5th and 7th Cavalry Brigades at Potreiro Marmoré to block the escape route to Cerro León.

Marshal Caxias, with 14,690 infantry, 4,011 cavalry, 408 artillery, and 306 pontoniers, left the town of Villeta at 2:00 a.m. on the 21st, his troops leaving their packs behind but donning their best uniforms, with their rifles freshly cleaned, for the seven-mile (11 km) march to the Lomas Valentinas range. It took this main Allied force until noon to concentrate ready to storm the

A contemporary illustration by A. Methfessel of the battle of Lomas Valentinas, 27 December 1868, showing the Argentine 'Legion Militar' capturing the Paraguayan positions.

95

Another painting of the battle of Lomas Valentinas, this time by Diógenes Hequet, shows Argentine troops advancing past the first line of entrenchments. (Courtesy of the Museo Histórico Nacional, Montevideo)

defences. The Brazilian artillery, with 26 pieces, had managed to reach its destination in time to begin a bombardment of the Paraguayan positions at 9:00 a.m., no doubt accompanied by cavalry and some infantry. A description of the Paraguayan defences is provided by George Thompson, who states that López 'had a ditch dug, two foot wide by two feet deep, and the earth thrown to the front, so that by sitting down on the inner edge of the ditch, the men would be somewhat protected from rifle bullets. This trench was garrisoned with all his troops, his escort, which was now well mounted, being kept in reserve, and guns placed all round it. With the view of keeping it out of rifle-range of his house [headquarters], the trench was made of an immense radius, so that it was thinly defended on the front. There was not time to dig this ditch all round, and the rear, towards Cerro León was completely open, and had no men to defend it.'[19] It would appear that a second line of entrenchments was also hastily dug, as Brazilian narratives of the battle record two defensive lines. In the morning López was reinforced by the 51st Infantry Battalion commanded by Lieutenant-Colonel Faustino Benegas, made up of about 500 men from Trinidad aged between 14 and 18 who had been enlisted the year before.

At 3:00 p.m. two columns of infantry commenced the assault. The first, commanded by General José Luís Mena Barreto with 6,000 men of the 3rd Infantry Division, marched against the western defences of Itá Ybaté, while the second, commanded by General Jacinto Machado de Bittencourt with 6,786 infantrymen of the 1st and 2nd Infantry Divisions and 1,800 cavalry from General Andrade Neves' contingent, including the General himself, attacked the northern defences of Loma

Acosta, including the hill of Cumbarity. As the Brazilian infantry advanced up the slope the Paraguayan defenders held their fire until it was most effective, the attackers encountering a line of abattis which added to their difficulties.

The extreme northerly entrenchment of Cumbarity was finally captured at sundown. The Brazilians sent in the 1st Infantry Division, with the 1st Infantry Brigade as its vanguard followed by the 12th and 16th Infantry Battalions in two columns of attack and the 4th Infantry Battalion hindmost. These were followed by the 9th and 13th Infantry Brigades advancing in battalion columns.[20] After bitter fighting, severe losses forced the Paraguayan commander of these defences, Major Ignacio Genes – who was himself wounded – to order a withdrawal. During the fighting the Rifles Battalion, commanded by Major Vincente Giménez, and a squadron of dismounted cavalry had been sent to reinforce Genes. When Major Giménez was killed, General Caballero was despatched to take command of the defences, but even he could not hold onto them.

With the capture of the defences at Cumbarity the Brazilians immediately set about pulling them apart, an Engineer section of 25 men and two officers commanded by First-Lieutenant Emilio Garcia Trois having been specially attached to the 1st Infantry Division for this purpose. (In addition they had helped to open up gaps in the line of abattis before the trenches.) A company of Pontoniers under Captain Martins was also sent to assist the engineers. Fourteen cannon were captured here, including the 32-pdr Whitworth that had been taken during the Second Battle of Tuyuti.

Now it was the turn of the 2nd Infantry Division to

advance and capture the remaining part of the hill. General Andrade Neves was mortally wounded during this assault, attacking with the 2nd Infantry Division and advancing on foot with his dismounted 3rd and 8th Cavalry Brigades beyond the captured trenches. He would die of fever in the Allied hospital in Asunción on 6 January 1869. The Paraguayan 40th Infantry Battalion, the Rifles Battalion, the 'Acaverá', 'Acaraiá', and 'Acomoroti' Regiments (the last newly formed during the war), and the Presidential Escort Regiment were all nearly annihilated during this bitter struggle, the Escort in the defence of López's headquarters and its counter-attack under the command of Colonel Felipe Toledo. Some of the Paraguayan artillery pieces sited along the entrenchments were placed on mounds of earth after being dismounted from their carriages by Allied artillery fire, so that they could continue to fire at the attacking infantry. Total Brazilian casualties in this assault were listed as 157 killed including eight officers, 1,084 wounded including 76 officers, and 70 missing. The 16th Infantry Battalion lost 22 officers killed and wounded out of 28, and 209 men killed and wounded from a total of 358 other ranks.

The assault by General José Luís Mena Barreto on the defences of Itá Ybaté was not so successful, despite being carried out with energy and impetuosity. This division lost 220 killed including 13 officers, 1,344 wounded including 98 officers, and 282 men missing including five officers.

Marshal Caxias positioned the 5th Cavalry Division of Colonel Câmara as his rearguard near Villeta, but decided that the 10th Cavalry Brigade would be sent towards Angostura to stop any attempts to send out counter-attacks against either his main army or General Mena Barreto's column. Total Brazilian losses in the day's fighting were 377 killed, 2,428 wounded, and 352 missing, not including any casualties suffered by Mena Barreto's column or the troops of General Gelly y Obes, which I have been unable to ascertain. Nor are Paraguayan losses known. The number of defenders is variously given as 6–8,000 men, and I would go along with General Juan C. Centurión (a colonel at the time) who states that 6–7,000 troops of various ages and fighting conditions were stationed along the ridge of Lomas Valentinas.

On 22 December 1868 Marshal Caxias ordered the Argentine and Uruguayan troops, with the Brazilian artillery and infantry brigade of Colonel Silva Paranhos based at Las Palmas and along the Pikysyry, to advance towards the heights of Lomas Auxilio. This corps, which also included twenty 32-pdr Whitworth field-pieces under the command of Colonel Emílio Luís Mallet, which would be very useful for the final assault, reached the Brazilian lines the next day. Three thousand Brazilians were left to contain Angostura. The same day, López was reinforced by an infantry battalion of about 500 men from Cerro León, and on the 25th by another infantry battalion and a cavalry regiment from Caá Pucú and an infantry unit from Ypoá, a grand total of 1,600 men. These reinforcements were divided into four battalions, one of which, under the command Lieutenant-Colonel Julián Godoy, was renumbered the 40th. Many of its soldiers were aged between just 12 and 14 years.[21]

By the 23rd the full cost of the fighting to the manpower of the Brazilian Army had become apparent, and Marshal Caxias ordered many Volunteer Battalions to be dissolved and their men and officers distributed to other battalions. The units disbanded were the 24th, 25th, 29th, 32nd, 33rd, 34th, 36th, 38th, 39th, 41st, 47th, and 49th Battalions. The remaining infantry battalions were reorganised into seven brigades formed into two divisions.

A contemporary illustration by A. Methfessel showing Paraguayan prisoners taken at the Battle of Lomas Valentinas.

Photograph of Argentine Engineer officers taken between 1865–70, showing levita *(frock coats) and loose tunics being worn. Note also the number of buttons on cuff seams and the rank lace on the cuffs. The* levita *could be either single-breasted or double-breasted: the officer with crossed arms in the front row is wearing a double-breasted one; it would also appear that he is wearing shoulder bars rather than cuff rank insignia.* (Courtesy of the Archivo General de la Nacion, Buenos Aires)

On the morning of the 24th Marshal Caxias sent a message to López demanding that he surrender to avoid further unnecessary bloodshed. This was refused. Consequently two hours after sunrise on the 25th an Allied bombardment of the Paraguayan defences by 46 field-pieces commenced, each gun firing 50 shells into the entrenchments at Itá Ybaté. This bombardment lasted for three hours. With only six cannon left that had not been dismounted, the defenders still managed to stop a number of assaults by General Bittencourt's infantry, while a body of 230 Paraguayan cavalry was formed and made a sudden sally against the Brazilian 14th National Guard Cavalry of Colonel Vasco Alves' division stationed at Potreiro Marmoré. At this the three remaining National Guard cavalry regiments (the 13th, 17th, and 18th) counter-attacked, killing 150 men and capturing 30, only 50 Paraguayans managing to return. None of the Paraguayan positions were captured during the day.

The 26th saw another bombardment and a few Brazilian assaults on the defences, which were turned back. The following day Marshal Caxias decided to use General Gelly y Obes' infantry to assault the Paraguayan lines. These comprised 4,826 Argentines and 600 Uruguayans, who had seen little action during December and were keen to be utilised in the coming battle. The artillery units from both Argentina (one battery of 384 men) and Uruguay (one battery of 200 men) were also brought into action. The Paraguayan defenders had meanwhile been reduced to just 2,500 men plus the reinforcements that had arrived between the 23rd and 25th, while the forces available to their attackers stood at 15,752 Brazilians, 5,210 Argentines, 800 Uruguayans,

and 46 field-pieces, plus 202 Brazilian and 375 Argentine engineers and pontoniers.

Marshal Caxias ordered the 2,413 cavalrymen of Colonels Vasco Alves Pereira and Caetano Goncalves to the extreme left flank. Also on the left, but not so distant, were the 700 cavalrymen of General João Manuel Mena Barreto. The 2,400 Argentine troops of the 1st Argentine Corps, under General Rivas, were to attack the left flank, along with 4,739 Brazilian infantry under the command of General Bittencourt. The 600 Uruguayans under General Enrique de Castro, 1,105 Brazilians under General Silva Paranhos, and the 2,426 men of the 2nd Argentine Corps under Colonel Pedro José Aguero were to assault the left and centre positions. The 5,252 Brazilian infantry of General José Luís Mena Barreto were to attack the centre and right positions and any movement of Paraguayan reinforcements from the right flank.

The entrenchments, with the usual line of abattis, were taken by the 1st Argentine Corps in their first assault, and 14 guns were captured, most of them damaged. The Argentine 4th Infantry Battalion and the 1st Corrientes Infantry Battalion was first over the defences, and charged towards López's headquarters, which General Caballero defended to cover the President's retreat. Following this success a general assault was ordered which also attained its objectives, the Argentine Córdoba and Santa Fe battalions capturing their sections of entrenchments, while the Argentine reserve battalions of the 1st Division Buenos Aires and the Rosario Regiment kept up the momentum by capturing the second line of defences. The Uruguayan troops under the command of Lieutenant-Colonel Vázquez also managed to unite with the attacking Argentines.

It was during this stage of the fighting that López, with Elisa Lynch and 60 men of the 'Acaverá' cavalry regiment[22] acting as his escort, managed to make their escape. Generals Resquín and Caballero and a few dozen cavalrymen also got away. How López managed to slip through the Allied lines beggars belief. The Brazilian 54th Volunteer Infantry Battalion was sent to catch his party but somehow missed them: cavalry units could not be sent because they had already been despatched to attack other groups of retreating Paraguayans.

Paraguayan losses were 1,500 killed and 1,500 captured, many of them wounded. Argentine losses were reported to be 64 men killed including six officers and 283 wounded including 28 officers. Reported Brazilian losses were five killed including one officer and 33 wounded including four officers. The total losses inflicted on the 54th Volunteer Battalion during the battles of the 21st and 27th were 17 officers killed and wounded out of a total of 21 and 470 men killed and wounded from a total of 560.[23] Uruguayan losses are reported to have been 80 killed and wounded.

The failure to capture López meant that the war would continue, a situation that Marshal Caxias had hoped to end with this battle. He had been told that he must make progress towards ending the conflict by early January 1869, as the Brazilian chambers were meeting on 8 January to vote on future policy, and if he could not gain an effective victory before then a conditional peace would be arranged. Another political factor which doubtless weighed on the Marshal's mind was that the

Government of President Sarmiento in Buenos Aires had voted in early December to recall all of the Argentine National Guard units to Buenos Aires.

Two days after the fall of Lomas Valentinas the commanders of Angostura, Lieutenant-Colonels George Thompson and Lucas Carrillo, were requested to surrender the garrison. In Thompson's memoirs he writes: 'The garrison of the two batteries consisted of 3 jefes [field officers], 50 officers and 684 men, of whom 320 were artillerymen; and we had just ninety rounds of ammunition per gun. After the Pikysyry trenches were taken, on the 21st, we had an additional 3 jefes, 61 officers, and 685 soldiers, most of them having lost their arms [weapons], and the greater part being small boys. Besides these, we received 13 officers and 408 men, all badly wounded, whom we had to accommodate in the soldiers' quarters, and about 500 women'. Nevertheless, he would only surrender if the Allied victory at the heights was confirmed by five officers from his staff who were permitted to visit the battlefield. On receiving their report attesting to the Paraguayan defeat Colonel Thompson agreed to capitulate, full military honours being allowed to the garrison while the officers were placed on parole. When it surrendered at 11:00 a.m. on 30 December the garrison numbered 1,907 men, of whom 800 were wounded.

THE CONDE D'EU TAKES COMMAND

Following the capture of Angostura the Brazilian navy was able to steam up to Asunción unhindered, landing an advance force of 1,700 troops under the command of General Juan da Souza da Fonseca Costa on 1 January 1869. Two days later Marshal Caxias also reached the outskirts of Asunción with the larger part of his army, this force entering the city on the 5th. The following day saw Generals Osório and Alexandre Gomes de Argollo Ferrão both ask to be relieved of their commands of the 1st and 2nd Army Corps respectively, due to ill health. General José Luís Mena Barreto was then given command of the 1st while General Jacinto Machado Bittencourt was given the 2nd. These two corps were now composed of: 1st Corps, the 3rd and 5th Cavalry Divisions and the 2nd Infantry Division; 2nd Corps, the 1st and 2nd Cavalry Divisions and the 1st Infantry Division. The 1st Infantry Division contained the 1st, 2nd, 3rd, and 4th Infantry Brigades, while the 2nd Infantry Division contained the 5th, 6th, 7th, and 8th Infantry Brigades. The brigade of General Paranhos remained with the Uruguayan troops, while the engineers and the corps of pontoniers, plus an artillery brigade, remained under the control of the commander-in-chief. Brazilian troops initially remained in the city while the Argentines and Uruguayans went on to the town of Luque. The dockyards at Asunción now became available for use by the Brazilian fleet, which was badly in need of them.

Just as Osório and Argollo had the previous week, on 12 January 1869 Marshal Caxias himself asked to be relieved of his command because of ill health. Two days later he proclaimed that the war was over. Unsurprisingly, following his return to Brazil he was called to face a Senate inquiry, not only to explain this declaration but also to give some account of how López had managed to evade capture. However, his explanations were accepted and on the 26 March he was awarded the title of Duke.

During January 1869 Counsellor José Maria da Silva Paranhos, a special representative of the Brazilian Government, arrived at Asunción. One of his tasks was to organise a provisional administration, but no Paraguayan civilians could be induced to fill its posts. Faced with this dilemma it was decided to appoint officers from the Paraguayan Legion. They in turn obtained a number of signatures to petition the Allied governments for permission to elect a Provisional Government and carry on the war against López. This was allowed in June 1869, when representatives from the Allied governments signed a treaty in Asunción giving the right of free elections to all Paraguayans residing in the liberated portions of the country. It was hoped that such actions would erode support for López. The Provisional Government, headed by a triumvirate, was installed on 15 August, and was to hold its authority until López was either killed or expelled from the country. Only in military matters was it to be subject to the orders of the commander-in-chief of the Allied armies.

On 5 January a Brazilian naval squadron set out to find and destroy such Paraguayan ships as remained afloat. These were reported to be on the river Manduvirá. The Brazilian squadron consisted of the ironclad *Bahia*, the monitors *Pará*, *Alagoas*, *Ceará*, *Piauhy*, and *Santa Catarina*, and the gunboats *Ivaí* and *Mearim*. However, as they set out the level of the River Paraguay quickly dropped, so that it was only safe for the monitors to proceed to their destination. These were under the command of Captain Jerónimo Francisco Goncalves.

The following day the monitors sighted eight Paraguayan ships and an old steamer. These had been crewed by only 30 men under the command of Lieutenant Viera, but reinforcements under Captain Romualdo Núñez from the encampment of the Naval Battalion at Azcurra, and the 'Acamorotí' Cavalry Regiment under the command of Major Blas Montiel, arrived in time to assist them. Though the monitors tried to capture the Paraguayan vessels they managed to get away in time, though they were forced to leave behind many light craft and two small steamers (the *Coititeí* and *Rosário*), the crews of which jumped aboard the larger ships. The Paraguayans escaped down a narrow creek as yet unexplored by the Brazilians, forcing the latter to anchor at its mouth for the night. The monitors set out in pursuit the following morning, but after a few hours without any sight of the enemy it was decided to turn back; the creek being too narrow for the monitors to turn round, they had to reverse out, being careful to avoid two vessels scuttled by the Paraguayans to cover the escape of the other six.

Another attempt to destroy or capture the Paraguayan squadron began on the 25th. This time the ironclad *Colombo* and the gunboat *Belmonte* remained at the mouth of the river, where they disembarked units of infantry and cavalry who were to assist another ironclad, the *Araguary*, as it sought to find and destroy the Paraguayan ships. By the 29th this force had reached the Paraguayan mooring, but found that the river had been blocked by stakes, chains, carts full of stones, and mines. The *Araguary* hit a mine which failed to explode, while the land forces engaged a unit of Paraguayan infantry, capturing some of them. Though a third attempt was made on 23 April, it was not until June that the

Paraguayan vessels were finally destroyed, and then it was their own crews which set fire to them to prevent them falling into Brazilian hands. The six ships destroyed were the *Apa*, *Paraná*, *Yporá*, *Guairá*, *Amambaí*, and *Pirabebe*.

Another Brazilian naval squadron, consisting of the gunboats *Mearim*, *Ivaí*, *Iguatemí*, *Henrique Dias*, *Felipe Camarão*, and *Fernando Vieira*, and the steamer *Jaguareté*, with 250 sappers, was sent from Asunción on 14 January to take control of towns along the River Paraguay in the Brazilian province of Mato Grosso, that had been invaded and captured by López at the beginning of the war. These included Cuiabá, Coimbra, and Corumbá.

To replace Marshal Caxias as commander-in-chief of the Allied forces, the 26-year-old Conde d'Eu, the Emperor's son-in-law and grandson of Louis Philippe of France, was selected. He arrived at Asunción on 14 April 1869 and took command at the Army Headquarters in Luque two days later. During the interim period command was given to General Guilherme Xavier da Souza. This period also saw Admiral Ignacio retire to Brazil because of illness (he died during the return journey). He was replaced by Admiral Eliziáro dos Santos. In fact before the Conde d'Eu arrived in Asunción, many Brazilian officers requested permission to go back to Brazil on grounds of ill health, family problems, and the like, and most such requests were granted. This was indicative of the general state of mind of the Brazilian army, the morale of which was at an all-time low after having gone through so much during the past few years only to find that victory was not yet in sight. The wages of the Brazilian troops were also slow in being paid (some were reported to be in arrears by nine months), which produced the unpleasant spectacle of soldiers begging on the streets. Brazilian commanders did not wholly deny this fact, but they did justify late payment of up to three or four months – as proposed by Marshal Caxias – on the grounds that their soldiers had all they wanted, and that the issue of money was a signal for all manner of disorders. Many officers now urged that peace negotiations should be opened with López, an opinion which also began to be voiced in governmental circles. It was only stopped by Emperor Dom Pedro II hinting that he would abdicate if the war against López was not allowed to continue.

The month of March 1869 saw numerous Allied cavalry excursions to gather information on enemy-held terrain and positions. On the 17th the fleet was divided into two divisions, of which the first, under *Capitão de Mar e Guerra* Vitório José Barbosa da Lomba was to guard the rivers of the Paraguay, while the second, under Admiral Garcindo de Sá, was to protect the waterways of the Paraná.

5 April saw the Allied army organised as follows: at Luque, the army's main base, were the 8,769 men of the 2nd Army Corps; the Argentine Corps of 3,400 infantry and 700 cavalry under the command of General Emilio Mitre; 600 Uruguayan infantry and 70 cavalry under General Henrique Castro; and 800 men of the Paraguayan Legion under the command of Colonel Baez; at Rosario were 1,907 men under Colonel José de Oliveira Bueno; at Lambaré were the 6,024 men of the 1st Army Corps; at Juqueri was the 3rd Cavalry Division of the 2nd Corps, with 3,547 men; at Humaitá was a garrison of 2,084 men, not including hospital staff, under the command of Colonel Piquet; at Asunción were 2,856 men under the command of Colonel Hermes Ernesto da Fonseca; and on the River Paraná was General José Gomes Portinho with 1,300 men.

With the arrival of the Conde d'Eu a shake-up of the available troops was put in hand, and improvements in the morale of the Brazilian troops and their determination to see the war to a speedy conclusion that incorporated the demise of López began to take hold. Things improved further with the return of General Osório from hospital on 6 June to take command of the 1st Army Corps, despite still having to wear a black silk scarf to bind his chin and being restricted to a diet of liquids because of his wound. As Charles J. Kolinski (1965) writes, 'it was clear that the return of the army's most popular general represented a distinct psychological factor which would be valuable in the forthcoming campaign.' The Conde d'Eu retained the army's two-corps structure, but reduced the 1st Corps to just one infantry division (the 2nd) under the command of Brigadier José Auto da Silva Guimarães and one cavalry division (again the 2nd) under Brigadier José António Corrêa da Câmara. The 2nd Corps, commanded by Lieutenant-General Polidoro da Fonseca Quintanilha Jordão, had one infantry division (the 1st), commanded by Brigadier Salustiano Jerónimo dos Reis, and two cavalry divisions (the 1st and 3rd) commanded by Brigadiers João Manuel Mena Barreto and Vasco Alves Pereira.

Meanwhile López had not allowed this time to be wasted. He had arrived at Cerro León after the Battle of Lomas Valentinas with no more than the few survivors who had managed either to escape with him or by themselves on horseback. He found that Colonel Luis Caminos with his column from Asunción was already there, as was a small garrison to guard the camp and hospital that was situated here. Thompson writes that there were also 'several thousand wounded here' from the previous battles. As the weeks went by stragglers continued to arrive in small groups or in ones and twos. Some brought wild Indians from the Chaco with them, who had sheltered the soldiers when they were cut off from their units and now volunteered to fight against the Allies.

It took López just six weeks to put together a new army from these various resources, the men being despatched to acquire weapons, equipment, and food wherever and by whatever means they could, including raids on enemy outposts and searching through the detritus of the old battlefields of Lomas Valentinas and the surrounding area for discarded weapons that could be rendered serviceable. With firearms and ammunition proving scarce, many troops were issued with the long Paraguayan lance. Thirteen light cannon were successfully cast at Caacupé from equipment that had been saved from the arsenal at Asunción and brought downriver before the city fell. A further five guns were already in the area, and by August over 40 field-pieces had been scratched together – though what their calibre or condition may have been can only be guessed at. Doubtless some were taken off the ships that had been bottled up by the Brazilian navy and were destroyed in June.

A defensive line was constructed, its western flank

on the edge of the Paraná plateau with its marshes while the eastern flank edged the railway line and the heights of Azcurra. Its construction may have been useful in uniting the Paraguayan troops in a common task while the wounded healed, but to defend this line from flanking attacks would have required more than the 9,000 men and boys available to López, a portion of whom had already been sent to defend the towns of Piribebuy and Caacupé, plus the vanguard positions at Tacuaral and Pirayü.

General Juan C. Centurión writes that in 1869 López created four infantry divisions: the I Division (Lieutenant-Colonel Silvestre Carmona) with three battalions; the II Division (Lieutenant-Colonel Bernardo Franco) with three battalions; the III Division (Colonel Juan B. Delvalle) with three battalions; and the IV Division (Colonel Patrico Escobar) with four battalions (the 6th, 7th, 20th, and 21st). Among these battalions were the 'Riflero', 'Maestranza', 'Suelto', 'San Isidro', 'Marinos', and 'Acámorotí', each with 300–350 men. A cavalry division was also organised, consisting of five regiments under the command of General Bernardino Caballero. Its 1st Brigade (Lieutenant-Colonel Ignacio Genes) comprised the 1st and 5th Regiments; the 2nd Brigade (Lieutenant-Colonel Victoriano Bernal) comprised the 12th and 24th Regiments; while the

Vanguard consisted of the 11th Regiment and two light artillery pieces, commanded by General Caballero himself. Units of spies and arsonists were also organised, usually in groups of eight to ten men, the most famous of these being led by Captain Fortunato Montiel, who was killed in action.

On the railway track at Cerro León were six flatcars and an engine. López, seeing this as a means of surprising the Allied troops stationed further up the line, decided to place two of his newly-cast cannon on one of the flatcars while manning the rest of the train with infantrymen. In April he sent it on its way. The train got as far as Aregua, where, firing their cannon and firearms, the Paraguayans caught the encamped Brazilians completely by surprise. The Paraguayans then leisurely reversed the train back along the track, leaving confusion and some 40 of the enemy dead and wounded in their wake. Slowing to pick up two wounded men who had fallen off during the attack, the train was attacked, but, as Burton observes of the event, though 'the steam-engine was charged by the Rio Grandenses, lance in hand ... no one had the presence of mind to lay a log, or to cut the throat of a horse across the rails in rear.'

Other raiding parties were sent to capture more horses and weapons, stepping up pressure on the Allied

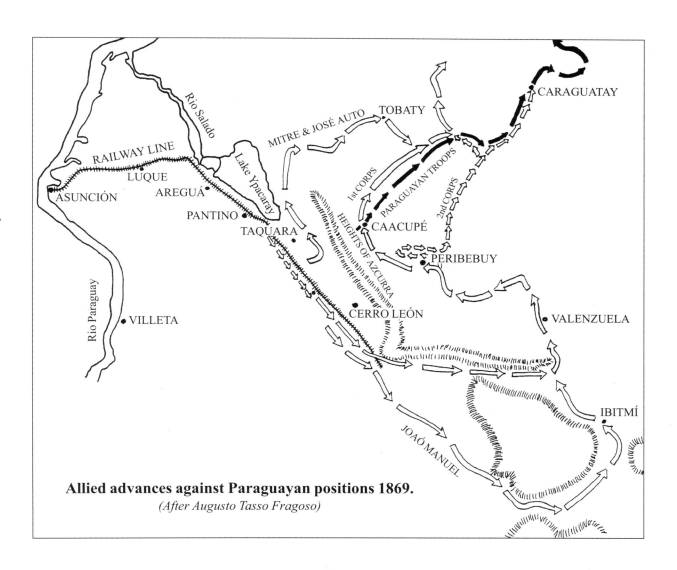

Allied advances against Paraguayan positions 1869.

(After Augusto Tasso Fragoso)

field commanders to react to this annoyance. Three railway bridges were also damaged during this period, including the one across the Juquery, which was only about 4–5 miles (6–8 km) from the Allied headquarters at Luque.[24] Other targets were the telegraph lines that connected Luque with Asunción.

THE BATTLE OF TUPI-HÚ

The Conde d'Eu reorganised his two Army Corps again in early May. The 1st Corps now comprised the 1st Cavalry Division (1st, 7th, and 9th Cavalry Brigades), the 3rd Cavalry Division (2nd, 5th, and 8th Cavalry Brigades), and the 2nd Infantry Division (2nd, 6th, 8th, and 9th Infantry Brigades). The 2nd Corps consisted of the 2nd Cavalry Division (3rd, 5th, 6th, and 10th Cavalry Brigades), the 4th Cavalry Division (5th and 9th Cavalry Brigades; this division was with General Portinho), and the 4th Infantry Division (1st, 3rd, 4th, 5th, and 10th Infantry Brigades).

After a long march from Asunción, on 17 May a column of 86 Uruguayan cavalrymen under the command of Mayor Hipólito Coronado attacked the Paraguayan encampment of Ibycuí, where there was a large iron works, capturing its commander, Captain Julián Insfrán. The Paraguayans lost 28 men killed and 56 were taken prisoner. Also at the works were found 86 Allied prisoners of war who had been made to work in the foundry, Captain Insfrán being subsequently executed for allegedly mistreating them.

Next day the two Brazilian Army Corps renewed their offensive. The column of General João Manuel Mena Barreto, consisting of the 1st Cavalry Division, the 2nd and 6th Infantry Brigades, and the 2nd Artillery Regiment, set out towards Itá. Lieutenant-Colonel João Sabino Mena Barreto's cavalry brigade was sent to Jaguarão to make sure that no enemy troops were stationed there; he then rejoined the main column at Itauguá on 24 May. The Paraguayan positions at Tacuaral and Pirayü were captured by Allied columns on the 25th, and forward positions at Cerro León were attacked by the column of Colonels Manuel Cipriano de Moraes and Manuel Deodoro da Fonseca (from the 1st Corps) the same day. By the 29th the Allied Vanguard, commanded by General Vaso Alves, had reached the Paraguayan defensive works before Cerro León and the heights of Azcurra.

Meanwhile, on 19 May the 2nd Cavalry Division, commanded by Brigadier José António Corrêa da Câmara, consisting of the 11th, 19th, and 21st Provincial Cavalry Corps and the 11th and 23rd Volunteer Battalions with four artillery pieces, had been transported from Asunción to Rosário, where it was reinforced with the troops of Colonel Oliveira Bueno. At 7:00 a.m. on 21 May the Villa de San Pedro, north of the River Jejuí, was captured in a surprise attack by 600 men under Colonel João Nunes da Silva Tavares. Brigadier Câmara then brought up the rest of his troops by ship to San Pedro. By the 28th this force was composed of the 11th, 18th, 19th, and 21st Provincial Cavalry Corps, the 11th Line Battalion, 23rd, 35th, and 53rd Volunteer Battalions, and four guns. On the 30th a force of just 1,052 Paraguayans, commanded by Lieutenant-Colonel Manuel Galeano, was ordered to make a stand against these troops, before whom they has been retreating since the 21st. Composed

of one infantry battalion, three cavalry regiments, nine field-pieces, and 50 veteran or garrison troops, the Paraguayans awaited the advancing enemy along the dried riverbed of the Aguaraí-guassú. Here they were assailed by the Brazilian infantry, supported by covering artillery fire and flank attacks by the cavalry, and were pushed back, the action being over in an hour. The Paraguayan commander and his adjutant Lieutenant Giménez had fled the field, leaving their unit commanders to continue the fight. They suffered 500 men killed, 87 wounded, and 350 captured, and lost four cannon. The Brazilians lost 15 men killed and 111 wounded. This battle is called Tupi-hú. Lieutenant-Colonel Galeano was later captured by the Paraguayans and executed for cowardice in the face of the enemy.

THE FALL OF PERIBEBUY

On 9 May 1869 the column of General José Gomes Portinho, consisting of the 5th and 9th Cavalry Brigades, the 12th Infantry Battalion (sent from Humaitá), and a horse artillery battery of five guns, was sent to capture the town of Encarnación. Resistance was met at the various villages along the route, although Encarnación itself was only lightly defended by 65 Paraguayan infantry. These only quit the town on 1 June, after having suffered 41 casualties. A Paraguayan counter-attack was then mounted to recapture the town under Colonel Rosendo Romero, with Major Manuel Bernal as his second-in-command. This force comprised just 1,500 men and four guns. Although outnumbered, the Paraguayans managed to dislodge the Brazilian troops, who retreated to the River Tebicuary and managed to board the monitors moored there. They lost 200 men killed, while the Paraguayans suffered 150 casualties. Fighting between these two columns continued into July, the Brazilian column attacking again at the Passo de Yuty, north-west of Encarnación, on 29 June, forcing the Paraguayans to retreat; at Pirapó on 8 July; and at Baré-cué on the 21st. This last encounter cost the Paraguayans 140 killed, wounded, and captured, compared to a Brazilian loss of 70 killed and wounded. During these advances the Brazilians were assisted by the ships *Henrique Martins*, *Santa Catarina*, *Ceará*, *Herval*, and *Ipiranga*. By 24 July Paraguayan resistance in this area had been eradicated, and the Brazilian troops were transported back to Asunción. The 12th Infantry Battalion arrived there on 10 August and the remainder of the Division disembarked on the 21st.

It was also during June that General João Manuel Mena Barreto's 1st Cavalry Division, consisting of the 1st, 7th, and 9th Cavalry Brigades (with two cavalry regiments in each) and a battery of four La Hitte horse artillery pieces, began a long expedition from Pirayü to Ibitimí, which was captured on the 2nd. Informed of this incursion, López sent General Bernardino Caballero with a mixed force of 3,000 men to stop it. Arriving at Ibitimí on 6 June, General Caballero found that it had been abandoned the day before. The Brazilian column had divided into two, one element reconnoitring as far as the River Tebicuary while the other headed towards the town of Ibycuí and its surrounding factories. A Paraguayan force of 600 men under Majors Manuel Bernal, Rufino Ocampos, and Eduardo Vera had hastily entrenched itself at Sapucaí in an attempt to block the latter element, their position being attacked by troops under Colonel Bento Martins. The fight lasted for two hours, during which time 200 Paraguayans were killed and wounded. Although the Brazilians had been delayed by their sacrifice, they not been halted long enough for General Caballero's main force to be any use. After visiting Ibycuí and making sure that the factories there were completely destroyed, General Mena Barreto's column returned to Pirayü.

By August 1869 the Allied Army was in position ready to begin the last phase of the war. Leaving a holding force at Pirayü under General Emilio Mitre (Brazilian 7th Infantry Brigade, the Argentine 'Santa Fe' and 'Cordoba' Infantry Battalions, the 4th Battalion National Guard of Buenos Aires, the Infantry Regiment of Rosário, and the San Martin Cavalry Regiment) and General José Auto da Silva Guimarães (5th and 9th Infantry Brigades, 12th and 14th Provincial Corps of Cavalry, and 12 La Hitte and six Whitworth guns from the 1st Foot Artillery Battalion of the 4th Provincial Artillery Corps), a wide flanking movement was set in motion against the Paraguayan left. Commanded by General João Manuel Mena Barreto, this comprised 4,040 men, made up of the 1st Cavalry Division (minus the 2nd and 3rd Line Regiments), the 8th Infantry Brigade, part of the 1st Horse Artillery Regiment, and a squad of Engineers; General Osório, with 7,440 men from the 1st Corps (made up of the 3rd Infantry Division, the 3rd Cavalry Division, the 2nd Cavalry Regiment, the Engineer Battalion, the Paraguayan Legion, the Uruguayan contingent, 900 Argentine troops under Colonel Luis Maria Campos, the 2nd Artillery Regiment with a battery of four light guns from the 1st Artillery Battalion, and a battery of rockets); and General Polidoro with the 7,710 men of the 2nd Corps (composed of the 1st Infantry Division, the 2nd Cavalry Division, part of the 1st Horse Artillery Regiment, and the Corps of Pontoniers). These three forces would constitute the main attacking force.

General Mena Barreto's cavalry column captured the town of Ibitimí on 5 August and then headed towards Pirajura to unite with the 1st and 2nd Corps. Also on the 5th, the defences at Sapucay were taken by the 1st, 4th, and 6th Infantry Brigades and General Castro's Uruguayan troops. On the 7th the town of Valenzuela also came under Allied control. With this the road to Peribebuy lay open.

Peribebuy was defended by 1,600 men under the command of Lieutenant-Colonel Pedro Pablo Caballero and Captain Manuel Solalinde, supported by 12 guns commanded by *Sargento Mayor* Hilario Amarilla. However, since the town was surrounded by hills the Brazilians were able to emplace six batteries (a total of 47 field-pieces and four rocket stands) overlooking it and its defences, these guns being under the command of Colonel Emílio Luís Mallet. A peace envoy from the Conde d'Eu was sent to ask for the town's surrender, but this was refused; a second request later in the day was also refused.

At 4:00 a.m. on the 12th the Brazilian batteries opened up on Peribebuy's defences, this barrage lasting for four hours. Then at 8:00 a.m. a general assault was made on three sides by infantry under covering fire from the hill batteries. When the infantry had taken the trenches the Brazilian cavalry charged through the camp and town. The Paraguayans lost 730 men killed, 700

wounded, and 170 captured in this brisk fight, many of them being mere boys, aged from eight upwards. The town's women are also reported to have taken up arms, although they are not listed as combatants. Among the dead was Lieutenant-Colonel Caballero, who, it is said, was killed after his surrender. Of the Allies, the Brazilians lost 53 men killed and 446 wounded, and the Argentines 15 men killed and 96 wounded. These included General João Manuel Mena Barreto, who was mortally wounded while leading a cavalry charge through the northern breastworks. The fall of this popular officer led to many Brazilians refusing to take prisoners during the later stages of the assault, although after the battle the reality of just how many boys had been killed compared to adult males shocked the Brazilian officer corps.

On 8 August a combined force commanded by Generals Emilio Mitre and José Auto da Silva Guimarães advanced from Pirayü, which the 7th Brazilian Infantry Brigade and the 54th Volunteer Battalion were left to garrison. This column was composed of the 5th Cavalry Brigade, the 5th and 9th Brazilian Infantry Brigades, the Argentine San Martin Cavalry Regiment, the Santa Fe Battalion, two companies of the Cordoba Battalion, the 4th Battalion of the Buenos Aires National Guard, the Infantry Regiment of Rosario, three batteries of La Hitte cannon with four guns in each, and a battery of six Whitworths. It advanced against the Paraguayan right flank through mountainous terrain, to reconnoitre and capture the towns of Altos, Atira, and Tobatí before heading on to the outlying defences of Caraguatay.

THE WAR ENTERS ITS FINAL STAGE

News of the defeat at Piribebuy caused López to retreat from his Azcurra camps. Knowing now that the columns of Generals Mitre and Silva Guimarães on his right flank had been diversions, he headed north-east towards Caraguatay, allowing the Allied 1st Corps to take possession of Caacupé on 15 August, where they found 1,200 Paraguayan wounded. It was at this time that both General Osório and General Polidoro asked to be relieved of their commands, citing ill health as the reason, and they were replaced by Generals José Luís Mena Barreto and Victoriano Carneiro Monteiro respectively.

With the capture of Caacupé the Conde d'Eu sent the 2nd Corps via Barreiro Grande in an attempt to cut off López's retreat, while closely pursuing him with the 1st Corps. The column of Generals Mitre and Silva Guimarães would unite with the 1st Corps along the way (this occurred on 18 August).

With this Brazilian force so close to the main concentration of Paraguayan troops, López decided that his best tactic was to attack them before they could be reinforced. On 15 August he therefore divided his army into two divisions: the first, under General Resquín, was to stay with López, while the second, under General Bernardino Caballero, was to be the rearguard. The following day the Conde d'Eu and the Brazilian 1st Corps came into contact with the Paraguayan rearguard at Campo Grande – called Acosta Ñú by the Paraguayans – on the River Yagarí, where cavalry were prevented from operating by broken ground along the riverbank. Here General Caballero had taken up a defensive position with his back to the river. His force numbered 3,646 men and boys and 12 cannon, only the 6th Infantry Battalion, commanded by Lieutenant-Colonel Bernardo Franco, containing a majority of veteran troops. It was organised in two divisions. The first, under Caballero himself, with Lieutenant-Colonel Florentin Oviedo as his second-in-command, consisted of 36 officers and 1,816 men and boys, while the vanguard division, commanded by Colonel Angel Moreno with Lieutenant-Colonel Franco as second-in-command, consisted of 29 officers and 1,765 men and boys.

The infantry of the Allied 1st Corps attacked the Paraguayan vanguard positions along the nearer riverbank at 8:00 a.m., their advance being assisted by artillery. Lieutenant-Colonel Franco was killed in a counter-attack, and the Brazilian horse-artillery caused great havoc amongst the Paraguayans as they retreated across the river, firing 683 shells (the 2nd Provincial Artillery Regiment were to fire a total of 1,700 shells during the battle). At the same time a right flanking movement was implemented by the 4th Cavalry Brigade, which had been ordered to cross the Yagarí anywhere downriver that it could.

Meanwhile the 2nd Corps, hearing the artillery fire on their left, sent the 1st, 9th, and 10th Cavalry Brigades to assist, followed by the 1st, 3rd, and 10th Infantry Brigades. The remainder of the 2nd Corps continued towards the junction of the roads from Caacupé, Caraguaty, and Piribebuy. These reinforcements from the 2nd Corps took three hours to reach the Paraguayan rear, but their eventual arrival had the desired effect: the Paraguayans could no longer retreat from the field.

The battle was fiercely fought, but the outcome was inevitable. After the fighting was over the Paraguayan dead and prisoners were again found to include a large percentage of boys from the age of ten years upwards, who had fought wearing false beards. A Brazilian lieutenant, Dionísio Cerqueira, noted that after the battle his men had commented 'there is no pleasure in fighting with so many children.' Many of the Paraguayans were also found to have been armed with old flintlock muskets and blunderbusses that would normally be found in museums. Also among the weapons captured was a Wilhelm Wagener's modern Congreve rocket-launcher. The Paraguayans had lost 2,000 killed and 1,500 wounded and captured, as well as three flags and all 12 cannon. Brazilian losses were 182 men killed and 420 wounded.

After these defeats López and his remaining 6,000 troops moved into the wooded area to the north, from where he planned to wage a guerrilla war against the Allied forces. However, this became more of a continual retreat northwards than a real guerrilla campaign. His first camp was at Caraguatay, where a trench was hastily dug and 1,200 men with 12 cannon were designated to defend it; in command was Colonel Pedro Hermosa. This defensive work was taken by the Brazilian 2nd Corps on 18 August after two hours' of fighting, the Paraguayans losing 260 killed and 530 taken prisoner plus all their guns, while the Brazilians lost 13 killed and 153 wounded. López then headed for San Estanislao, but left here on 30 August and went on to Itanará.

21 August saw the last engagement of the war for the Argentine troops, when a force of Brazilians and Argentines under the command of Colonel Carlos Bethbezé de Oliveira Néri attacked a supply column under the command of Colonel Ignacio Genes. The Allied force lost five men killed and 26 wounded, the Argentine infantry commander, Colonel Ayala, being amongst the dead. The Paraguayans had 26 men killed and lost three cannon and three wagons.

On 7 September López sent a force of 2,500 men and boys designated the IV Division, under the command of Colonels Gabriel Sosa and Juan B. Delvalle, to occupy the site of Panadero near the River Verde in the department of San Pedro, to guard against any flank attack from this direction.

29 October saw an attack on the Brazilian forward position of Colonel Fidélis Paes da Silva, at San Isidro de Curuguaty, by 500 men under the command of Major Verón. This was beaten back. On the same day this Paraguayan force was itself attacked by Major Francisco Adorna. Total losses to the Paraguayans were 257 killed and wounded.

On 24 November 1869 it had been agreed by the Allies to begin to reduce their respective armies stationed in Paraguay, the Uruguayans being the first to leave on 1 December, while the Brazilian 17th, 40th, and 53rd Volunteer Battalions began their homeward journey on 3 February 1870.

By December 1869 López had only 4,000 men and boys left with which to continue the fight, and many of these were sick or walking wounded. On 2 January 1870 the IV Division was recalled to Cerro Corá to be with López, but they were attacked en route by the column of Colonel João Nunes da Silva Tavares, and their 18-day retreat caused the division considerable suffering and loss. On 11 January the column of Colonel Ignacio Genes was found and attacked at Lomarugua, near San Pedro, by General José António Corrêa da Câmara; the campsite was captured and 154 prisoners taken. In a letter to the Conde d'Eu dated 14 January, General Câmara sent these details of the Paraguayan forces that had opposed him, obtained from prisoners captured on the 2nd, 3rd, and 11th:

2nd Infantry Battalion: 69 men in four companies
    including a Grenadier company.
4th Cavalry Regiment: 100 men in two squadrons with
    two companies in each.
7th Cavalry Regiment: 92 men in three squadrons with
    two companies in each.
8th Cavalry Regiment: 95 men in four squadrons with
    two companies in each.
12th Cavalry Regiment: 87 men in three squadrons with
    two companies in each.
13th Cavalry Regiment: 120 men in three squadrons with
    two companies in each.
19th Cavalry Regiment: 72 men in three squadrons with
    two companies in each.
29th Cavalry Regiment: 80 men in two squadrons with
    two companies in each.
Total: 715 men.

In February 1870 an Allied column under Colonel Bento Martins de Menezes, searching to the north, learned from a captured deserter that an encampment of 400 Paraguayans was situated near the River Aquidaban; and it was reported that López was with them – as indeed he was, for just two days later, at Cerro Corá, he reviewed

Table 8: The Paraguayan Army, at Cerro Corá February 1870

		Field officers	Company officers	Sergeants	Corporals	Other ranks
1st Cavalry Regiment						
1st Squadron	1st Company	1	2	1	1	4
	2nd Company	–	1	1	–	2
2nd Squadron	1st Company	–	1	–	1	2
	2nd Company	–	1	1	–	3
3rd Squadron	1st Company	–	1	1	–	3
	2nd Company	–	1	1	–	2
6th Cavalry Regiment	1st Company	1	1	1	1	3
	2nd Company	–	1	1	1	4
25th Cavalry Regiment	1st Company	–	3	3	4	4
	2nd Company	–	3	3	4	4
30th Cavalry Regiment	1st Company	–	2	–	1	5
	2nd Company	–	1	–	1	5
32nd Cavalry Regiment	1st Company	–	2	3	2	3
	2nd Company	–	2	3	2	3
46th Cavalry Regiment						
1st Squadron	1st Company	1	2	1	–	3
	2nd Company	1	2	–	1	2
2nd Squadron	1st Company	–	2	–	1	2
	2nd Company	–	4	1	–	2
3rd Squadron	1st Company	–	3	1	–	2
	2nd Company	–	4	–	1	1
Battalion 'Suelto'	1st Company	–	4	1	1	9
	2nd Company	–	4	–	1	9
Battalion 'Maestranza'	1st Company	1	4	7	2	23
	2nd Company	1	3	6	2	13
Battalion No.18	Grenadier Company	1	2	1	1	3
	1st Company	–	2	1	–	3
	2nd Company	–	1	1	–	3
	3rd Company	–	1	1	–	2
Battalion No.19	Grenadier Company	–	1	1	1	3
	1st Company	–	1	1	–	2
	2nd Company	–	1	1	2	2
	3rd Company	–	1	1	1	1
	4th Company	–	–	1	–	1
Battalion No.24	Grenadier Company	–	1	2	1	5
	1st Company	–	1	1	–	3
	2nd Company	–	1	1	1	5
	3rd Company	–	–	1	2	2
Battalion No.25	1st Company	1	1	1	–	–
	2nd Company	–	–	–	1	–
	3rd Company	–	1	–	–	1
	4th Company	–	1	–	–	1
	Cazadore Company	–	2	–	–	1
Battalion No.39	Grenadier Company	1	2	1	–	3
	1st Company	–	1	1	–	2
	2nd Company	–	2	–	–	2
	3rd Company	–	1	1	–	2
Battalion No.40	1st Company	–	1	1	2	3
	2nd Company	–	2	2	2	3
	3rd Company	–	1	1	2	2
	4th Company	–	1	2	2	1
	5th Company	–	2	2	2	2
	Band	–	1	1	1	2
Battalion No.42	Grenadier Company	–	2	1	1	3
	1st Company	–	3	1	1	2
	2nd Company	–	2	1	1	2
	3rd Company	–	2	1	–	1
Battalion No.46	Grenadier Company	–	2	1	1	2
	1st Company	–	1	2	–	2
	2nd Company	–	1	2	1	1
	3rd Company	–	1	2	1	2

his troops there. This force consisted of 268 infantry and 148 cavalry, although the latter's mounts might not be considered very good. A list of the units reviewed on 20 February still exists (see page 105). It is revealing to note that a 'company' could consist of as little as one sergeant and one private. The actual lists also show that a small number of musicians existed (a trumpeter in the 1st and 46th Cavalry Regiments, a drummer and fifer in the 42nd

Infantry Battalion), though I have included these men under the heading of 'other ranks'. A column of a further 40 men under the command of General Bernardino Caballero had been sent out from this camp earlier on a foraging expedition.

Colonel Menezes' force was not close enough or strong enough to act on the deserter's information, although it would be in a good position to block the

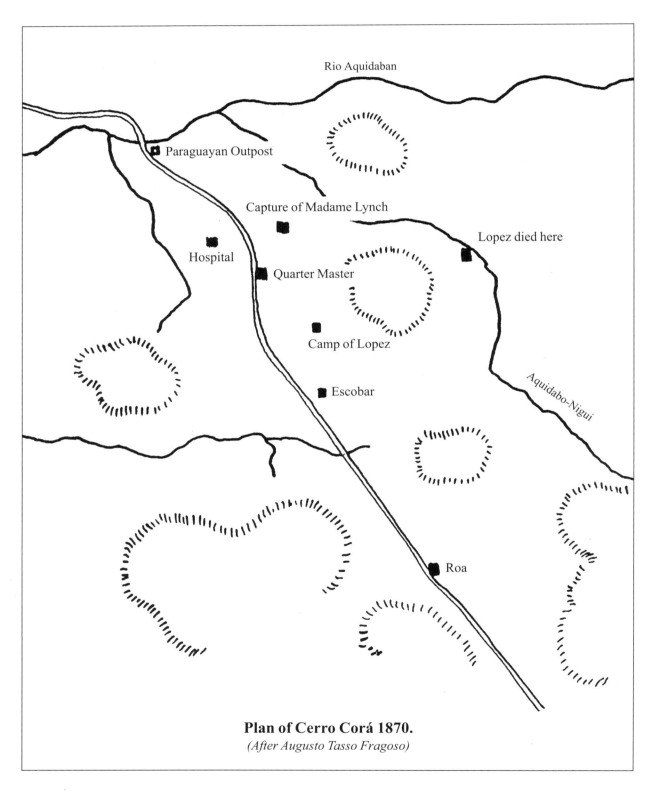

Plan of Cerro Corá 1870.

(After Augusto Tasso Fragoso)

Paraguayans' escape route if the camp was attacked. He therefore relayed the information back to General José Corrêa da Câmara, who upon receiving it on 18 February decided to make contact with the enemy as soon as possible, even though the whole complement of his column was not available. Colonel António da Silva Paranhos was therefore ordered to stop his advance towards the Rio Negla and join the main column as it headed towards Cerro Corá. The two forces united on the 25th.

On 1 March the Allied vanguard under the command of Lieutenant-Colonel Francisco Antonio Martins was close enough to attack the Paraguayan camp, and at 7:00 p.m. three columns set off. The first comprised the dismounted squadron of the 18th Provincial National Guard Corps commanded by Captain Pedro José Rodrígues; composed of 90 men with two field-pieces, this was to take the forward position that guarded the entrance to the valley, sited on the River Taquará. The second comprised the 21st Provincial National Guard commanded by Captain José Alexandre de Brito, who was to attack the flank, while the third comprised the 4th infantry company of the 9th Battalion under Major Floriano Vieira Peixoto, whose orders were to evade the Paraguayan pickets and attack the campsite. The unexpected Allied attack on the Paraguayan forward position allowed very little time for its defenders to organise a strong resistance, although a runner was sent back to warn the main camp. The other two Allied columns bypassed the forward position and continued 2.8 miles (4.5 km) until they reached the camp, the second column overrunning another Paraguayan detachment on the River Aquibadan that cleared the way to the main site, which was attacked as soon as the Allies reached it.

On hearing of the attack on his forward position in the pass, López had instructed Lieutenant-Colonel Solis to go with ten men to confirm the accuracy of the report, while also ordering General Francisco Roa to bring his troops from the far end of the valley to the main campsite. However, both men were overtaken by events. Fearing that the surprise attack was by a larger force, many Paraguayan civilians began to flee the campsite as best they could. Meanwhile the Brazilian reserve cavalry of the 1st and 19th Provincial National Guard (the 1st comprising only one squadron), commanded by Colonel João Nunes da Silva Tavares, charged into the camp, reaching it at the moment when the Paraguayan panic was at its height.

In the midst of the confusion some Paraguayans mounted horses to flee, amongst whom were General Resquín, Vice-President Francisco Sánchez, the Secretary of State Luis Caminos, and López himself with some of his bodyguard. However, the broken and swampy ground around the campsite prevented fast travelling, which enabled a force of Brazilian cavalry to cut off their retreat. Luis Caminos and Francisco Sánchez were both killed, the first by a carbine shot, the second by a lance thrust. General Resquín was surrounded after his mule stumbled, and surrendered after receiving a promise that his life would be spared. As for López, his horse could make little headway through the soft mud of the river. He was called upon to surrender by a six-man cavalry unit, but refused, firing his revolver and wounding one trooper. A lance thrust into his abdomen by corporal José Francisco Lacerda then caused him to

fall from his horse. Struggling to his knees, he was assisted by Captain Francisco Arguello and *Alférez* (Ensign) Norberto Chamorro of his staff. They fired into the Brazilians and, escaping from the patrol, reached the Aquidaban-Niqüi stream. However, López could not climb the steep further bank on account of his wound (it would appear that by now they were all on foot), and his companions set out to find an easier slope for him, leaving him half in the water grasping a branch from a tree at the water's edge. It was in this state that the Brazilians found him. He was again called on to surrender by an officer but replied with his revolver. This time a Brazilian trooper, João Soares, crossed the river and grabbed López, and, pushing him face down against the riverbank, fired his Spencer carbine into his back at close range. López died a few minutes later, muttering the words '*Muero con mi Pátria*' ('I die with my native land'). An autopsy subsequently found that the lance wound itself was mortal, and that the carbine shot had merely hastened his end.

The Paraguayans had lost 200 killed during the fight for the campsite, including 36 officers and four priests, with 245 taken prisoner including another 51 officers, three doctors, eight priests, and one secretary. Two flags and 16 cannon were also captured. Civilian casualties are not listed. The President's eldest son, Juan Francisco 'Panchito' López, who at 15 had recently been made a colonel by his father, also died in the battle, being killed by a lance thrust through the window of the carriage in which he was riding with the remainder of his family: they had been called upon to surrender and 'Panchito' in answer had fired his revolver at the Brazilian cavalrymen. Brazilian losses are given as seven men wounded.

On 3 March the following Paraguayan units surrendered to Colonel Deodoro da Fonseca near Curuguatí: the 1st, 6th, 7th, 8th, 10th, and 11th Infantry Battalions, and the 10th and 13th Cavalry Regiments. No details of the number of men per unit are given. After news of the death of López reached him General Caballero and his men surrendered to the Brazilian column of Major Francisco Marques Xavier on 8 April.

So ended the Paraguayan War. The loss to the Paraguayan people had been very great indeed, through both casualties and disease. In the census of 1846, 238,862 people were registered in Paraguay, but when the Allies produced a census in 1872 it showed just 232,000, whereas allowing for an average population growth of perhaps 5% per annum it could have been expected to show a total of some 590,000 by 1865. The Paraguayan government's own census of 1886 listed 231,878 people, this last figure showing that there were 137,010 females compared to just 94,868 males, and that of the latter 63,200 were aged below 20, 21,200 were 21–30, and only 10,300 were aged over 31. But the dramatic reduction of its population was not the only area where Paraguay suffered. Its economic, social, and international standing was also shattered, all of which would take many years to rebuild. Was this down to one man? Many think so, although in Paraguay itself Francisco Solano López is looked upon as a defender of the *Patria* or homeland, and a glowing example of self-sacrifice for the sake of one's country.

There were 23,917 Brazilian battle casualties during the war. This figure includes killed in action, wounded, and missing in action. In addition Argentina lost 9,861 killed, wounded, or missing, and Uruguay another 1,240 killed and wounded. All these figures could easily be doubled if desertions and deaths from illness were added.

The countries of the Triple Alliance may have won the war, but they did not enjoy the fruits of their labours long before internal problems toppled the Brazilian Empire and brought a sequence of military *Juntas* and strong men to power, who would dominate South American politics throughout the 20th century. If Francisco Solano López had been a better general and diplomat the Allies would have had a much harder struggle on their hands, and could well have been forced to make terms as their own power bases were threatened and the Triple Alliance agreement dissolved in tatters. It is also worth pointing out that matters may have turned out otherwise but for the considerable loans obtained by Brazil and Argentina to finance their participation in the war. Most of these came from European banking houses, mainly British, which some historians believe gives credence to contemporary opinion that the British Government desired the downfall of López and his replacement by a Liberal/Capitalist orientated government. This is not my own view, but anyone interested in forming an opinion of their own should read E.N. Tate's *Ibero-Amerikanisches Archiv* article 'Britain and Latin America in the Nineteenth Century' (1979), or the State Papers of the period.

NOTES

1 Persons of Spanish parentage born in the Americas.
2 A naval rank equivalent to commander.
3 A *caudillo* was a provincial leader, usually a large landowner or ranch owner.
4 This followed the recent example set by Rosas, whose followers wore a red ribbon with the legend *Viva Los Federales! Mueran Los Salvajes Unitarios!* ('Long live the Federals! Death to the Unitarian savages!').
5 The 'Blanco' party would not be in government again until 1958.
6 A large collection of cutlasses found aboard these captured ships was later issued to the 6th Infantry Battalion.
7 During efforts by the *Iguatemi* and *Ipiranga* to refloat the *Jequitinhonha* later the same day the *Ipiranga* also became grounded, but not for long, being refloated on 13 June.
8 The same number of animals per gun or caisson was used by all of the armies involved in this war.
9 In Brazil slaves were taken into the army as a way of combatting the effects of sickness in the field, and were promised their freedom after the war had ended. In addition some Brazilian plantation owners sent slaves rather than members of their family to serve in the army. The Volunteer Battalions found replacements for casualties in this manner. Of the 140,000 men sent by Brazil to fight against Paraguay during the war, only 18,000 were from the regular army, while 8,000 were blacks, all ex-slaves enlisted into the army in one way or another. Commander A.J. Kennedy RN saw a Brazilian battalion of 600 blacks. He wrote that they 'appeared in poor condition, the officers [who were of course white] told us their men found great difficulty in marching, not being accustomed to wearing boots, in fact they did not wear them and in consequence, a long march knocked them up. The officers had revolvers and the inevitable opera-glass and said they expected to get Spencer rifles for the men soon, their present arms being smooth-bores.' He also noted that Brazilian *Caçador* battalions were manned by either white or mulatto troops, no blacks being

drafted into them.
10 This was a neat little semi-circular brick fort which normally mounted two or three guns, situated on a high point known as Diamante. At the beginning of the war the Paraguayans had placed an additional two 8-inch cannons here.
11 Being mounted, Colonel Aquino had been the first to reach the enemy and was wounded in the waist. Picked up by the advancing Paraguayan infantry and sent back for treatment, he was promoted to General of Brigade by López but died two days later.
12 Static torpedoes were contact ignited and several dozen had been anchored in this part of the river, a fact known to the Allied ship commanders. A.J. Kennedy says that they 'consisted of an iron cylinder with several cases of powder in it. This was floated a short distance under water by being attached to light demi-johns on the surface. A pole secured to the cylinder and projecting above the water, communicated at its lower end with some detonating composition which ignited the powder on the pole being struck by an advancing ship. The apparatus was moored in its place by an anchor and cable, but the great strength of the current in the river rendered it extremely difficult to ensure these machines remaining in the required position long enough to be of any service, and notwithstanding the great number of them used by the Paraguayans, few were successful in damaging the Brazilian ships.'
13 Even in the Allied army relations between Argentine and Brazilian troops were not always as friendly as one would think. In one camp later in 1867 Richard Burton saw that a trench had been dug to separate the troops of the two nations.
14 Hydrogen for the balloon flights was produced by a field generator, using a supply of iron filings and sulphuric acid, but it was impossible to produce enough gas to lift the larger balloon until adequate supplies of these materials had become available. This took several months.
15 I have listed the cavalry brigades as totalling only four regiments rather than the six recorded to have taken part, since four of them had only one squadron each rather than the normal two. I do not know which units these were.
16 A Brazilian infantry brigade had also been despatched from Tuyucué in the direction of the sound of fighting, consisting of the 27th, 34th, and 49th Volunteer Battalions, but it did not arrive in time to fight.
17 1,500 men (four battalions) and two artillery pieces, under the command of Lieutenant-Colonel Germán Serrano, actually arrived later, during one of the Brazilian attacks, but are included in this overall total of 5,000 men.
18 One of the reasons for not committing the 1st Corps to the forthcoming battle was that Marshal Caxias had been warned of the possibility of attack by the Paraguayan troops of Colonel Luis Caminos from Asunción, and half expected this column to attack his rear.
19 López had moved his headquarters from Cumbarity to a more central position within his defences.
20 It would appear that this method of 'columns of attack' was favoured by Allied commanders for use against entrenchments throughout the war.
21 At Cerro Corá in 1870, this unit would have a fighting strength of only 38 men, made up of eight officers, seven sergeants, ten corporals, and 13 soldiers, under the command of Captain Pascual Aranda.
22 The 'Acaverá' Regiment's commander, Lieutenant-Colonel Francisco Ozuna, had been killed during the Allied assault.
23 This unit consisted largely of blacks, as was very often the case in Volunteer Battalions after 1867. It should be noted that the Paraguayans always referred to the Brazilian troops as monkeys and illustrated them as such in their newspapers; Emperor Dom Pedro was called '*el caraí de la macacada*' (chief of the monkey tribe). Although Paraguay too had both black slaves and free blacks, these constituted only 7.19% of the population in 1846, a much lower figure than in Brazil. The Paraguayan army also included units of *Pardo* (black) troops, such as the 2nd and 3rd Infantry Battalions and various cavalry

units (many Paraguayan slaves being used as ranch-hands on the rolling grasslands just north of the River Tebicuary). In 1842 the Paraguayan government enacted the Law of the Free Womb, whereby any child born of slave parents after 31 December 1842 would be classified as *Libertos de la República* and would, on reaching the age of 24 (women) or 25 (men), become fully free. But until they reached that age the *Libertos* would have to serve as if they were slaves. Slavery continued to exist in Brazil until late in the 19th century.

24 The Allies used the railway to bring supplies, etc, to their camps situated along the line, but the engine they used had to be brought down from Buenos Aires, since the Paraguayans had left only one dilapidated engine at Asunción and little rolling stock, although leaving the track intact. Burton notes that the Paraguayan failure to pull up the track probably saved the Allied army some two months' work.

ORGANISATION AND UNIFORMS

The figure drawings in this section illustrate only a portion of the uniforms worn in this region between the years 1826 and 1870. I have tried to include as many as possible from the earlier part of this period without detracting from this book's main theme, the Paraguayan War.

THE ARGENTINE ARMY 1826

This consisted of one battalion of artillery with six companies, each company with 100 men; a company of *zapadores* (sappers), four battalions of infantry each with six companies of 100 men (four of fusiliers, one of grenadiers, and one of *cazadores*); and seven regiments of cavalry, each of four squadrons, with two companies of 100 men per squadron. Each regiment had a staff corps of 13 men. The Argentine troops which accompanied General Carlos María de Alvear against the Brazilians in 1826 were in three Army Corps:

I Corps (General Lavalleja)
9th Regiment of Cavalry (2 squadrons)
Regiment 'Colorados' (2 squadrons)
Mounted Uruguayan Militia

II Corps (General Alvear)
1st Regiment of Cavalry (3 squadrons)
4th Regiment of Cavalry (2 squadrons)
8th Regiment of Cavalry (2 squadrons)
16th Regiment of Cavalry (2 squadrons)
Squadron 'Coraceros' (cuirassiers) (2 companies)
Cavalry Militia of Colonia

III Corps (General Solar)
1st & 2nd *Cazadores* Battalions (5 companies each)
3rd & 5th *Cazadores* Battalions (6 companies each)
2nd Regiment of Cavalry (3 squadrons)
3rd Regiment of Cavalry (2 squadrons)
Cavalry Militia of Mercedes
Regiment of Artillery (2 squadrons)

FIGURES

Sources for these illustrations are: documents in the Archive General of the Nation, Buenos Aires; paintings, illustrations, and documents in the Museo Historico Nacional, Buenos Aires; and plates by Jorge F. Rivas.

1 & 2. INFANTRY 1826 At the time of the war with Brazil over the Banda Oriental del Uruguay, or Cisplatina Province, the Argentine Army's four regular line infantry battalions wore a uniform consisting of a blue felt shako and dark blue tunic and trousers. The shako had a black leather top and band, with a bottom black leather band, a black leather visor edged in brass, a brass shako plate, a national cockade, and brass chin-scales. The Argentine cockade was actually light blue-white-light blue, but in some contemporary paintings the central light blue disc has faded almost to white; in addition the cockade holder strap sometimes entirely covered the central disc. In such cases I have decribed the cockade as simply light blue and white, since this is as much of it as can be seen in the source illustration. The 'carrot'-style plume and shako cords for each battalion were: 1st white, 2nd red, 3rd green, and 4th yellow. A French-style stable cap might also be worn. This was in dark blue cloth with piping and

Argentine chasseur or light cavalry officer's jacket of c.1826 in the Museo de Luján, Argentina. It is blue-black, with dark green velvet collar, cuffs, cuff bars, turnbacks and lapels, all piped in red, and gilt buttons. There are gold lace horns and flaming grenades on the collar. The shoulder bars are green velvet with a gold lace leaf design, and the aiguillettes are also in gold lace. (Photograph by David Prando in the author's collection)

tassel in battalion colour, and had a brass battalion number at the front. Piping and facing colours of the jacket and trousers were:

	Collar	Cuffs	Piping	Turn-backs	Trouser piping
1st Bn	red	red	white	red	white
2nd Bn	blue	blue	red	red	red
3rd Bn	green	green	green	green	green
4th Bn	red	red	red	red	red

The epaulettes of the fusilier companies had a red board with a yellow half-moon and fringe, the grenadier company had a red board with a brass half-moon without a fringe, and the *cazadore* (light) company had a red board with a yellow half-moon and a green fringe. All buttons were brass, and on the cuffs were three gold lace bars. The turnback ornamentation was a flaming grenade in yellow. Each Battalion had a large brass number on the collar.

All grenadier companies (Figure 2) wore the same uniform. Their black bearskins had red cords, a brass plate with flaming grenade, a national cockade in light blue and white, and a white plume with a red top. The tunic was dark blue with red collar, cuffs, cuff flaps, and turnbacks. Piping was white except for the pocket piping, which was red. On the collar and cuffs were gold lace stripes (there was no number on the collar) – one on the collar and two on the cuffs. There was a gold lace flaming grenade on the turnbacks. Trousers were white, buttons brass.

Cazadore companies also all wore the same uniform. Their shako was as for the fusilier companies, except in having a dark green pompom and cords. The tunic was dark blue with dark green lapels, collar, cuffs, and turnbacks, piped in red; pocket piping was also red. The turnback ornamentation was a gold lace hunting horn. The collar had two gold lace bars, the cuffs three. The trouser stripe was red, while the stable cap had a dark

blue top with a dark green base, yellow piping and tassel, and a brass hunting horn on the front. The overcoat for all infantry was of dark blue cloth, and the backpack was of brown leather. All straps and belts were white leather.

3. GENERAL OFFICER 1826 Full dress. Bicorne black felt with red feathers, national cockade (light blue-white-light blue), gilt feather holder and chin-scales, gold lace tassels and cockade holder, black silk edging. Tunic dark blue, collar, cuffs and turnbacks also dark blue. Collar has red piping and gold lace laurel branches, cuffs have two rows of red piping plus gold lace laurel branches. Turnbacks piped in red with gold lace grenade insignia, epaulette board in medium blue with gold lace edge, half-moon, and bullion fringe, aiguillettes in gold lace. Front of tunic piped red. Red waist-sash, breeches dark blue with gold lace laurel leaves on seam, sword slings red edged in gold lace, gilt hilt with white sword knot, steel scabbard with gilt fittings, black boots, steel spurs.

4. LIEUTENANT-COLONEL, ADC TO THE GENERAL STAFF 1826 Bicorne black, gold lace edge, tassels, and cockade holder, national cockade (on right side), gilt buttons, white feather crest. Tunic dark blue, collar and cuffs red with gold lace laurel branch and edging. Epaulettes have a black board with gold lace edge, half-moon, and bullion fringe, gold lace on chest, gilt buttons. Waist-sash red with gold tassels, trousers white, black boots, steel spurs, white waistbelt and sword slings, gilt fittings. Scabbard black leather with gilt fittings, hilt gilt, sword knot in gold lace.

5. LIEUTENANT-COLONEL, 1st INFANTRY BATTALION 1826 Bicorne black with silver lace edge, gold lace tassels. Tunic blue, collar, cuffs, turnbacks, and lapels green, red piping on all, plus pocket piping. Gold lace on collar and cuffs, gold lace hunting horn on turnbacks, gold lace epaulettes, gilt buttons, white breeches, black boots. Waistbelt and sword slings black

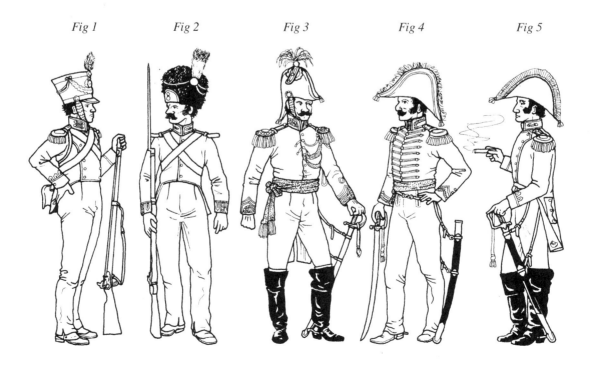

Fig 1   Fig 2   Fig 3   Fig 4   Fig 5

Fig 6   Fig 7   Fig 8   Fig 9

leather with gilt buckle and fittings. Scabbard black leather with gilt fittings, hilt gilt with gold lace sword knot, steel spurs. During the war this battalion was commanded by Lieutenant-Colonel Correa, who was accompanied by just five companies.

6. OFFICER, 2nd INFANTRY BATTALION 1826

Service dress. Bicorne black, gold lace edge and tassels. Shell jacket green with red collar, cuffs, and buttoned-back lapels or jacket lining, gold lace on collar and cuffs. White waistcoat, black trousers with white side stripe, white waistbelt and sword slings with gilt buckle and fittings. Steel scabbard with gilt fittings, hilt gilt with gold lace sword knot. This battalion was commanded by Colonel Francisco Sánchez de Zéliz.

7. CUIRASSIER OFFICER 1826

Full dress. Cap of blue cloth with gold lace trim and lines, black leather visor edged in gilt. Tunic blue with red collar and cuffs, gold lace flaming grenade on collar, gold lace contre-epaulette. Trousers blue with red stripe. Cuirass steel with gilt rivets and shoulder scales. Black leather waistbelt, pouch belt red edged in gold lace, black pouch, steel scabbard with gilt fittings, gilt hilt and gold lace sword knot. Shabraque blue with red edge lace and gold lace flaming grenades, black leather harness etc. Another figure is shown in the original wearing a shako with red pompom and gold lace cords and flounders, gold lace top and bottom bands, gilt plate and fittings. He is also wearing a sabretache which has a dark blue field edged in gold lace, in the centre of which is the national coat of arms within two laurel branches, all in gold lace, and he

wears two epaulettes, making him a field officer.

8. CUIRASSIER, 6th LINE CAVALRY 1826

Shako black, red 'carrot'-style plume, brass plate, chin-scales, and visor edging, national cockade with yellow holding cord and brass button, top band yellow lace, bottom band black leather. Jacket dark blue with red collar, cuffs, and turnbacks without piping, yellow flaming grenade on collar and turnbacks, red pocket piping, brass buttons. Overalls dark blue with red stripe. Steel cuirass with brass rivets and edges, shoulder-straps black leather with brass buckles, waistbelt and sword slings the same. Steel scabbard with brass fittings, brass hilt with white sword knot. White sheepskin with red cloth edging, dark blue roll, black leather harness and straps. Wooden lance shaft with red-over-white pennon. This unit was composed of one lieutenant-colonel, one major (*sargento mayor*), one adjutant, one captain, one first-lieutenant, one second-lieutenant, three ensigns, seven sergeants, two trumpeters, 15 corporals, and 170 troopers. It became the 6th Line Cavalry on 10 July 1826, giving up its old title of *Blandengues* or border guards. On 9 October 1827 its commander was Lieutenant-Colonel Mariano García.

9. TROOPER, 7th LINE CAVALRY 1826

Campaign dress. Shako black with green plume and cords, brass plate, chin-scales, and visor edging, yellow lace top and bottom bands, national cockade under plume. Jacket dark blue, collar, cuffs, lapels, and turnbacks also dark blue, all piped red, brass buttons. No epaulettes worn but shoulder button and holding strap part of jacket. Yellow lace flaming grenade on turnbacks. Breeches dark blue

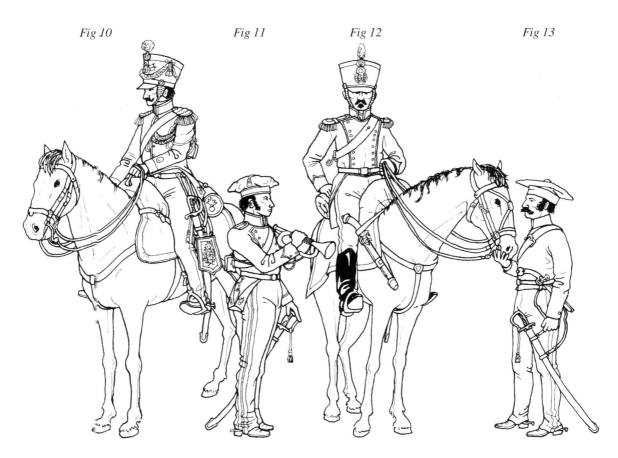

Fig 10   Fig 11   Fig 12   Fig 13

with red stripe, black boots. Carbine sling and waistbelt are buff in colour with brass fittings. All-steel scabbard, sword hilt brass with green sword knot. This regiment's commander was Colonel Ramón Estomba.

10. OFFICER, 15th LANCERS 1826 Full dress. Shako dark blue felt with top and bottom bands in black leather, red pompom, national cockade, gold lace cords and flounders, gilt plate, chin-scales, and edge to black leather visor. Tunic dark blue with red collar, cuffs, and turnbacks, no piping to cuffs or turnbacks. Collar has blue piping, front of tunic has red piping. Gilt scales on epaulettes with gold lace fringe. Gold lace flaming grenade on turnbacks, gold lace aiguillette. Trousers dark blue with red stripe, white leather waistbelt, sword and sabretache slings. Sabretache has a field of dark blue, a gold lace edge, and the national coat of arms between two laurel branches. Shabraque dark blue with gold lace edging and flaming grenade, valise same. Harness etc in black leather. This unit was created on 4 August 1826, commanded by Lieutenant-Colonel José de Olavarria, who had arrived back from Peru after commanding the Hussars of Junín Regiment. Its troops came from the militia of Luján and Lobos.

11. TRUMPETER, 16th LANCERS 1826 Campaign dress. Cap sky blue with red tassel and band. Tunic sky blue with red collar, cuffs, and turnbacks, gold lace flaming grenade ornaments on turnbacks. Lapels sky blue piped red, pockets piped red, shoulder straps sky blue piped red, white buttons. Overalls sky blue with double red side stripe and black leather false boot bottoms. Brass trumpet with red cords. Steel scabbard,

brass hilt, white leather sword knot and sword slings.

12. TROOPER, COLORADOS DE LAS CONCHAS 1826 Shako black with red 'carrot'-style plume above national cockade, brass plate, chin-scales, and visor edging, yellow lace band around top of shako. Jacket dark blue with red collar, cuffs, lapels, and turnbacks all piped white. Epaulettes are red, buttons brass. Breeches dark blue with red stripe, black boots, white leather straps and belts with brass buckles. Steel scabbard with brass fittings, brass hilt, white sword knot. Shabraque dark blue, valise dark blue with red braid. Black leather harness with brass fittings. First raised in 1812 as a mounted company, by 1826 this unit's strength was 350 men. At the Battle of Ituzaingo it had four squadrons and a mounted band.

13. TROOPER, LIBERTY DRAGOON REGIMENT 1826 Campaign dress. Cap dark blue with red piping and band. This style of cap was commonly used when the French style of stable cap was too expensive to produce – mainly in provincial militia and volunteer units. Shell jacket dark blue, collar red. Overalls dark blue with red stripe. Black leather straps, belts, and pouch with brass buckles. Black boots with steel spurs, steel scabbard with brass fittings, hilt brass with black grip.

14. OFFICER, NATIONAL DRAGOONS 1826 Campaign dress. Cap dark blue with gold lace piping and tassel, red band, gilt chin-scales and visor edging, black leather visor. Jacket dark blue, collar, cuffs, and turnbacks red. Collar, turnbacks, and front of jacket piped yellow. Gold cuff lace, gilt shoulder scales. Waistcoat yellow, breeches dark blue with yellow stripe. Black boots with white stockings. Belts and straps white leather with gilt fittings, steel scabbard with gilt fittings, gilt hilt with ivory grip and gold lace sword knot.

15. INFANTRY PRIVATE 1827 A new uniform was decreed for the Argentine Army in 1827, to standardise the dress of its various branches and thereby reduce the cost of manufacture. Although these uniforms did bring about some degree of standardisation they were short-lived, and it would appear that only the Artillery received them during the war.

Helmet black leather with brass comb, plate, and visor edging, pale green cap lines, red pompom, black leather chinstrap, brass boss. Tunic medium blue with collar, cuffs, lapels, and turnbacks in green, piping red, brass buttons. No epaulettes. Waistcoat and trousers white linen, overcoat medium blue. All leather straps are white, brass waistbelt buckle.

16. CUIRASSIER 1827 Helmet as per Figure 15, but with red cap lines. Tunic medium blue, collar medium blue with a yellow flaming grenade, cuffs and turnbacks red, brass buttons. Turnbacks have a yellow flaming grenade. Trousers are medium blue with a thick red stripe. Black boots, steel spurs, white leather sword slings, steel sword scabbard with brass fittings. Brass hilt and black grip, white sword knot. Cuirass steel with brass trim, rivets, and shoulder scales, and black leather side straps with brass buckles.

17. LANCER 1827 Helmet as per Figure 15, but with white cap lines. Tunic medium blue, collar and cuffs as per Figure 15, lapels medium blue piped red, turnbacks medium blue piped red. Waistcoat white linen, trousers medium blue, no side stripe. Black boots, sabre etc as per Figure 15. Waistbelt white leather with brass buckle. Lance pennon red over white, wooden shaft with brass ferrule.

18. ARTILLERYMAN 1827 Helmet as per Figure 15,

but with black cap lines (a surviving artilleryman's helmet in the Museum of Luján, Argentina, appears to be all-metal rather than leather). Tunic medium blue, collar and cuffs as per Figure 16, turnbacks red with yellow flaming bomb (collar has flaming bomb rather than grenade), lapels medium blue without piping. White waistcoat, medium blue breeches, black boots, steel spurs. Sidearm brass hilt with black grip, black leather scabbard with brass fittings. White leather crossbelts. There was also a Naval Artillery unit, which had the same uniform as the normal artillery except: cuffs were medium blue piped red, collar insignia was an anchor, not a bomb, lapels had red piping. On 9 May 1826 the *Regimiento de Artillería Ligera* was created, consisting of two squadrons with two companies in each. A company of artillery comprised one captain, two first-lieutenants, two second-lieutenants, two ensigns (*alféreces*), one first-sergeant, four second-sergeants, six first-corporals, six second-corporals, six trumpeters, 44 artillerymen first class, and 50 artillerymen second class. The 1st Artillery Regiment was commanded by Colonel Tomás de Iriarte.

19. OFFICER, 5th INFANTRY BATTALION 1827 Shako black with black leather top and bottom bands, red 'carrot'-style pompom, national cockade, gilt plate, visor edging, and chin-scales, gold lace cords. Tunic blue, collar and cuffs red, collar piped white, lapels and turnbacks white piped red, pockets piped red, epaulettes in gold lace. Breeches white, black Hessian boots with gold lace and tassels. Scabbard black leather with gilt fittings, hilt gilt with black grip. This unit was created on 4 August 1826 under the command of Colonel Felix de Olazábal.

20. TROOPER, URUGUAYAN VOLUNTEER CAVALRY 1827 This is a *Tiradore Ligeroz* or Mounted Rifleman. Carlist-style cap dark blue with red band and tassel. Jacket dark blue, collar and cuffs dark blue piped red, turnbacks red, front piping to jacket red, brass buttons. Breeches dark blue, black boots, white leather

Fig 14   Fig 15

Fig 16   Fig 17

Fig 18   Fig 19   Fig 20   Fig 21

belts and straps with brass buckles. Steel scabbard, brass sword hilt, white sword knot.

21. URUGUAYAN DRAGONES ORIENTALES 1826

Campaign dress. Cap dark blue with red piping and base band. Jacket dark blue with red collar and cuffs. Trousers white, apron pale blue cloth, waistbelt natural leather with silver studs. Black leather scabbard with brass fittings, sword hilt brass with white sword knot. His toeless boots are *bota de potro*, which were made from a horse's fetlock by cutting off the hoof and pulling out the bone and flesh, then turning it inside out and cleaning it. The spur straps held the boot in place.

BRAZIL c.1820–50

A decree of 1 December 1824 divided the Brazilian infantry into First and Second Line units. The First Line units were composed of the 1st Battalion of Grenadiers (Imperial Guard of Honour), which became the 1st Line; the 2nd Battalion of Grenadiers, which became the 2nd Line; the 1st–4th Battalions of *Caçadores* from Rio de Janeiro, which became the 1st–4th *Caçadores*; the 1st and 2nd *Caçadores* of São Paulo, which became the 5th and 6th *Caçadores*; the Infantry Legion of São Paulo, which became the 7th *Caçadores*; the Battalion of *Caçadores* from Santa Catarina, which became the 8th *Caçadores*; the Battalion of Infantry and Artillery from Curityba, which became the 9th *Caçadores*; the 1st and 2nd Battalions of Free Blacks (*Libertos*) of Montevideo, which became the 10th and 11th *Caçadores*; the infantry company and a corps of light cavalry from Espírito Santo, which were reorganised into the 12th *Caçadores*; the 1st–3rd *Caçadores* of Bahia, which became the 13th–15th *Caçadores*; the battalion from Alagoas, which became the 16th *Caçadores*; the 1st–3rd Battalions from Pernambuco, which were reorganised as the 17th and 18th *Caçadores*; the battalion from Parahya, which became the 19th *Caçadores*; the infantry units from Piauí, Rio Grande de Norte, Ceará. and Maranhão, which

became respectively the 20th, 21st, 22nd, and 23rd *Caçadores*; units from Pará, which became the 24th and 25th *Caçadores*; and foreign *Caçador* units, which

Federal Infantry Battalion No.3 junior officer's hat, c.1840, in the Museo de Luján, Argentina. It is red with yellow piping along the seams, and a brass number '3' on the front. A thin gold lace trim goes along the bottom edge of the hat, while at the end of the flap there is a small red cloth ball to which a tassel would have been attached (in this case I believe it would have been of gold lace rather than yellow wool). (Photograph by David Prando in the author's collection)

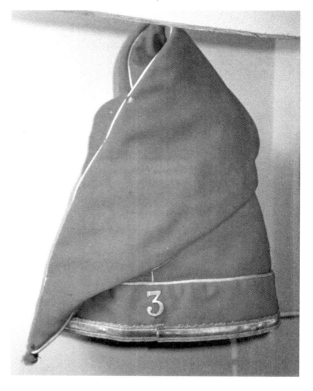

became the 26th and 27th *Caçadores*. The 28th *Caçadores* were added in 1825.

First Line cavalry units were created from the Imperial Guard of Honour, which became the 1st Regiment of Cavalry; the regiment from Minas, which became the 2nd Regiment; the Cavalry Legion of São Paulo and a squadron of cavalry from the city, which were reorganised to become the 3rd Regiment; the squadron from São Pedro do Rio Grande do Sul, which became the 4th Regiment; the Dragoons of Rio Pardo, who became the 5th Regiment; the Dragoons of Montevideo, who became the 6th Regiment; and the Dragoons of União, who became the 7th Regiment.

The First Line artillery were created from the artillery regiment from Rio de Janeiro, which became the 1st Corps of Artillery; the artillery battalion from Rio de Janeiro, which became the 2nd Corps; the artillery from Santos, which became the 3rd Corps; the artillery from Santa Catarina, which became the 4th Corps; the artillery from Montevideo, which became the 5th Corps; the artillery from Espírito Santo, which became the 6th Corps; the artillery from Bahia, which became the 7th Corps; the artillery from Pernambuco, which became the 8th Corps; and the artillery from Piauí, Ceará, Maranhão, and Pará, which became the 9th, 10th, 11th, and 12th Corps respectively.

Five Horse Artillery corps were created: the Mounted Artillery Brigade of the Court became the 1st Corps of Horse Artillery; the horse artillery from the Legion of São Paulo became the 2nd Corps; the horse artillery from São Pedro do Rio Grande do Sul became the 3rd Corps; the horse artillery from Alagoas became the 4th Corps; and the horse artillery from Paraíba do Norte became the 5th Corps.

The Second Line units were composed of four regiments of line infantry, 89 battalions of *caçadores*, 38 regiments, or units, of cavalry, and many small units of Artillery.

FIGURES

Sources for the following drawings of Brazilian soldiers are: *Uniformes do Exercito Brasileiro* by Gustavo Barroso, illustrated by J. Washt Rodrigue (1922); articles by C.A. Norman published in *El Dorado*, the journal of the South and Central American Military Historians Society; *Os Voluntários da Pátria na Guerra do Paraguai* by General Paulo de Queiroz Duarte (1983); and a letter by Reginaldo J. da Silva Bacchi, published in *Military History* magazine in October 2002.

22. LIEUTENANT-COLONEL, REGIMENT OF *CAÇADORES* 1823 Full dress. Shako black felt, green feather plume, gilt bugle, crown, and plume holder, black leather visor, black shako cords. Jacket dark blue, collar, cuffs, and turnbacks white. Gold lace laurel leaves on collar, gold rank lace on sleeve, black chest lace, black buttons. Crimson waist-sash. Trousers white, black boots, belts, and straps, gilt buckles. Black leather scabbard with gilt fittings, hilt gilt with black grip and black sword knot.

23. PRIVATE, REGIMENT OF *CAÇADORES* 1823 Full dress. Shako and cap lines black, brass bugle, crown, and plume holder, plume white, visor black leather.

Federal cuirassier, c.1840, from a painting by D'Hastrel in the Museo Histórico Nacional, Buenos Aires. The cap and jacket are red, the cuirass is of blackened metal with brass fittings and red cloth trim, and the chiripá *is of brown cloth over a white lace undergarment. The scabbard is steel with brass fittings. His footwear is that of the gauchos, which involved taking a horse's fetlock, cutting off the hoof, and removing the bone; pulled over the foot, this left the rider's toes free to grip the stirrups.*

Various types of Federalist troops, c.1840, an original watercolour by José Balaguer. The first figure is an infantry drummer dressed entirely in red except for his cap tassel, collar, cuffs, jacket piping, and cuff lace, which are all black. His drum is red with yellow top and bottom bands and white stretchers. The second figure is a cazadore de monte, *who is also dressed in red except for his cap tassel and the piping on cap, jacket, cuffs, pockets, and collar, which are all yellow. There are yellow lace flaming grenades on the collar, and the buttons are yellow metal. Footwear is of brown leather. His sword has a steel scabbard with brass fittings, a brass hilt, and a red knot. Next is an infantry officer wearing a red cap with black leather visor and strap and gilt metal buttons; a red jacket with yellow cuffs, collar, turnbacks, and piping, and red shoulder bars with gold lace trim; white trousers; a white leather waistbelt with gilt buckle; and black shoes. His sword scabbard is steel, the hilt gilt, and the sword knot red. The final figure is a cuirassier in a red cap with red tassel and an all-red jacket. His leather cuirass is black with gilt fittings and a brown leather waistbelt (I have seen a cuirass made from thick hide in the Museo Historico del Ejército Argentino at Ciudadela in Buenos Aires. The hide was translucent; it was also very light.) His brown cloth chiripá is worn over a white lace undergarment, and his toeless footwear is of brown leather. The scabbard is steel with white leather slings, the sword hilt brass with a red knot, and the spurs steel.* (Author's collection)

Jacket dark blue, collar, cuffs, and turnbacks green. Collar has a black lace zigzag design and edge piping, shoulder straps and crests black, chest lace and buttons also black. Trousers dark blue, belts black leather with brass fittings, hanging musket brush and pricker brass with black cords. Bayonet socket brass. Another regiment of *caçadores* which existed in 1823 was made up of German mercenaries. Their uniform was the same but with these differences: shako had a plate with number stamped on it (same style as the grenadier battalions), no crown just a bugle, cap lines are not shown as being worn, the collar lacked the zigzag lace design, and the bayonet socket was steel rather than brass.

24. PRIVATE, REGIMENT OF *CAÇADORES* 1824
Winter dress. Shako as per Figure 23, without plume or cords. Overcoat dark blue, trousers and spats dark blue, black leather waistbelt and pouch, brass buckle.

25. OFFICER, 1st GRENADIER BATTALION 1823
Full dress. Shako black, gilt plate, plume holder, and visor edging, national cockade, black ribbon tied into a bow on side with a sprig of leaves placed into it, plume green with yellow top section, black leather visor. At this date the cockade consisted of four concentric circles (yellow-green-yellow-green) surrounding a small central yellow disc. Jacket dark blue, collar dark blue with gold lace edging, cuffs red with rank in gold lace, piping along front of jacket red, turnbacks red, buttons gilt. Rank epaulettes gold lace. Trousers and spats white, black shoes, waist-sash red. Crossbelt and sword slings white leather, scabbard black leather with gilt fittings. Hilt gilt with black grip and red and gold sword knot.

26. PRIVATE, 1st GRENADIER BATTALION 1823
Full dress. Black shako as per Figure 25, without the sprig of leaves, and brass rather than gilt metal. Jacket dark blue, collar green with flaming grenade and piping in yellow lace, cuffs green piped yellow, turnbacks red, a vertical back pocket flap with three buttons, shoulder straps and crests red with a white top on the crests, red piping to the front and bottom of jacket, brass buttons. Trousers and spats white with black boots. Crossbelts white leather, black pouch, bayonet scabbard black leather with brass fittings, white musket strap.

Two thousand Irishmen, who it would appear had

Fig 22   Fig 23   Fig 24   Fig 25   Fig 26

sailed to Brazil in 1827 to make a new start in life, were pressed into the army on disembarking and formed into two further battalions of Grenadiers under a Colonel Crotter. Of these, the uniform of the 1st Irish Battalion was the same as that described above, but with these differences: collar and cuffs red piped white, piping to the front and bottom of jacket white, turnbacks white, shako plume red and smaller. The 2nd Irish Battalion mutinied

A contemporary print from the 1840s, artist unknown, showing Federal cuirassiers and infantry. (Author's collection)

and its men were shipped off to Canada after a year.

27. FIFER, 1st GRENADIER BATTALION 1824
Summer dress. Stable cap dark blue, with red lace, piping, and tassel, brass flaming grenade badge. Shell jacket, trousers, shirt, and spats white linen. Boots black, crossbelts white leather. Fife case brown leather. Sidearm has brass hilt, black leather scabbard with brass fittings.

28. PRIVATE, 2nd REGIMENT OF MILITIA, RIO DE JANEIRO 1822 Campaign dress. Shako black with national cockade, white metal plate, unit disc and plume holder. Plume yellow with green tip. Jacket dark blue, collar and cuffs green piped white, piping to front and bottom of jacket white, turnbacks white, shoulder straps and crests yellow with a green top to the crests. On his left sleeve would have been a chevron and cockade as described under Figure 32. Trousers and spats white. Black boots, crossbelts white leather. Brass hilt to sidearm. Backpack and pouch black leather, overcoat roll dark blue, black hanging tassel, dish strapped to pack steel.

29. CORPORAL, 1st REGIMENT OF CAVALRY 1824 Shako black with yellow lace top band, brass plate, chin-scales, plume holder, and visor edging, national cockade. Plume (when worn) green with yellow tip. Jacket dark blue, collar and cuffs red with white piping, turnbacks and piping to the front and bottom of jacket white, brass shoulder scales and buttons. Yellow lace chevrons. Trousers dark blue. Black boots, white slings and belts with brass buckles. Steel scabbard and hilt, white sword knot. A picture of an officer of this unit shows him wearing overalls with an inch-wide red stripe.

30. CAPTAIN, 1st REGIMENT OF MILITIA CAVALRY 1824 Shako black with red plume, gold lace top band, gilt chin-scales, white metal/silver shako plate, plume holder, and visor edging, national cockade. Jacket

dark blue with white collar and cuffs not piped, epaulettes silver, turnbacks and piping to front and bottom of jacket red, silver buttons. Red waist-sash, trousers white, boots black, belts and slings black leather with silver buckles. Steel scabbard and hilt, black sword knot, black leather sabretache. A picture of a major of the 2nd Regiment of Militia Cavalry in full dress shows him in the same uniform but with a red collar, dark blue trousers with red stripe, yellow-tipped green shako plume, and silver sword knot.

31. LIEUTENANT, FOOT ARTILLERY 1823 Full dress. Shako black with black plume, gold lace top band, gilt plate, visor edging, and plume holder, national cockade. Jacket dark blue, collar and cuffs red with gold lace edging, gold lace rank epaulettes, gilt buttons. Trousers white, boots black, black leather belts, slings, and sabretache with gilt fittings. Steel scabbard and hilt with red and gold lace sword knot.

32. TROOPER, HORSE ARTILLERY 1823 Full dress. Black fur busby, brass unit plates and plume holder, yellow cords, green plume with yellow tip, black leather visor. Jacket dark blue, green collar and cuffs with yellow lace edging, shoulder cords yellow, piping to jacket yellow, brass buttons. Chevron on sleeve is yellow with a plain green cockade above it; on the chevron is the legend 'Independencia ou Morte'; such chevrons were worn during the war of independence against Portugal by those troops which supported the Brazilian Emperor. They were worn only on the upper left arm. Trousers white, black leather belts, straps, and sabretache with brass fittings. Steel scabbard and hilt with black grip and sword knot.

33. GUNNER, FOOT ARTILLERY 1827 Campaign dress. Stable cap dark blue with yellow piping. Jacket dark blue with collar, cuffs, and turnbacks red piped yellow, shoulder straps yellow, brass buttons. Trousers

Fig 27   Fig 28   Fig 29   Fig 30   Fig 31

Fig 32   Fig 33   Fig 34   Fig 35

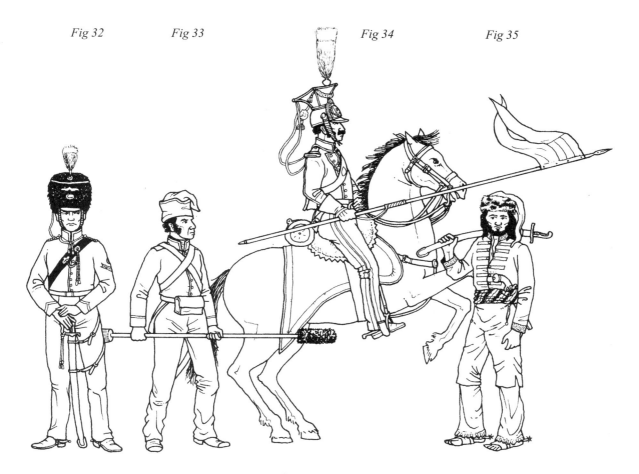

white, black leather boots, belts, and belly pouch, brass hilt to sidearm.

34. TROOPER, GERMAN LANCER REGIMENT 1826 This was one of Brazil's 38 Second Line cavalry units. *Czapka* black leather skull and visor, brass plate, chin-scales, and visor edging, red top, white cords and flounders, brass plume holder (ball), plume green with yellow tip. Jacket blue, collar, turnbacks, and cuffs green, lapels blue. (Ron Poulter's May 1990 *Military Modelling* article on the Battle of Ituzaingo has a colour plate of a German Lancer from the left-hand side, wearing green lapels, which could mean that this illustration shows the lancer with his lapels buttoned back.) Yellow lace on collar, cuffs, lapels, back-seams, and back arm-seams – none on turnbacks, but they have a yellow/gold crown and shield device. Fringeless epaulettes white, brass buttons. Overalls blue with two yellow stripes, white leather straps and belts. Saddle sheepskin black edged in yellow cloth, shabraque blue with green lace edge, and thin yellow outer edge piping. Lance pennon has green top, yellow bottom; top corner has red-black-yellow horizontal bars. On the left arm would have been a chevron (see caption to Figure 32), yellow with green edge and black legend, surmounted by a green rosette.

35. TROOPER, SÃO PAULO MILITIA 1826 Campaign dress. Brown fur cap with blue cloth bag. Jacket blue with collar and cuffs red, collar piped white, chest lace white, silver buttons. Waist-sash white, red, and blue diagonal stripes. Green breeches with black buttons (two at each side of drop-front fly), white linen

undergarment in the style of gaucho *calzoncillos* (see caption to Figure 46). Natural leather belts and straps. Steel scabbard and hilt with dark wood grip. His toeless boots are *bota de potro* (see Figure 21).

36. TROOPER, VOLUNTEER CAVALRY 1826 Campaign dress. Black top hat, green shirt, white trousers, red neckerchief, grey poncho with yellow and blue stripes. Black leather waistbelt. Footwear as Figure 35, steel spurs. Lance pennon has green top, red middle, and yellow bottom. Black hilt to the dagger worn at his back.

37. GAUCHO TROOPER, VOLUNTEER CAVALRY 1826 Campaign dress. Hat grey, shirt white, brown cloth *chiripá*, blue undergarment, green poncho with black stripes. Footwear as Figure 35, steel spurs. Waist-sash red and blue with grey fringe. The *chiripá* is a square of cloth or leather worn around the waist to help protect a rider's legs.

TROOPS OF THE UNITARIOS AND CONFEDERATION ARMIES

The emergence of Rosas as the main power in Argentina was accompanied by a period of colourful uniforms. Green uniforms were not allowed in his army, as this was the colour favoured by his enemies, commonly known as *Unitarios* (Unitarists, or Centralists); red and blue therefore became the two main colours for uniforms worn by troops that supported Rosas, who were commonly known as the Federal or Confederation Army.

Sources for the illustrations in this section were documents in the Archive General of the Nation, Buenos Aires; documents, paintings, and illustrations in the Museo Historico Nacional, Buenos Aires; and plates by Jorge F. Rivas.

38. CORPORAL, *BLANDENGUES* CAVALRY REGIMENT, CONFEDERATION ARMY 1834

Shako black with yellow lace top band, black leather bottom band, white cords and flounders, brass shako plate, chin-scales, cord holder, and visor edging, black leather chinstrap, white plume, national cockade sky blue-white-sky blue, with brass holding strap. Tunic dark blue with collar and cuffs also dark blue, both piped red. Piping to front and bottom of tunic red, pocket piping (under red chest ribbon) red, rank chevron red lace, brass buttons. Waistbelt white leather with brass buckle. Breeches red with thin red piping to side seam, boots black with steel spurs, sword scabbard black leather with brass fittings. Sword hilt brass with black grip, sword sling white leather. Lance natural wood, white sling, pennon red, steel blade and ferrule.

Created on 17 August 1832 from the 2nd Line Cavalry Regiment and the *Guardia Argentina* garrison from Bahia Blanca, the *Blandengues* regiment comprised two squadrons with two companies in each. Its commander was Colonel Martiniano Rodríguez.

39. TRUMPETER, *BLANDENGUES* CAVALRY REGIMENT, CONFEDERATION ARMY 1834

Shako as for Figure 38 except plume and cords are yellow not white. Tunic is red with collar and cuffs also red. Collar, cuffs, and jacket all piped yellow, chest lace also

yellow, brass buttons. Waistbelt white leather with brass buckle. Breeches red with yellow side stripe, boots black, steel spurs. Scabbard black leather with brass fittings, sword hilt brass with black grip, sword slings white leather. Shabraque dark blue with yellow lace edge, same for pistol covers and valise. Horse furniture black leather.

40. CAVALRY OFFICER, *UNITARIOS* ARMY OF GENERAL JOSÉ MARIA PAZ 1832

Black top hat with national coloured ribbon (sky blue over white), gilt badge on front. Shell jacket blue with green collar and cuffs, white piping to jacket, pockets, and collar, gold lace fringeless epaulettes, gilt buttons. White waistcoat, blue trousers with a white stripe and fringe to bottom of trouser leg. White leather belts and slings, steel scabbard with gilt hilt. The core elements of General Paz's army were from the old Republican Army, and included the 2nd and 5th Infantry Battalions and the 2nd Line Cavalry Regiment. Part of the Light Artillery also joined him.

41. LANCER, *UNITARIOS* ARMY OF GENERAL JOSÉ MARIA PAZ 1832

Cap blue with green piping, sweatband sky blue over white. Shell jacket blue with green collar and cuffs, red piping to jacket and collar. White collarless shirt, brown cloth *chiripá*. Natural leather waistbelt with silver buckles and buttons, buff leather soft boots with dark brown straps. He has a silver *facon* or dagger, common to all provincial cattlemen or 'gauchos' even in the 21st century. Note also the *boleadoras* at his waist. Consisting of three stones wrapped in hide and attached to leather thongs that were joined together, this was used to bring down cattle, horses or men by entangling their legs. Lance pennon sky blue

Fig 36 *Fig 37* *Fig 38* *Fig 39* *Fig 40*

Fig 41   Fig 42   Fig 43   Fig 44   Fig 45

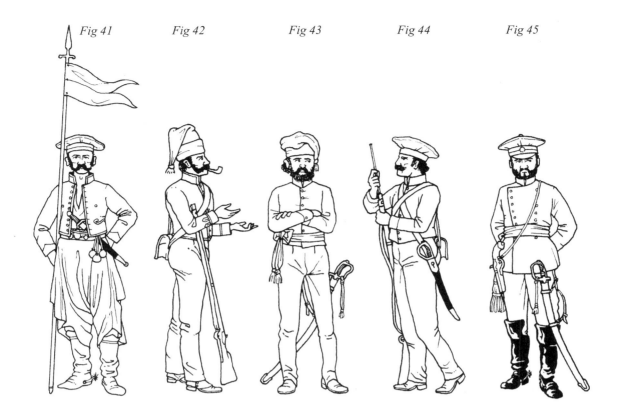

over white. There were two regiments of lancers in Paz's army: the *Lanceros Republicanos*, recruited mainly from Indians; and the *Lanceros Argentinos*. Both had three squadrons.

42. *CAZADORE, UNITARIOS* ARMY OF GENERAL JOSÉ MARIA PAZ 1832 This depicts a private of the *Cazadores de la Libertad*. Formed from the Civic Battalion (*Batallón Cívico*), this unit included free blacks. Stable cap green with white piping and tassel. Shell jacket blue with green collar and cuffs, yellow piping to jacket, collar, and cuffs, yellow cuff lace bars. Trousers blue, boots black, crossbelts white leather with black pouch.

43. AIDE-DE-CAMP, *UNITARIOS* ARMY 1840 This is Colonel José M. Nadal, ADC to General Lavalle. Cap dark blue with red band and gold tassel. Jacket dark blue, collar and cuffs red, gilt buttons. Waist-sash red with gold tassels, trousers white, sword knot white.

44. INFANTRY PRIVATE, LAVALLE'S DIVISION OF *LIBERTORAS, UNITARIOS* ARMY 1840 Cap dark blue, sky blue band. Jacket dark blue, brass buttons. White trousers, crossbelts white leather. General Lavalle's division had five Legions, named after their respective commanders – Vilela, Salvadores, Rico, Méndez, and Torres – with a total of 3,360 men.

45. GENERAL JUAN GALO LAVALLE, *UNITARIOS* ARMY 1840 Cap dark blue, sky blue band with bottom section white (this could be the chinstrap), button on top and badge on front gilt, visor black. Tunic dark blue, collar and cuffs red, gilt buttons. Waist-sash red with gold tassels. Breeches dark blue, red stripe.

Black boots and sword slings. Pistol cord red, sword knot white.

46. LEGION *LIBERTORAS* LANCER, *UNITARIOS* ARMY 1840 Cap blue with sky blue band, visor and chinstrap black leather. Jacket dark blue, collar and cuffs sky blue. *Chiripá* brown cloth, *calzoncillos* white linen, *bota de potro* natural leather. Lance pennon was sky blue over white. *Calzoncillos* were long underpants that were fashionable gaucho wear (see also, for example, Figures 21 and 35 amongst others). Mainly white, they were usually heavily laced around the bottom edge if the wearer had money.

47. STANDARD BEARER, CONFEDERATION ARMY 1840 Carlist-style cap medium blue with red band, gold lace piping and cord with tassel, black leather visor with gilt edge, and gilt chin-scales on a black leather strap. Shell jacket medium blue, collar and cuffs red both with gold lace edging. Jacket is piped red along the front and bottom edge, pocket is piped red, chest ribbon is also red. Mameluke-style trousers and spats red, shoes black. Waistbelt is black leather with gilt plate. Steel sword scabbard with black leather slings, gilt hilt with black grip and red sword knot. The flag is of the type described under Figure 48c. It has a red bow and hangers, while the staff is of natural wood with steel fittings.

48. FLAGS Figure 48a is the provincial flag of Corrientes, 1832. This comprises blue–white–blue horizontal stripes, with a sky blue triangle adjacent to the staff. The flag depicted in 48b was used by the Division *Libertoras* of the *Unitarios* Army in 1840. Its vertical stripes are sky blue–white–sky blue, with a gold sun and rays on the white stripe. This standard can be seen in the

Fig 46 *Fig 47* *Fig 48* *Fig 49*

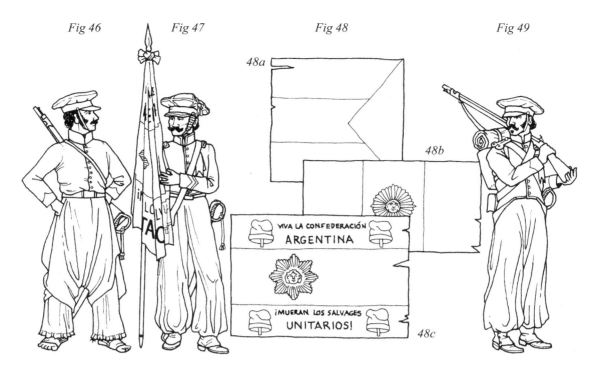

48a

48b

VIVA LA CONFEDERACIÓN ARGENTINA

¡MUERAN LOS SALVAGES UNITARIOS!

48c

Museo Historico Nacional, Buenos Aires. The third flag is of a style used by many units of the Confederation Army during the 1840s. The legend varied, but always expressed the same general sentiments (the flag carried by Figure 47 is of this type). It has medium blue stripes above and below a central white stripe, on which a sun is embroidered in gold lace. The legend is in black, while the Phrygian caps are red.

49. INFANTRY *TIRADOR*, CONFEDERATION ARMY 1840 The *Tiradores* or 'Marksmen' was one of the smaller units raised by Rosas, and was not numbered during the 1840s. Carlist-style cap medium blue with red band, black leather visor with brass edge, brass buttons, and black leather chinstrap. Tunic medium blue, collar and cuffs red, shoulder cords white, piping to jacket red, turnbacks white not piped, brass buttons, red chest ribbon. Mameluke-style trousers and spats red, black shoes. Crossbelts white leather, black leather backpack with white leather straps, medium blue blanket roll. Black leather ammunition pouch and sabre-bayonet scabbard with brass fittings.

50. PRIVATE, BATTALION RETIRO, CONFEDERATION ARMY 1840 *Retiro* were retired veteran troops who had re-enlisted to serve the cause. With the fall of Rosas such units were disbanded and disappeared. Stable cap blue with red piping and tassel. Shell jacket blue with blue collar and cuffs piped in red, front of jacket also piped in red, brass buttons. Trousers blue with a red side stripe, black boots. White leather crossbelts.

51. PRIVATE, BATTALION LIBRES VOLUNTARIOS DE BUENOS AIRES, CONFEDERATION ARMY 1841 Stable cap red with yellow piping and tassel, brass unit badge. Coat red with cuffs and roll-over collar also red, brass buttons. Trousers white, black boots. Waistbelt and crossbelts white leather, sabre-

bayonet scabbard and pouch black leather. Blanket roll dark blue with white straps.

52. PRIVATE, BATTALION RESTAURADOR, CONFEDERATION ARMY 1840 Peaked cap with red top and tassel, dark blue band, black leather visor and chinstrap. Jacket red, collar, cuffs, and turnbacks red with white piping, the collar with a single yellow lace bar with button, white piping to front of jacket, brass buttons. Trousers dark blue with white stripe, black boots. White leather crossbelts. Musket sling is shown as red. This unit was created in 1835.

53. GUNNER, COASTAL ARTILLERY, CONFEDERATION ARMY 1840 Shako black with red cords, plume, and bottom band, gold lace top band, national cockade under plume, brass 'fouled anchor' unit badge, chin-scales, and visor edge. Jacket red with blue collar, cuffs, shoulder boards, and turnbacks, all piped white, front of jacket also piped white. Brass buttons and waistbelt buckle. Red Mameluke-style trousers and spats. Black boots, white crossbelts, straps, and waistbelt, red sidearm knot, black scabbard.

54. SERGEANT, 1st LINE CAVALRY REGIMENT, CONFEDERATION ARMY 1840 Full dress. Shako black with red lace side chevrons, pompom, and bottom band, national cockade under pompom, yellow lace top band, brass shako plate, chin-scales, and visor edging. Jacket red, collar and cuffs red, the collar with a yellow embroidered crossed sword and laurel branch device. Collar piped in dark blue. Turnbacks are dark blue, epaulettes are red with yellow lace edging to board, half-moon, and fringe, front of jacket piped dark blue, brass buttons and buckles. Rank lace on forearm is yellow on a backing of red cloth. Waistbelt loop to either side of jacket red piped dark blue. Trousers white with a wide red stripe. Black boots and steel spurs, white leather straps and belts. Scabbard steel with brass fittings, hilt brass with black grip and red sword knot. Lance pennon red. Shabraque and valise red with yellow lace trim and sword and laurel branch device. Brown leather pistol holsters under flaps. Black harness etc.

55. TROOPER, 6th LINE CAVALRY REGIMENT, CONFEDERATION ARMY 1840

The 6th was a cuirassier regiment. Stable cap red with yellow lace, tassel, and regimental number on front. Blouse red, collar and cuffs red. Steel cuirass with brass rivets and shoulder straps. (Some units were issued with cuirasses made from leather more than a quarter of an inch thick.) Black leather sword slings and cuirass waistbelt with brass buckle showing unit number. *Chiripá* dark blue with yellow piping, white *calzoncillos*, natural leather boots. Steel spurs and scabbard, brass hilt, white sword knot.

56. TROOPER, *MONTE CAZADORES*, CONFEDERATION ARMY 1840

Units of light cavalry were raised in the 1830s. Stable cap red top piped yellow with a yellow bottom band and tassel. Jacket red, collar and cuffs red, no piping on cuffs. Collar has a yellow embroidered flaming grenade and piping. Jacket has yellow piping to front and bottom edge, a yellow lace loop on both sides of chest, brass buttons. *Chiripá* red, white linen *calzoncillos*, natural leather *bota de potro*, steel spurs. Steel scabbard with brass fittings, brass hilt with black grip. The red ribbon on his chest denotes he is a supporter of Rosas.

Note the horse-whip hanging from his right hand, typically carried by gauchos. Various designs appear, this particular one consisting of a wristband, then a length of leather filled with sand that could be used as a blackjack, and at the end a flat leather strap with which to whip his horse while breaking it in.

57. TROOPER, PALERMO LANCERS, CONFEDERATION ARMY 1840

The Palermo Lancers were a volunteer cavalry unit commanded by Colonel Juan José Hernández. Very loyal to Rosas, they fought at the Battle of Caseros. Carlist-style cap red with black-and-white fringed tassel. Shell jacket dark blue with collar, cuffs, and shoulder bars in red, no piping, brass buttons. Red ribbon on chest. Waistcoat red with brass buttons. Overalls white with red cloth half-boots, black boots, steel spurs. Scabbard steel with brass fittings, brass hilt with red sword knot. Lance pennon red, lance strap white leather. Another picture shows the red pennon having a yellow skull and crossed bones with an illegible legend embroidered in black above and below.

58. INFANTRY SERGEANT, CONFEDERATION ARMY 1842

Taken from a plate depicting the Battle of Arroyo Grande. Shako black, red cords, plume, and ball plus bottom band, yellow lace top band, brass plate, chin-scales, and visor edge. Jacket dark blue, collar, cuffs, and turnbacks red, turnbacks piped white, front of jacket piped red, brass buttons. Shoulder straps and wings red, wings with gold lace rank stripes. Diagonal rank stripes on the forearm are gold lace on a red cloth base that shows as edging. Red ribbon on chest. Trousers white. Privates wore same uniform without the rank insignia.

59. SAPPER, BATTALION GUARDIA ARGENTINA, CONFEDERATION ARMY 1843

Full dress. Busby is black fur with red bag piped yellow, white feather plume with red tip, brass skull badge. Tunic medium blue with collar, cuffs, and epaulettes red, collar and cuffs piped white, front of tunic piped red, brass buttons; the yellow/gold lace cuff bars show that this is an elite unit. Arm badge of two crossed axes in red cloth.

Fig 50   *Fig 51*   *Fig 53*   *Fig 54*

Fig 52

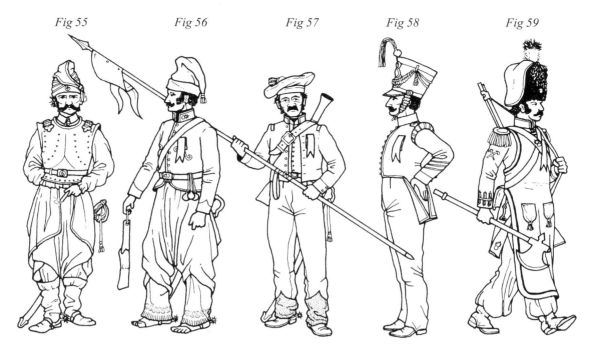

Fig 55   Fig 56   Fig 57   Fig 58   Fig 59

White turnbacks with yellow flaming grenade but no piping, turnback pockets piped red. Red ribbon on chest. Mameluke-style trousers red with red spats and black shoes. Apron is white cloth/leather with red pockets and black piping about an inch from the edge. Sidearm is in a black leather scabbard with brass fittings and hilt. Crossbelts white leather with brass flaming grenade, axe pouch black leather. Axe shaft has a brass ferrule. Service dress was the same except for medium blue Mameluke trousers and spats, plus a brown fur backpack with a medium blue roll, backpack straps all of white leather. Daily or garrison dress also the same except for the Mameluke trousers and spats being white, the epaulettes being replaced by shoulder straps in medium blue piped red, and the busby being replaced by a cloth stable cap in medium blue piped red, apparently with a long flap wound around the top.

In 1840 this battalion was composed of seven sappers, 16 sergeants of the band, 32 musicians, 22 sergeants of fusiliers, five sergeants of grenadiers, 64 grenadiers, and 254 fusiliers, under the command of General Mariano Benito Rolón.

60. DRUMMER, BATTALION GUARDIA ARGEN-TINA, CONFEDERATION ARMY 1843 Full dress. Shako black, yellow top and bottom bands, white plume with red tip, brass plume holder, shako plate, chin-scales, and edging to black leather visor. National cockade dark blue-white-dark blue, cords and flounders red. Tunic medium blue with red collar, cuffs, turnbacks, and piping to front of tunic and back pockets, collar piped white, yellow flaming grenade on turnbacks. Fringeless epaulettes are white with red piping to the board. Chest and arm lace yellow, red chest ribbon, brass buttons. Trousers and spats white, black shoes. Drum brass with red top and bottom bands, white cords, white leather tighteners and belts. Brass waistbelt buckle and drumstick holder. Apron is jaguar skin.

61 & 62. MUSICIANS, BATTALION GUARDIA

ARGENTINA, CONFEDERATION ARMY 1843 Figure 61 is in parade dress. Medium blue stable cap piped red. Medium blue shell jacket piped red with red collar and cuffs piped white, medium blue shoulder straps piped red, three rows of brass buttons. White Mameluke-style trousers and spats with black shoes. Brass trumpet with red cords. White waistbelt with brass buckle. In full dress a shako as described for Figure 60 was worn, plus a tunic in medium blue with red collar and cuffs piped white, turnbacks white piped red, lapels white piped red, fringed epaulettes white with red piping to board, brass buttons, red chest ribbon, white stock, red Mameluke-style trousers and spats, and black shoes.

Figure 62 is in daily or garrison dress. He wears a stable cap like that described for Figure 61, but here folded in a different fashion. The shell jacket is white piped red, collar and cuffs are red piped white, single row of brass chest buttons. Trousers are white with a red side stripe, black boots. White leather waistbelt with brass fittings and sidearm hilt, black leather scabbard with brass fittings.

63. CORPORAL, BATTALION GUARDIA ARGEN-TINA, CONFEDERATION ARMY 1843 Full dress. Bearskin black fur, bag red with yellow piping, white plume with red tip, national cockade under plume dark blue-white-dark blue, brass flaming grenade badge. Tunic medium blue, collar and cuffs red piped white, fringed epaulettes all red, red piping to front and bottom of tunic and turnback pocket, brass buttons. Cuffs have three yellow 'elite' lace bars. Turnbacks are white, not piped, with a yellow flaming grenade badge. Rank lace from seam to seam on left forearm is yellow with red edging. Red chest ribbon. Mameluke-style trousers and spats red, black shoes. Bayonet and sidearm scabbards black leather with brass fittings, crossbelts white leather with brass ornaments, black leather pouch. Rifle sling white leather. Service dress was the same except for the Mameluke-style trousers and spats being medium blue not red. Daily or garrison dress comprised a Carlist-style

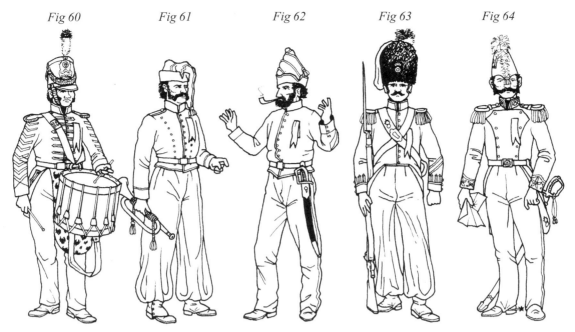

Fig 60 *Fig 61* *Fig 62* *Fig 63* *Fig 64*

cap in medium blue with red band, piping, cord, and tassel; a medium blue shell jacket, collar and cuffs red piped white, the cuffs with three yellow lace elite bars, red piping to jacket front and bottom, shoulder straps medium blue piped red; white Mameluke-style trousers and spats; and black shoes. Equipment same as service or full dress.

64. COLONEL, BATTALION GUARDIA ARGENTINA, CONFEDERATION ARMY 1843 Full dress. Bicorne black felt with white feathers and gold lace tassels and cockade holding cords, gilt button. Tunic medium blue, collar red with gold lace trim, cuffs medium blue with gold lace trim, lapels and turnbacks

white without piping, the turnbacks with a flaming grenade in gold lace and pockets piped red, gilt buttons. Epaulettes have a gold bullion fringe with board in silver lace with gold lace edge, holding strap silver lace. Red chest ribbon. Waist-sash red with gold lace tassels, waistbelt red with two thin gold stripes, gilt buckle. Trousers white with gold lace side stripe, black shoes with gilt spurs. Sword scabbard black leather with gilt fittings.

65. OFFICER, BATTALION GUARDIA ARGENTINA, CONFEDERATION ARMY 1843 Full dress. Shako black, gold lace top band, cords, and flounders, gilt plume holder, shako plate, and chin-scales, national

Fig 65 *Fig 66* *Fig 67* *Fig 68* *Fig 69*

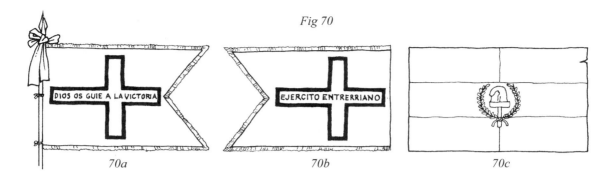

Fig 70

70a   70b   70c

cockade under plume holder dark blue-white-dark blue, white plume with red tip. Tunic as described for Figure 64 with these differences: collar and cuffs red piped white, collar with two gold lace bars; gold lace fringed epaulettes, not bullion, with medium blue holding strap; gilt buttons and gorget. Trousers medium blue with gold lace side stripe, black shoes.

Daily dress comprised a Carlist-style cap in medium blue with red band edged in gold lace, red piping, gold lace cord and tassel. Shell jacket medium blue piped red, collar and cuffs red, collar piped white with gold lace bars, cuffs with gold lace, gilt buttons, red chest ribbon. Waistcoat red with gilt buttons. Waistbelt black with gilt 'S' buckle. Trousers white, black shoes. Steel scabbard with gilt fittings, black sword slings, gilt sword hilt with black grip and gilt wire.

66. GENERAL ANGEL PACHECO, CONFEDER-ATION ARMY 1845 This depicts General Pacheco as he appeared at the Battle of San Cala. Cap has a white top, gold lace band, black leather visor, gilt chin-scales and bosses. Coat dark blue, collar and cuffs red edged in gold lace, chest lace silver, gilt buttons, epaulettes gold bullion, chest ribbon red. Crimson waist-sash, white trousers, steel sword scabbard with black leather slings.

67. OFFICER, CAVALRY REGIMENT 'ESCORTA LIBERTAD', CONFEDERATION ARMY 1845 Parade dress. Shako black, red plume, gold lace top band, black leather bottom band, red cords, gilt shako plate and chin-scales, black leather visor with silver metal edge. Jacket red, collar and cuffs blue with gold lace, the collar also piped red, gold lace epaulettes. Jacket piped blue, gilt buttons, red chest ribbon. Breeches blue with red stripe, black boots, gold lace sword knot, steel scabbard.

68. ARTILLERY OFFICER, CONFEDERATION ARMY 1845 Shako black, gold lace top and bottom bands, gilt shako plate and chin-scales, black leather visor with gilt metal edge. Tunic red piped white, cuffs and collar blue, the cuffs with gold lace, collar piped white, gilt buttons, red chest ribbon. Fringeless epaulettes gold with red holding strap and lining cloth underneath. Waistcoat red with gold lace and gilt buttons. Overalls blue with red stripe. Steel scabbard, gold lace sword knot.

69. LANCER OF THE ARMY OF URQUIZA 1850 Cap all red. Blouse red with blue collar and pocket flaps, cuffs red with blue piping. Red neckerchief, red cloth *chiripá*, white linen *calzoncillos*, natural leather *bota de*

potro boots, white leather belts and slings. Lance pennon sky blue-white-sky blue.

70. FLAGS Figures 70a and 70b show both sides of the personal standard of General Urquiza as carried at the Battle of Caseros. The field is red silk, while the central cross is red with a black lace border, and bears the legends DIOS OS GUIE A LA VICTORIA on one side and EJERCITO ENTRERRIANO on the other, embroidered in black. The fringe is of gold lace, and the bow is red. Figure 70c is the flag of General Urquiza's army. The central stripe is white, while the stripes at top and bottom are sky blue on the left and red on the right. The central design is a red liberty cap on a deep red staff surrounded by two green laurel branches.

THE IMPERIAL BRAZILIAN ARMY 1864–70

The forces mobilised by the Brazilian Empire for the Paraguayan War fell into three major categories. First there was the regular army, which, even after mobilisation and expansion, remained relatively small. The second, and largest, element consisted of the *Guarda Nacional* or National Guard, which was mobilised en masse in 1865 and continued to expand throughout the war, though many of its units served behind the lines on garrison and line-of-communications duties. The third category was a separate corps of volunteers, the *Voluntários da Pátria* ('Volunteers for the Fatherland'), which was formed to draw in men not otherwise liable for service in existing units. The *Voluntários* proved an unqualified success, eventually providing more manpower than the regular army.

THE REGULAR ARMY

E.C. Jourdan (1893) provides the following figures for the Brazilian regular army as it stood in 1864:

Staff Corps officers	511
1 x Engineer battalion	4 companies
1 x Horse Artillery regiment	6 companies
4 x Foot Artillery battalions	32 companies
1 x Foot Artillery corps	4 companies
1 x Foot Artillery corps	2 companies
4 x Companies of pioneers	4 companies
1 x Corps of pioneers	2 companies
5 x Cavalry regiments	40 companies
16 x Infantry battalions	128 companies

1 x Garrison/Depot infantry battalion 6 companies
1 x Infantry corps   6 companies
5 x Infantry corps   20 companies
4 x Infantry corps   8 companies
2 x Infantry companies   2 companies

In all there were 1,733 officers (including 12 sub-lieutenants at school and the 511 Staff Corps officers) and 15,091 other ranks.

At the beginning of the Paraguayan War the regular army comprised 14 infantry battalions, five cavalry regiments (each of three companies totalling 618 men), four battalions of Foot Artillery (each of eight companies totalling 690 men), and a detached Corps of Horse Artillery (of four companies totalling 557 men). The engineering branch comprised an 'Imperial Corps of Engineers' formed of trained engineer officers, a 'Battalion of Engineers' (of four companies) to provide trained manpower, and an 'Artificer Corps' of technical specialists. The various support services tended to be rather rudimentary, neither numerous nor well organised, though a squadron of Train was raised in 1865.

Of the infantry battalions, the 1st–7th were designated *Fusileiros* (line or heavy infantry), and the 8th–14th *Caçadores* (light infantry). Barroso notes that the 1842 regulations established a *Fusileiro* battalion at eight companies (no elite companies) totalling 882 men, and a *Caçador* battalion at six companies totalling 552 men; since no subsequent changes are noted I assume this establishment continued in use.

In addition to all of the above, there were various small units designated as 'Garrison' or 'Fixed' corps. Due to the shortage of regular troops many of these had been raised and maintained by the various provinces, and often had only the most tenuous connection with the regular army. Initially they were known by a variety of names – *Pedestres*, *Ligeiros*, *Caçadores de Montanha*, etc – and served a variety of functions as local garrison troops, gendarmerie or police agents, customs agents, guards of various sorts, and so on. During the 1850s the Federal Government began a general reform of these semi-independent corps, drawing them increasingly under army control and progressively reorganising them as auxiliary units of the regular army. Their foot units were generally redesignated as *Caçadores*, their old designations being officially abolished. During the early days of the Paraguayan War a number of these auxiliary corps did valuable service in resisting Paraguayan invasion forces until the army could be mobilised, but following the official declaration of war the 'Fixed Corps' were ordered to be abolished and incorporated into the regular army.

The disbanded 'Fixed Corps' provided much of the manpower for the army expansion which followed the declaration of war almost immediately. The infantry was expanded to 14 numbered battalions, of which the first seven remained *Fusileiros* while the remainder were designated *Caçadores*. Of the cavalry, the 1st Regiment was slated to remain at Court throughout the war to guard the Emperor; the 2nd and 3rd were immediately mobilised to join the field forces; and the 4th and 5th were ordered to be broken up and used as a nucleus for the formation of five new corps of *Caçadores a Cavalaria* ('Mounted Rifles'), each of four companies with 638 men. The Corps of Horse Artillery was to provide a cadre for the raising of a second Provisional Corps, while the Foot Artillery was to be augmented by a fifth battalion. The Corps of Engineers remained basically unchanged but at a higher establishment.

At the outbreak of war the army was still wearing the uniforms established by the dress regulations of 7 August 1852. For the *Fusileiros*, this consisted of a rather low 'Yeoman-crowned' shako and a single-breasted dark blue coatee for full dress, with a dark blue tunic and kepi for the 'second uniform' worn for daily and service dress. The *Caçador* battalions wore similar uniforms but with the base colour dark green instead of blue, and generally somewhat simpler and plainer in style. All battalions were distinguished by battalion-coloured facings worn on the collar and cuffs, according to the following scheme:

	Collar	Cuffs
Fusileiros		
1st Battalion	white	yellow
2nd Battalion	yellow	light blue
3rd Battalion	red	yellow
4th Battalion	light blue	red
5th Battalion	red	light blue
6th Battalion	yellow	red
7th Battalion	light blue	yellow
Caçadores		
8th Battalion	yellow	white
9th Battalion	red	red
10th Battalion	dark green	dark green
11th Battalion	dark green	red
12th Battalion	yellow	yellow
13th Battalion	yellow	dark green
14th Battalion	dark green	yellow

All piping for Fusiliers was red, with brass buttons; and for *Caçadores* black, with bronzed buttons.

In the same year, 1852, the 7th Fusilier Battalion was disbanded for mutiny, the 8th Battalion was renumbered as the 7th, and all the *Caçador* battalions were moved up by one number, the vacant number 14 being taken up by an existing German volunteer battalion, which was moved onto the line establishment. The limited evidence available would seem to suggest that the battalions retained their existing distinctive colours (thus the new 7th Battalion would have continued to wear the distinctions it had formerly worn as the 8th, etc), but it's not clear what distinctions were adopted by the new 14th Battalion.

Winter trousers matched the upper garment, therefore dark blue for Fusiliers (except for the 1st Battalion, which was uniquely authorised to wear blue-grey) and dark green for the *Caçadores*, worn over short black gaiters. Pictures occasionally show red piping down the outer seams of Fusilier trousers, though it's unclear to what extent this was worn. For summer wear both trousers and gaiters were of white linen or cotton. Belts were to be white for Fusiliers and black for *Caçadores*. See the figure captions for further details.

Following the expansion of the army for war service, it was decided to modify and simplify uniforms, the modifications being spelled out in Decree No.3,620 of 28 February 1866. Full dress coatees were abolished and replaced by the undress tunic for all orders of dress,

Illustration by Jorge H. Fernández Rivas depicting Brazilian officers in daily dress uniforms. The first has a white-covered kepi, a plain blue tunic with only gold cuff lace and gilt buttons, light brown trousers tucked into black canvas gaiters, black shoes, a white waistbelt over a crimson waist-sash, and a steel sword scabbard. The second figure wears a shorter style tunic with red piping down the front, red cuff flaps and cuffs, and gold rank lace above the red cuff piping. The collar has red patches and piping, the shoulder bars are blue with a gold lace edge, and the buttons are gilt. His kepi has a white cover, and his trousers are also white. The boots are black, the holster, water bottle and strap are brown leather, and the waistbelt and sword slings are white leather, the former with a gilt buckle. The sword hilt is gilt and the scabbard steel. The third figure is depicted in summer dress. He has a white-covered kepi with neck curtain, and light brown tunic and trousers, the tunic having red piping down the front and on the cuffs and cuff flaps. His gold lace rank lace is positioned above and below the cuff piping. The collar has a red patch and piping, and the fringeless epaulettes have a blue board edged in red with gilt half-moons and buttons. His waist sash is red with a gold lace toggle and red fringe. The waistbelt and sword slings are black leather, the scabbard steel, and the sword hilt gilt with a gold lace knot. Shoes are black. The last figure has a blue kepi with a white band and red piping, a gold lace unit badge and strap, and a black visor. His gilt-buttoned frock coat is blue, the collar having red patches and piping. The cuffs, cuff flaps, and front opening are also piped red, the blue shoulder bars have gold lace edging, and the gold rank lace on his cuffs consists of two rows below the piping and a third above it. Waistcoat and trousers are white, shoes black. (Author's collection)

while the shako was retained for parade and ceremonial wear but was seldom seen during the war, being replaced on most occasions by the undress kepi. The *Caçadores'* green uniforms were abolished and replaced by dark blue, virtually identical to those of the Fusiliers. The various battalion distinctions were also abolished at this time and replaced by branch of service-coloured piping edging the tunic, the kepi, and the outer seams of the trousers; this was red for the *Fusileiros* and yellow for the *Caçadores*, the Fusiliers having in addition a red, roughly square-shaped patch on either side of the collar front (missing from *Caçador* uniforms). The various types of epaulettes formerly worn were simplified (exact details are somewhat obscure), being replaced by plain dark blue shoulder-straps piped with branch of service colour for daily and service dress.

A number of new items of dress were also introduced, including a barracks cap of French *bonnet de police* form for fatigue wear, which seems to have been widely worn on campaign during the war. Two entirely new uniforms introduced at this time were a summer/tropical uniform entirely of white duck, and a fatigue/working uniform of a light brown duck or sailcloth. Both were usually piped and trimmed with branch colour in much the same fashion as the woollen uniform. Gaiters were abolished.

Once on campaign, dress regulations tended to go by the board and a wide variety of outfits were worn, resulting in various unauthorised combinations of regulation and civilian items of dress and a wide range of field improvisations. Felt slouch hats became extremely popular, along with straw hats, the kepi (sometimes privately purchased and of non-regulation form), and the barracks cap. White cotton covers were widely worn over the kepi, sometimes with neck curtains (Barroso mentions cases of units dyeing these cotton covers in various colours as unit distinctions, but, unfortunately, quotes no examples). As a general rule, units of the 1st Army Corps of General Osōrio tended to wear the kepi, while those of the 2nd Army Corps of the Conde de Pôrto Alegre are said to have generally worn the slouch hat.

Footgear was equally varied, many preferring high-shafted marching boots, while perennial shortages of army boots led to widespread use of sandals and canvas *espadrilles*, or bare feet if no footwear could be acquired. Civilian coats or trousers were not uncommon replacements for worn-out uniform items. Bad weather gear would include ponchos, ordinary blankets wrapped around the body, or overcoats made of duck or sailcloth, in addition to the regulation dark blue woollen greatcoat (which seems to have been in rather short supply anyway). Gaucho-style clothing had a considerable vogue, though it seems to have been more common in mounted units, particularly those from the province of Rio Grande do Sul, where it was the normal style of dress.

In the field of armament, variety seems to have also been the rule. The most that can be stated with any degree of certainty is that most infantry carried muzzle-loading percussion arms of a wide variety or makes. Enfield and Belgian Liège-made arms seem to have been particularly common. The Fusiliers were theoretically armed with long muskets and socket bayonets, although various rifled Minié arms became their standard weapon as the war progressed. At the beginning of the conflict a decision was made to use only 14.66 mm bullets, and all of the Army's Enfield rifles were returned to the arsenal in Rio de Janeiro to be re-rifled to the correct size. The *Caçadores* carried shorter rifled *carabines* with sabre-bayonets and had trumpeters in place of drummers. The 15th *Caçadores* were armed with 'German breech-loaders' (900 Dreyse needle-guns were bought), but threw them away and picked up Minié rifles dropped by casualties from other Brazilian units during the attack on the Cierva redoubt on 18 February 1868.

The *Voluntários da Pátria*

Although Brazil had a large National Guard, Brazilian law stated that its individual provincial units could only be used beyond the national boundary when their respective provinces were attacked by outside forces. The Paraguayan invasion of the states of Mato Grosso and Rio Grande do Sul therefore meant that only these two provinces could send National Guard units to assist the Brazilian Army. As a result the call went out for volunteers to reinforce the army in the field, who were formed into battalions known as *Voluntários da Pátria*. The following *Corpo de Voluntários da Pátria* ('CVP') were created during the course of the war:

1st CVP: Commanded by Lieutenant-Colonel Carlos Betbeze de Oliveira Nery. Was at the siege of Uruguayana.

2nd CVP: Commanded by Major Campos Mello.

3rd CVP: Commanded by Lieutenant-Colonel Rocha Galvão. Was at the siege of Uruguayana.

4th CVP: Commanded by Lieutenant-Colonel Francisco Pinheiro Guimarães. Saw action at Uruguayana and guarded the prisoners taken there.

5th CVP: Commanded by Lieutenant-Colonel Augusto Francisco Caldas. At the siege of Uruguayana.

6th CVP: Commanded by Major S. Valente. Disbanded on 12 December 1868.

7th CVP: Raised in São Paolo. This was the first of all the CVP battalions to become ready for war.

8th CVP: On 20 July 1867 was in the 12th Infantry Brigade with the 39th and 51st CVP.

9th CVP: Raised in Pôrto Alegre. Commanded by Lieutenant-Colonel J. Bueno. Later became the 39th CVP.

10th CVP: Raised in the province of Bahia, mainly from the Police Corps. Commanded by Lieutenant-Colonel D'Araujo. Disbanded by the Marquis of Caxias on 23 December 1868 due to losses but reformed in 1870 as the 41st CVP with other volunteers from Bahia.

11th CVP: Commanded by Major J. Cavalcante. Became the 42nd CVP in November 1866.

12th CVP: Raised in the province of Rio de Janerio, mainly from the Military Police of Niteroi. Commanded by Major Floriano Vieira Peixoto. Became the 44th CVP in December 1866.

13th CVP: Recruited from elements of the Pará Military Police and National Guard.

14th CVP: Raised in the province of Bahia.

15th CVP: Raised in the province of Bahia. Later became the 45th CVP.

16th CVP: Raised in the province of Goiás. Fought alongside the 17th CVP in Mato Grosso commanded by Major Manoel Batista Ribeiro de Faria, who died of malaria 10 June 1866; replaced by Major do Corpo. Another CVP unit initially given the same number was later given the title of 16th *Corpo de Voluntários Auxiliar*. The latter was raised in Montevideo, was sometimes called the *Batalhão dos Garibaldinos* (Battalion Garibaldi), and later became the 48th CVP.

17th CVP: Raised in Ouro Preto, the capital of the province of Minas Gerais, on 18 February 1865, this contained elements drawn from the Police Corps. It was initially called the 1st *Corpo de Voluntários Mineiros*, before becoming the 17th CVP on 27 April 1865. Colonel Carlos de Morais Camisão was given command on 3 June. It was in one of the two columns that saw service in the Mato Grosso campaign. With the death of Colonel Camisão in 1867 Lieutenant-Colonel Antonio Eneas Gustavo Galvão took command. He was succeeded in late 1868 by Major (Lieutenant-Colonel) José Maria Borges, and the unit participated in the advance to Asunción. Brigaded with the 40th and 53rd CVP on 27 January 1870 by the Conde de d'Eu. This brigade was despatched home on 3 February 1870; a week later the 17th is listed as having 34 officers and 460 men.

18th CVP: Raised in the town of Outro Preto, this consisted of elements drawn from the Police Corps, National Guard, and volunteers from the town and district of Uberado in the north of the province. Initially called the 2nd *Corpo de Voluntários Mineiros* and under the command of Lieutenant-Colonel Antonio Martins do Amorim Rangel, changing its title to the 18th CVP on 27 April 1865. Placed in the 2nd Army Corps under the command of Baron de Pôrto Alegre, this unit was sent back to Santa Catarina, Brazil, on 13 August 1867.

19th CVP: Organised from elements of the Police Corps from the provinces of Ceará and Sergipe, with an additional company from the Police Corps of Piauí. Commanded by Lieutenant-Colonel Domingos José da Costa Pereira. Placed in the 1st Army Corps under the command of General Osõrio. Disbanded on 20 December 1866, its troops being transferred to the 50th CVP.

20th CVP: Raised in the town of Maceió, capital of the province of Alagoas, from elements of the Police Corps, National Guard, and volunteers. Commanded by Lieutenant-Colonel Carlos Cirilo de Castro, in September 1865 it consisted of 39 officers and 345 men, forming part of 1st Army Corps. Disbanded on 20 December 1866, its men being used to reinforce the 52nd CVP.

21st CVP: Raised in the town of Paraíba, capital of the province of Paraíba do Norte, from elements of the National Guard and volunteers from the interior of the province. Part of 1st Army Corps. Disbanded by General Osõrio on 9 August 1865 at the Aiui-Chico camp. A second unit with this number was formed by General Osõrio at the Tala-Cora camp in 1866 from various contingents of volunteers, the bulk coming from Pernambuco. This was commanded by Major Genuino Olimpio de Sampaio, and later by Major A.J. Bacellar.

22nd CVP: Raised in São Luís, the capital of Maranhão province, from National Guard units and volunteers. 1st Army Corps. Disbanded by General Osõrio on 17 July 1865 at the Juqueri-Grande camp. A second unit issued with this number, commanded by Lieutenant-Colonel Albuquerque, was organised by General Osõrio at the Tala-Cora camp on 1 March 1866, and disbanded by Marshal Polidoro da Fonseca at the camp of Tuiuti on 1 August.

23rd CVP: Raised in Salvador, capital of the province of Bahia, from elements of the National Guard. 2nd Army Corps. Disbanded by Baron de Pôrto Alegre at the Vila de São Borja camp on 1 January 1866. A second unit of the same number, ex 1st *Corpo de Voluntários da Corte*, was raised in the Corte do Rio de Janerio in 1868, and placed in the 10th Infantry Brigade on 27 April. Initially commanded by Colonel Mena Barreto, replaced by Major João Pinto Homem due to promotion that year, it consisted of 50 officers and 687 men in 1868. Along with the 35th and 53rd CVP battalions took part in the expedition to San Pedro in May 1869. Its strength in April 1869 was 39 officers and 541 men. Major Augusto Rodrigues Chaves took command in 1869 after Major Homem was wounded at Tupium on 30 May. On 8 March 1870, at Montevideo, unit strength stood at 48 officers and 463 men.

24th CVP: Raised in Salvador, Bahia, from National Guard units from the interior, notably the towns of Lencois and Santa Isabel. 2nd Army Corps. Commanded by Captain Valporto. Disbanded on 23 December 1868 between the two battles for Lomas Valentinas.

25th CVP: Commanded by Major Afonso José de Almeida Côrte Real in December 1867. Disbanded 23 December 1868.

26th CVP: Raised in the province of Ceará. Commanded by Lieutenant-Colonel Figueira de Mello. Disbanded by the Marquis of Caxias on 12 December 1868 after the Battle of Avay, where it was commanded by brevet Major (*Comandante*) Domingo Alves Barreto Leite (promoted full major 20 February 1869), its surviving 376 men being used to strengthen the 1st Line Battalion and the 34th CVP. Reformed on 8 March 1870 by the Conde d'Eu, and command given to Lieutenant-Colonel Antonio Tiburcio Ferreira de Souza. On 15 March 1870 consisted of 45 officers and 437 men.

27th CVP: Ex 4th *Corpo de Voluntários da Corte do Rio de Janerio*, raised in Rio de Janerio. Became 27th CVP on 27 November 1866, commanded by Colonel Hermes Esnesto da Fonseca. On 6 January 1870 he was given command of the 7th Infantry Brigade (10th and 16th Line Battalions and 27th CVP) and was replaced by Major (later Lieutenant-Colonel) José Maria Ferreira de Assuncão. On 12 February 1869 this unit contained 35 officers and 409 men; on 6 April 1870 it contained 30 officers and 412 men.

28th CVP: Commanded in December 1867 by Major José Clarindo de Queirós. Placed in the 10th Infantry Brigade on 27 April 1868. Disbanded after the Battle of Avay, 12 December 1868.

29th CVP: In September 1867 placed in the 11th Infantry Brigade with the 11th Line Battalion and the 29th, 32nd, 37th, 43rd, and 47th CVP battalions. Disbanded 23 December 1868.

30th CVP: Raised in the province of Pernambuco. Commanded by Major Apolinario Florentino de Albuquerque Maranhão, on 5 January 1869 this battalion was placed in the 6th Infantry Brigade. Later part of the Auxiliary Brigade based in Asunción (6th and 13th Line Battalions and 30th CVP, a total of 1,599 men of whom 403 were from the 30th).

31st CVP: In 1868 was in the 7th Infantry Brigade with the 39th and 55th CVP battalions. Commanded by Colonel Machado da Costa.

32nd CVP: In September 1867 placed in the 11th Infantry Brigade with the 11th Line Battalion and the 29th, 37th, 43rd, and 47th CVP battalions. Disbanded 23 December 1868.

33rd CVP: Raised in Rio Grande do Sul, commanded by Lieutenant-Colonel Francisco Agnelo de Souza Valente. Disbanded 23 December 1868.

34th CVP: In December 1867 commanded by Captain José de Almeida Barreto. Reinforced with men from 26th CVP on 12 December 1868 after the Battle of Avay, but disbanded on the 23rd.

35th CVP: Took part in the expedition to San Pedro in May 1869 with the 11th Line Battalion, 23rd and 53rd CVP, and the 11th, 18th, 19th, and 21st *Corpos Provisorios de Cavalaria*.

36th CVP: Commanded by Major Francisco Manuel da Cunha junior in December 1867, when it was placed in the 9th Infantry Brigade with the 6th Line Battalion and the 43rd, 44th, and 49th CVP. Disbanded 23 December 1868 between the two battles for Lomas Valentinas.

37th CVP: In September 1867 placed in the 11th Infantry Brigade with the 11th Line Battalion and the 29th, 32nd, 43rd, and 47th CVP battalions. Commanded by Lieutenant-Colonel Fernando Machado. Disbanded 9 March 1868.

38th CVP: Commanded by Lieutenant-Colonel Freire de Carvaiho. Disbanded 23 December 1868.

39th CVP: Organised in the province of Piauí based on a core of men from the disbanded 9th CVP.

Commanded by Major Antonio Pedro Heitor, replaced in 1867 by Lieutenant-Colonel José de Oliveira Bueno (promoted Colonel 31 January 1868). On 20 July 1867 this unit was placed in the 12th Brigade with the 8th and 51st CVP battalions. 30 September saw Lieutenant-Colonel Tome Fernandes Medeiros de Castro placed in command. In the 7th Infantry Brigade with the 31st and 55th CVP battalions in 1868. 1st Army Corps. At the Battle of Avay the battalion was commanded by Major João Teodoro Pereira de Mello. Disbanded by the Marquis of Caxias on 23 December 1868, 179 men being sent as reinforcements to the 50th CVP.

40th CVP: Raised in the province of Bahia. Incorporated into the 2nd Infantry Brigade, 2nd Army Corps, in January 1869, when it was commanded by Major João da Gama Lobo Bentes Juvenis and comprised 39 officers and 574 men. In April 1869, commanded by Colonel Antonio Augusto de Barros e Vasconcelos, it was placed in the 3rd Infantry Brigade, its strength standing at 36 officers and 670 men. Brigaded with the 17th and 53rd CVP on 27 January 1870 by the Conde de d'Eu. On 31 January command passed to Lieutenant-Colonel Pedro Jaime Lisboa. On its passage home on 10 February 1870 the 40th consisted of 37 officers and 457 men.

41st CVP: Created by the Conde d'Eu on 13 March 1870 from men of the old 10th CVP and replacements from Bahia. Commanded by Lieutenant-Colonel Joaquim Mauricio Ferreira (ex-commander of the Military Police in Bahia). On 14 April 1870 it consisted of 45 officers and 514 men, having lost 82 killed and 244 wounded in one month. Lieutenant-Colonel Antonio da Silva Paranhos was its final commander.

42nd CVP: Ex 11th CVP. Raised in the province of Pernambuco and commanded by Colonel Antonio Gomes Leal. Renumbered the 42nd CVP in November 1866, it was disbanded by the Marquis of Caxias on 12 December 1868 after the Battle of Avay, its troops being dispersed into the 46th and 54th CVP. Reformed 13 January 1870, commanded by Captain (later Major) João Capispara de Aguiar Montarroyos and, later, by Major José do Rego Barros, when its strength stood at 41 officers and 418 men.

43rd CVP: Raised in the province of Bahia. Commanded by Lieutenant-Colonel Manoel Jeronimo Ferreira. Placed in the 9th Infantry Brigade with the 45th CVP battalion on 30 June 1867. In September 1867 commanded by Major Caetano da Costa Araujo e Melo and placed in the 11th Infantry Brigade with the 11th Line Battalion and the 29th, 32nd, 37th, and 47th CVP. In December 1867 it was placed in the 9th Infantry Brigade with the 6th Line Battalion and the 36th, 44th, and 49th CVP. Disbanded 9 March 1868, its band being transferred to the 15th Line Battalion.

44th CVP: Ex 12th CVP. Placed in the 9th Infantry Brigade in September 1867. Disbanded by the Marquis of Caxias on 12 December 1868 after the Battle of Avay and incorporated into the 9th Line Battalion. Reformed on 12 March 1870 by the Conde d'Eu and Lieutenant-Colonel Luis Antonio Correa de Albuquerque given the command, its strength standing at 44 officers and 525 men.

45th CVP: Ex 15th CVP. On 30 June 1867 placed in the 9th Infantry Brigade with the 43rd CVP. Commanded by Major Benedito José de Barros from December 1866. At his death in June 1867 replaced by

Major Timoleao Perez de Albuquerque Maranhão. Disbanded by the Marquis of Caxias on 9 March 1868.

46th CVP: Raised in the province of Bahia. Commanded by Major Joaquim Aniceto Vaz. On 27 April 1868 placed in the 10th Infantry Brigade with the 6th Line Battalion and the 23rd and 28th CVP, 2nd Army Corps. Reinforced from the disbanded 42nd CVP in December 1868. On 20 February 1869 command was given to Major Frederico Cristiano Buys. As part of the 2nd Infantry Brigade, in April 1869 it contained 26 officers and 551men. Later Major Francisco de Lima e Silva was given command. In June 1869 this unit was transferred from the 4th Brigade, 1st Division, 2nd Army Corps, to the 6th Brigade, 3rd Division, 1st Army Corps.

47th CVP: Raised in the province of Paraíba do Norte. In September 1867 placed in the 11th Infantry Brigade with the 11th Line Battalion and the 29th, 32nd, 37th, and 43rd CVP battalions. Commanded by Lieutenant-Colonel Luis Inacio Leopoldo de Albuquerque Maranhão, on 3 December 1868 this unit was placed in the 10th Infantry Brigade with the 23rd and 50th CVP. This brigade was commanded by the 47th's old commander, Albuquerque Maranhão, who was replaced as battalion commander by Major Antonio Pedro de Silva. Disbanded by the Marquis of Caxias on 23 December 1868.

48th CVP: Ex 16th CVP. Raised in Montevideo, this unit was sometimes called the *Batalhão dos Garibaldinos* (Battalion Garibaldi). Served with the Uruguayan Army Corps in April 1865, commanded by Major José Groppi, but being made up of Brazilians living in Uruguay it came under the command of the Brazilian Army and not the Uruguayan. Commanded by Colonel Fidelis Paes da Silva, it marched with the Vanguard army and took part in the Battle of Yataí, the siege of Uruguayana, and the battles of Estero Bellaco and Tuyuti. Disbanded by the Marquis of Caxias on 13 October 1867. It would appear that it was subsequently reformed as it is also listed among the units disbanded on 12 December 1868 after the Battle of Avay.

49th CVP: Commanded by Lieutenant-Colonel Antonio Martins de Amorim Rangél in December 1867, when it was placed in the 9th Infantry Brigade with the 6th Line Battalion and the 36th, 43rd, and 44th CVP. Disbanded 23 December 1868.

50th CVP: Raised in the province of Mato Grosso. Reinforced with the remnants of the 19th CVP in December 1866 after suffereing heavy losses. Reinforced again on 23 December with 179 men from the disbanded 39th CVP. Placed in the 10th Infantry Brigade by December 1868. In 1869 saw service in the 4th Brigade, 2nd Army Corps, alongside the 23rd CVP and the 3rd and 9th Line Battalions. Commanded by Lieutenant-Colonel Joaquim Cavalcanti de Albuquerque Belo.

51st CVP: On 20 July 1867 was in the 12th Infantry Brigade with the 8th and 39th CVP, commanded by Lieutenant-Colonel F. Villar.

52nd CVP: On 20 December 1866 received reinforcements from the disbanded 20th CVP. Commanded by Lieutenant-Colonel Carlos Cirilo de Castro. Disbanded on 9 March 1868.

53rd CVP: Took part in the expedition to San Pedro in May 1869 alongside the 23rd and 35th CVP and other units. Brigaded with the 17th and 40th CVP on 27 January 1870 by the Conde d'Eu. This Brigade was sent home on 3 February 1870.

54th CVP: Commanded in December 1867 by Lieutenant-Colonel Manuel Gonçalves da Cunha. Reinforced from the disbanded 42nd CVP in December 1868. Assisted the 17th CVP at Asunción in 1869.

55th CVP: In the 7th Infantry Brigade during 1868 with the 31st and 39th CVP battalions. Disbanded 12 December 1868 after the Battle of Avay.

The Government promised volunteers a grant of land at demobilisation. Many later sold these titles to land speculators for a small percentage of their value because they were often situated in distant and unfavourable locations. When the number of volunteers began to wane, recruits were obtained in other ways. The authorities tended to 'club-and-rope' recruits amongst migrants, the un- and underemployed, rogues, criminals, orphans, and ex-slaves, the bulk of enlisted men therefore coming largely from what their superiors considered the dregs of society. Regiments could consist of white or black soldiers, but the majority were of mixed race.

The 'freed slaves' were slaves made free men at the end of the war. They were often 'volunteered' by their masters to take the place of the latter's relatives, or were sold to the Government. Of the latter category, 218 were bought for Army service and 1,300 for Navy service. However, in some cases – such as in the state of Bahia – it was cheaper to buy an exemption than a healthy slave. These ex-slaves were integrated into the various units. Nearly all were sent to the most inhospitable regions where the initial wave of volunteers had not survived very well.

The Cavalry

The cavalry arm as established by regulations of 1842 and 1852 comprised four regiments of regular horse. A fifth regiment was raised in 1854, so that there were five in existence at the outbreak of the Paraguayan War. As we have seen, the reorganisation of 1866 reduced this total to three regiments of regular cavalry but added five new 'Corps' of *Caçadores a Cavalaria*, this strength

Table 9: Brazilian volunteers mobilised during the Paraguayan War

Province	CVP	National Guard	Freed slaves	Total	% of vols.	% of pop.
North Region						
Amazonas	367	285	53	705	0.57	0.61
Para	2,084	1,440	303	3,827	3.11	2.79
North-East Region						
Maranhão	2,385	1,787	364	4,536	3.69	3.58
Piauí	1,420	1,134	251	2,805	2.29	2.08
Ceará	2,037	3,096	515	5,648	4.59	7.43
Rio Grande do Norte	814	348	149	1,311	1.07	2.42
Paraíba	1,472	599	383	2,454	1.99	3.86
Pernambuco	5,793	1,104	239	7,136	5.79	8.54
Alagoas	1,591	787	278	2,656	2.15	3.17
East Region						
Sergipe	1,405	724	125	2,254	1.83	1.72
Bahia	9,164	5,312	721	15,197	12.34	14.39
Minas Gerais	2,158	1,768	164	4,090	3.32	20.71
Espírito Santo	625	285	56	966	0.79	0.79
Rio de Janeiro	4,667	2,315	869	7,851	6.38	7.19
Corte	7,128	1,851	2,482	11,461	9.31	2.93
South Region						
São Paulo	4,824	1,125	555	6,504	5.28	8.69
Paraná	613	1,296	113	2,020	1.64	1.32
Santa Catarina	1,103	264	170	1,537	1.25	1.47
Rio Grande do Sul	3,200	29,967	636	33,803	27.46	4.05
West Central Region						
Goiás	275	108	43	426	0.35	1.63
Mato Grosso	1,417	4,074	20	5,511	4.47	0.62
City of Montevideo	450	–	–	450	0.35	–
Totals	*54,992*	*59,669*	*8,489*	*123,150*	–	–

The '% of vols.' column denotes the percentage of all Brazilian volunteers represented by the individual provincial figures. The '% of pop.' column denotes the percentage of the province's population who volunteered.

remaining unchanged thereafter until the end of the war.

The dress regulations of 7 August 1852 gave the cavalry dark blue uniforms similar to those of the line Fusiliers, with shako and coatee for full dress, and kepi and tunic for service and undress (the so-called 'second uniform'). Facings were to be in variations of red and dark blue, initially distinguished by white piping, with brass buttons. These regulations quoted red collars for full dress, the different regiments being distinguished by variations in their cuffs and cuff flaps as follows:

1st Regiment – Red cuffs with dark blue flaps
2nd Regiment – Red cuffs without flaps
3rd Regiment – Dark blue cuffs with red flaps
4th Regiment – Dark blue cuffs without flaps

On the undress tunic the red collar was reduced to a red patch on either side of the front, and cuffs were dark blue with flaps of the colour of the full dress coatee cuff. When it was raised in 1854 the 5th Regiment was distinguished by a red collar and cuffs. Shortly after this the system was slightly modified for the 1st Regiment, which was to discontinue its full dress cuff flaps, and the 2nd Regiment, which was to have plain dark blue coatee cuffs edged in red piping.

The dress regulations of 1866 gave the cavalry a standardised uniform based on the undress uniform formerly worn by the 1st Regiment, with dark blue collar and cuffs, red collar patches and cuff flaps, and uniformly white piping. Details, including new uniforms and clothing items, were generally as outlined for the infantry. The newly-raised *Caçador* cavalry were given a uniform almost identical to the infantry *Caçadores*, being entirely dark blue trimmed with yellow piping, with black belts in place of the white used by the line cavalry.

The Artillery

The reorganisation of the regular army in 1866 had seen an increase in artillery strength by the addition of a second corps of horse artillery and a fifth battalion of foot artillery. The horse artillery were largely recruited in the province of Rio Grande do Sul and had a distinctly 'gaucho' tradition. In 1852 both bodies of the artillery were wearing dark blue uniforms similar to those of other branches, distinguished by facings in crimson and/or black. Horse artillery uniforms were similar to those of the cavalry, with entirely crimson facings and brass buttons. In full dress they wore the coatee with brass contre-epaulettes and the low 'Yeoman-crowned' shako with a red-tipped black standing plume (a 'waterfall' plume of cock feathers in the case of officers). Their 'second' (service or undress) uniform comprised the tunic, generally with brass shoulder chains, and the kepi, following the patterns in use in other branches. The foot artillery followed essentially infantry patterns, their dress coatee distinguished by battalion variations: crimson collar and black cuffs for the 1st Battalion, black collar and crimson cuffs for the 2nd, both black for the 3rd, and both crimson for the 4th, all other piping and trim being crimson. Their shako was conical, wrapped with cords which fell in flounders on the right breast. On the front was a device of brass crossed cannon with an Imperial crown above and battalion tassels and number below. As a special distinction the 1st Battalion had their shakos

covered with crimson cloth wrapped with black cords; the other battalions had black shakos with yellow cords. Shako plumes were of the hanging or 'waterfall' variety, of cock feathers for officers, or black horsehair emerging from a black ball pompom for other ranks. Their 'second uniform' followed much the same pattern as for infantry, distinguished by various crimson or black collar patches and cuff flaps according to battalion.

The dress regulations of 1866 retained what was

Brazilian generals' rank insignia: dark blue collars with white outer piping, an inner edging of gold lace, and gold oakleaf embroidery indicating rank.

a: Marshal: A double row of wavy gold oakleaf embroidery, joined at the ends to form a sort of frame around the collar (and full dress cuffs).

b: Lieutenant-general: A single row of embroidery with leaves on both sides of the branch.

c: Marechal de campo: A single row of embroidery with leaves only on the top side of the branch.

d: Brigadeiro (brigadier): A spray of oakleaf embroidery at the front of the collar reaching to about an inch past the shoulder seam of the jacket.

e: Marshal's epaulette: Barroso includes a detail sketch of a marechal's *epaulette, which is distinguished by an embroidered device of the world globe within a wreath, with the Imperial Crown above on the strap. Unfortunately, he gives no details of the epaulette devices, if any, of other generals' ranks (or for that matter, of other officer's ranks).*

f: Brigadeiro's full dress cuff: On the full dress (coatee) cuff a brigadeiro *was distinguished by a sort of star-shaped spray of oakleaf embroidery with a single edging line of gold lace just inside the white outer piping. Other generals wore the same pattern of embroidery on their collars, plus a varying number of gold lace edgings (two for a* marechal de campo *and three for a lieutenant-general; a* marechal *had only a single slightly wider lace, which had a scalloped edge on the inner side). Note: these varied lace edgings were only worn on the cuffs, collars having a single plain lace for all ranks.*

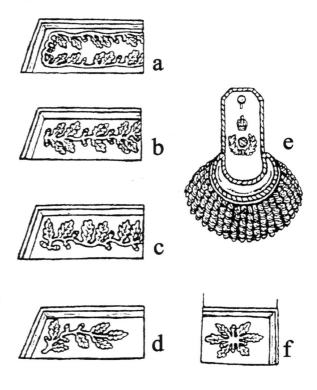

essentially the former 'second uniform' as the only authorised artillery uniform. This remained virtually unchanged for the horse artillery while all foot artillery adopted the 'second uniform' as formerly worn by the 1st Battalion, with crimson collar patches and black cuff flaps. In theory all artillery were now to have a gold or yellow (according to rank) flaming grenade on the collar patches, but its use seems to have been sporadic at best. For full dress the former shakos continued in use. For the foot artillery these were now to be universally black wrapped with crimson cords and with a new plume for lower ranks. Other uniform items and equipment were much as for other branches of service. Curiously, the foot artillery kepi was now to be crimson for all units.

General Staff and Engineers

Barroso gives few details of the composition or strength of the various elements of the General Staff, or of their different functions. Basically, the General Staff consisted of General Officers, General Staff officers of the first and second classes (with no indication of the functions of either), and a secretariat of administrative officers and clerical staff. Attached to the General Staff were the Imperial Corps of Engineers (a corps of trained engineer officers) and an Artillery General Staff (which formed the administrative headquarters of the artillery).

Two units which appear to have been dependencies of the General Staff without actually being considered part of it were the Battalion of Engineers, comprising a force of trained manpower at the disposal of the Imperial Corps of Engineers; and a specialist corps of Artificers (trained carpenters, metal workers, wheelwrights, etc), which may have been a dependency of the Artillery General Staff, since their uniform resembled that of the foot artillery more than the engineers. Alterations to the strength and organisation of these bodies during the war seem to have been relatively minor.

In 1823 the General Staff adopted a uniform based on that of the Portuguese General Staff; this was entirely dark blue edged with white piping, with gold buttons and trim. However, the uniforms in use in 1865 were those of the dress regulations of 1858, which were themselves a modification of the 1852 uniforms. The full dress uniform consisted of a long-tailed coatee and bicorne hat, edged with white ostrich-feather plumage for General Officers. Other staff officers had instead a 'waterfall' plume of variously coloured feathers according to corps. The 'second uniform' comprised a tunic in the same colours as the coatee, worn with either the bicorne without plume or a kepi. A General's rank was distinguished by various patterns of gold oakleaf embroidery on the collar and cuffs of the dress coatee (prior to 1858 this embroidery had also been worn on the breast and the edging of the tails), plus epaulettes. On the tunic this embroidery was worn only on the collar, and epaulettes were generally not worn. Other staff officers had only a corps badge embroidered on either side of the collar, with rank indicated by the normal officers' epaulettes on the coatee and sleeve lace on the tunic. The Corps of Engineers and Artillery General Staff officers wore essentially the same uniform with black velvet collars and their own distinctive collar badges and hat plumes. These uniforms remained largely unchanged throughout the war, though the full dress uniform was seldom worn

and campaign uniforms were submitted to numerous field modifications.

The Battalion of Engineers never had a full dress uniform, only a rather simple dark blue 'second uniform' with plain black facings and trim, worn for all orders of dress. The Artificers Corps, however, did have a full dress uniform, consisting of a dark blue coatee with dark blue collar piped red, red round cuffs, turnbacks, and front piping, and an infantry-style shako with brass chinscales, a brass oval front plate (the design of which is not very clear), and a standing white-over-black plume. Their 'second uniform' is depicted in Figure 115. The Battalion of Engineers' uniform seems to have continued virtually unchanged throughout the war, except for the adoption of certain new items from the 1866 dress regulations, such as barrack caps and summer and working uniforms. The same probably applied for the Artificers, though no wartime uniforms are depicted in Barroso.

FIGURES

71 & 72. FUSILIERS, 1st BATTALION c.1865 Figure 71 wears summer full dress. Black shako with brass 'rayed' front plate (incorporating the battalion number), above this the national cockade (since 1831 a yellow five-pointed star on a green field with a narrow yellow border). White cords and flounders, and a tallish red plume tipped white. Dark blue coatee with white collar and turnbacks and yellow round cuffs, all edged with red piping, as too are the front opening and pocket flaps on the turnbacks. Brass buttons. On the shoulders, epaulettes with red straps and pads, the former edged with white piping, smooth brass crescents, and white fringe. White trousers, gaiters, gloves, waistbelt, and musket strap. Clearly visible here is one of the more unusual distinctions of the period: a white leather strap attached to a button on the right breast, from the lower ends of which are suspended a needle and small brush for clearing the musket's touchhole; normally the lower end would be tucked under the waistbelt (as here) to keep it from entangling the wearer's arms or equipment, but in battle it might be left hanging free ready for use.

Figure 72 wears instead the 'second' or undress uniform. The kepi has dark blue top and white (battalion colour) band, both piped with red, white leather chinstrap, and a small national cockade on the front. Dark blue tunic with red front piping, brass buttons. On this garment the white collar colour is reduced to a smallish patch on either side, piped with red on three edges, and the yellow cuff colour is reduced to a three-button flap (also piped with red) on the outer side, the collar and cuffs themselves being dark blue with red piping along the top. The fringed full dress epaulettes are replaced by soft dark blue straps piped red, the outer ends carrying large white woollen crescents rather similar to those used by British centre company troops during the 1830s–40s. White trousers and gaiters. The white waistbelt equipment was patterned on the French model, with three-part shoulder straps supporting the pack with dark blue greatcoat roll strapped on the top. The small black pouch visible on the front of the waistbelt to the right of the brass plate was presumably for percussion caps.

73–75. FUSILIER OFFICERS c.1866–70 Figure 73 is a colonel in undress uniform. Kepi in a white cotton

Fig 71   *Fig 72*   *Fig 73*   *Fig 74*   *Fig 75*

cover. The long dark blue tunic is a privately acquired, non-regulation item, almost a frock-coat, with red rectangular collar patches (no collar piping), red piping down the front opening and edging the dark blue cuff flaps, gilt buttons, and three wide gold rank laces circling the cuff. Plain dark blue epaulette holding straps on the shoulders. White cotton or linen trousers and waistcoat, white shirt, and a black scarf wrapped around the neck in place of a stock.

The lieutenant depicted in Figure 74 is shown in the 'regulation' 1866 service dress uniform, worn in the authorised manner. Dark blue kepi with red band and vertical piping on front, side, and rear seams, national cockade on the front, white leather strap, black peak. Dark blue tunic with red collar patches, and red piping edging the top of the collar, the front opening, the dark blue cuffs and cuff flaps, and the rear pocket flaps. Gilt buttons and two narrow gold lace rank stripes circling the cuff just below the red piping. On more 'dressy' occasions stiffened dark blue shoulder straps were worn with gilt metal crescents and red piping edging the straps. Dark blue trousers with red piping down outer seams. A white waistbelt is worn over the darkish red or crimson waist-sash. White sabre knot. The uniform's dark blue base colour was very dark, more or less a 'blue-black'.

Rank insignia conformed to the dress regulations of 1852: an ensign (*alferes*) wore one narrow lace stripe of button colour circling the cuff; a lieutenant (*lieutenant*) two narrow lace stripes; a captain (*capitão*) one broad lace stripe; a major (*major*) one broad stripe with a narrow stripe below; a lieutenant-colonel (*lieutenant coronel*) two broad stripes; and a colonel (*coronel*) three broad stripes. Normally these were worn in the following manner: ranks from ensign to captain wore their stripes on the cuff, below the piping; majors and lieutenant-colonels wore the top lace stripe above the cuff piping and the bottom one below the piping; and colonels' rank lace almost covered the cuff and was normally worn with the centre lace covering the piping. However, there seems to have been a good deal of variation in this, many

officers suiting themselves in this regard. Some also wore a second set of rank laces circling the kepi band, though this was not authorised by regulations.

Figure 75 is a captain wearing campaign dress. The kepi has a white cover. In place of the regulation tunic he wears a plain dark blue campaign coat (apparently a common practice) distinguished only by the gilt buttons and rank lace circling the cuffs. His lightish brown trousers are probably part of an other ranks' working uniform, which was not authorised for officers. Black gaiters and boots. Crimson waist-sash, white leather waistbelt and sabre knot, sabre with gilded hilt and steel scabbard. A brown-covered container (a water-bottle?) is slung form his left shoulder. Blanket roll is dark blue.

76. FUSILIER DRUMMER c.1866–70 Campaign dress. Kepi with white cotton cover and white chinstrap. Dark blue tunic with dark blue collar, shoulder straps, cuffs, and cuff-flaps, all edged with red piping. Red collar patches and piping down the front opening, brass buttons. White duck trousers tucked into black marching boots. White belts and straps, brass belt plate, sliding bars for attachment of the pack support straps, and drum stick carriers on the drum belt. Brass drum with red hoops and white tightener cords. Pre-war, musicians often wore elaborately laced uniforms, but all such gaudiness was abolished in 1866 to reduce battlefield visibility. Thereafter they normally wore the same uniform as the rest of their unit. This particular uniform combination, with the woollen tunic and white trousers and kepi cover, seems to have been particularly prevalent as combat dress.

77. FUSILIER NCO c.1866–70 This figure depicts an *anspessada* – a lance-corporal, or private first-class (the term translates as 'broken lance' and dates back to the middle ages, when it denoted a gentleman who had somehow lost his horse and was constrained to serve with the lowly infantry) – wearing campaign dress. His headwear comprising a dark blue barracks cap with

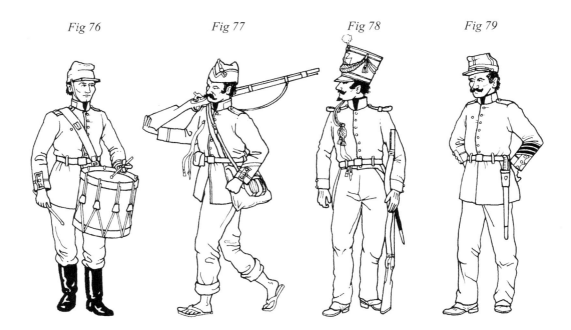

Fig 76   Fig 77   Fig 78   Fig 79

yellow turn-up and tassel is unusual, as *Fusilieros* normally wore caps with red trim and a red five-pointed star on the front of the turn-up; possibly it is a *Caçadores* cap, or simply a non-standard variant. Tunic and trousers are of light brown duck, the tunic having red collar patches and piping of the same pattern as on the woollen tunic. The light brown duck trousers sometimes had side piping as well, though white duck trousers seldom, if ever, did so. The tunic buttons are almost invariably depicted as being a darkish, brownish colour: might they have been bronzed, or of some non-standard material such as wood or horn, or are they simply tarnished brass? The waistbelt and the cap pouch to the right of the belt plate are white, as is the breast-strap with its brush and needle, here worn hanging loose ready for instant use. His sandals are brown. On his lower left sleeve he wears a red diagonal rank stripe; for further details of NCO rank insignia see Figure 79.

On his left hip hangs a haversack of light brown duck, and a natural wood water-bottle strapped with iron, suspended on a white strap. Backpacks were of black leather with white straps, and had an iron mess tin strapped to the rear flap and a dark blue greatcoat wrapped horseshoe-fashion round the outside.

Sir Richard Burton, who observed Brazilian infantrymen in 1868, commented that 'the men are well dressed. Their fatigue suits are blouses and overalls of brown drill, besides the kepi and strong highlows [laced ankle-boots]; in "grand tenue" they wear tunics and pants of good broadcloth, with red facings and black leathers – clay pipe not being here a favourite. On the march they carry light knapsacks, and wear white forage caps with red bands, and white or blue trousers, tucked up, not tucked in.'

78 & 79. CAÇADORES, 8th BATTALION c.1865
Figure 78 is a private in winter full dress. Black shako with bronzed Maltese Cross plate, national cockade above, black cords and flounders, green pompom. Very dark green coatee with red collar and round cuffs, dark green skirt turnbacks, bronzed buttons, stiff black

shoulder-straps with brass crescents resembling epaulettes. Dark green trousers over black gaiters. Black waistbelt with brass plate, white gloves. Black leather carbine strap and brass-hilted sabre bayonet. The breast strap with brush and needle is also of black leather, but is almost hidden by the shako cords and flounders, which attach to the same button on the right breast.

Figure 79 is a 'clerk', wearing the 'second' or undress uniform. Dark green kepi with red band and vertical seam piping, black chinstrap. Dark green tunic with red collar patches and three-button cuff flaps, dark green collar, shoulder-straps, and cuffs (the last edged with black piping on the top), bronzed buttons. White trousers worn with black gaiters. Black waistbelt with brass plate and sliding bars.

On his lower left sleeve are three black diagonal rank stripes backed with red cloth. NCO's rank insignia conformed to the regulations of 1852, and consisted of diagonal stripes on the lower left sleeve, running from seam to seam. In theory these stripes were to be of branch of service-coloured wool, though the range of unit facing colours in use prior to 1866 frequently led to variations (regulations were tightened up in this regard after 1866), generally backed/edged with a contrasting colour. The ranking system was as follows: *anspecada* or *anspessada* (lance-corporal or private first-class) one stripe; *cabo* (corporal) two stripes; clerk (quartermaster) three stripes; second *sargento* (second sergeant) four stripes; and first *sargento* (first sergeant – this rank was sometimes referred to as *sargento mor* or sergeant-major) five stripes.

80. CAÇADOR OFFICER c.1866–70 This is an ensign in campaign dress. Kepi has a white cotton cover and black chinstrap; kepis seem to have been sometimes made entirely of white cotton, with no woollen backing – entirely non-regulation, needless to say. Entirely dark blue tunic trimmed with yellow piping, including the rear skirt slash and irregularly shaped three-button rear pocket flaps. Gilt buttons and one gold cuff lace just below the yellow piping, dark blue epaulette loops on the shoulders (epaulettes not being normally worn on campaign). White cotton or linen trousers tucked into black marching boots. Black waistbelt over crimson sash, brown leather bag for personal effects on the right hip, dark blue greatcoat or mantle in a roll over the right shoulder. In the latter part of the war officers' uniforms could be entirely of cotton or linen in the summer months, dyed light brown, with a white kepi and neck-cover.

Using Figure 74 as a guide a colonel of *Caçadores* in undress uniform can be visualised. Dark blue kepi with yellow band and vertical piping, black chinstrap, small national cockade on the front. Dark blue tunic with dark blue collar, cuffs, and cuff flaps, all edged with yellow piping, yellow front piping, gilt buttons and three wide gold lace cuff stripes. Dark blue shoulder-straps edged with yellow piping and gilt metal crescents. Dark blue trousers with yellow side piping. Black waistbelt with gilt plate, worn over a sash – officially crimson – with gold lace knot and crimson tassels. White gloves, black sabre knot.

81–83. CAÇADORES c.1866–70 All three of these figures wear campaign dress. Figure 81's dark blue barracks cap is trimmed with yellow piping, and has a black tassel and yellow hunting horn device on the front of the turn-up (see Figure 82). Entirely dark blue tunic has yellow piping edging the collar, shoulder-straps, front opening, cuffs, cuff flaps, rear skirt slash, and pocket flaps. Brass buttons. Dark blue trousers with yellow side piping. Black belts and cartridge pouch. Black leather pack with black straps, white metal mess tin attached to the rear flap, and dark blue greatcoat roll strapped to the top. There is a brown canvas haversack on his right hip, and in the original it can be seen that he carries a second, unclear, article on his left hip, possibly a second haversack.

Figure 82's headgear is a special tropical or summer version of the barracks cap with white (cotton?) top, dark blue turn-ups without piping, yellow hunting horn device on the front, black tassel, and white curtain.

Tunic and trousers of light brown duck, piped with yellow as for the dark blue woollen uniform, depicted with darkish buttons. Black belts and cartridge pouch, the latter pulled around to the front for easier access in combat. Dark blue greatcoat strapped to the top of the pack. The branches attached to the pack provided additional shade from the sun, plus an incidental measure of camouflage.

Figure 83 is a *cabo* (corporal). Hat natural straw. Tunic and trousers of light brown duck trimmed with yellow piping as for the last figure, dark (brown or black – the original picture is unclear) buttons, and two yellow rank lace stripes backed with black cloth on the lower left sleeve. White canvas *espadrilles* with rope soles. Black belts and pouch. He carries his dark blue greatcoat rolled over the right shoulder (a blanket roll, in a variety of neutral colours, would be equally likely), a light brown haversack on the left hip and some sort of white metal water-bottle on a brown strap on the right hip. His *carabine* would have steel fittings and a black strap; its brass-hilted sabre-bayonet is carried in a black scabbard with a brass chape.

84. CAPTAIN, 1st CAVALRY REGIMENT c.1865 Full dress. Black shako with gold plate and chinscales, gold lace top band, national cockade above the plate, 'waterfall' plume of red feathers. Dark blue coatee with red collar and cuffs, entirely edged with white piping including the front opening, white skirt turnbacks, gold buttons and epaulettes. Dark blue trousers with a red side stripe. Crimson waist-sash with gold knot and crimson tassels. White belts and gloves, full dress sabre knot of gold cord.

85. CABO DE ESQUADRA, 1st CAVALRY REGIMENT c.1865 'Second uniform'. *Cabo de esquadra* means 'squadron corporal'. Dark blue kepi with red band, white piping on top and vertical side seams and edging the band, white leather chinstrap, Dark blue tunic with dark blue collar and cuffs, red collar patches and cuff

Fig 80   *Fig 81*   *Fig 82*   *Fig 83*

137

flaps, all edged with white piping, as is the front opening. Brass buttons and 'chainmail' shoulder straps of linked brass rings. On the lower left sleeve are two red rank stripes, edged white on the outer sides only. White summer trousers. White belts with brass fittings, black sabre knot. The plain black leather sabretache has a crowned brass number on the flap which presumably denotes his unit (though Barroso invariably depicts the number '1'). For full dress, other ranks wore a shako similar to the officer's with a smaller standing plume, and plain dark blue winter trousers without a stripe. A plain dark blue kepi was also in use, though it's not clear under what circumstances it was to be worn.

Using this figure as a guide, the appearance of a cavalry lieutenant in service/campaign dress of 1866–70 can be pictured. Dark blue kepi with red band edged with white piping, white side piping, white leather chinstrap, and *two* small gold rank laces circling the band (non-regulation, but not uncommon). Dark blue tunic with dark blue collar and cuffs, red collar patches and cuff flaps, all edged with white piping, white front piping, gold buttons and two gold rank laces circling the cuff. Dark blue epaulette loops on the shoulder, but no epaulettes worn. Dark blue trousers with red stripe, black riding boots, crimson waist-sash.

86. CAVALRY CAPTAIN 1866–70 Summer undress. Kepi in white cover. White linen trousers. Tunic as described for the last figure, with gold contre-epaulettes lined white (which shows as an edging all around). The gold rank lace is sewn on in an entirely non-regulation fashion, covering the centre of the cuff flap. Crimson waist-sash, white belts and sabre knot.

87. CAVALRY TRUMPETER 1866–70 Campaign dress. Plain dark blue kepi with brass front device (crown above regimental number) and white leather chinstrap.

Dark blue tunic with dark blue collar and cuffs, red collar patches and cuff flaps, white piping, brass buttons and brass 'chain' shoulder straps. Note the collar variation, with no piping on the rear. Plain dark blue trousers tucked into black boots. White belts, cap pouch, waistbelt, and carbine sling. Dark blue mantle roll worn over the right shoulder, beige or off-white haversack on the left hip. Brass trumpet with green cords and tassels.

Barroso also shows a cavalryman in campaign dress, wearing a kepi with a white cover (slightly rucked-up at the rear to show the edge of the red band), its white chinstrap worn around the back of the head. His tunic is as for the figure depicted, except that the collar is piped along the back. Trousers, belts, and sabre knot are white, and he wears soft black leather boots in the popular 'gaucho' style, which had a tendency to collapse in folds around the ankles.

88 & 89. CAVALRYMEN 1866–70 The campaign dress of these two figures displays elements of the 'gaucho' style that was particularly popular among mounted troops. Figure 88 wears a brown felt hat with chincords, a dark blue poncho with red lining, light brown trousers (probably from the regulation duck working uniform), a red neckerchief, and soft black 'gaucho' boots. Lance pennon is red over white, the 'sleeve' around the pole being entirely red. Lances seem to have been widely used by cavalry, both before and during the war, but their official status is unclear.

The officer depicted in Figure 89 wears a black felt hat with natural leather band, and a light brown fringed poncho with a pattern of dark red-white-dark red lines round the edge. Though it cannot be seen here, his plain dark blue trousers are reinforced with a second layer of the same material between the legs. His pink neckerchief has an edging of double white lines. Boots are black. In this guise, he is virtually indistinguishable from his men,

Fig 84   Fig 85   Fig 86   Fig 87   Fig 88

Fig 89   *Fig 90*   *Fig 91*   *Fig 92*   *Fig 93*

many officers making a deliberate effort to 'blend in' on campaign.

90. CLERK, 1st CAVALRY REGIMENT 1866–70 Full dress. Black shako with brass plate and chinscales, national cockade above the plate, yellow lace top band, red plume. Tunic as described for Figure 85, with fringeless brass epaulettes, and three red rank stripes edged white on the lower left sleeve. Dark blue trousers with red stripe, white gloves, belts and sabre knot, black leather sabretache (as depicted in Figure 85). The 1st Cavalry Regiment, which spent the war guarding the Imperial Court in Rio de Janeiro, would have been one of the few units to wear the full dress uniform on a fairly regular basis during the conflict.

91 & 92. *CAÇADOR* CAVALRY OFFICERS 1866–70 Figure 91 depicts a captain in full dress. Black shako with gold fittings and top lace band, national cockade, plume of dark green cock feathers. Dark blue tunic, collar, cuffs, and cuff flaps, all with yellow piping, front opening also piped yellow. Gold buttons and epaulettes. Dark blue trousers with yellow side piping. Crimson and gold waist-sash, white gloves, black belts and sabretache, gold full dress sabre knot. By regulation, officers were to continue to distinguish their rank by means of epaulettes with the full dress uniform, but in practice many simply substituted their 'second uniform' tunic (with cuff lace), with detachable epaulettes, for the full dress tunic.

Figure 92 is a lieutenant-colonel in undress/service uniform. Dark blue kepi with black chinstrap, yellow band and side and top piping (there seems to have been considerable variation in kepi trim during this period). Dark blue tunic, including collar, cuffs, and cuff flaps, all with yellow piping, yellow piping also edging the rear

pocket flaps. Gold buttons and contre-epaulettes, two gold rank stripes on the sleeve (one above and one below the yellow cuff piping). Dark blue trousers with yellow piping down the outer seam. Crimson waist-sash with gold knot and crimson tassels. Black belts with gilt or brass fittings. Gilt crowned number '1' on the flap of the sabretache. There is also an unclear gilt device on the pouch flap on his back (not visible here). A water-bottle in a buff or beige cover is suspended at his left hip from a black strap. Black leather holster and revolver lanyard.

A picture of a *Caçador* trooper in service/campaign dress of this period, resembling Figure 85, shows him wearing a kepi with white cover and black chinstrap; a brass-buttoned dark blue tunic with dark blue collar, cuffs, cuff flaps, and shoulder-straps (not the brass chain type of Figure 85), all edged with yellow piping; and white summer trousers. Belts are black with brass fittings, and the sabre knot is black.

93. *CAÇADOR* TROOPER 1866–70 Summer campaign dress. Brown felt slouch hat. Tunic of white duck, the collar, front opening, cuffs, cuff flaps, and shoulder-straps all edged with yellow piping in the same pattern as on the woollen tunic (no rear pocket flaps, however). Buttons are dark, either uncleaned or perhaps bronzed. Plain white duck trousers, black belts and sabre knot. The saddlecloth is dark blue with a white-edged red stripe across the bottom. Dark blue holster covers and mantle roll behind the saddle; a brown poncho or blanket hangs down below the mantle. The combination of rifled carbine and cavalry sabre suggests a 'general purpose' type of corps, able to function as either cavalry or mounted infantry. The Brazilian cavalry were issued with 2,000 Spencer carbines in 1869, after they had been thoroughly tested.

139

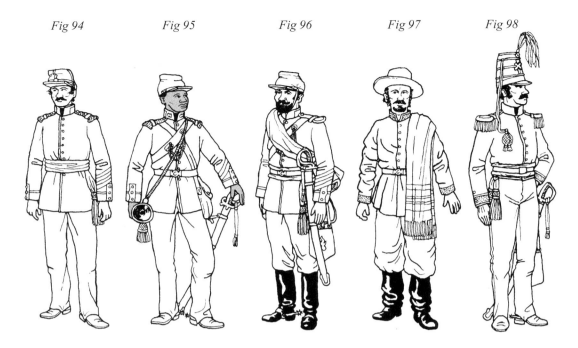

94. SECOND-SERGEANT, HORSE ARTILLERY c.1865 'Second uniform'. Dark blue kepi with crimson band and vertical piping, black peak and chinstrap, national cockade on the front. Dark blue tunic with crimson collar patches, cuff flaps, and piping edging the collar, front opening, and cuffs. Brass buttons and chain shoulder straps. Crimson rank stripes, backed in black. White cotton summer trousers, crimson or red waist-sash. (Sergeants appear to have frequently worn a crimson or red woollen waist-sash as part of their rank insignia, but details of the circumstances governing its use are unclear.)

By referring to Figure 86, the appearance of a captain of Horse Artillery in service uniform of the period c.1866-70 can be visualised. Dark blue kepi with crimson band, no vertical piping, national cockade on the front (a common variant type). Dark blue tunic with crimson collar patches, cuff flaps, and front and cuff piping, no piping on collar. Gold buttons, contre-epaulettes, and cuff lace below the piping (not going over the cuff flap this time). Dark blue trousers with crimson piping down the outer seams. Crimson waist-sash with gold knot. Black and gilt belts, white gloves, black leather undress sabre knot.

Similarly, reference to Figure 84 will enable an ensign (*alferes*) of Horse Artillery of c.1865 to be visualised in full dress. Low black shako with gold fittings and top lace, narrow gold bottom lace with a crimson centre line, plume of green-black cock feathers in a gilt 'tulip' holder, above the national cockade. Oval shako plate embossed with a crowned shield bearing the Imperial arms, surrounded by a laurel wreath. Dark blue coatee with rather short tails, crimson collar, cuffs, turnbacks, and front piping, no piping to collar or cuffs. Gilt buttons and epaulettes (one contre-epaulette and one fringed epaulette). Dark blue trousers with crimson side stripe. Black belts with gilt fittings, crimson waist-sash with gold knots and crimson fringe, white gloves, gold sword knot.

95–97. HORSE ARTILLERY c.1866–70 Figure 95 depicts a corporal-trumpeter in undress uniform. Kepi with white cover and black chinstrap. Dark blue tunic with crimson collar patches, cuff flaps, and piping, brass buttons and chain shoulder straps, yellow flaming grenades on the collar patches. Crimson rank stripes edged black. White trousers, black belts and sabre knot, off-white haversack. Brass trumpet with crimson cords. Smaller figures manning a gun in the background of the illustration from which this figure comes wear the same tunic with black slouch hats and light brown duck working trousers.

Figure 96 is a second sergeant in marching uniform. Kepi in white cover which leaves a portion of the crimson band visible at the rear. White duck summer uniform with crimson collar patches, cuff flaps, and piping edging the collar, cuffs, and front opening, dark (bronze?) buttons, brass contre-epaulettes (though I've seen one copy of this plate which shows brass shoulder chains). Crimson rank stripes backed with black cloth. Crimson waist-sash, black boots, belts, and sabre knot, dark blue mantle roll over the right shoulder. The brass device on the black sabretache appears to be a flaming grenade.

As noted earlier, Brazil's horse artillery were largely recruited in the province of Rio Grande do Sul, and commonly wore elements of gaucho dress. A somewhat extreme example is provided by Figure 97, whose non-regulation uniform is of a type which was widely worn within Rio Grande do Sul during the 1850s, particularly by troops involved with the Farrapos and Platinos rebellions. It comprises a black slouch hat, red flannel blouse with black collar, cuffs, and buttons, white *bombacho* (sailcloth) trousers tucked into black 'gaucho boots', and a black waistbelt with brass clasp. Over his left shoulder is a light brown fringed poncho, with red-brown and black stripes at its ends. Unfortunately the sources provide no details of the continued use of this type of uniform; however, one hypothesis is that it may have been issued initially to elements of the new 2nd

Provisional Corps, pending the availability of stocks of the regulation uniform.

Brazilian field-pieces are depicted as brass, on carriages painted a darkish grey. In addition, Congreve and Hales rockets were used in the Brazilian Artillery from the 1840s on, although by this time they were manufactured in Brazil rather than imported from Britain or the USA. Those used during the Paraguayan War were painted dark grey, and their individual pieces had numbers painted on them for speedier assembly on the battlefield.

98 & 99. 1st BATTALION OF FOOT ARTILLERY c.1865 Figure 98 depicts a captain in full dress. Crimson shako with black leather top band and cords, white/silver bottom band, gold front plate with national cockade above, plume of green-black cock feathers. Dark blue coatee with crimson collar, skirt turnbacks, and front piping, black cuffs piped crimson, gilt buttons and epaulettes. Dark blue trousers with crimson side piping. White belt over crimson and gold waist-sash, white gloves, gold full dress sword knot. Sabretaches seem to have been used by mounted officers until 1866, and were then abolished.

The artilleryman depicted in Figure 99 wears his 'second uniform'. Dark blue kepi with crimson band and vertical piping, white chinstrap. Dark blue tunic with crimson collar patches and piping edging the front opening and the dark blue collar and cuffs. Black cuff flaps piped crimson, brass buttons, dark blue shoulder straps piped crimson with large black woollen crescents. White trousers and belts, black gaiters.

100–104. FOOT ARTILLERY c.1866–70 The first figure is a lieutenant in undress. Entirely crimson kepi trimmed with gold horizontal and vertical lace (the double vertical laces may have been an indication of rank, but unofficial), white chinstrap, national cockade on the front. Dark blue tunic with crimson collar patches and piping, black cuff flaps piped crimson, gold buttons and cuff rank lace, gold flaming grenades on the collar

patches. Dark blue contre-epaulettes piped crimson with a narrow inner edging of gold lace, gold crescents, dark blue holding straps. Dark blue trousers with crimson piping. White belt over crimson and gold waist-sash. White gloves and undress sword knot. Another illustration shows a Foot Artillery captain of this period wearing the same uniform except that his kepi has a white cover and a gold flaming grenade on the front, his tunic has no epaulettes, and he substitutes white trousers tucked into black riding boots.

The officer portrayed in Figure 101 wears campaign dress, comprising a dark brown slouch hat, a plain, gilt-buttoned, dark blue greatcoat with attached hood, and black boots. The sword knot is white leather. It is not clear whether his greatcoat is official issue or a type that was in common usage.

Figure 102 depicts an artilleryman in 'second' or undress uniform. Barracks cap with crimson top and dark blue turn-ups, piped crimson, black tassel. Dark blue tunic with crimson collar patches and front and cuff piping, black cuff flaps piped crimson, brass buttons. Dark blue shoulder-straps piped crimson with black woollen crescents. Dark blue trousers with crimson piping. White belt and musket strap. The foot artillery seem to have been armed with an assortment of long and short muskets during the war, generally with a sabre-bayonet.

Barroso's plates show a number of variations in other ranks' barracks caps – with or without dark blue piping on the seams of the top; with or without crimson piping edging the band; black or crimson tassel, etc – so there may not have been an established pattern for this item of dress, only a sort of general pattern. Unfortunately, Barroso never depicted the other ranks' kepi for this period, so it's unclear whether or not it had any sort of trim. Virtually all the men in his plates are depicted in barracks caps, except for a couple in the full dress shako; might this therefore have been the norm for foot artillery?

Figure 103 wears campaign dress. Summer barracks cap with white top, dark blue turn-ups piped

Fig 99   Fig 100   Fig 101   Fig 102   Fig 103

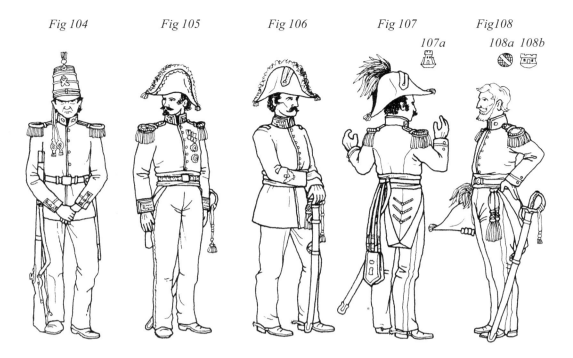

Fig 104   Fig 105   Fig 106   Fig 107   Fig 108
107a   108a 108b

crimson, crimson tassel, and national cockade on the front (some copies of the plate from which he is taken show a grenade instead of the cockade). The tunic is depicted as pale cream to beige – probably indicating a very faded brown working tunic – with crimson collar patches and collar and cuff piping, black cuff flaps piped crimson, and dark buttons. The shoulder-straps are depicted the same pale beige colour as the tunic, with black woollen crescents Other versions of the original picture show crimson piping down the tunic front and edging the shoulder-straps, these variations resulting from the fact that the plates were hand-coloured. The trousers are decidedly white. White belts and musket strap, pale beige haversack, water-bottle in a dark brown cover. Black backpack with large roll on top that appears to be covered in a black oilcloth.

Figure 104 shows a foot artilleryman in full dress. His black conical shako is wrapped with crimson cords with hanging flounders and tassels on the breast, brass crossed cannons and flaming bomb devices on the front, national cockade, and crimson tufted pompom. His dark blue tunic is the same as that of Figure 99 except for having small yellow flaming grenades on the collar patches, dark blue epaulettes piped crimson with brass crescents and crimson fringe (as worn for full dress pre-war, except that the straps were also crimson), and white waistbelt, the brass plate of which was embossed with the same devices as worn on the shako. Trousers dark blue with crimson piping. There are no gaiters. Muskets are generally shown with brass fittings, the bayonets with steel hilts, wooden grips, and brass and black leather scabbards.

Note that while the Barroso colour plates depict three single cords circling the foot artillery shako, a black and white detail drawing in his text shows three double cords instead; it is perhaps due to the reduced size of the colour figures that these appear to show single cords. Also, the shako cords are placed horizontally, and not in a spiral. The plates also show variations in the cuff flaps,

some having crimson piping edging the rear face, and some not.

105–108. GENERAL STAFF c.1865 Figure 105 is a Marshal in full dress. Dark blue coatee including collar, cuffs, and tail lining (Generals' tails were without turnbacks), white piping edging the collar, cuffs, and front opening, gilt buttons and epaulettes. Gold embroidery on collar and cuffs, including gold lace edging just inside the outer piping (scalloped on the cuff). Dark blue trousers with a broad stripe of gold oakleaf embroidery down the outer seam. Black bicorne hat with scalloped gold lace edging and cockade loop on the right-hand side (see next figure), gold end tassels, white feather plumage. No cockade. Gold laced waistbelt over a red sash, white gloves. Generals had a distinctive sword with a Mameluke-style hilt and straight or very slightly curved blade, entirely gilded, including the scabbard. The grip could be either ivory or ebony, with gold lace knot.

Figure 106 is a Brigadier in 'second uniform'. Bicorne hat as described for the last figure but without the gold lace edging. Dark blue tunic with white piping edging the dark blue collar and front opening, no cuffs. Gilt buttons and epaulette loops, gold embroidery and inner lace edging on the collar. The gold-embroidered device on the lower sleeve is unexplained. It appears to consist of the world globe (or possibly the Imperial crown) above an open wreath, and may indicate a member of the Imperial War Council – a post indicated by gold chevrons and a crown worn in the same position according to the 1852 regulations – but this is purely speculation. White linen summer trousers, gold belt, red waist-sash with gold knots and tassels.

Figure 107 depicts an officer of the Imperial Corps of Engineers in full dress. Black bicorne hat with gold cockade loop and tassels, and black-over-white feather plume. Dark blue coatee with black velvet collar and dark blue round cuffs, both edged with white piping, white skirt lining and turnbacks (for all General Staff officers

142

below General's rank), gilt buttons and epaulettes. The three skirt buttons are trimmed with black silk twist in herringbone pattern, while on either side of the collar is a gold embroidered tower (detail 107a). Dark blue trousers with gold lace stripe. Black belt over red waist-sash. The black leather sabretache has an unclear gold device on the flap (probably the tower with a crown above). Officers of the Artillery General Staff wore the same uniform with gold flaming bombs on the collar, and hat plumes of plain green-black cock feathers.

Figure 108 is a General Staff officer of the first class, also in full dress. Bicorne hat with gold cockade loop and tassels, red-over-white feather plumes. Dark blue coatee with dark blue collar and cuffs, white piping and skirt turnbacks, gilt buttons, epaulettes, and world globe collar device (detail 108a). Dark blue trousers with gold lace stripes. Black waistbelt, red waist-sash with gold knots and tassels, white gloves, gold sword knot. Officers of the General Staff of the second class were distinguished by a gold five-pointed star on the collar and green-over-white plumes on the bicorne. The castle device depicted in detail 108b was the collar badge of Administration and secretaries; unfortunately Barroso did not record the colours of their hat plumes.

109–111. GENERAL STAFF 1866–70 The first figure
is a General in campaign dress. Kepi in white cover with national cockade on the front. Plain dark blue campaign coat with gilt buttons, the white-piped collar bearing his gold-embroidered rank insignia. White trousers in black boots. Black waistbelt over red sash. A lightish brown fringed blanket or poncho with black end stripes is slung over his right shoulder.

Figure 110 is a General in undress uniform. Entirely dark blue kepi with gold rank embroidery circling the hat band, gold piping around the top of the band and on the side seams, national cockade on the front. Plain dark blue tunic with gilt buttons and rank embroidery on the collar, the latter without piping. White shirt, tie, and waistcoat. Plain dark blue trousers. The red waist-sash with gold tassels is twisted around his waist.

Figure 111 shows a general in campaign dress.

Dark blue poncho with dark blue collar and lining. The front opening is edged with a wide strip of gold embroidery, on the lower part of which is what appears to be a black pouch or square; it is not entirely clear if this is part of the pattern for the neck opening or something hanging from the neck and protruding through it. Loose dark blue trousers tucked into black boots. The standard General's sword has been replaced by a heavier sabre for campaign use, this having a gilded hilt and scabbard and a black leather knot.

Reference to Figure 75 will enable the undress uniform of a colonel of the General Staff of the first class, c.1866–70, to be visualised. Kepi top dark blue, the band apparently being white with a touch of gold at the rear overlapping onto the chinstrap (extrapolating from other figures I would conjecture the band to be encircled by a wide gold lace with white piping above and on the vertical seams). National cockade on the front and gold lace chinstrap. Plain blue tunic of a non-regulation cut, virtually a frock coat, with gilt buttons, gold cuff lace and collar device on plain blue collar, no shoulder bars. White cotton or linen waistcoat and trousers.

112–114. ENGINEERS Figure 112 is a *cabo de esquadra* (squad corporal) of the Battalion of Engineers in service dress of c.1865. Dark blue kepi with black band and chinstrap; the vertical seams also appear to be piped black, but this is not entirely clear. Dark blue tunic with black collar and cuff flaps (the cuffs appear to be without piping), brass buttons, yellow (metal) collar badge, dark blue epaulettes edged white with large woollen crescents, and two black rank stripes piped white on the lower left sleeve. Dark blue trousers. Black gaiters, belts, and pouch, the cartridge pouch on the front of the waistbelt suggesting that he might be armed with a musketoon on campaign.

An officer in campaign dress is shown wearing a dark blue kepi with a black band and white horizontal and vertical side piping, with the national cockade on the front. Tunic dark blue, collar black with gilt tower badge (see detail 107a), dark blue cuffs, white piping edging the collar, cuffs, and front opening. Gilt buttons and cuff rank

Fig 109   *Fig 110*   *Fig 111*   *Fig 112*

Fig 113 *Fig 114* *Fig 115* *Fig 116*

lace. Dark blue trousers, black waistbelt, red waist-sash, and black leather sabretache and slings. Steel sword scabbard, the sword having a gilt three bar hilt. No epaulettes or straps are shown on his shoulders.

Figure 113 is an engineer of the Battalion of Engineers in campaign dress of the period 1866–70. Kepi in white cover. Dark blue tunic with black collar, cuff flaps, and cuff piping, brass buttons and collar badge, epaulettes as for the last figure. White trousers, black belts and equipment. The brown cowhide pack has some sort of black cloth hanging down on the left side, while the dark blue roll on the top appears to be wrapped in black oilcloth. A light brown haversack hangs at his right hip, and a dark grey or black water-bottle at the left. Armament consists of a short musketoon and a sabre-bayonet, for which a needle and brush hang from a black strap on the right breast. About the only visible wartime change to the uniform is the abandonment of the gaiters. The Barroso plates are rather sketchy about the placement of piping on certain elements of the uniform – the cuffs, for instance, the vertical seams of the kepi, and possibly even the front opening of the tunic. Presumably this is due primarily to the lack of contrast between the dark blue base colour and the black facings. Whether the variations in the figures he depicts mirror reality, or are due to sloppy colouring, or simply a lack of precision in the source material, is problematic.

Figure 114 is an engineer in working dress of the same period as the last, taken from a background sketch depicting two engineers apparently digging a trench. One wears a plain light brown working uniform with dark buttons and no other trim, while the other has a lightish grey uniform of almost identical cut but with brass buttons (possibly a pre-war working uniform). Both wear 'tropical' barracks caps with white tops, plain dark blue turn-ups, and black tassels, one having a white neck curtain.

115. ARTIFICER c.1865 'Second uniform'. Entirely dark blue kepi trimmed with red piping, white chinstrap. Dark blue tunic with dark blue collar and cuffs piped red, red cuff flaps and front piping, black collar patches piped

red, brass buttons, and red epaulettes piped dark blue with black woollen crescents. White summer trousers over black gaiters. White belts and breast straps for the brush and pricker.

116. *ALFERES*, BATTALION OF ENGINEERS c.1865–70 Service dress. Dark blue kepi with black band, national cockade on the front. Dark blue tunic, cuffs, and epaulette loops, black velvet collar, black cuff flaps and cuff piping, gilt buttons, gold cuff lace and tower device on the collar (see detail 107a). Dark blue trousers. Black waistbelt and holster, red waist-sash with gold lace knots and red tassels, white gloves, black sabre knot.

'FIXED' OR 'GARRISON' CORPS c.1865–66

As already mentioned, Brazil's limited number of regular troops led to the various provinces raising their own units for local defence. These initially answered to no authority above that of the local government and, as a result, their organisation, designations, and functions varied widely. During the 1850s these semi-independent local corps began increasingly to be drawn into the orbit of the regular army establishment. Being already in place, they were to function as local garrison forces, precluding the necessity of assigning regulars to that role. The year 1860 saw a major reorganisation of these 'Fixed' forces, all existing infantry corps being redesignated as *Caçadores*; at the same time all *Pedestre* corps – a term which translates, very roughly, as 'walkers' or 'those who go on foot' – were ordered to be abolished. (Judging from the very limited available evidence, the *Pedestres* appear to have functioned as a sort of local gendarmerie.)

Following the Paraguayan invasion of Mato Grosso province in 1865, many of the 'Fixed Corps' were, of necessity, pressed into service to try to hold the breach until the army could be mobilised. In the course of the reorganisation and expansion of the army in 1866 these local corps were abolished, their personnel generally being used as the nuclei of new formations. Barroso gives histories of most of these local corps; I reproduce details of just three of them, to give a general idea of the evolution of such units prior to the Paraguayan War.

The first of these is Mato Grosso. The local forces of this province were descended from a 'Legion of Mato Grosso' which existed toward the end of the 18th century. Following the War of Independence (1822–25) existing local forces were reorganised as a corps of *Ligeiros* ('Lights'). In 1832 this force was organised into eight companies; five of *Caçadores*, two of Artillery, and one of Marine Artillery. In 1840 the province raised a company of cavalry and the artillery companies were combined into a battalion of 465 men. In 1842 this force was officially designated as a 'Fixed Corps', auxiliary to the army, a company of *Pedestres* was added, and the artillery battalion was taken into the regular army as the 4th Battalion of Foot Artillery.

In 1843 a new artillery battalion was formed and the entire force was reorganised as two 'Fixed Corps', the first comprising four companies of *Caçadores*, two of artillery, one of cavalry, and one of artificers, total 768 men; the second comprising two companies of *Caçadores* and two of artillery, total 438 men. Somewhat later, this force was rationalised as two equal corps of *Caçadores* of six companies each, an artillery corps of four companies, an artificer company, and a squadron of cavalry. The general reform of 'Fixed Corps' in 1851 saw the reorganisation of the *Caçadores* into a single battalion and the cavalry into a 'half-regiment', the artillery remaining unchanged.

At the tine of the Paraguayan invasion in 1865, the Mato Grosso 'Fixed Corps' totalled, on paper, 1,327 men; in reality, however, only about 600 could be mustered to defend the province. The artillery corps, assisted by Indians and local volunteers, defended the fortress of Coimbra; the *Caçador* battalion, assisted by local National Guards and volunteers, held the line of the Rio Apa for some weeks; while the 130 cavalrymen, under Lieutenant-Colonel Antonio Dias, conducted a holding action around Nioac and along the line of the Rio Feio. Eventually, in the face of overwhelming numbers, the remainder of the corps formed a nucleus around which local refugees and National Guards could coalesce, and conducted a fighting retreat to Laguna.

In 1824–25 a corps of militia was formed in Goiás province to replace the ancient (and almost useless) corps of *Ordenanças* dating back to the 17th century. An order of 1831 abolished the heterogeneous assortment of militias, *Ordenanças*, and Municipal Guards forming the then existing reserve forces. By 1839 the province had a company of 100 *Ligeiros*, reduced to just 39 men two years later. In 1841 there was a 'Fixed Corps' of one company of *Caçadores*, expanded to two companies, plus a company of cavalry, the following year. In 1850, the above force having 'disappeared' in the meantime, the government raised a new company of *Caçadores*. With the general reform of 1860 this was expanded to a battalion of *Caçadores* and a company of cavalry. Following the outbreak of war with Paraguay this force was sent to São Paulo to take part in a projected invasion of enemy territory. While there, due to a shortage of horses the cavalry company was combined with dismounted cavalry from São Paulo and Minas Gerais provinces to form a battalion of foot *Caçadores*, which was later taken into the regular army as the 20th Line Infantry.

Local defence in Minas Gerais province was initially in the hands of the 'Divisions of Rio Doce', established in 1820 to protect the local populace from the attacks of hostile Indians; this totalled 268 men. In 1840 this force was retitled the *Caçadores de Montanha* and expanded by two companies of *Pedestres*, to which a company of cavalry and two more of *Caçadores* were added in 1851. In 1860, following the general abolition of *Pedestre* units, the local 'Fixed Corps' comprised a battalion of four companies of *Caçadores* and a cavalry company. On the outbreak of war with Paraguay the *Caçador* battalion was accepted into the *Voluntários da Pátria* organisation as the 17th Corps of Volunteers, and took part in the expedition to retake Mato Grosso province. The subsequent history of the province's cavalry company is noted in the preceding paragraph.

The 'Fixed Corps' appear in army dress regulations for the first time in 1852, their uniforms formerly having been determined by their respective local authorities. The 1852 uniforms followed much the same pattern as other army units, but tended to be simpler. They were never authorised the coatee, but instead wore the tunic for all orders of dress; initially the full dress tunic had the entire collar and round cuffs in the authorised provincial facing colour(s), the 'second' or undress tunic having collar patches and three-button cuff flaps as used by other corps. From 1856 the flapped cuff was authorised for all orders of dress, the full dress tunic continuing to be distinguished by a facing-colour collar and the 'second uniform' tunic by collar patches. The full dress headgear was the low bell-crowned shako as used by other corps, with a brass badge on the front comprising the provincial initial or initials surrounded by a wreath with imperial crown above. Plumes were of branch of service colour: green for *Caçadores*, red for cavalry, and black with a red tip for artillery. Undress headgear was initially a small round cap (see Figure 127), later replaced by the kepi. Other items of uniform were much the same as those used by the rest of the army.

The various corps were distinguished by the colours of their collars, cuffs, and piping. Barroso provides details of these distinctions as listed in the 1852 dress regulations:

Caçadores – Mato Grosso: green collar, red cuffs and piping; Bahia: red collar, dark blue cuffs, green piping; Piauí: dark blue collar, yellow cuffs, green piping; Ceará: yellow collar, dark blue cuffs, green piping; São Paulo: light blue collar and cuffs, red piping; Minas Gerais: dark blue collar and cuffs, green piping; Goiás: red collar, cuffs and piping; Rio Grande do Norte: dark blue collar and piping, green cuffs; Espírito Santo: green collar and piping, dark blue cuffs; Paraíba: green collar, dark blue cuffs and piping; Sergipe: dark blue collar, green cuffs and piping; and Pernambuco: red collar and cuffs, dark blue piping.

Cavalry – Mato Grosso: red collar, cuffs and piping; Bahia: red collar, dark blue cuffs, green piping; Minas Gerais and São Paulo: light blue collar, dark blue cuffs, red piping; Goiás: red collar and piping, dark blue cuffs; and Pernambuco: dark blue collar and piping, red cuffs.

On the 'second uniform' tunic, the collar patches were the colour of the full dress collar, and the cuff flaps were the same colour as the full dress cuffs. These distinctions varied a bit over the years as new provincial forces were raised, and other corps modified their facings. No complete list is known for their final years, but some examples are noted in the captions to the figures.

'Fixed' Artillery Corps were only raised in the provinces of Mato Grosso, Amazonas, and Pará, that of Pará being dissolved in 1842 to leave only two provincial corps in existence. See Figure 99 for details of their uniforms. They had plain shoulder straps without the black woollen crescents shown in Figure 99. These still had the piping along the edge, but it was red for Matto Grosso and light blue for Amazonas.

As noted earlier, all these units vanished in the reorganisation of 1866, when they served either as the nuclei of new line, national guard, and volunteer units, or were broken up and used as reinforcements.

117. *CAÇADOR*, CORPS OF SÃO PAOLO c.1852
Full dress. Black shako with brass badge ('S.P.' within a wreath), national cockade, green plume, black cords, flounders, and tassels. Dark blue tunic with light blue collar and cuffs piped red, red piping down the front opening and edging the dark blue shoulder straps, brass buttons, black (possibly detachable?) woollen shoulder rolls. Plain dark blue trousers (no stripe or piping), white gloves, black belts and gaiters. This is the original full dress uniform, as authorised in 1852. Within a few years it was modified by extending the cuff flaps of the 'second uniform' to the full dress tunic (for São Paulo, these would be light blue on dark blue cuffs, all piped red).

118. *CAÇADOR* HORNISTS c.1865
Detail 118a depicts a hornist (*corneta*) of the *Caçadores* of Mato Grosso in full dress. Shako as for the last figure except for having

the initials 'M.G.' on the plate (the standard pattern shako plate for 'Fixed Corps' being a wreath of laurel branches with the Imperial crown above and the provincial initials inside). Dark blue tunic with green collar and cuff flaps, dark blue cuffs and shoulder straps, all edged with red piping including the front opening – a number of Barroso plates show the cuff flaps coming to a point at the top as depicted here. Black shoulder rolls, brass buttons. A broad yellow tape with red centre stripe edges the collar and cuffs, and runs down the front and rear seams of the sleeves. Dark blue trousers, white gloves, black belt and gaiters. Brass horn (see main figure) with green cords and tassels.

The main figure shows a *corneta* of the *Caçadores* of Pernambuco in 'second uniform'. Dark blue kepi with red band, yellow horizontal and vertical piping (presumably indicating a general uniform modification rather than a special musicians' distinction), national cockade on the front, black chinstrap. Uniform the same as that described above except for having dark blue collar and cuffs, red rectangular collar patches, and dark blue cuff flaps, all piped yellow.

119. *CAÇADOR*, CORPS OF SERGIPE c.1865
'Second uniform'. Dark blue kepi and band, trimmed with green piping. Dark blue tunic, collar, collar patches, cuffs, and shoulder straps, all with green piping, green cuff flaps, brass buttons. White summer trousers, black gaiters and belts. His pouch belt is depicted in the original as having a square or rectangular brass plate on the breast. 'Fixed Corps' seem to have used a variety of equipment models, some being depicted with only a waistbelt, while others have mixed equipment, with the pouch on a bandolier combined with a waistbelt.

Fig 117   *Fig 118* *Fig 119*   *Fig 120*   *Fig 121*   *Fig 122*

118a

Fig 123   *Fig 124*   *Fig 125*   *Fig 126*   *Fig 127*

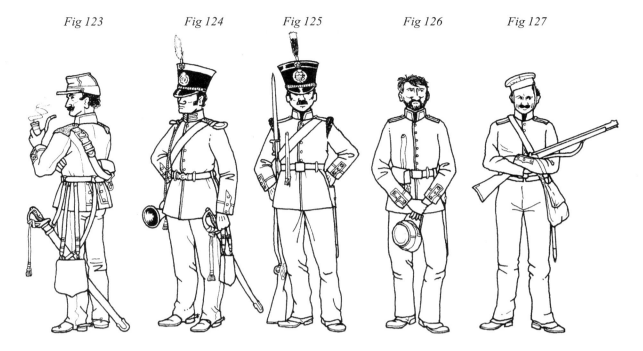

120. *CAÇADOR*, CORPS OF RIO GRANDE DO NORTE c.1865 Campaign dress. Dark blue kepi and band, green piping, white curtain. The dark blue tunic appears to have exactly the same distinctions as the last figure: dark blue collar patches and cuffs, green piping and cuff flaps – a clear modification from the 1852 regulations; dark blue trousers; and black gaiters, belts, (percussion cap?) pouch, and cravat. A dark blue roll is worn over the right shoulder, and there is an off-white haversack at the left hip and an iron water-bottle on the right. The needle and brush for the musket hang from a black strap buttoned to the right breast, as for other elements of the army. This is one of two figures depicted by Barroso with a curious device of three small yellow discs or ovals arranged in a triangular form on the front of the kepi, the significance of which is unknown.

121. *CAÇADOR*, CORPS OF PARAÍBA c.1865 Fatigue uniform. Dark blue kepi with green band, no visible piping (indicating dark blue piping perhaps?), and a yellow frontal device as for the last figure. Plain white cotton jacket and trousers with brass buttons (note the three buttons on his sleeve, placed so as to imitate cuff flaps), black gaiters. He wears his kepi over a red bandanna.

122. *CAÇADOR*, CORPS OF ESPÍRITO SANTO c.1865 Service dress. Dark blue kepi with green band and vertical piping, black chinstrap. Dark blue tunic with green collar patches, cuff flaps, and piping (including the slit and pocket flaps on the rear of the skirts), dark blue collar and cuffs, brass buttons. White trousers, black gaiters, belts, and pouch.

123. CAVALRY TROOPER, CORPS OF PARANÁ c.1865 'Second uniform'. Dark blue kepi with light blue band and piping (including around the crown), white chinstrap. Dark blue tunic with dark blue collar, cuffs, and cuff flaps, light blue collar patches and piping, brass buttons, and brass chain shoulder straps. Dark blue

(winter) trousers, white belts with brass fittings, plain black leather sabretache.

Refer to Figure 86 for the appearance of an officer of this corps in 'second uniform'. This would be basically the same as that described for the trooper, except for having gilt buttons, gold epaulettes in place of the chain shoulder straps, gold cuff rank lace, gilt belt fittings, white gloves, and a dark red or crimson waist-sash with gold knot and crimson tassels. The leather sabre knot would be white. The original source shows him in white linen (summer) trousers.

124. CAVALRY TRUMPETER, CORPS OF MATO GROSSO c.1865 Full dress. Black shako with brass plate and chin-scales, yellow tape circling the top, red plume. Dark blue tunic with red collar, cuff flaps, and piping, dark blue cuffs, brass buttons and shoulder-scales, two white tapes or laces on either side of the collar. Dark blue trousers, white belts, gloves, and sabre knot, green trumpet cords.

125. ARTILLERYMAN, CORPS OF MATO GROSSO c.1865 Full dress. Black shako with brass plate and chin-scales, national cockade, black plume with red tip. Dark blue tunic with black collar and cuff flaps, dark blue cuffs and shoulder straps, all piped red, black shoulder rolls, brass buttons. Dark blue trousers, black gaiters, white belts and gloves.

126. ARTILLERYMAN, CORPS OF AMAZONAS c.1865 'Second uniform'. Dark blue kepi and band, light blue piping, white chinstrap. Dark blue tunic with dark blue collar, cuffs, cuff flaps, and shoulder-straps, black collar patches, all edged with light blue piping, brass buttons. Dark blue trousers, black gaiters. White belt with brass plate and smallish black percussion cap pouch on right hip.

127. *ANSPESSADA* OF *PEDESTRES* c.1860 Although all *Pedestre* units were ordered abolished in 1860, this *anspessada* of the Corps of Santa Catarina province is included as a guide to their uniform and armament while they existed. He wears a small dark blue cap with black band and chinstrap. Plain dark blue waist-length jacket, red cuff flaps and rank stripe on the lower sleeve, white piping edging the shoulder straps, brass buttons. White (or dark blue) trousers, black gaiters and waistbelt, white haversack. *Pedestres* were distinguished by various provincial facings, though these appear to have been rudimentary compared to other 'Fixed Corps' units: Barroso depicts the *Pedestre* corps of Bahia province wearing much the same uniform as that depicted here, distinguished by light blue collar patches (and rank stripes for a corporal) and dark blue cuffs. *Pedestres* were armed with a carbine or musketoon (no bayonet), with a sabre briquet as sidearm.

THE *GUARDIA NACIONAL*

The *Guardia Nacional* or National Guard was the largest single source of manpower for Brazilian armies during the Paraguayan War. Unfortunately, it is also the force on which the least information is available. Barroso includes a small section devoted to the *Guardia* at the end of his book, but it totals only three-and-a-half pages of text and six plates to cover the force's entire history. Consequently I've included a few figures from other sources in this section in an effort to fill some of the gaps. However, coverage remains sketchy.

During the war of 1825–28 with Argentina, Brazilian reserves and second-line forces were provided by a hotchpotch of militias, *Ordenanças*, municipal guards, and so on, with little standardisation or co-ordination between them. Needless to say, their performance during this conflict left a good deal to be desired. After the war it was decided to abolish these miscellaneous corps and replace them with a single standardised reserve force. Accordingly, the Decree of 18 August 1831 created the *Guardia Nacional*, comprising all three major combat arms – infantry, cavalry, and artillery. Each infantry battalion was to include two companies of *Caçadores*, but there was to be no separate corps of such troops. Units were to be recruited, organised, and administered by the individual provinces, which necessarily led to some diminution of the expected standardisation.

The Imperial Court also raised its own National Guard units from the country at large, as if it were a province in its own right. These units 'of the Court' tended to be better trained and equipped than ordinary provincial units, and seem to have often served as 'model' units for the corps as a whole.

The *Guardia* was completely reorganised in 1851, when a range of new uniforms were introduced. The 1851 Dress Regulations were accompanied by an album of explanatory lithographs which form the basis for a number of Barroso's plates, though there is little additional information in his text. Despite some alterations during the period 1858–65 these basic uniforms appear to have still been in use at the outbreak of the Paraguayan War.

In 1865, Decree No.3,383 mobilised some 14,796 *Guardias Nacionales* for war service, some to be sent to join the field armies, others to perform 'police' functions behind the lines or to relieve regular troops in provincial garrisons. The National Guard continued to recruit throughout the war, as the demand for units for all sorts of duties continued to grow. To the best of my knowledge there are no available figures for how many National Guards were eventually mobilised. Barroso provides a hint by noting that the province of Rio Grande do Sul alone mobilised a total of 43,500 during the war, of whom 29,200 saw combat. Equally, I know of no complete listing of the number of units raised. This is probably not too surprising considering that the war seems to have seen a continual process of units being raised, disbanded, amalgamated, renumbered, etc, to the point where even attempting to follow the history of a single unit can be tortuous. To complicate the picture even further, there were also units designated as 'Provisional Corps' which seem to have nevertheless been considered part of the National Guard. Available evidence suggests these were ad hoc units formed of drafts from various sources and 'provisionally' attached to the regular line, though their exact status remains unclear.

As regards dress, the outbreak of war saw a fairly rapid disappearance of the last of the fancy, and rather old-fashioned, 1851 uniforms. No new dress regulation was ever promulgated for the National Guard during the war, management of such matters being generally left to the individual provinces. As a general rule National Guard units seem to have worn uniforms based on those of the regular army, but simplified and plainer, with little extraneous decoration. As with the regulars, field improvisations were widespread on campaign, and many units seem to have been largely dressed in civilian clothing (whether they started out that way, or if it resulted from a shortage of replacement uniforms, is another question). They seem to have worn roughly the same range of dark blue woollen winter and white cotton summer uniforms as the regular army, with little indication of the use of the brown drill working uniform.

The following quotation from Alexander Majoribanks' *Travels in South and North America* (1853) provides a valuable snapshot of the general appearance of National Guard troops at about mid-century: '2nd July [1852] during my residence there [at Bahia]. There was a review of all the troops on that day both cavalry and infantry, including the militia or national guard of the town. The regular Brazilian infantry are dressed in white woollen cloth and caps of the same with blue facings; but the national guard have dark blue short coats, with dark green facings, black covered buttons, black epaulettes, white cotton trousers, with green feathers in their caps. I never saw a more plain elegant dress. The men however were singular looking beings. Nearly one-fifth of them were jet black negroes, and a number of boys, not more than 14 or 15, were interspersed amongst them, some of them not exceeding four feet and a half in height; and the operation of shouldering arms seemed nearly to capsize them altogether ... The cavalry were the most wretched looking beings I ever saw, ill-mounted, ill-dressed, and badly accoutred'.

128. NATIONAL GUARD INFANTRY FUSILIER

1851 Full dress. Black shako with brass 'sunburst' plate bearing the provincial unit number, national cockade, red plume, and white cords. Dark blue coatee with white collar, cuff flaps, and skirt linings, red cuffs and piping

Fig 128   *Fig 129*   *Fig 130*   *Fig 131*   *Fig 132*

edging the collar, cuff flaps, and front opening, brass buttons, a yellow 'disc' on either side of the collar, and epaulettes with red strap and pad and brass crescents with white fringe. White belts, trousers, gaiters, and gloves. The collar 'disc' is a feature of most of the 1851 uniforms depicted by Barroso, but is not explained in his text. I would suspect it to be the 'world globe' from the Brazilian coat of arms, possibly embroidered, though it could also conceivably be of metal.

129. NATIONAL GUARD *CAÇADOR* 1851 Full dress. Black conical shako with brass bugle and Imperial crown on the front, national cockade, and dark green plume, wrapped with black cords. Dark green coatee with black collar and cuffs, white skirt linings, brass buttons, dark green contre-epaulettes with brass crescents, white discs on the collar. White trousers and gloves, black belts. Curiously, this is the only dark green uniform depicted in Barroso among the various Model 1851 uniforms. A *Caçador* officer depicted wears an almost identical uniform (barring the distinction of rank), except that his coatee appears to be dark blue rather than green. An officer and *Caçador* depicted in 'second uniform' are also dressed in dark blue. Assuming this is not simply a printing error, I could not even hazard a guess as to the reason for this variation. It is unclear if these *Caçador* companies survived the reorganisation of the National Guard in 1865–66. Personally, I suspect they were probably 'standardised' out of existence at this point.

130. NATIONAL GUARD *CAÇADOR* 1851 'Second uniform'. Wide-topped shako in black oil-cloth cover fastened by a row of brass buttons down the left side. Dark blue waist-length jacket with black collar and cuff flaps, brass buttons, white collar disc and trousers. These 'second uniforms' would probably have constituted the field uniforms of the period and show considerable variation from one branch to another. The totally different shako model worn with undress remains unexplained. An officer depicted in 'second uniform' wears similar dress,

but with a tunic in place of the jacket, having a gold rank stripe circling the cuff.

131. NATIONAL GUARD ARTILLERY OFFICER 1851 Full dress. Black shako with gilt plate and chin-scales, national cockade, red 'waterfall' plume issuing from a black ball pompom. Dark blue coatee with what appear to be dark green collar and cuffs (though they might be intended as black, or discoloured), both edged with red piping, red tail lining and turnbacks, gold buttons, epaulettes, and collar discs. Red or crimson waist-sash (with tassels on the right hip), white trousers, black gloves, sabre with gold knot on a white bandolier with gilt breast plate.

132 & 133. NATIONAL GUARD RESERVE INFANTRYMEN 1851 Figure 132 wears full dress. Black cylindrical shako, brass elongated star plate and chin-scales, national cockade and white plume. Dark blue tunic with dark blue collar and cuffs, all edged with white piping, white collar discs, brass buttons, dark blue contre-epaulettes with white strap edging and brass crescents. White trousers and gloves, black waistbelt and musket strap.

Figure 133 wears his 'second' or undress uniform, which is much the same as that of the preceding figure except that the shako is replaced by a dark blue cap with yellow band, and the epaulettes are missing. The rear skirts of the tunic have a triple row of white vertical piping, as well as piping edging the pocket flaps. I would presume the brass-hilted sidearm is a sword-bayonet, since no additional bayonet is shown (on the other hand, no cartridge pouch is depicted in the original either).

134. TROOPER, 1st NATIONAL GUARD CAVALRY REGIMENT OF THE COURT 1858 Full dress. Steel helmet with brass crest, front badge, and chin-scales, red horsehair mane. Dark blue coatee with white collar and cuff flaps, both edged with red piping, as are the dark blue cuffs and front opening. Brass buttons and shoulder-scales, red turnbacks, two yellow lace loops on either side of the collar. Dark blue trousers with red double stripe. White belts with brass or gilt fittings, white gloves and sabre knot. The uniform depicted was newly adopted in 1858, apparently by this regiment alone.

According to the 1851 regulations, cavalry were to wear a wide-topped shako similar to that of other units. A trooper of the 2nd Cavalry c.1851 shown in Barroso wears the shako with brass front plate and chin-scales, yellow lace encircling the top, and a rather short red plume. The rest of his uniform is much as depicted here except that the collar and cuff flaps are dark blue instead of white, the former with some sort of white device (possibly intended as the world globe). On the other hand, an officer of the 1st Regiment (it is not stated if this is the 'Court' regiment or a provincial unit) depicted in *grande gala* or full dress wears a red coatee with yellow collar and piping, red cuffs, green cuff flaps, gold buttons and rank epaulettes; black trousers with a red double stripe; and the shako with a 'waterfall' plume of red feathers. It would therefore appear that considerable variation was allowed in the cavalry uniform.

135. NATIONAL GUARD INFANTRYMAN OF THE COURT c.1865–70 Campaign dress. From Barroso, after a contemporary lithograph. Kepi covered by a white Havelock. Plain dark blue tunic and trousers with brass buttons. Black belts, pouch, boots, and musket strap, white haversack. The pack appears to be of black canvas, with an iron mess-tin strapped to the rear and a black or dark grey roll on the top.

136. NATIONAL GUARD INFANTRYMAN c.1865–70 Campaign dress. This figure comes from a contemporary newspaper engraving, described as 'National Guards waiting to enter the line'. Although no colours are indicated, the uniforms are shaded and would most likely have been plain dark blue with brass buttons. The upper garment is a sort of smock or 'shirt', of a type which seems to have been widely worn by both National Guards and Volunteers. It generally had a pleated breast with a reinforcing yoke covering the upper breast and

shoulders. Some models were open all the way down the front (as here), while others were only open to the waist and were pulled on over the head.

137. TROOPER, *LANCERO REGIMENT DA RIO GRANDE DO SUL* c.1865–70 Campaign dress. From a watercolour sketch in the National Historical Museum, Rio de Janeiro. Although not designated as a National Guard in the title, it seems likely that is what this figure is. White kepi cover and chinstrap, black peak. Plain dark blue tunic with brass buttons. White trousers tucked into black boots. Black waistbelt, circular brass plate. Brown saddle, black straps, dark blue saddle blanket and mantle roll. His lance has a steel blade and a plain red pennon.

138. NATIONAL GUARD CAVALRYMAN c.1865–70 Campaign dress. From a newspaper engraving: the uniform is unshaded in the original and would therefore probably be the plain white cotton summer variety. Hat, belts, and boots appear to be black. Note the sabre slings hooked together; whether this indicates a shortage of weapons, or that the trooper has simply left his sabre in his tent as an encumbrance, is unclear.

139–141. PROVINCIAL CAVALRYMEN c.1866–70 Barroso depicts three figures from what he describes as 'the celebrated Provisional Corps of National Guard Cavalry forming the Division of General Andrade Neves'. These units were recruited in Rio Grande do Sul province and seem to have largely worn the local gaucho-style dress.

Figure 139 wears a red hat, the turned-up brim of which shows a black lining (possibly leather). White cords circle the crown and are tied under the chin. His open black jacket is worn over a white shirt. The loose red *bombacho* trousers have a convoluted strip in the same colour (some sort of lace or embroidery) down the outer side. The soft heel-less boots are of natural leather. A dark brown fringed blanket or poncho is wrapped around his shoulders, the ends decorated with alternating stripes of black and ochre yellow. A brown bag of some

Fig 133   *Fig 134*   *Fig 135*   *Fig 136*

Fig 137   Fig 138   Fig 139   Fig 140   Fig 141

sort, possibly leather, hangs at his right hip, and an entirely steel sabre with black leather strap and knot at his left.

Figure 140 wears a black hat with yellow chincords. The visible part of the hatband appears mainly white, but might well be an attempt to depict a highlight on a dark leather band. Plain dark blue jacket worn over a red shirt. Light pink neckerchief, white trousers, dark brown boots. Wide dark brown leather waistbelt, the divided ends of which are fastened with three small brass buckles. A fringed yellowish-brown blanket or poncho, the ends decorated with three mid-brown stripes, is slung over his right shoulder. Hanging from his left wrist are natural leather straps, used as a horsewhip.

Figure 141 wears a brown hat with a white cord (or conceivably a thin chain) going under his nose, worn over a red headscarf. Plain lightish brown poncho, black trousers, natural leather boots, dark brown sabre knot. Visible at the neck, under the poncho, is what appears to be some sort of red scarf, but this is poorly delineated and might be intended to be a shirt.

In 1868 Sir Richard Burton saw a review of a Brazilian cavalry corps numbering six full troops. He writes: 'they were mostly Brazilians, Rio Grandenses, not liberated negroes. These Provincials, riders from their babyhood, are reputed as the best cavaliers throughout the Empire, where the "man on horseback" is universal. Some were lancers; their heavy wooden weapons, not nearly so handy as the bamboo of Hindostan, were decorated with white stars on red pennons, they carried regulation sabres and coarse horse-pistols, and the European trappings made them look much more soldier-like than the infantry ... The dragoons had swords, Spencer [eight-round] carbines, and in some cases pistols.'

THE *VOLUNTÁRIOS DA PÁTRIA*

As already mentioned, the *Voluntários da Pátria* became a major source of manpower during the war, with many of the earlier units seeing action and then being reformed into new units. Barroso's text includes the following unit numbers and the regions from which they were recruited:

At Court – 1st, 2nd, 4th, 9th, 31st, 32nd, and 38th
Amazonas – 14th
Bahia – 3rd, 10th, 14th, 15th, 23rd, 24th, 29th, 40th, 41st, 43rd, 46th, 53rd, 54th, the Zouave Battalion, and a unit called the Cuirassiers
Ceará – 26th
Espírito Santo – 47th
Goiás – 16th
Maranhão – 22nd, 36th, and 37th
Mato Grosso – 50th
Minas Gerais – 17th, 18th, and 27th
Pará and Piauí – 13th, 34th, 39th, and 55th
Paraíba – 25th
Paraná – 20th
Pernambuco – 11th, 21st, 30th, 44th, 51st, 52nd, and 56th
Rio Grande do Norte – 28th
Rio Grande do Sul – 33rd, 35th, 48th, and 49th
Rio de Janeiro – 5th, 6th, 8th, and 12th
Santa Catarina – 29th
São Paulo – 7th, 42nd, and 45th
Sergipe – 19th

If you look through this list carefully, however, you will notice that several unit numbers are duplicated.

It would appear that as the war continued the Volunteers' initial uniforms were replaced by the more practical style depicted in Figures 144, 146, and 148.

142. OFFICER, 7th *CORPO DA VOLUNTÁRIOS DA PÁTRIA* Hat black with gilt badge and red tuft. Jacket and trousers dark blue, collar, cuff bars, and shoulder-straps also dark blue, gilt buttons. Gilt Volunteers hero on left sleeve. Red waist-sash with gold lace toggles and red tassels. Black leather belts, steel scabbard and hilt, white sword knot and gloves.

Another Barroso illustration shows an officer of the 5th CVP. His hat is the same as that depicted, but the jacket and trousers are in an early form of olive-green, with black collar, gold lace on shoulder-straps, black cuff bar with a gold lace rank stripe, silver buttons and buckles. His belts are black leather, with steel scabbard and hilt and silver sword knot.

143. SERGEANT, 11th *CORPO DA VOLUNTÁRIOS DA PÁTRIA* This figure is wearing a uniform that, although smart, may not have lasted very long on campaign. The hat is a small peaked cap in blue with a yellow lace tassel and toggle on its top, brass unit badge ('VP'), and black leather visor. Tunic and trousers are medium blue. Collar and cuffs are medium blue with a yellow cloth patch and brass number '11' on the collar, cuff bar red, yellow rank lace (four stripes) on left forearm. Brass buttons, buckle, and Volunteers unit badge on left sleeve. Black waistbelt over a red sash tied on the right hip.

144. SERGEANT, 13th *CORPO DA VOLUNTÁRIOS DA PÁTRIA* Summer dress. Hat black, chinstrap black. Jacket and trousers white linen, collar white with red patches, cuffs and shoulder straps white, front of jacket piped in red, brass buttons, buckles, and Volunteers unit badge on sleeve. Red rank lace on left forearm. Black leather belts and straps, white percussion cap pouch, brass chape on black leather bayonet scabbard. The cords to his brass rifle brush and pricker are green. At his left hip is a brass case with a green cord and tassel and yellow toggle; this is believed to be a fife case. Black shoes, brown blanket roll.

145. PRIVATE, 16th *CORPO DA VOLUNTÁRIOS DA PÁTRIA* This is the unit that subsequently became the 16th *Corpo da Voluntários Auxiliar*, also known as the Battalion *Garibaldino*. It was named after the Italian hero Giuseppe Garibaldi, who before helping to liberate his own country had served in Uruguay, where he and his men had first begun to wear their famous red shirts. The colour red had been chosen because gauchos from the Brazilian state of Rio Grande do Sul, where Garibaldi had participated in the rebellion of 1838 before moving to Uruguay, wore red shirts so that the blood of slain cattle would be less noticeable.

Kepi red with green base band piped white, brass button, black leather visor and chinstrap. Blouse red, collar, cuffs, pocket flaps, and button fly green piped white. Trousers green. Black leather straps and equipment, black buttons, brass buckle and bayonet fittings. The 16th became the 48th CVP in 1867, but I'm uncertain if this uniform continued in use.

146. PRIVATE, 20th *CORPO DA VOLUNTÁRIOS DA PÁTRIA* 'Second uniform'. Kepi blue, base band blue, piping green, small square brass unit badge with '20' stamped through it, brass button, black visor and chinstrap. Jacket and trousers dark blue, collar and cuffs dark blue, brass buttons, buckle, and Volunteers badge on left sleeve. Dark blue blanket roll, black leather belts, straps, and shoes, white linen haversack. Water-bottle is white with a black strap.

A picture of a private of the 25th CVP in 1867 shows him wearing the same uniform but with the following changes: kepi with white sun cover, black visor and chinstrap, brass '25' above visor; water-bottle grey metal; rifle brush and pricker suspended from black straps; white trousers. Another illustration of this unit, dating to 1866, shows a private with dark blue trousers and a green waist-sash tied on the left side. Yet another picture, showing a private of the 25th in 1869, from a description by the Conde d'Eu, shows him wearing a black hat like Figure 142. The cockade is a yellow star on a green rosette, while the jacket style is as per Figure 146.

Fig 142   Fig 143   Fig 144   Fig 145   Fig 146

Fig 147   Fig 148   Fig 149   Fig 150

The jacket and trousers are all dark blue except the shoulder straps, which are red. Brass buttons, black leather equipment.

147. PRIVATE, 28th *CORPO DA VOLUNTÁRIOS DA PÁTRIA* His green jacket is of a longer cut. Collar, cuffs, and shoulder-straps are also green. The trousers are white linen. Blanket roll blue, belts and straps black. A picture of an officer of this unit, from a description by the Conde D'Eu, shows him in the same style hat but with a gold lace star on the green rosette rather than brass. His buttons and the Volunteers badge on his sleeve are gilt. His cuff bar, like that of Figure 142, is green with gold rank lace, while his waist-sash is crimson with a gold lace toggle and crimson fringe. White trousers, black leather sword slings, steel scabbard and hilt, silver lace sword knot.

A private of the 26th CVP is shown wearing the same hat as Figure 146 but with a brass number '26' under the cockade. Although the style of his blue jacket looks superficially the same as that of Figure 146 it has two large side pockets under the waistbelt. It has yellow shoulder-straps. Trousers are white, blanket roll dark blue, and backpack and straps black.

148. PRIVATE, 33rd *CORPO DA VOLUNTÁRIOS DA PÁTRIA* Campaign dress. Kepi with white cover and chinstrap, brass unit number, and black visor. It would appear that his dark blue jacket is not in the pleated style but is a normal type of tunic. It has red patches on the dark blue collar and red shoulder-straps. White shirt and trousers, brown leather sandals. White belts and straps, brass buttons and buckles, dark blue blanket roll. A black metal cooking utensil sits atop his backpack.

Other depictions of soldiers of this unit include a private resembling Figure 146. Forage cap with dark blue crown and green base, the tassel in yellow lace. Jacket and trousers are sky blue, collar, cuffs, and shoulder-straps also sky blue, brass buttons, buckles, and Volunteers badge. Blanket roll blue. White leather belts and straps, black leather ammunition pouch and shoes. Another private resembles Figure 147, with a brass '33' under the rosette; his jacket and trousers are the same as

the previous description. An officer resembling Figure 142 wears a blue kepi with red base band and gold rank lace, black visor and chinstrap, national cockade, and a yellow star on a green rosette; it would appear that no unit number is shown. His jacket and trousers are sky blue, collar, cuffs, cuff bar, and shoulder-straps also sky blue. Gold rank lace on cuffs, gilt Volunteers badge on sleeve. Waist-sash crimson with gold lace and toggles and crimson fringes. Black leather shoes, waistbelt, and sword slings, with gilt fittings. Steel scabbard and hilt, silver sword knot.

149. COLONEL, 41st *CORPO DA VOLUNTÁRIOS DA PÁTRIA* 'Second uniform'. Kepi dark blue with black leather visor, gold rank lace over red base band, showing as though it was piped red. Unit badge of gilt laurel leaves surrounding the unit number. Tunic dark blue, collar red, cuffs dark blue with red cuff bars and wide gold rank lace, front of tunic piped red, gilt buttons and buckles. Fringeless epaulettes, dark blue strap with red piping, gilt half-moon and gold lace holding strap. Waist-sash red, tied on the left side. Black leather waistbelt and sword slings, steel scabbard and hilt, white sword knot.

A captain of the 38th *Corpo da Voluntários da Pátria* is shown in a similar uniform. His kepi is the same but has more of the red band showing. Collar and cuffs dark blue piped red, no cuff bar. Blue shoulder straps but no epaulettes. Red waist-sash with gold lace toggles and red tassels is tied on right side. Black lace sword knot.

150. PRIVATE, ZOUAVE BATTALION OF BAHIA Red fez with light blue tassel. Shirt and waistcoat dark blue, yellow lace to both. Trousers red, waist-sash dark blue. White waistbelt and spats, black backpack and straps, dark blue blanket roll.

ARGENTINA 1864–70

On 26 February 1864 the Argentine Army was reorganised by President Mitre, with a view to reducing the standing army from eleven battalions to six, each of

400 men. Each battalion had five companies of 80 men, there being one company of grenadiers, one of *cazadores*, and three of fusiliers. The battalions which survived this overhaul were the 1st, 2nd, 3rd, 4th, and 6th, and the *Legión Militar*. The artillery was to remain at a strength of one regiment of 400 men, while the cavalry remained at eight regiments of 400 men, each regiment having two squadrons made up of two companies.

With the declaration of war on 16 April 1865, the National Guard was mobilised to be drafted into the regular army. The next day the formation of the *Ejército Nacional en Campaña* was announced, which was to comprise 19 battalions with 500 men in each. A total of 25,000 men would be raised, 10,000 to go to the regular army while the rest would form National Guard units.

In 1865 the National Guard gave the following returns of troops to the Government:

City of Buenos Aires	9,282
Province of Buenos Aires	32,320
Province of Catamarca (data given in 1863)	3,783
Province of Córdoba (data given in 1863)	8,000
Province of Corrientes (data given in 1863)	9,340
Province of Entre Ríos	19,316
Province of Jujuy	4,264
Province of La Rioja (no data given)	–
Province of Mendoza (data given in 1863)	5,708
Province of Salta	14,255
Province of San Juan	7,365
Province of San Luis	5,164
Province of Santa Fe (no data given)	–
Province of Santiago del Estero (data given in 1863)	19,514
Province of Tucumán	14,164
Total	154,478

A law of 5 June 1865 declared that it was obligatory for all married men aged between 17–45, and bachelors aged 17–50, to enrol in the active National Guard. Such individuals were destined to join the army for two years, while those found guilty of desertion had to serve for four years. National Guard Battalions that saw action in the war against Paraguay were:

Infantry
Battalion San Nicolás (Lieutenant-Colonel Juan Carlos Boerr)
Legión Militar (Lieutenant-Colonel Lezica)
1st Regiment National Guard, Battalion No.1 (Lieutenant-Colonel Juan Cobo)
1st Regiment National Guard, Battalion No.2 (Lieutenant-Colonel Carlos Urien)
3rd Regiment National Guard, Battalion No.1 (Lieutenant-Colonel Mateo Martínez)
3rd Regiment National Guard, Battalion No.2 (Lieutenant-Colonel José María Morales)
4th Regiment National Guard, Battalion No.2 (Lieutenant-Colonel José Luis Amandeo)
Battalion National Guard No.2 (Buenos Aires) (Colonel Martín Arenas)
Battalion National Guard No.3 (Buenos Aires) (Lieutenant-Colonel Juan Manuel Serrano)
Battalion National Guard No.4 (Buenos Aires) (Colonel Miguel Martínez de Hoz)
Battalion National Guard No.5 (Buenos Aires) (Lieutenant-Colonel Carlos Keen)

Major Julio A. Roca in the uniform of the Salta Battalion. Promoted to lieutenant-colonel before his 27th birthday, he became commanding officer of the 7th Line Battalion. (Photograph in the collection of his granddaughter Agustina Roca de Uriburu)

Battalion Corrientes No.1 (Lieutenant-Colonel Desiderio Sosa)
Battalion Libertad No.2 (Santa Fe) (Colonel José Esquivel)
Battalion General Paz No.3 (Santa Fe) (Lieutenant-Colonel Fidel Paz)
Battalion No.1 (Santa Fe) (Colonel José María Avalos)
Battalion Códoba No.1 (Colonel Cesáreo Domínguez)
Battalion Códoba No.2 (Lieutenant-Colonel Olmos)
Battalion Tucumán (Lieutenant-Colonel Juan A. Casanova)
Battalion San Juan (Lieutenant-Colonel Juan Giuffra)
Battalion Pringles (San Luis) (Lieutenant-Colonel José María Cabot)
Battalion Mendoza (Lieutenant-Colonel Manuel Morillo)
Battalion Cazadores de la Rioja (Lieutenant-Colonel Julio [Gaspar] Campos)
Battalion Salta (Lieutenant-Colonel Manuel del Prado)
Battalion Entre Ríos (Colonel José Santos Caraza)
Battalion Libertad de Catamarca (Lieutenant-Colonel Máximo Matoso)
Battalion of Sappers (Lieutenant-Colonel J. Martínez)

Cavalry
General San Martín Regiment (Buenos Aires) (Colonel Esteban García)

Officers of the 1st National Guard of Corrientes Battalion, 1865. Some are wearing chest frogging, while all have elaborate rank lace on their forearms. (Courtesy of the Archivo General de la Nacion, Buenos Aires)

General Lavalle Regiment (Colonel Pantaleón Sotelo; Lieutenant-Colonel Mariano Orzábal after Sotelo was promoted to command of a brigade)
Squadron of Guides (Lieutenant-Colonel Romero)
Regiment of Cavalry (Corrientes) (Lieutenant-Colonel Paiva)
Regiment of Cavalry (Corrientes) (Lieutenant-Colonel López)
4th Squadron of Santa Fe (horse artillery) (Lieutenant-Colonel Leopoldo Nelson)
Plantel de Voluntarios Santafecino (Santa Fe) (Colonel José Agustin Fernández)
Regiment Blandengues de Belgrano (Santa Fe) (Lieutenant-Colonel Faustino Joaquim Arámbulo)
National Guard Cavalry Regiment of Santa Fe (Lieutenant-Colonel Goytea)
Squadron of Horse Artillery (Entre Ríos) (Lieutenant-Colonel Andrés Simón de Santa Cruz)

After the capture of the capital of Corrientes the Governor, Lagraña, began to organise new volunteer units to hamper the invading Paraguayan army and regain their homeland. These units, which were concentrated at San Roque, were the cavalry regiments of Paraná (the 1st and 2nd from Curuzú Cuatiá, the 3rd from Pay Ubre, the 4th, 5th, and 6th from Saladas), the Legión Empedrado, the Legión Lavalle, and the Legión Victoria. On the banks of the Río Uruguay two more cavalry regiments were formed, recruited in Bella Vista, along with a battalion of

infantry plus the militia from Lomos, San Cosme, Itatí, and Empedrado. These infantry units constituted the 1st Corrientes Battalion. The first few months of the war also saw 5,000 volunteers from Corrientes enlist. A battalion of students was also raised, but since most of its personnel were only 15 years old the authorities declined to accept its services, although the medical students in its ranks were enlisted to help in military hospitals.

By 24 August 1865 there were 11 battalions of the line (numbered 1, 2, 3, 4, 5, 6, 7, 8, 9, 11, and 12) and the 1st and 2nd Legions of Volunteers. It would appear that only the 7th and 11th Battalions took no part in the Paraguayan War. The strength of battalions was increased to six companies with 80 men in each. The commanders of these units were as follows (where units appear to have two or more commanders simultaneously it is usually because one or more of them had been promoted to the brevet rank of brigade commander):

1st Battalion
Major Benjamín Basavilbaso (killed at Tuyuti, 24 May 1866)
Lieutenant-Colonel Manuel Rossetti (killed at Curupaytí, 22 September 1866)
Major Pedro Retolaza (September 1866–67)
Major Ruperto Fuentes (October 1867)
Lieutenant-Colonel Juan Ayala (October 1867–70)
Major Angel Zavalía (November 1868)

2nd Battalion
Major Francisco Borges (1865)
Lieutenant-Colonel Adolfo Orma (1865–67)
Colonel Francisco Borges (1868–75)
Lieutenant-Colonel Emiliano Sáenz (1868–75)

3rd Battalion
Colonel Ignacio Rivas (1865)
Lieutenant-Colonel Felipe Aldecoa (killed at Yataiti-Corá, 11 June 1866)
Major Lindolfo Pagola (killed at Tuyuti, 24 May 1866)
Major Alejandro Díaz (killed at Curupaytí, 22 September 1866)
Major Pablo Alegre (1866–68)
Lieutenant-Colonel Teófilo R. Ivanowski (1868)
Major Teodoro García (1868)

4th Battalion
Lieutenant-Colonel Manuel Fraga (1865, killed at Curupaytí, 22 September 1866)
Colonel Florencio Romero (1866, killed at Lomas Valentinas, 27 December 1868)
Major Liborio Bernal (September 1867)
Lieutenant-Colonel Liborio Bernal (1868–79)
Sargento Mayor Gregorio Pereyra (1870)

5th Battalion
(This Battalion was reformed on 29 August 1865 from the 3rd Squadron of the 2nd Cavalry Regiment and the 2nd Company of the Fija de Martín García Battalion.)
Sargento Mayor Pedro Ximeno (1865)
Lieutenant-Colonel Rufino Victorica (1865–67)
Lieutenant-Colonel Alejandro Díaz (1866; killed at Curupaytí, 22 September 1866 – see 3rd Battalion; he must have been transferred after his promotion)

Lieutenant-Colonel Luis A. Pereyra (1867)
Lieutenant-Colonel Miguel F. Martínez de Hoz (1868)
Lieutenant-Colonel Nicolás Levalle (February 1869–78)

6th Battalion
Colonel José María Arredondo (1865)
Lieutenant-Colonel Luis María Campos (1865)
Sargento Mayor Belisario Liendo (July–August 1868)

7th Battalion
Lieutenant-Colonel Juan A. Casanova (June 1865)
Lieutenant-Colonel José Natalio Romero (May 1866)
Lieutenant-Colonel Hilario Lagos (April 1867–68)
Major Julio A. Roca (July 1867)
Major Domingo Gutiérrez (1868)
Lieutenant-Colonel Julio A. Roca (September 1868–74)

8th Battalion
Sargento Mayor Pedro Sagari (1865; killed at Corrientes, 25 May 1865)
Lieutenant-Colonel Juan Bautista Charlone (1865; killed at Curupaytí, 22 September 1866)
Colonel Manuel Caraza
Lieutenant-Colonel Baldomero F. Sotelo (1868–71)
Major Agustín Valerga
Lieutenant-Colonel Ramón Gómez Morales
Major Leonidas Pico
Lieutenant-Colonel Esteban Chousiño
Major José Orfila

9th Battalion
(This battalion was reformed on 1 May 1865 from the 3rd Squadron of the 5th Cavalry Regiment.)
Lieutenant-Colonel Benjamín Calvete (1865)
Major Joaquim Lora (1865)
Major Octavio Olascoaga (May 1867)

11th Battalion
(This battalion was reformed on 30 June 1865; in November 1868 it became the 9th Cavalry Regiment.)
Sargento Mayor Alvaro Barros (1865)
Captain Manuel Montenegro (1865)
Captain Juan G. Giles (1866)
Captain Luis Chausiño (1867)
Colonel Alvaro Barros (1868)
Lieutenant-Colonel Joaquim Lora (1868)

12th Battalion
(This battalion would later become the 1st and 2nd Volunteer Legions.)
Sargento Mayor Juan Ayala (October 1865)
Major Lucio V. Mansilla (October 1865)
Lieutenant-Colonel Lucio V. Mansilla (October 1867)
Major Eduardo Racedo (December 1867)
Lieutenant-Colonel Eduardo Racedo (June 1870)

Volunteer Legion
Lieutenant-Colonel José 'Pippo' Giribone (1865)

1st Volunteer Legion
Colonel António Susini

2nd Volunteer Legion
Lieutenant-Colonel José 'Pippo' Giribone

The only cavalry regiments to take part in the war were the 1st, 2nd (3rd Squadron only), 3rd, 8th, and 11th (part of which was used in 1870 as the nucleus of the Regiment 'General Lavalle' of the National Guard, which also participated in the war). Commanders of these regiments were:

1st Regiment
Lieutenant-Colonel Segovia (1865–70)
Major Amaro Catalán (1865–70)

2nd Regiment
Lieutenant-Colonel Benito Villar (1865)
Major Adolfo Cortina (1865)
Lieutenant-Colonel Bernadé Díaz (October 1867)
Major Clodomiro Villar (March 1868)
Colonel Francisco de Elías (April 1868)
Lieutenant-Colonel Hilario Lagos (August 1868)
Major Salvador Maldonado (January 1870)

3rd Regiment
Colonel Eustaquio Frías (1865–70)
Lieutenant-Colonel Emilio Vidal (1865–70)
Major Marcelino Bims (1865–70)
Major Pedro Timote (1865–70)

8th Regiment
(This regiment had three squadrons. On 17 January 1865 the Squadron of Guides and the Squadron 'Nueva Creación' were amalgamated with the single-squadron 8th Regiment and became its 2nd and 3rd Squadrons respectively.)
Lieutenant-Colonel Francisco del Prado (3rd Squadron) (1865–70)
Major António Benavídez (1st Squadron) (1865–70)
Major Fortunato Solano (2nd Squadron) (1865–70)

11th Regiment
Lieutenant-Colonel Pantaleón Sotelo (1865–68)
Major Cruz Cañete (1865–68)
Colonel Mariano Orzábal (1868)
Lieutenant-Colonel Cruz Cañete (1868)
Major Nicanor Ramos Mejía (1868)
Lieutenant-Colonel Alfredo Danel (August 1869)
Major Juan Rivademar (September 1869)

The Escort to the Governor
(Created 26 April 1865. It had two squadrons of 100 men, which were taken, one from each, from the 1st and 5th Cavalry Regiments.)
Lieutenant-Colonel Pedro C. Díaz

On 20 April 1865 a Company of *Zapadores* (Sappers) was formed, composed of 100 men commanded by Colonel Juan Cetz. On 1 June a Battalion of Engineers was created from this company, with half of it being sent to the front straight away under the command of *Sargento Mayor* Alejandro Díaz.

The 1st Regiment of Artillery consisted of light artillery organised in two squadrons, commanded by Colonel Julio de Vedia (July 1865) and Lieutenant-Colonel Ramón Ruiz (November 1865), later replaced respectively by Colonel Joaquim Viejobueno (November 1868) and Colonel Martin Arenas (December 1868). It was garrisoned in Buenos Aires at the start of the war. 15

March 1867 saw the formation of the *Brigada de Artillería de Plaza*, which was composed of three companies with 100 men in each. This unit was to take the place of the line artillery, which had been sent to the front line.

The *Cuerpo Médico Militar* (Medical Corps) was created by a decree of 9 May 1865. It was composed of a surgeon major with the rank of colonel, two 'first surgeons' with the rank of lieutenant-colonel, four army surgeons with the rank of *sargento mayor*, 16 regimental surgeons with the rank of captain, 20 medical assistants with the rank of adjutant, one chemist with the rank of adjutant, and 16 pharmacists with the rank of lieutenant.

ARMS

The outbreak of war in 1865 found Argentina's National Guard units equipped with many different makes and types of muskets and rifles, even including some old flintlocks. Alongside locally-produced weapons and Spanish imports there were Austrian Werndl muskets, Russian 11.4-calibre Berdans, and American 15-calibre Roberts percussion rifles. The regular line battalions and cavalry regiments, however, were issued with the Minié rifle or carbine of 14.66 calibre, and as the dire need to standardise ammunition became more pressing the Minié was gradually adopted for all Argentine units. By the end of the conflict the Argentine artillery were using field guns obtained from a variety of suppliers that included Whitworth, Krupp, and Hotchkiss.

FIGURES

Sources for the figures in this section are: paintings by Candido López in the Museo Historico Nacional, Buenos Aires; prints by Eleodero Marenco; the 'Coleccion Whitcomb' in the General Archives of the Nation, Buenos Aires; *Reseña Historica de la Infanteria Argentina* (1969); *Reseña Historica y Organica del Ejército Argentino* vol.2 (1971); *Los Números de Línea del Ejército Argentino*, vols.1 and 2, by Adolfo Saldías

(1912); *Los Cuerpos Militares en la Historia Argentina 1550–1950*, by Julio Mario Luqui-Lagleyze (1995); *Historia de la Artilleria Argentina*, by Colonel Pedro E. Marti Garro (1982); and notes and illustrations supplied by José Balaguer and Alberto del Pino Menck.

151. GENERAL BARTOLOMÉ MITRE Hat black with sweatband in national colours (light blue/white/light blue). Coat dark blue with gilt buttons and gold lace shoulder straps. Breeches are white, boots black.

152 & 153. GENERAL W. PAUNERO In Figure 152 he wears a blue kepi with gold rank lace and piping, sky blue-white national cockade, and black visor. Tunic is dark blue with black silk edging, gold cuff rank lace, crimson waist-sash with gold lace tassels, and gold lace aiguillettes. Waistbelt and sword slings black leather with gilt buckles. Breeches red with gold lace stripe. Black boots, steel scabbard, gilt hilt, gold lace sword knot. White cloth cloak. The Argentine system of officers' rank insignia followed that of the French when worn. In Figure 153 the crown of his kepi has a white cover. Jacket dark blue, collar and cuffs dark blue, gold lace shoulder bars, black silk lace edging. Trousers red with gold lace stripe, boots black.

154. ADJUTANT TO THE GENERAL STAFF Kepi all blue with gold rank lace and black visor. Tunic dark blue, collar and cuffs dark blue, cuff lace and shoulder bars gold lace, gilt buttons. Trousers red with gold lace stripe, shoes black.

155. OFFICER, STAFF CORPS Kepi with white cover and curtain and black visor. Shell jacket dark blue, collar and cuffs yellow, gold lace on cuffs and shoulder bars. Waistcoat white, gilt buttons. Trousers blue with gold lace stripe. Boots black, steel sword scabbard.

156. STAFF OFFICER Kepi red with blue bottom band, gold rank lace, national cockade, and black visor. Coat dark blue with gilt buttons and gold lace shoulder bars.

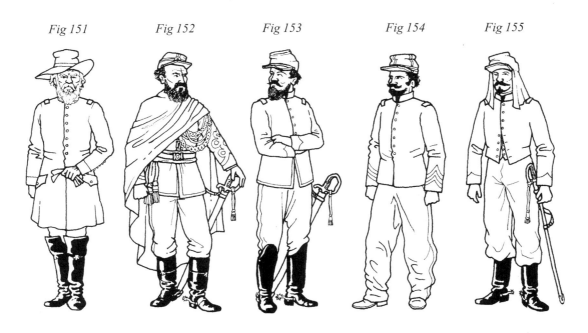

Fig 151   Fig 152   Fig 153   Fig 154   Fig 155

Waist-sash crimson silk with gold lace tassels, black leather waistbelt and sword slings. Breeches red with gold lace stripe.

157. OFFICER, 'ESTADO MAYOR' This figure comes from a painting by Candido López. Red kepi with blue bottom band, gold lace, national cockade, black visor, and gold lace chinstrap. Frock coat dark blue, red collar and cuffs, gold rank lace on arms. Waistcoat blue, baggy trousers red with gold lace stripe, shoes black. Gold lace sword knot, steel scabbard.

158. COLONEL IGNACIO RIVAS Hat yellow/buff felt with black sweatband, tunic blue with gilt buttons, blue collar and cuffs, and gold rank lace on cuffs. Trousers red with gold lace stripe, black boots. Black waistbelt and sword slings, gilt buckles, gold lace sword knot, gilt hilt, steel scabbard.

159. LINE INFANTRY OFFICER Kepi with white cover and curtain and black peak. Tunic dark blue, collar and cuffs dark blue, gilt buttons, gold cuff rank lace and shoulder bars. Waist-sash and tassels crimson, waistbelt and sword slings black. Trousers dark blue with gold lace stripe, shoes black. Scabbard steel, hilt gilt, sword knot gold lace. Satchel and strap black leather. Another picture of an officer of Line Infantry shows him wearing the same style coat as Figure 151. His kepi has a white cover and black visor. Frock coat is blue with blue collar and red pointed cuffs, gold lace shoulder straps, and gilt buttons. White shirt with black bow tie, white trousers, black shoes. Sometimes the kepi would be worn with a white neck curtain but no cover – this would probably only have been seen early in the war, as I'm sure that complete covers would have been made as soon as demand warranted it.

A further illustration shows an officer in the same style coat as Figure 159, but worn open, without waist-sash or belt. It would appear that this was daily dress, as he is wearing a forage cap in blue with gold lace and tassel. Cuffs are green with gold rank lace and shoulder bars, and the collar is folded over rather than upright. He

is wearing a black cravat, and white shirt, waistcoat, and baggy trousers tucked into riding boots. His waistbelt is concealed under the waistcoat, from which his sword is suspended on black slings. Steel scabbard, gilt hilt.

160. OFFICER Red kepi with blue bottom band, gold rank lace, national cockade, and black visor. Topcoat blue with black silk edging and frogging and gold sleeve lace. Trousers crimson with gold stripe, black shoes.

161. MOUNTED OFFICER Blue kepi with red bottom band, gold rank lace, black visor and chinstrap, white neck curtain. Jacket dark blue, collar and cuffs dark blue, buttons gilt, gold lace piping to false back pockets and cuffs. Breeches red with dark blue stripe, brown boots and straps. White sword knot, gilt hilt, steel scabbard. In the original picture from which this figure is taken, his horse has a plain blue shabraque and valise, black pistol holsters, and a brown leather satchel.

162. ADJUTANT Red kepi with blue bottom band, gold rank lace, black visor and chinstrap. Tunic dark blue, collar and cuffs dark blue, cuff rank and shoulder bars gold lace, gilt buttons. Trousers dark blue with red stripe, black boots. Waist-sash crimson, tassels also crimson. Waistbelt and sword slings black leather, satchel brown leather with black strap.

163. INFANTRY OFFICER Kepi all dark blue, gold rank lace. Jacket dark blue, collar and cuffs red, shoulder straps red with gold lace edging, gilt buttons. Waist-sash crimson with gold lace tassels. Trousers red with gold lace stripe. Black shoes, steel sword scabbard, brown leather binocular case and strap.

164. LINE INFANTRY OFFICER Red kepi with blue bottom band, gold rank lacing, black visor and chinstrap. Coat dark blue, collar and cuffs also dark blue, gold rank lace on cuffs, gilt buttons. Waist-sash crimson with gold lace tassels, trousers red with gold lace stripe. Black shoes, steel sword scabbard, gilt hilt, gold lace sword knot.

Fig 156   *Fig 157*   *Fig 158*   *Fig 159*   *Fig 160*

Fig 161   Fig 162   Fig 163   Fig 164   Fig 165

165. STANDARD BEARER, 1st INFANTRY BATTALION Red kepi with blue bottom band, gold rank lace, black visor and chinstrap. Tunic blue, collar and cuffs blue, gold rank lace on cuffs, golf lace epaulette and contre-epaulette, green piping to front of tunic. Trousers red with gold lace stripe, black boots. Waistbelt and sword slings black leather, steel scabbard. Standard and sash in national colours (sky blue-white-sky blue), with gold lace fringe on both, and a gold lace sun with rays in the central white stripe. The bow has two

streamers, on which the regimental or battalion name would be embroidered, usually in gold lace.

166. STANDARD BEARER, 1st CAVALRY REGIMENT Colours the same as Figure 165, except tunic has no piping or epaulettes and trousers are red with a blue stripe. Black riding boots, steel spurs.

167. CORPORAL, LINE INFANTRY 1865 Parade dress. *Morrion* (shako) black felt, top and bottom bands

Fig 166   Fig 167   Fig 168   Fig 169   Fig 170

black leather, side chevrons red lace, plume green with brass holder and unit plate, black leather visor and chinstrap. Tunic dark blue, collar, cuffs, and piping green, rank chevron yellow, brass hunting horn on collar, epaulettes green with yellow strap and half moon, brass buttons. Trousers red with green piping to side pockets, shoes black. Spats are white with a buff leather top section. Straps and pouch are black leather, backpack brown leather with black straps, blanket roll light blue. Musket sling is white leather.

168. FIRST-SERGEANT, LINE INFANTRY 1865

Tropical dress. Red kepi with blue bottom band and blue piping, visor and chinstrap black. Tunic white with green collar, white cuffs, brass buttons, rank chevrons yellow lace. Trousers white with green stripe, shoes and spats as last figure. Black waistbelt, brass buckle. Commander A.J. Kennedy saw a parade at Corrientes on New Years' Day 1867 at which the Argentine 3rd Infantry Battalion was present: he writes that 'their uniform was dust coloured with red facings, tunic and trousers made of coarse cotton cloth, leather leggings, small kepi shako the same colour as the tunic with red band and regimental number in front, they were armed with smooth bores and bayonet.'

The Argentine NCO rank system at this period consisted of inverted chevrons worn on the right upper arm. One chevron denoted a corporal, two chevrons a second sergeant, and three chevrons a first sergeant. These were of yellow lace when worn on parade or full dress occasions, but when worn with service dress or fatigues were of red lace for infantry and artillery, or white lace for cavalry.

169. INFANTRY PRIVATE

From an illustration in Enrique Udaondo's book, published in 1922. Hat *paja* (straw), black sweatband, white neck curtain. Coat dark blue with red collar and cuffs, epaulettes all red, trousers red, spats white. Black leather boots, waistbelt, pouch, and bayonet scabbard, brass buckles and bayonet fittings. Rifle sling was white.

170. PRIVATE, 6th INFANTRY BATTALION

Blue kepi with green bottom band, green piping to top of kepi, black visor and chinstrap. Blue tunic with green collar, cuffs, and piping, blue trousers, black boots, white gaiters with buff leather top, white haversack and belts.

171. INFANTRYMAN IN TROPICAL UNIFORM

From a painting by Candido López. Kepi cover white, visor black. Coat all white, brass buttons, red chevron (erroneously depicted on the left arm by López). Trousers white with red stripe. Black leather waistbelt, bayonet scabbard and frog, and shoes. White cloth bag and strap.

172. OFFICER, BATTALION 'SANTA FE'

From a painting by Candido López. Red Carlist-style cap with silver lace tassel and cord. Frock coat dark blue, collar and cuffs red, gold rank lace on arms. Waistcoat blue, waist-sash red, trousers red with double dark blue stripes, shoes black. Another officer from this unit is depicted wearing a white Carlist-style cap with gold lace tassel and cord. His frock coat is dark blue with red collar and cuffs, gold lace shoulder bars, a single gold rank lace on pointed cuffs, and a row of seven small buttons from cuff edge to below the point of the rank lace. Buttons and waistbelt buckle are gilt, waistbelt and sword slings are white leather. Colours are otherwise the same as described above.

173. INFANTRY OFFICER

White cap with gold lace tassel and cord. Tunic dark blue with black silk lace edging, dark blue cuffs and collar with gold lace trim. Trousers are red with double blue stripes. The poncho is white cloth with gilt buttons, the collar and button section in red. Black shoes, steel scabbard, black sword slings, gilt hilt.

174. OFFICER

Blue kepi with red bottom band, gold rank lace, national cockade, black visor. Jacket blue with black silk frogging and edging, gold rank lace on cuffs, gilt buttons, gold lace shoulder bars. Waistcoat red with gilt buttons, waistbelt and sword slings black leather, gilt buckles. Trousers blue with green pocket piping (in

Fig 176   Fig 177   Fig 178   Fig 179   Fig 180

another picture white trousers are depicted being worn with this type of jacket). Black boots, gold lace sword knot, steel scabbard.

175. OFFICER, 1st VOLUNTEER LEGION Kepi has white sun cover and curtain, black visor. Jacket red with blue collar and cuffs, gold lace on sleeves and edges of jacket, black silk frogging with gold toggles. Trousers blue with red stripe, white sword slings.

176. OFFICER, NATIONAL GUARD Kepi black with gold lace bands and gilt chin-scales, green feather plume. Frock coat dark blue, collar and cuffs green, gold rank lace on arms, gilt buttons, front of coat piped green. Trousers crimson with double green stripes. Waistbelt and sword slings white leather, scabbard black leather with gilt fittings, gilt hilt with gold lace sword knot. Another National Guard officer is depicted as resembling Figure 164. His green kepi has a red bottom band, gold rank lace, sky blue-white-sky blue national cockade, and black visor. Frock coat is dark blue, with green collar and cuffs, gold rank lace on cuffs, green piping to the front of the coat, and gilt buttons. Trousers crimson with green double stripes. White waistbelt with gilt buckle, white sword slings.

177. PRIVATE, *LEGIÓN MILITAR* 1865 Kepi cover white, black visor. Blouse dark blue with red lace to cuffs and buttons on chest, brass buttons. Zouave waistcoat dark blue with red lace on edges, etc. Red trousers, white gaiters. Black shoes, waistbelt, straps, and pouches. Backpack brown, grey roll, white straps to roll, white musket sling.

Another contemporary description of this unit's uniform notes 'we wore dark green tunics, white linen "pumphosen" [baggy trousers] with gaiters for the hot months from September to April, and blue linen, somewhat thicker and tighter fitting, for the cooler season from April to September. On the front of our kepis we carried the letters "L.M."' This account comes from the diary of Ulrich Lopacher, who in 1868 arrived in Buenos Aires 'along with some 100 other Swiss veterans of the

Papal service'. On landing they were enrolled 'almost directly off the ship' into the *Legión Militar* and were rushed to join the Argentine field army in Paraguay. Lopacher's description suggests that after a year or two of combat the Zouave-style dress depicted in the drawing had been replaced by a more functional uniform.

178. PRIVATE, NATIONAL GUARD BATTALION 'CORRENTINO' Red kepi with green bottom band and piping, brass unit badge of laurel branches, black leather visor. Tunic dark blue, collar and cuffs dark green both edged in a lighter green lace, tunic frogging black lace, brass buttons. The front and bottom of the tunic are edged in the same green lace as the collar and cuffs. Trousers dark blue. Black shoes and equipment, pouch and strap white cloth.

An illustration of Colonel D. Sosa of this battalion has him wearing a uniform along the same lines. His red kepi has a dark green bottom band, gold rank lace, national cockade, and black visor. Frock coat is dark blue, collar and cuffs green, gold rank lace on cuffs; the collar has a gold lace edging which also runs along the bottom. Shoulder straps are dark blue with a gold lace edge. Trousers dark blue with double gold lace stripes, waist-sash crimson with gold lace tassels. Sword scabbard black leather with gilt fittings, sword knot gold lace.

179. PRIVATE, NATIONAL GUARD BATTALION 'SAN NICOLAS' Kepi with white cover, black visor. Tunic lead grey, collar and cuffs sky blue, buttons brass. Trousers sky blue with white stripe, shoes black. Black leather belts, straps, and pouch, white cloth haversack, blue blanket roll.

180. OFFICER, NATIONAL GUARD BATTALION 'SAN NICOLAS' His uniform is much the same as that of the preceding figure, except for the addition of gold lace shoulder bars and the substitution of dark blue trousers with a red stripe. Pistol holster is black leather, and the blanket roll across his left shoulder is blue. Steel scabbard with brass fittings, hilt gilt with black grip and

Fig 181   Fig 182   Fig 183   Fig 184   Fig 185

gold lace sword knot. Belts and straps black leather.

181. COMMANDER OF THE CORPS OF SAPPERS
This figure comes from a picture of *Sargento Mayor* Alejandro Díaz. Kepi with all blue cover and black peak. Jacket blue, collar and cuffs blue, cuff rank and shoulder bars in gold lace, gilt buttons. White waistcoat with gilt buttons, white breeches, black boots, steel sword scabbard.

182 & 183. TROOPERS, ESCORT TO THE GOVERNOR Figure 182 wears the parade dress of a trooper of General Mitre's Escort. Shako black with black leather top and bottom bands, red side chevrons, red plume, brass plate, black leather visor and chinstrap, white cords and flounders. This type of shako was made from a heavy duty felt; the black leather top was to help combat rain. Tunic dark blue, collar, cuffs, turnbacks, and lapels red. Trousers dark blue with red stripe. Black half boots, waistbelt, and sword slings, natural leather carbine sling with brass plate.

Figure 183 wears campaign dress. Shako black with red plume, brass plume holder and plate, national cockade, and black leather bands and visor. Jacket dark blue with red collar and cuffs, brass buttons. Red *chiripá*, white lace *calzoncillos*. Black boots, white leather sword slings and waistbelt.

184. TROOPER, SQUADRON OF GUIDES from the Province of San Juan. Black *morrion* with black leather top and bottom bands, black lace chevrons on each side, sky blue-white national cockade, brass plate, black leather visor and chinstrap. Tunic all white, brass buttons. Breeches dark blue, boots black, waistbelt and sword slings white leather, carbine strap brown leather. White sword knot, steel scabbard.

185. COLONEL OF CAVALRY Red kepi with blue bottom band, gold lace and button, national cockade, black visor and chinstrap. Jacket dark blue with red cuffs,

gold lace on sleeves and front edge of tunic, gilt buttons. Black cravat, red breeches with double gold stripes, black boots, dark blue cloak with red lining. White sword slings, gold sword knot.

186. CAVALRY OFFICER Red kepi with blue bottom band, gold rank lace. Tunic dark blue, collar and cuffs red, gold rank lace on arms, gilt buttons. Breeches red with gold lace stripe. Black boots, brown blanket roll, white sword knot, steel scabbard. Another cavalry officer is shown wearing a uniform consisting of a kepi with a white cover and neck curtain and black visor; a dark blue shell jacket with red collar and cuffs (pointed cuffs with no rank lace), and red shoulder straps edged in gold lace; white trousers cut in the fashion of those worn by Figure 163; a brown waistbelt with gilt buckle; and a steel scabbard and white sword knot, plus a pistol worn through the waistbelt without a holster.

187. OFFICER, CAVALRY REGIMENT 'GENERAL SAN MARTIN' Blue kepi with white bottom band, gold lace, national cockade, black visor and strap. Jacket dark blue, white collar and cuffs, gold lace on sleeves and around edge of jacket, black frogging on chest with gold toggles. White waist and pouch belts. Trousers dark blue with white stripe.

The blouse or *camiseta* worn by troopers of this regiment was in the same style as that of Figure 195, although with a different shape of pocket flap (detail 187a). It was dark blue with white collar, cuffs, and pocket flaps. The kepi had white lace, and the *chiripá* was blue with white lace under it. Boots were black, belts and straps white.

188. CAVALRY OFFICER Red kepi with dark blue bottom band, gold rank lace, national cockade, gold lace knot on top. Tunic dark blue, collar and cuffs also dark blue, shoulder straps red with gold lace edging, gilt buttons. Trousers red with gold lace stripes, shoes black. Holster and strap brown leather.

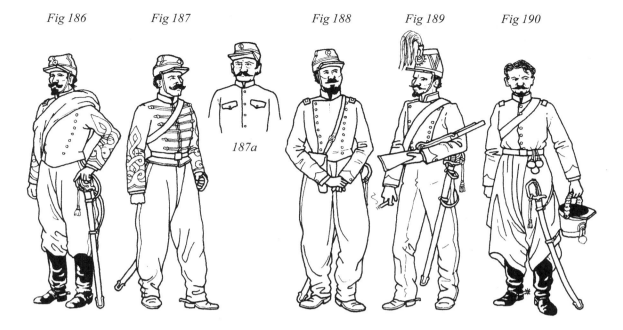

Fig 186   Fig 187   187a   Fig 188   Fig 189   Fig 190

189. TROOPER, 3rd CAVALRY REGIMENT Black felt *morrion* with black leather top, yellow horsehair plume, chevrons, and top and bottom bands, national cockade with yellow lace holder, brass buttons and plume holder, black leather chinstrap and visor. Tunic dark blue, collar, cuffs, short turnbacks, and lapels yellow, brass buttons. Trousers dark blue with yellow stripe. Black shoes and equipment, brass sword scabbard.

190. TROOPER, 4th CAVALRY REGIMENT Shako black, black leather top band, yellow lace bottom band, brass chin-scales, yellow pompom, national cockade, yellow lace holding strap and brass button. Tunic dark blue, collar, cuffs, turnbacks, and shoulder bars yellow, *chiripá* grey cloth with white undergarment. Black boots, white sword knot, white leather belts and straps.

191. LANCER From a painting by Candido López. Red kepi with blue piping, national cockade, black leather visor. Blouse dark blue, red collar, pocket flaps, cuffs, and front button fly, brass buttons. Breeches dark blue with red stripe, boots black, sword knot white, lance strap white leather, pennon red over white.

192 & 193. TROOPERS, NATIONAL GUARD CAVALRY Campaign dress. Figure 192 wears a red kepi with blue bottom band, black leather visor and chinstrap. Dark blue blouse with red shoulder bars and cuffs, blue *chiripá* with white undergarment, black boots, steel spurs. Black leather belt and scabbard, brass fittings.

Figure 193 wears a blue hat with red bottom band and tassel, a blue blouse and *chiripá*, white linen *calzoncillos*, and natural leather boots with steel spurs. Waistbelt is brown leather with silver studs. His saddle is covered with a sheepskin. The blanket thrown over his arm is brown, and the tuft on his lance is red.

194. SECOND-SERGEANT, NATIONAL GUARD CAVALRY OF ENTRE RÍOS Carlist-style cap red with yellow lace tassel and cord. Tunic dark blue, collar and cuffs also dark blue, cuffs piped black, rank chevrons red.

Sky blue trousers, black shoes and equipment, white leather carbine sling. Pouch slung at right hip white cloth.

195. TROOPER, CAVALRY REGIMENT OF BUENOS AIRES Carlist-style cap red with yellow tassel. Jacket red with blue collar, cuffs, and pocket flaps, brass buttons. *Chiripá* as that of Figure 192. Black boots, white belts and sword slings.

An unknown Uruguayan artillery major photographed in Asunción in 1869. (Courtesy of the Museo Histórico Nacional, Montevideo)

Fig 191   *Fig 192*   *Fig 193*   *Fig 194*   *Fig 195*

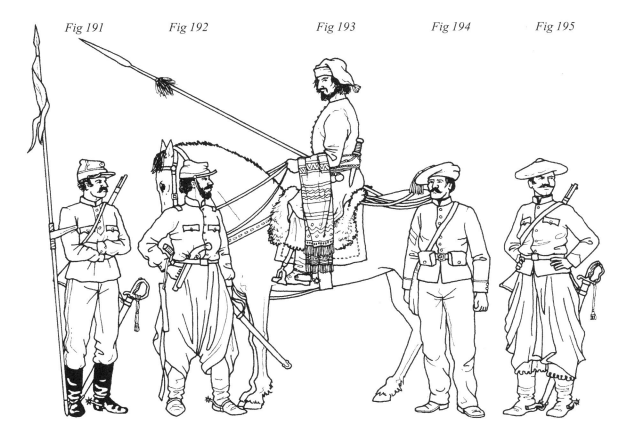

I have not included any figures depicting the uniform of the Argentine Artillery during this war, as the only details I have found are not contemporary. The earliest is a line drawing by Janet Lange that was published in an Argentine newspaper just after the Paraguayan War. It shows an artilleryman wearing a uniform in the style of Figure 168, but in the colours of winter dress: blue kepi with red band and piping, blue coat, red baggy trousers with blue stripe, white spats and waistbelt, and black shoes. The jacket has epaulette straps in blue with a button near to the collar (red epaulettes would have been worn with the jacket in full dress). He also wears three medals, whence my belief that the figure represents a gunner of the post-war period. Another artillery figure, dated 1865, is shown in Enrique Udaondo's book. He looks much like Figure 179, but without the equipment. His kepi is all dark blue with red piping, the jacket and trousers are blue, with blue collar and pointed cuffs, both piped red, red trouser stripes, and a black waistbelt. A third artillery figure, in a set of plates by E. Marenco published in 1973, resembles the Udaondo illustration, but is shown with red piping along the front and bottom of the jacket, and brass buttons.

URUGUAY 1852–70

In his *Armed Forces of Latin America*, Adrian English notes that in 1852 the Uruguayan army consisted of two battalions of infantry, four squadrons of cavalry, and a brigade of artillery, and had a total strength of 1,830 men, all ranks. The infantry consisted of the Battalion 'Voltijeros' and the 2nd Battalion 'Cazadores'. Though the name of the latter implies the existence of a 1st Battalion of *Cazadores* it is possible that the 1st Battalion

was actually the same as the 'Voltijeros', as these were originally recruited from Uruguayans of European descent whereas the 'Cazadores' consisted of men of Spanish descent, whence the unit's Spanish title. The Uruguayan army present at the Battle of Caseros in 1852 as given in Table 1 (see p.17) actually lists four infantry battalions rather than two, but of these the 'Resistencia', 'Guardia Oriental', and 'Orden' were made up of volunteers, and only the 'Voltijeros' were regular troops. One presumes that after the war against Rosas these volunteer battalions were stood down as an economy measure, and that the details provided by Adrian English probably reflect the downsized army list as it stood at the end of the year.

In 1858 the two regular battalions were also abolished and a National Guard was established, whereby all male citizens between the ages of 17 and 47 were obliged to serve, continuing in reserve status until the age of 55. By 1860 the regular army consisted of 9 Generals, 386 officers, and 895 other ranks, while at the same date the National Guard comprised 766 officers and 16,012 other ranks. As one can imagine, the National Guard units tended to see their allegiance as being to their local *caudillo* rather than the central government.

León de Palleja's *Diario* provides the order of battle for the Army of the Vanguard (*Ejército de Vanguardia*), commanded by General-in-Chief *Señor Gobernador* Don Venancio Flores, President of the Republic of Uruguay, that was despatched to the province of Corrientes in Argentina in 1865. This was a mixed corps that contained all of the units that Uruguay was to send to the war against Paraguay. The artillery, under Major J. Yance, consisted of six field-pieces, 12 officers and 210 gunners, drawn from the 2nd Squadron of Horse-

Artillery (the 1st Squadron being left behind in Uruguay). The cavalry consisted of the Regiment 'Escolta' – the President's escort – under Lieutenant-Colonel M. Mendieta (20 officers and 274 men) and three regiments from the *Guardia Nacional Oriental*, the 1st, 2nd, and 3rd, with a combined strength of 90 officers and 613 men. The 1st Regiment was commanded by Lieutenant-Colonel T. Albín, the 2nd by Lieutenant-Colonel N. Ramirez, and the 3rd by Lieutenant-Colonel A. Castro. The infantry contingent comprised the Infantry Battalions 'Florida' (Colonel L. de Palleja), '24 de Abril' (Major M. González), 'Voluntários de la Libertad' or 'Voluntários Garibaldinos' (Lieutenant-Colonel C. Bustamante), and 'Independencia' (Lieutenant-Colonel F. Elías). Each infantry battalion was to have six companies (one of *Cazadores*, one of Grenadiers, and four of Fusiliers), although the Battalion 'Florida' had eight, a figure which was reduced to four in 1866. Individual battalion strengths were:

'Florida' – 28 officers and 592 men
'24 de Abril' – 21 officers and 486 men
'Voluntários de la Libertad' – 30 officers and 294 men
'Independencia' – 17 officers and 332 men

The change of the 'Voluntários Garibaldinos' name to the 'Voluntários de la Libertad' may have resulted from the existence of a Brazilian *Voluntários da Pátria* unit with the same title.

Also sent were a medical section with nine officers, a supply train with one officer and 24 men, a supply staff of eight officers and 32 men, and a staff corps of 28 officers and seven men.

A brief history of the Infantry Battlion 'Florida' will help to give a flavour of the chequered lineages of the Uruguayan units. This battalion, recruited initially in the town of Florida from freed slaves, was raised in 1825 as the *Libertados Orientales*, to participate in Juan Antonio Lavalleja's uprising against the Brazilian authorities. It was initially commanded by Colonel Felipe Duarte, and later by Colonel Pablo Zufriategui. The following year it was incorporated into the army of the United Provinces (Argentina) as the *3 de Cazadores*, and came under the command of Colonel Eugenio Garzón, a native of the United States and a veteran of the wars of independence in Chile and Peru. When peace came, the battalion was transferred back into the Uruguayan army on 24 February 1829 as the 1st *Cazadores*, still under the command of Colonel Garzón, assisted by Lieutenant-Colonel Andrés Gómez. On 1 July 1831 it was renamed the *Batallón de Infanteria de Linea*. It participated in the Battle of Arroyo Grande on 6 December 1842. In 1843 some of its men

Two Uruguayan infantry officers, the first in full dress, dating to 1866; the second, in frock coat, convalescing from a wound. (Both pictures courtesy of the Museo Histórico Nacional, Montevideo)

Senior Uruguayan cavalry officer, 1867. (Courtesy of the Museo Histórico Nacional, Montevideo)

were detached to form the 2nd *Batallón de Infanteria de Linea*. In 1849 the 1st Battalion was given the new name of *Voltijeros*, and in 1852 it took part in the Battle of Caseros. With the restructuring of the *Ejército Nacional* or National Army it was given the new title of *Batallón 1° de Cazadores*, and on 18 April 1860 it became the *Cazadores de la Unión*. It was granted the title of Battalion 'Florida' by General Venancio Flores when he took over the presidency in February 1865, in recognition of its support for his political cause. By, this time, however, its recruits were drawn from every part of Uruguay.

ARMS

At the beginning of the war the Uruguayan Army was equipped with a mixture of firearms. Colonel León de Palleja noted that his Battalion 'Florida' was armed with rifled percussion muskets that used Minié ammunition, while the Battalion '24 de Abril' had two companies equipped with flintlock muskets while the rest carried percussion weapons; he does not record the calibre or make. As the war progressed, 14.66-calibre Minié rifles and carbines were gradually issued to all infantry and cavalry units respectively, this rearmament coinciding with Brazilian standardisation of its own weaponry from 14.8 mm Modêlo Brasileiro and Modêlo Inglês Miniés to the 14.66 mm French St Etienne model in 1866. Officers

are noted as purchasing their own handguns, weapons from the maker Lefucheaux being mentioned by Alberto Pino del Menck.

FIGURES

Sources for the figures in this section are: Diogenes Hequet, Museo Historico Nacional, Montevideo; illustrations by Alberto del Pino Menck; paintings by Candido López, Buenos Aires; and illustrations by A. Samson.

196. OFFICER, INFANTRY BATTALION 'FLORIDA' Parade dress. *Morrion* crimson felt, gold lace top band, green bottom band and side chevrons, piped crimson, gilt chin-scales and unit badge, national cockade under green feather falling plume, black visor. (The national cockade was all sky blue at this period, but to judge from photographic evidence was not a common feature on the kepi.) Frock coat dark blue, collar and cuffs green piped crimson (note crimson piping with cuff buttons), epaulette and contre-epaulette gold lace, crimson piping to front of coat, gilt buttons. Trousers crimson with double green stripes. Waist-sash crimson with gold lace toggles but crimson fringe. Sword scabbard black leather with gilt fittings, gilt hilt with shark-skin grip, black strap to gold lace sword knot. Black leather sword slings, waistbelt, and shoes.

197. PRIVATE, INFANTRY BATTALION 'FLORIDA' Parade dress. Uniform as described under Figure 196, except: brass in place of gilt metal, *morrion* top band is green, and a brass bugle badge is added to the collar. Belts and straps white, belly pouch and sidearm scabbards black leather with brass fittings, gloves and sidearm frog white.

198. COLONEL LEON PALLEJA Red kepi with green bottom band, rank in gold lace, black leather visor and chinstrap, gilt button. Jacket dark blue with collar and cuffs green piped crimson, collar has a gold lace flaming grenade, pocket flaps are green piped crimson, front of jacket piped green, shoulder straps gold lace, gilt buttons. Breeches crimson, boots black. Gilt sword hilt and gold lace sword knot, steel scabbard, black leather sword slings.

199 & 200. OFFICERS, INFANTRY BATTALION 'FLORIDA' Campaign dress. Figure 199 wears a red kepi with green bottom band, gold rank lace, black visor and chinstrap, and gilt button. Jacket dark blue, collar and cuffs green, collar with gold lace flaming grenade and black silk piping, black silk frogging and jacket edge, gold rank lace on sleeves, gilt buttons. Trousers crimson, shoes and slings black leather. Steel sword scabbard with gilt hilt and gold lace sword knot.

Figure 200 has a crimson kepi with green edges to gold rank lace band, gold lace on top part of kepi, black visor. Jacket dark blue, green cuffs edged in crimson piping, green collar with gold lace flaming grenade and crimson piping, gilt buttons, gold rank lace on cuffs, gold lace shoulder straps, crimson piping to jacket, black lace loops for buttons. Trousers crimson with green side stripes, black boots. Steel scabbard, gold lace sword knot, black leather holster, belts, and slings.

201 & 202. STANDARD BEARERS, INFANTRY BATTALION 'FLORIDA' Both are officers. Figure 201 wears a red kepi with green bottom band, gold rank lace, black visor and chinstrap, and gilt button. Jacket dark blue with green collar, cuffs, and pocket flaps all piped crimson, front and bottom of jacket edged in black silk, gilt buttons. Trousers dark blue with green side stripes. Black shoes and sword slings, steel scabbard. Standard consists of the national flag – white and light blue horizontal stripes, with a gold lace sunburst in a white canton. It has a plain wooden staff, steel blade and fittings, sky blue silk bow, and a gold lace fringe. It appears that regimental and battalion standards were not issued in the Uruguayan army, and that the national flag was used in their place. Whether flags used in this way had the unit's name embroidered on either the white stripes or the tassels hanging from the bow is unclear. Figure 202's uniform is much the same; his standard sash is crimson with a gold lace fringe.

203. NCO, INFANTRY BATTALION 'FLORIDA' Campaign dress. Crimson kepi or *morrion* with green bottom band and green chevron on each side, black visor. Tunic dark blue with green collar and cuffs, brass buttons. Rank chevrons are yellow lace with a green centre stripe. Trousers white, shoes black, pouches, belts, and straps black leather. White canvas haversack and strap, grey blanket roll. A picture of a private in summer dress shows him wearing a stable cap with a red top and green base (detail 203a), and a white jacket and trousers with white collar and cuffs. His equipment remains as described above.

The Uruguayan NCO rank system was as follows: first and second sergeants wore, respectively, four or three yellow lace chevrons edged in green on each upper arm, while first and second corporals wore four or three diagonal lengths of green-edged yellow rank lace 3 ins (75 mm) below each elbow. Details 203b and 203c show coporals' stripes as worn with service (203b) and parade dress.

204. PRIVATE, INFANTRY BATTALION '24 DE ABRIL' 1865 Parade dress. *Morrion* dark blue felt, green top and bottom bands with thin red piping, brass chin-scales, cockade holding yellow lace, sky blue national cockade with brass button and ball for red hanging horsehair plume, black leather visor. Coat dark blue, collar, cuffs, and epaulettes green with red piping, red piping down the front, brass buttons. Trousers dark blue with green stripe. White spats, black shoes, straps, and belts, white gloves, dark blue blanket roll, natural leather musket sling.

205. OFFICER, AUXILIARY CORPS OF POLICE 1865 Parade uniform, from a picture of the unit's commander, Lieutenant-Colonel Fortunato Flores. Red *morrion* with gold lace around top, dark blue bottom band with gold lace chinstrap fastened above black leather visor, gold lace chevrons on either side, gilt bugle horn badge under sky blue national cockade. The green falling plume conceals a gilt holder. Tunic is dark blue piped red with red collar and cuffs, gold sleeve lace, epaulettes in gold lace with a white five-pointed star and the national coat of arms plus gilt buttons. Waistbelt is gold lace over a red sash with gold lace tassels. Trousers red with gold lace side stripes. Black shoes, white gloves, gold lace sword knot.

The Auxiliary Corps of Police originated as a single company with a *sargento mayor*, two captains, two first-lieutenants, one sub-lieutenant, six first-sergeants, seven second-sergeants, eight corporals, and 71 soldiers. In June 1865 unit strength was increased by two companies and a staff company, but in February 1866 it was disbanded and its personnel were used as the basis of the Infantry Battalion 'Libertad'.

206. OFFICER, NATIONAL GUARD OF MONTEVIDEO This is *Sargento Mayor* Simon Patino, commander of the 2nd Battalion of the *Guardia Nacionales de la Infanteria de la Capital* in July 1865. Shako dark blue with gold lace top band and red bottom

Fig 196   Fig 197   Fig 198   Fig 199   Fig 200

band, gold lace chinstrap above black visor, gold chin-scales tied behind plume, plume white and sky blue, gilt badge with a red centre containing gilt number '2', sky blue national cockade. Tunic as per that of Figure 196, but waist-sash has Uruguayan-style tassels rather than Argentine. Trousers dark blue, shoes black, gloves white. The medal (for the Battle of Monte Caseros) is silver with a light blue ribbon. This unit was disbanded in 1866. In all, three infantry battalions and one cavalry regiment of National Guard had been raised from Montevideo in 1865 to fight against Paraguay.

207. CAPTAIN, HORSE ARTILLERY SQUADRON

Parade dress. Kepi dark blue with red bottom band, gold rank lace, piping, and chinstrap, gilt unit badge, black visor. Coat dark blue with red collar, cuffs, and piping, gilt buttons, gold cuff lace, gold lace epaulettes and holding bars. The collar has a gold lace embroidered flaming bomb. Trousers dark blue with double red stripes. Black shoes, waistbelt, and sword slings, crimson waist-sash and tassels, steel sword scabbard, gilt hilt with gold lace sword knot.

208. FIRST-LIEUTENANT, HORSE ARTILLERY 2nd SQUADRON

Kepi dark blue with red bottom band, gold rank lace and chinstrap, gilt unit badge, black visor. Coat dark blue with red collar, cuffs, pocket flaps, and piping. Waistcoat dark blue piped red, gilt buttons. Trousers dark blue with double red side stripes, black shoes. Steel scabbard with gilt fittings, sword slings black.

209. MAJOR, CAVALRY REGIMENT 'SORIANO'

This unit was created on 17 May 1865. Kepi dark blue with red bottom band, gold rank lace and chinstrap, black visor. Tunic dark blue with red collar, cuffs, pocket piping, cuff button piping and piping to edge of coat, gold lace shoulder bars. Waistcoat dark blue piped red with gilt buttons. Brown poncho, white trousers, black boots, gilt spurs. Waistbelt and sword slings black leather, gilt buckle, steel scabbard.

210 & 211. OFFICERS, INFANTRY BATTALION 'LIBERTAD'

Figure 210 wears a white cap with gold lace tassel. Jacket dark blue with black silk edge and gold lace frogging, collar dark blue with black silk edge, gilt buttons. Trousers crimson with black side stripes, black boots, waistbelt, and holster, gilt buckle. Steel scabbard, gilt hilt, gold lace sword knot. Figure 211 wears the same style of cap. His jacket is dark blue with red collar and cuffs, its front and bottom edged in black silk. Gilt buttons, gold lace shoulder straps. Trousers are white with black boots and steel spurs.

212. STANDARD BEARER, INFANTRY BATTAL-ION 'LIBERTAD'

Cap white with gold lace tassel. Jacket dark blue edged in black silk, with red collar and cuffs. Trousers crimson, shoes, holster, and straps black leather. Steel scabbard, gilt hilt, gold lace sword knot. Standard comprises wooden staff with steel fittings and blade, sky blue silk bow, and national flag with a gold lace fringe.

213. OFFICER, INFANTRY BATTALION 'LIBER-TAD'

Cap white with gold lace tassel, jacket dark blue with red collar, cuffs, and pocket flaps and gilt buttons, trousers red. Black shoes, black leather sword slings and scabbard with gilt fittings. Gilt hilt with gold lace sword knot.

214. PRIVATE, INFANTRY BATTALION 'LIBER-TAD' 1865

Cap red, blouse dark blue with red collar, cuffs, button flap, and pocket flaps, trousers crimson.

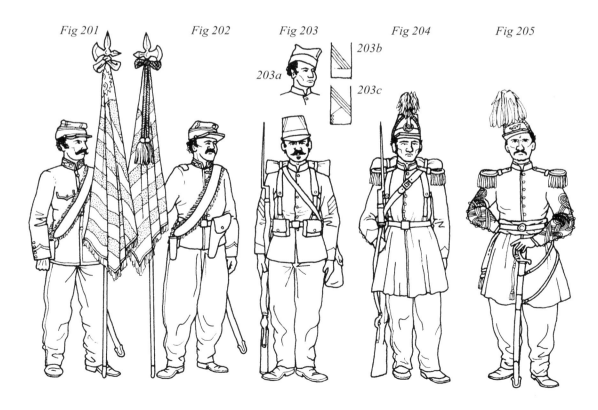

Fig 201   *Fig 202*   *Fig 203*   *Fig 204*   *Fig 205*

203a   203b   203c

Fig 206   Fig 207   Fig 208   Fig 209   Fig 210

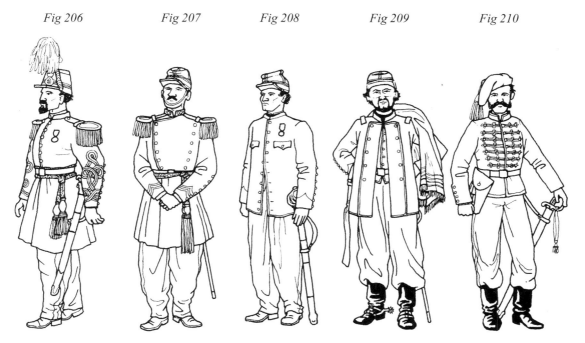

Black boots with brown gaiters. Waistbelt black leather, shoulder belt white, musket sling black.

PARAGUAY c.1780–1870

At the close of its period as a colony Paraguay had a population of just c.120,000. Of these only 200 were *Peninsulares*; a further 50,000 were Mestizos, 40,000 were settled Indians, a further 20,000 were nomadic Indians, and there were 10,000 *Pardos* (people of mixed African and Indian descent). By no means all of the last group were slaves, although slavery existed.

In the colony's early days defence had been based on a militia, which was faced with serious threats from wild Indian tribes and the Portuguese. The city of Asunción had its own militia, the infantry commanded by 16 officers, the cavalry by a further 16, and the artillery by three officers. All the officers were men of substance, drawn from the wealthy Creole elite. Elsewhere, up to the governorship of Pedro Melo de Portugal (1778–82), the militia was formed of small urban units, untrained and often poorly armed, in which all males aged 16–45 were liable for service. Melo de Portugal reformed the system – and it is interesting to compare his reforms with those

Fig 211   Fig 212   Fig 213   Fig 214

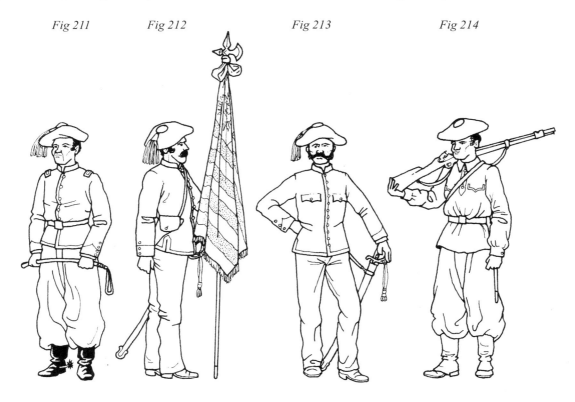

carried out elsewhere in the Spanish colonies, notably Mexico, which are well known. He introduced the *filiardo* system, of semi-professional units which were available for more than local use. In 1790 there were four cavalry regiments totalling 2,884 men, one battalion of infantry totalling 568, and a 70-strong company of artillery (these figures should only be taken as a rough guide to strength, as not all the people listed would be available for immediate use). There were 28 small, old cannon available, but these were scattered across the country's 27 forts and guard posts.

Further reform of the *filiardo* system in 1800 reduced the cavalry to two volunteer regiments of 1,200 each, and two artillery companies, all of which were kept up to full strength. These were officered by Creoles with permanent salaries, who were usually drawn from the most prominent families – Yegros, Montiel, Cavañas, and Iturbe. There were also some professional advisers. However, the strength of these units was still inadequate for defence, while pay was late and equipment remained poor. There was much discontent amongst the men and inspections revealed serious shortcomings.

In 1806 Governor Velasco, an experienced brigadier, was called upon to serve as Major and Sub-Inspector against the British attack on Buenos Aires. He led a contingent of nearly a thousand troops from Paraguay, the majority from the 1st *Filiardo* Regiment, these taking part in the campaign against the British at Buenos Aires and Montevideo.

When the independence movement gathered pace in Buenos Aires, Paraguay – dominated by its small population of *Peninsulares*, and united in its dislike of the *Porteños* (people from the port of Buenos Aires) – remained loyal. When General Belgrano invaded with his army of 1,500 men, Velasco called on Paraguay's ill-armed but well-mounted militia, raising 6,000 men. In the battle that followed, the *Peninsulares* ran away after Belgrano's initial success, leaving the militia under its Creole officers to win the day. The *Filiardo* colonels Manuel Atancio Cavañas and Manuel Gamarra pursued Belgrano out of the country with their 2,000 mounted troops. The Peninsular officers were subsequently arrested, and, with the exception of Lieutenant-Colonel Juan Valeriano de Zevallos, were all relieved of command. Governor Velasco was deposed and a five-man *junta* was appointed to rule in his place. Gradually all *Peninsulares* were excluded from office and, by heavy fines and restrictions, were destroyed as a distinct economic and social group.

The army initially dominated the Congress subsequently summoned from all Paraguay, but by his endeavours José Gaspar Rodriguez Francia was eventually able to impose his will, and set about dismantling the old Creole-dominated army. In 1813 he was confirmed as one of the two consuls who ruled Paraguay, with control over half the country's arms and ammunition and with a new infantry battalion under his direct command. By 1814 he had consolidated his authority further, posting suspect officers to distant garrisons, promoting and selecting loyal officers for duty in the capital, and creating the Horse Grenadier Company as a guard unit. In addition he established a salaried army of company-sized units, replacing the old *filiardo* system which he regarded as dangerous under its existing officers.

In the face of blockade by Argentina, great efforts were made to procure, repair, and manufacture weapons. The first Paraguayan-built ship was launched in 1815, and by 1816 guns were being produced in Paraguay and cloth was being woven, dyed, and tailored for uniforms. Gunpowder, leather, and bullets were all produced locally, and the state raised cattle to feed the army. The armed forces took 64% of the country's total budget, but its troops were also used for public works projects.

The *filiardo* units were integrated into the urban militia, and militia and regular troops took over national defence and security. In the capital were 16 companies of regulars (eight infantry, two artillery, three hussars, and three horse grenadiers), and there were three main barracks, 70% of all the regulars being stationed in the capital while there were smaller garrisons in Pilar, Ytapúa, and Concepción. No officer was given a large command, they were rotated between stations regularly, the highest rank they could aspire to was captain, and there was mandatory early retirement. By the time of the 1816 Congress, no officer remained in the army who had been in the first forces raised against Belgrano. By now the entire officer corps had started their careers as private soldiers, and only Francia had the authority to appoint officers. Strict behaviour was expected of officers, who, being drawn from the ordinary people, faced instant dismissal if they abused their position.

For other ranks, recruiting was limited to unmarried volunteers aged 18–30, but the local *commandante* in charge of recruitment was charged by Francia to be 'especially careful not to accept any that are of bad reputation in their public conduct, but only those from whom honour, proper subordination, and the fulfilment of their obligation in the service to which they are destined can be expected.'

Commandantes governed the larger population centres outside the capital, the most senior being those who looked after vital frontier areas or commercial districts, who had the title of *subdelegado*. There were three of these, in Pilar, Ytapúa, and Concepción. Another was established in Santiago at a time of crisis. The Ytapúa sub-delegate also had responsibility for the Candelaría Misiones area claimed by Paraguay, while the Concepción sub-delegate looked after the northern frontier. These men were military officers, usually with the rank of captain, and had defence, commerce, and governmental responsibilities. Selected for their reliability, they still usually served for a maximum of only four years. Most had already served as military or political officers in one of the *partidos* or small towns. After the expiry of their term as sub-delegates, they were retired to some sinecure well away from Asunción. As delegates, they had to report to Francia in detail, daily, while he sent them the most detailed orders three times a week.

Companies were generally of 60–100 men, with three to four non-commissioned officers and an ensign or lieutenant in command of each company. Equipment for cavalrymen consisted of a sabre, pistol, and carbine for hussars, chasseurs, dragoons, and horse grenadiers, while lancers substituted a lance for the carbine. By 1820 Francia had increased army strength to 1,793 men (compared to 842 men in 1816, and 1,413 in 1818). A further 5–10,000 militia were also mobilised during 1820–21

The uniform during the 1820s consisted of a blue coat with coloured cuffs, white trousers, and a round hat. Infantry and cavalry had different laces. Lancers had a white coat without buttons, a red waistcoat, white trousers, and a red *bonnet de police*. The cockade colours were red, blue, and white. Dragoons and horse grenadiers were issued with parade uniforms, but details have not yet been found. In 1821 a *corps de joune gens* (cadet corps) was created.

The Candelaría Misiones were reoccupied by Paraguay after 1821, and patrols were sent out to expel intruders and re-establish control. The area began to flourish under protection, and trade increased – especially with now-independent Brazil – along the internal rivers. Special terms made the import of weapons particularly attractive to traders.

By 1824 the Army consisted of 5,500 troops of the line and 25,000 militiamen. All troops of the line were white, with the exception of the lancers. Although raised as an escort, the lancer companies created by Francia were paid at a lower rate than the rest of the army because they were *Pardos* – although they were free blacks, they were still generally regarded as of lower status than whites, even if they were not slaves. Parts of the 2nd and 3rd Infantry Battalions were also *Pardo*, as were some other cavalry units; their officers, however, were mostly non-*Pardo*. Officers continued to be regularly rotated, and no officer or official was ever able to gain any insight into the full details of the army. Each battalion theoretically consisted of six companies, with a peacetime strength of 700 men per battalion.

A return of 31 May 1828 lists the Paraguayan army as comprising five rifle companies, four companies of horse grenadiers (one lieutenant, four sub-lieutenants, 11 sergeants, 18 corporals, and 159 men), three infantry companies, three cavalry companies (107 men), and two artillery companies (32 men), a total of 1,167 men. There was only one captain and four lieutenants in the whole force, plus 18 sub-lieutenants, 32 sergeants, 77 corporals, and 450 soldiers, plus 107 cavalrymen, 32 artillerymen, three drummers, two buglers, a 'bleeder', and two helpers (these last three, being quite highly paid, were probably a surgeon and his assistants), plus 435 recruits. The number of troops actually fluctuated considerably, depending on the magnitude of outside threats. The years of greatest expansion for the army during Francia's rule were 1816–20, 1828–29, 1831–32, and 1835–45. Mid-1832 saw the import of 1,000 high quality muskets and 1,000 high quality sabres from Brazil.

Paraguayan budgets during the period 1816–40, with military expenditure expressed as a percentage of the national budget (all amounts in pesos), were:

	Total expenditure	Military expenditure	%
1816	158,711	133,123	83.88
1818	195,220	150,947	77.33
1820	217,504	175,200	80.55
1822	151,990	121,409	79.87
1823	123,772	104,865	84.57
1828	105,119	87,816	83.63
1829	130,165	116,215	89.4
1831	96,793	83,352	86.11
1832	113,047	98,601	87.26
1833	80,381	68,558	85.29
1834	56,119	42,819	76.43
1835	73,227	62,456	85.29
1837	126,363	115,627	91.48
1838	127,624	120,594	94.51
1839	108,872	96,629	88.75
1840	126,222	112,553	89.22

Returns for the years 1834, 1837, and 1839 show the army being composed of these units and troops:

30 April 1834: four infantry companies, three rifle companies, three companies of horse grenadiers (five sergeants, 19 corporals, and 100 men), one company of lancers and one new squadron being formed, and two artillery companies (70 men); total, 649 men, made up of a captain, three lieutenants, six first sub-lieutenants, five second sub-lieutenants, 24 sergeants, 47 corporals, 223 soldiers, 70 artillerymen, one master drummer, 10 drummers, two apprentice drummers, four flute players, one apprentice flute player, three buglers, and 249 recruits.

31 December 1837: four infantry companies, four rifle companies, four cavalry companies, three companies of horse grenadiers (eight sergeants, 22 corporals, and 177 men), three companies of lancers (nine sergeants, 16 corporals, and 122 men), one artillery company (107 men), and one military band (19 men); total 1,760 men. There were three lieutenants, 11 first sub-lieutenants, six second sub-lieutenants, 42 sergeants, 103 corporals, 14 drummers, seven flute players, three buglers, 107 artillerymen, 19 bandsmen, and 1,445 soldiers.

30 June 1839: four infantry companies, four rifle companies, six cavalry companies, three companies of horse grenadiers (seven sergeants, 20 corporals, and 170 men), three companies of lancers (nine sergeants, 14 corporals, and 106 men), one artillery company (86 men), and one military band (18 men); total 1,345 men. There were three lieutenants, 17 first sub-lieutenants, four second sub-lieutenants, 43 sergeants, 102 corporals, 86 artillerymen, 13 drummers, five flute players, two buglers, 18 bandsmen, and 1,052 men.

On Francia's death the garrison commanders took over and created a *junta*, arresting Patinó, Francia's much-hated secretary. However, in 1841 a coup was mounted by the sergeants of the infantry in favour of a Congress, an idea suggested by the able Don Carlos António López, a lawyer of ability who had kept his head well down during Francia's reign, as Francia became ever more suspicious of able men. López was one of the two consuls elected by the new Congress to serve for three years. Like Francia, his ability soon rendered him indispensable and he effectively became dictator, albeit a rather more benign one than Francia. On his death, his son Francisco Solano López was to succeed to the presidency.

In 1842 the new congress laid down the Republic's coat of arms and national flag. A census was ordered in 1845 and was carried out in 1846. It provides a fascinating picture of Paraguay before the devastation of the War of the Triple Alliance. Not entirely complete, it nevertheless gives a total of 238,862 people, plus around another 20,000 nomad Indians; 17,181 were black, 7,866 of them slaves. Whole areas were either underpopulated or deserted.

The army was modernised on 26 August 1845 and

also expanded. The Grenadier Battalion and the line infantry battalions (numbered 1–4) were each to have a battalion staff composed of one colonel, one major, one *alférez* adjutant, one *alférez* secretary, one *alférez* quarter-master, two standard-bearers, and one drum major. Each battalion was to have six companies, each composed of one captain, one lieutenant, one *alférez*, one first-sergeant, one or two second-sergeants, six corporals, 78 privates, two drummers, and a fifer. Light infantry battalions (numbered 1–6) were to be organised in the same way, except that the battalion staff had only one standard-bearer and there was a trumpet major rather than a drum major. Company organisation was the same except in having five corporals, 60–75 privates, one bugler, and no drums or fifes.

The cavalry regiments, numbered 1–4, were to have a regimental staff of one colonel, one major, one *alférez* adjutant, one *alférez* secretary, one *alférez* quarter-master, one standard-bearer, and one trumpet major. Each of a regiment's three squadrons was to be composed of one captain, one lieutenant, one *alférez*, one first-sergeant, one or two second-sergeants, five corporals, 75 troopers, and one trumpeter.

The two corps of artillery were to be known as the 1st and 2nd. Each was to have a corps staff of one colonel, one major, one *alférez* adjutant, one *alférez* secretary, one *alférez* quarter-master, and one drum major. Each corps was to contain four companies, each with one captain, one lieutenant, one *alférez*, one first-sergeant, one or two second-sergeants, four corporals, 60 gunners, and one drummer.

It was hoped that these new measures would stop marauding Indians from causing trouble, which had forced forts and guard posts to be established. The militia became better trained and their equipment improved. Retaliatory campaigns against the Indians then began, all southern pueblos being ordered to have a force of 'ready' militia to pursue raiders. This proved effective, and only in the Rio Apa area – where the Brazilians encouraged Indian raids – did trouble persist. Smallpox epidemics solved this problem, hitting the Indians particularly hard, as a result of which the Chaco became open to settlement. Military posts and army *estancias* then expanded into this area: larger outposts were established, the river was patrolled by canoes, and cannon were placed in the garrisons.

In the capital, a battalion-sized police force was established, which received army wages. By 1849 it comprised three companies of infantry totalling 194 officers and men, and 195 cavalry with four officers. Similar companies were established throughout the rest of the country. A National Guard was set up in 1845, a semi-professional militia that in theory enlisted all able-bodied men aged between 16 and 55. Divided on paper into battalions of infantry and regiments of cavalry, initially it amounted to only one infantry battalion of 407 officers and men in the capital. López's eldest two sons were company commanders.

During 1845, following the signing of a treaty with General José María Paz of Corrientes, a force from Paraguay was despatched to assist in the latter's struggle for home rule, and maybe independence, from the central government of Buenos Aires. These Paraguayan troops were under the command of Francisco Solano López, son of Carlos. Though a brigadier-general he was just 18 at the time, but was, luckily, assisted by Lieutenant-Colonel Wisner de Morgenstern, late of the Hungarian Cavalry, who acted as his chief-of-staff. The Paraguayan contingent was described as being in poor condition, Paz writing that they were 'an unformed mass without instruction, without organisation, without discipline, and ignorant of the first rudiments of war.' The infantry were described as so rustic that they didn't know how to load or fire their weapons. Of the cavalry, Paz wrote that they were 'so badly mounted, not through not having been given horses, but because they did not care for them and destroyed them in a few days.' Paz also protested at the lack of officers. Of López, he wrote that he was 'adorned with lovely personal qualities but he has no military knowledge and, what is more, not the slightest idea of war and how to wage it.' Unsurprisingly, this force ended up retreating back into Paraguay, while its allies were destroyed and Paz fled to Paraguay.

By the end of 1847 Rosas was in control of Argentina, and Paraguay was in fear of an attack. New military units were raised, militia embodied, a big military camp set up near the main ford at Paso de la Patria, and picked units of 50 cavalry were ordered to be stationed at all the pueblos along the Alto Paraná, ready for action. Wisner was ordered to take 600 cavalry and 1,000 infantry into Candelaría, along with an artillery battery; to establish garrisons and patrol up to the River Uruguay; and to arrange to buy 2,000 muskets from Brazil. It was an effective operation, and reinforcements were sent in 1849. A cavalry regiment, a company of artillery, and an infantry battalion were stationed at San Miguel, with another artillery company, several warships, and three infantry battalions, together with parts of two cavalry regiments and other smaller units, at Tranquera. Altogether some 2,656 well armed men with 117 officers were established in the area.

By this time there were too few officers, the highest having the rank of colonel, but these were few and most lacked field experience. No higher rank was held, except by Francisco Solano López himself, who was a General and later became a Marshal. In 1864 the remainder of the officer corps comprised five colonels, two lieutenant-colonels, ten majors, 51 captains, 22 first-lieutenants, and several hundred junior officers and NCOs. There was no military manual, and the salaries of all ranks were low, but the equipment of the army's regular troops had by this time improved considerably. The infantry carried European muskets, the officers revolvers, and the cavalry sabres plus short carbines when available (replaced by lances in lancer regiments).

The infantry was organised into battalions, which at full strength were to number 1,000 men. The 1st Battalion at Asunción numbered 977 officers and men, with four rifle companies, a grenadier company, a light company, a reserve, and two small bands. However, this was an elite unit and no other battalion stood at full strength. The 2nd Battalion numbered just 483 officers and men, which was the strength of an average battalion at this time.

The cavalry had nominally three squadrons to a regiment, each of two or three companies. There were also several unattached squadrons on service on the frontier and elsewhere. The 1st Regiment had two squadrons of three companies each, plus a large staff, and numbered 355 officers and men. The other regiments

Posed photograph of a Brazilian cavalry officer with a captured Paraguayan soldier. (Courtesy of the Arquivo Historico do Exercito, Rio de Janeiro)

connected by train to Asunción. On 2 April General Robles was named commandant of the camp. There were other military camps used for the training of troops but this was by far the largest.

By December 1864, 30 infantry battalions, 23 cavalry regiments, and four artillery regiments each of 18 field-pieces, had completed their training. The infantry and cavalry units were numbered 1–30 and 1–23 respectively. The Naval Battalion was by this time composed of six infantry companies and an artillery company. Each infantry battalion was likewise composed of six companies of 100 men each, of which the 1st, 2nd, 3rd, and 4th companies were designated grenadiers, while the 5th and 6th were designated *cazadores*, or light companies. When on a war footing, each company was to be increased to 120 men.

The cavalry regiments were made up of four squadrons with 100 men in each. On mobilisation these troops were issued with the 20,000 muskets that Carlos António López had bought from Brazil during 1845–50, surplus from the war against Rosas of Argentina. Only three infantry battalions were armed with percussion cap muskets (sometimes referred to as Witon rifles), the rest having flintlock muskets, many produced by Dupont. The 6th Infantry Battalion was later equipped with cutlasses, captured in Corrientes, as sidearms, which were more often used as machetes. Lances and sabres for the cavalry were in the process of being produced in factories at Ibycuí, only 2,000 sabres being available, and flintlock carbines were issued when available. The Presidential Escort contained only 250 men, but these were armed with rifled carbines made by Turner. The Regiment of Dragoons 'Acá-verá' ('Golden Heads') was also issued with this rifled carbine.

Prior to mobilisation the Paraguayan armed forces consisted of eight infantry battalions numbered 1–8 with 4,084 men, five cavalry regiments numbered 9–13 with 2,522 men, and two artillery regiments numbered 1–2 with 907 men. Following initial mobilisation these figures increased to: infantry 23,459 men (19,375 being mobilised), cavalry 13,228 men (10,706 being mobilised), and artillery 1,960 men (1,053 being mobilised). Officially, infantry battalions were supposed to contain 800 men, and cavalry regiments 500 men. Additional men – and boys – were mobilised as the war progressed, and various units are mentioned in reports for which I only have titles, such as the Guard Rifle Battalion, the Infantry Battalion Maestranza, the Acámoroti, San Isidoro, and Acáyvoti cavalry regiments, the Heavy Artillery Regiment, the Police Battalion, and the Mounted Police. In addition there were the Marine Infantry Battalion of 500 men and the Marine Artillery Battery.

Efraim Cardozo, in his *El Imperio del Brasil y el Rio de la Plata* (1961), states that at the beginning of 1864 the Paraguayan army's officers comprised one general, five colonels, two lieutenant-colonels, ten *sargento mayors*, 51 captains, and 22 first lieutenants.

Infantry battalions were organised into four rifle companies, a reserve company, a light company, a grenadier company, and two small bands. This organisation was replaced in newly raised battalions, which had four grenadier companies and two light companies per battalion. Cavalry regiments were normally composed of three squadrons of two or three

numbered around 200–300 men. Each unit had a rudimentary medical staff, tied to the Army Medical Service. This had a surgeon major, three surgeons holding the rank of captain, a pharmacist with the rank of lieutenant, and 43 other rank assistants. The Asunción Police Battalion was by now 576 strong.

In March 1864 the Army of Paraguay was distributed as follows:

– at Humaitá: the 1st Naval Battalion (called the Battalion Bogavante), the 2nd, 3rd, and 5th Infantry Battalions, the 10th Cavalry Regiment, and the 2nd Artillery Regiment.

– at Asunción: the 4th and 6th Infantry Battalions (the latter helped to man the telegraph posts at Villa Franca and Pilar), the 11th and 13th Cavalry Regiments, and the 1st Artillery Regiment. The 11th Cavalry Regiment was named 'Acá Carayá', and acted as the Presidential Escort.

– at Pátiño (Ypacaraí): the 7th Infantry Battalion (its men were working on an extension of the railway line).

– at Rosario: the 8th Infantry Battalion.

– at Concepción: the 9th and 12th Cavalry Regiments.

On 31 March that year López designated Cerro León as the training camp for the newly mobilised troops, and sent the 4th Infantry Battalion (under the command of Captain Cipriano Dávalos) and the 13th Cavalry Regiment (under the command of Captain Pedro Duarte) to organise it and to train the recruits, who were aged between 17 and 40. The site was well chosen, being

Table 10: The Paraguayan Army 1865–66

	Stationed (1865)	Commander (1866)	Generals	Field officers	Officers	Other ranks
Staff Corps			2	3	5	46
1st Inf Bn	Asunción	Lt-Col Domingo Resquin	–	1	9	751
2nd Inf Bn	Asunción	?	–	1	6	566
3rd Inf Bn	Humaitá	Lt Celestino Prieto	–	1	8	660
4th Inf Bn	Humaitá	Maj Ciprinao Dávalos	–	–	8	597
5th Inf Bn	Humaitá	?	–	?	?	?
6th Inf Bn	Alto Paraguay	Capt Santiago Florentino	–	1	10	640
7th Inf Bn	Alto Paraguay	S/Mayor António L. González	–	1	8	584
8th Inf Bn	Santa Teresa	Capt C. Baez	–	?	?	131
9th Inf Bn	Humaitá	S/Mayor Marcelino Coronel	–	–	5	502
10th Inf Bn	Miranda	Capt M. Mendez	–	–	8	223
11th Inf Bn	Humaitá	Capt Manuel Méndez	–	?	?	?
12th Inf Bn	Humaitá	Capt Eugenio López	–	–	5	447
13th Inf Bn	Cerro León	S/Mayor Manuel A. Giménez	–	–	5	320
14th Inf Bn	Cerro León	Capt Mereles	–	–	8	813
15th Inf Bn	Cerro León	Capt Campurno	–	1	3	809
16th Inf Bn	Cerro León	Lt Matino	–	–	5	820
17th Inf Bn	Cerro León	Capt Diogo Alvarenga	–	–	7	823
18th Inf Bn	Cerro León	Capt António Venegas	–	–	5	715
19th Inf Bn	Cerro León	Capt Leonardo Martínez	–	–	3	807
20th Inf Bn	Cerro León	Capt Justo Pastor Penayos	–	–	5	775
21st Inf Bn	Cerro León	Lt-Col José Osõrio	–	1	6	760
22nd In Bn	Cerro León	Lt Francisco Rojas	–	–	6	772
23rd Inf Bn	Cerro León	?	–	–	3	749
24th Inf Bn	Cerro León	Lt Agustin Moreno	–	–	6	782
25th Inf Bn	Humaitá	?	–	–	6	842
26th Inf Bn	Cerro León	?	–	–	8	794
27th Inf Bn	Asunción	Capt Bernardo Olmedo	–	–	8	778
28th Inf Bn	Pindo Poi	Lt Zorilla	–	–	13	812
29th Inf Bn	Humaitá	Capt Vincente Meza	–	–	8	599
30th Inf Bn	Gebiet (Alto Paraguay)	Capt Casimiro Báez	–	–	13	605
31st Inf Bn	Pindo Poi	Capt Ibanez	–	–	13	448
32nd In Bn	Villa Encarnación	Capt Avalos	–	–	6	794
33rd Inf Bn	Villa Encarnación	Capt Joel Rozario Tellez	–	–	11	449
34th Inf Bn	Cerro León	?	–	–	4	800
35th Inf Bn	Cerro León	?	–	–	6	419
36th Inf Bn	Asunción	Lt Pablo Carera	–	–	4	844
37th Inf Bn	Asunción	Capt José Orihuela	–	–	2	890
38th Inf Bn	Humaitá	Lt-Col Venancio Ortiz	–	?	?	?
39th Inf Bn	Humaitá	Lt-Col Angel Torres	–	?	?	?
40th Inf Bn	?	Maj José Díaz	–	?	?	?
41st Inf Bn	?	Capt Gabriel Sosa	–	?	?	?
42nd In Bn	?	Capt Francisco Correa	–	?	?	?
43rd Inf Bn	?	?	–	?	?	?
44th Inf Bn	Humaitá	Maj Hilario Marcó	–	?	?	?
1st Cav Regt	Humaitá	Maj Fidel Valiente	–	1	7	330
2nd Cav Regt	?	?	–	?	?	?
3rd Cav Regt	Humaitá	Lt-Col Manuel Esinola	–	–	6	306
4th Cav Regt	Cerro León	Lt-Col Carlos Brito	–	1	5	218
5th Cav Regt	Asunción	?	–	–	7	430
6th Cav Regt	Concepción	Capt Gregoria Escobar	–	–	3	422
7th Cav Regt	Concepción	Capt Blas Obando	–	–	10	411
8th Cav Regt	Concepción	Capt Juan Bautista Aguerro	–	–	6	353
9th Cav Regt	Concepción	Capt Francisco Peralta	–	?	?	?
10th Cav Regt	Asunción	Capt Luis António Sosa	–	?	?	?
11th Cav Regt*	Cerro León	Capt Isidro José Arce	–	?	?	?
12th Cav Regt	Cerro León	Lt-Col Ignacio Aguilar	–	?	?	?
13th Cav Regt	Cerro León	Capt José M. Delgado	–	?	?	?

Table 10: The Paraguayan Army 1865–66 (continued)

	Stationed (1865)	Commander (1866)	Field Generals	officers	Other Officers	ranks
14th Cav Regt	Cerro León	Capt Rafael Insaurralde	–	–	4	520
15th Cav Regt	Cerro León	Capt Manuel Lezcano	–	–	3	513
16th Cav Regt	Cerro León	Capt Santiago Arevalo	–	–	4	510
17th Cav Regt	Cerro León	Capt António Olavarrieta	–	–	4	486
18th Cav Regt	Cerro León	Lt-Col Marcelino Vázquez	–	–	4	491
19th Cav Regt	Pilar	Lt-Col Albertan Marin	–	–	6	488
20th Cav Regt	Pilar	Lt Fortunato Montiel	–	1	5	491
21st Cav Regt	Pilar	Capt José de Jesus Páez	–	–	6	485
22nd Cav Regt	Cerro León	Capt Gregorio Escobar	–	–	4	505
23rd Cav Regt	Cerro León	Lt-Col. Eduardo Correa	–	–	5	512
24th Cav Regt	Pindo Poi	?	–	1	6	539
25th Cav Regt	Pilar	S/Mayor M. Núñez	–	–	6	471
26th Cav Regt	Pindo Poi	Lt-Col Melitón Taboada	–	–	4	561
27th Cav Regt	Villa Encarnación	Maj López	–	–	2	279
28th Cav Regt	Villa Encarnación	Capt Centurion	–	–	5	527
29th Cav Regt	Cerro León	Capt Donato Servin	–	–	3	511
30th Cav Regt	?	Lt Manuel Rojas	–	?	?	?
31st Cav Regt	?	Capt Bernardo Amarilla	–	?	?	?
32nd Cav Regt	?	Lt-Col Tomas Ferreira	–	?	?	?
33rd Cav Regt	?	Capt Manuel Coronel	–	?	?	?
34th Cav Regt	?	Lt-Col Bonifactio Amarillia	–	?	?	?
36th Cav Regt	?	Capt Pedro Avalos	–	?	?	?
37th Cav Regt	?	Lt-Col Francisco Medina	–	?	?	?
40th Cav Regt	?	Capt Nazario Gimenez	–	?	?	?
46th Cav Regt	Ribera	Capt R. Prieto	–	?	?	?
Detachment	Miranda	?	–	?	?	?
1st Arty Regt	Asunción	S/Mayor Francisco Roa	–	–	11	429
2nd Arty Regt	Humaitá	Col J.M. Bruguez	–	–	6	461
3rd Arty Regt	Humaitá	?	–	?	?	?
4th Arty Regt	Humaitá	?	–	?	?	?
Fortress Arty Regt	Humaitá	Lt-Col J. Balbuena	–	?	?	?

*'Acá Caraya' (Presidential Escort).
S/Mayor = *Sargento Mayor*.

Sources for this information are Jürg Meister's *Francisco Solano López* (1987) and Victor Ayala Queirolo's 'Campaña de Mato Grosso', in *Historia Paraguaya* 11 (1966). The units strengths given are from 1865.

companies each, but a number of unattached squadrons also served, especially on the frontier, without regimental affiliation.

By March 1865 a further six infantry battalions and eight cavalry regiments had been organised, the additional infantry battalions being the 31st, 32nd, 33rd, 41st, 42nd, and 43rd, and the cavalry regiments the 26th, 28th, 35th, 36th, 37th, 38th, 39th, and 46th.

The garrison of Humaitá in 1865 was composed of the 1st, 2nd, 3rd, 5th, 9th, 12th, 13th, 18th, 19th, 20th, 22nd, 23rd, 25th, 26th, 29th, 34th, 35th, 36th, 37th, 38th, and 39th Infantry Battalions, plus the 1st, 3rd, 4th, 8th, 10th, 11th, 13th, 14th, 15th, 16th, 17th, 19th, 20th, 21st, 22nd, 23rd, and 25th Cavalry Regiments, with two artillery regiments.

FIGURES

Sources for the drawings in this section are: prints in the Museo Historico Nacional, Rio de Janeiro; contemporary newspaper prints; an illustration by B. Acosta Periodico entitled 'El Cabichu' and an illustration by Y. Aquino entitled 'Carga Caballeria Paraguaya', both in the Biblioteca Nacional, Buenos Aires; a painting by Francsico Fortuny in the Museo Historical Nacional, Buenos Aires; *Essai Historique sur la Revolution du Paraguay et le Gouvernement Dictatorial du Docteur Francia* by M.M. Rengger and Longchamps (1829); *Paraguay's Autonomous Revolution 1810–1840* by Dr Richard Alan White (1978); *Nights on the Rio Paraguay* by Albert Amerlan (1902); *The Rise and Fall of the Paraguayan Republic 1800–1870* by John Hoyt Williams (1979); the letters of John Parish Robertson and his brother William; various articles by Nick Dore published in *El Dorado*, journal of the South and Central American Military Historians Society; *Soldados de la Memoria: Imágenes y Hombres de la Guerra del Paraguay* by Miguel Andel Cuarterolo (2000); illustrations by Alberto del Pino Menck; and *Las Fuerzas Armadas (F.F.A.A.)* by Luis Vittone (1969).

215. INFANTRY CAPTAIN c.1863 *Morrion* black felt, top and bottom bands gold lace, gilt chin-scales, unit badge, and plume holder, black leather visor. The plume

Contemporary engraving of a Paraguayan sentry sticking to his post, come what may, based on a painting by Néstor González. (Author's collection)

has a red top, white centre, and blue bottom. Tunic is dark blue, with collar, cuffs, and cuff bar all red piped white, gilt buttons. Wais:-sash is red with gold lace tassels. Trousers dark blue, shoes black. Sword scabbard brass, gilt hilt, black waistbelt and sword slings. The waist-sash is all that identifies him as an officer. Note the tunic cord, which could be part of an award.

216. INFANTRY COLONEL c.1863 *Morrion* as per Figure 215, but note vertical side edging in black leather, also cap lines and flounders in gold lace. Tunic dark blue with red collar and cuffs, epaulettes gold lace, cuff and collar lace also gold, turnbacks red piped white, front of coat piped white, gilt buttons. Trousers red with gold lace stripe, waist-sash crimson with gold lace tassels. Black waistbelt, sword slings, and shoes. Brass scabbard with gilt sword hilt.

217. CAVALRY CAPTAIN c.1863 Kepi dark blue with red piping, black visor and chinstrap. Tunic dark blue, collar dark blue, gilt buttons, gold lace shoulder straps. White shirt, red trousers with gold lace side stripes, black boots, waistbelt and sword slings. Brass scabbard, gilt hilt.

218. AIDE-DE-CAMP This is Colonel José M. Aguilar, ADC to Marshal López in the pre-war period, commander of all cavalry regiments of the 'Division del Sud' in the Corrientes Campaign, and commander of the cavalry in the column of Colonel José E. Díaz and Hilario Marcó at Tuyuti on 24 May 1866. He was killed at Cerro Corá in March 1870. Hat black with white lace, national cockade on side (see caption to Figure 224), blue-white-red feather plume. Dolman red, collar and cuffs blue, gold lace on chest and sleeves, gilt buttons. Breeches white, waist-sash crimson with gold lace fringe, boots black with gold lace tops. Waistbelt and sword slings black leather, gilt fittings, gold lace sword knot, brass sword scabbard, gilt hilt. Sabretache red centre with blue piping, wide gold lace surrounding edge, central device (possibly the national coat of arms) in gold lace.

219. CAVALRY OFFICER 1866 From a picture of the First Battle of Tuyuti. Kepi black, ribbon in national colours around bottom, white metal fleur-de-lis badge, black leather visor and chinstrap. Jacket is red with black chest braid and cuff lace, cuffs red, collar red with black lace edge, buttons gilt. Trousers dark blue with double red stripes. Pouch belt, waistbelt, and sword slings white leather. Steel sword scabbard, white sword knot, brass hilt.

220. TROOPER, 'ACÁ-VERÁ' DRAGOON REGIMENT Taken from a woodcut print published in the *Jornao do Rio* in October 1864. Shako black felt with top and bottom bands in gold lace, black peak and chinstrap. Blouse red with black collar, cuffs, shoulder patches, pocket flaps, and button section. Trousers are white. Black boots and waistbelt, brass buttons and buckle, steel sword scabbard, brass sword hilt.

It is noted by George Thompson that because of its close proximity to the President, the Presidential Guard Cavalry Regiment 'Acá Carayá' made a good target for Allied artillery, and that since Lopez was extra careful 'that the enemy should not know where he was ... he abolished the brass helmets of his guard and also its banner'. It would appear from this note that the 'Acá Carayá' regiment was issued with the normal cavalry kepi after the first battle of Tuyuti. Its uniform consisted of a tunic of *punzó* (deep scarlet), white breeches, and horse grenadier boots. The helmets they had worn until this time were of brass with a flowing horsehair crest, the sides of the helmet having the red-white-blue national colours painted on them in vertical stripes.

221. GENERALS Detail 221a wears a dark blue tunic with red collar and epaulette board, gold lace and gold bullion epaulette fringe; while 221b wears a blue shell jacket with red collar and gold lace.

222. ENGINEER OFFICER All-blue uniform and kepi with gold lace, black collar and centre to shoulder bars. Waistcoat and trousers also blue. Black leather waistbelt and sword slings. Scabbard steel, gilt hilt.

223. INFANTRY OFFICER Kepi with red top and band, gold lace on band, piping, and rank lace, black leather visor and chinstrap, gilt button. Tunic dark blue with red collar and cuffs, both with gold lace rank,

Fig 215   *Fig 216*   *Fig 217*   *Fig 218*

shoulder bars red with gold lace edging, gilt buttons, red piping to front of tunic. Trousers white with red side stripes, boots black. Waistbelt black leather with gilt buckle. Gilt sword hilt with gold lace sword knot.

224. INFANTRY PRIVATE *Morrion* black with national cockade and ribbon. The cockade consisted of a red centre, surrounded by white, then a blue edge, but it is sometimes illustrated in modern books with red on the outer edge and blue in the centre. Ribbon was red at the top, white in the middle, and blue at the bottom. Blouse red with black collar, cuffs, and button stripe. Trousers white. Leather straps are white with black leather ammunition pouch and bayonet scabbard with brass fittings. An Argentine description (in Albert Amerlan's

Nights on the Rio Paraguay) of a meeting between two groups of infantrymen the day before the peace meeting of López and Mitre states that 'the Paraguayans ... with the exception of the commanding Lieutenant, were without shoes and trousers – a veritable lot of "sansculottes". Their whole dress consisted only of a red woollen blouse with black collar and trimmings, a belt with a cartridge box attached and a cap of leather, on the rim of which the national colours, red, white and blue, were painted in oil.'

225. INFANTRY PRIVATE 1869 *Morrion* black, black leather visor and chinstrap, ribbon and cockade as per Figure 224. Coat red, collar, cuffs, and shoulder straps also red. Trousers white. Crossbelts white leather,

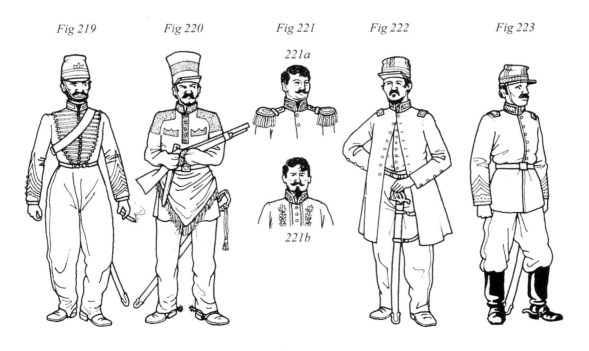

Fig 219   *Fig 220*   *Fig 221*   *Fig 222*   *Fig 223*

221a

221b

177

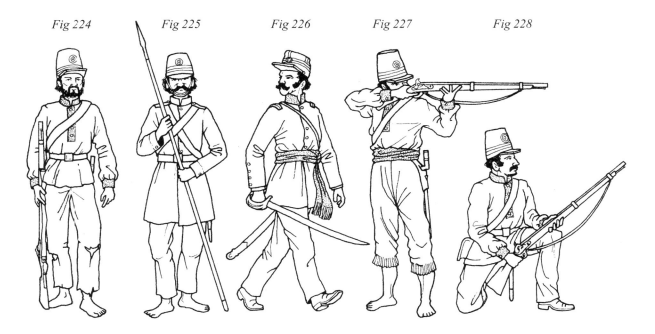

Fig 224   Fig 225   Fig 226   Fig 227   Fig 228

waistbelt black leather with brass buckle; the hilt of his attached sidearm is of natural wood. Since this private is armed with a spear his unit would appear to have been short of muskets.

226. INFANTRY OFFICER Kepi bright blue with gold lace and front star, black peak. Tunic medium blue with red collar and waist-sash, gilt buttons and shoulder bars. White trousers. Sword sling white leather, scabbard black leather with gilt fittings, gilt sword hilt. It should be noted that as the war progressed many officers were seen wearing the red blouses and white trousers of the other ranks, the only distinctions being their gold lace decorated kepi, pistol, and sometimes a sword.

227 & 228. INFANTRY PRIVATES 1866 These two regular infantrymen come from the painting 'Batalha di Curupayty' by Vijiera (1887), in the Museo Historico Nacional, Rio de Janeiro. Figure 227 has a bright blue shako with cockade and ribbon in the national colours (cockade: red centre-white-blue edge; ribbon: red top, white centre, blue bottom), black peak. Blouse bright blue with red collar, cuffs, button stripe, and waist-sash, brass buttons. *Calzoncillo*-style trousers white, crossbelt white leather. Figure 228's uniform is in the same colours, although he has a longer blouse and proper white trousers. White leather crossbelt and waistbelt, black leather ammunition pouch and bayonet scabbard with brass fittings, black shoes. Sir Richard Burton describes Paraguayan infantry drums as being 'with tricolour bands and inscribed: Republico del Paraguay – Vencer o morir.'

229 & 230. MILITIA INFANTRY PRIVATES Figure 229's shako is as per that of Figure 224, except that the cockade is replaced by three vertical white lines which are supposed to represent three feathers, although it would appear that the contemporary artist did not know what they represented. Blouse red with reinforced seams along shoulder and front, trousers white. Black leather waistbelt, sidearm belt, and scabbard, with brass belt buckle and fittings. Figure 230 substitutes a white cloth

chiripá for the trousers. Black leather waistbelt, belly ammunition pouch, backpack, backpack slings, and sidearm scabbard, with brass fittings. Blanket roll is brown.

231 & 232. MILITIAMEN Figure 231 has a shako as per Figure 224. White shirt, a grey blanket with red and white stripes, and a blue *chiripá* with black and red stripes. He is armed with a locally produced sword with wooden handle. Figure 232's shako is like that of Figure 229, and his *chiripá* is beige with wide green and thin red lines. Hanging from a black strap round his neck is a white bone amulet engraved with a cross.

233. MILITIA OFFICER Shako as per Figure 224. Blouse red, trousers brown, boots black. Waistbelt and sword slings black leather. Scabbard black leather with gilt fittings and sword hilt.

234. MILITIA CAVALRY TROOPER Shako as per Figure 229. Shirt red, *calzoncillo*-style trousers white. Notice he has tie-up cords rather than a belt, and wears an engraved cross amulet as per Figure 232. His wooden lance has a steel blade.

235. CAVALRY TROOPER Hat white straw with red sweatband, jacket red with collar and cuffs also red, trousers white, boots black with steel spurs. Black waistbelt with brass buckle, sword hilt brass with black grip, scabbard steel with white sword knot.

236. MILITIA CAVALRY OFFICER Shako as per Figure 224. Shirt white, *calzoncillo*-style trousers white, waist-sash blue/grey with red stripes, spurs steel on brown leather toeless socks. Shabraque is light brown with red outer edge. His lance pennon is in the national colours (red top, white centre, blue bottom).

237. REGULAR CAVALRY TROOPER *Morrion* red with national cockade and ribbon, black visor. Blouse red, *chiripá* blue, *calzoncillos* white linen. Blanket roll

Fig 229   Fig 230   Fig 231   Fig 232   Fig 233

dark blue. The original shows his shabraque as red. Black leather belts and straps, footwear as Figure 236.

238. MILITIA CAVALRY TROOPER Shako red, ribbon in national colours, stylised painted white feathers as described under Figure 229, black peak. Shirt is red, *chiripá* yellow/green with alternating red and green stripes, waist-sash dark brown. Note the bolas tied around his waist. Footwear as per Figure 236. The original depicts him mounted, with black fur over brown blanket shabraque. The flag he carries consists of red

(top), white (centre), and blue (bottom) horizontal stripes, with in the centre a red star with a red device above it, surrounded by green laurel branches on a white field piped red. Paraguayan units were issued with regimental and battalion standards, which were based on the national flag with the unit name or number on a streamer/tassel. Many were captured during the war, but I have not seen any, nor even illustrations of them, in museums.

239 & 240. INFANTRY PRIVATES 1869 These two

Fig 234   Fig 235   Fig 236   Fig 237

figures represent the general appearance of Paraguayan soldiers on the battlefield towards the end of the war, often famished and with few clothes, but always keeping their weapons and ammunition pouches close at hand. Contemporary newspaper illustrations show a hotchpotch of clothing being worn at this time. Figure 239 wears a white shirt and what look like rolled up trousers, while Figure 240 has his red shirt with blue cuffs tied around his waist. How clean and in what condition such pieces of clothing actually were can only be imagined. Their *morrions* are a smaller version of that worn by Figure 227, in the same colours, although the cockades have blue in the centre. A photograph of Paraguayan prisoners of war shows many of them wearing straw hats, plus some soft kepis, a *morrion*, felt hats, and a top hat (I think the top hat is made of straw rather that felt); this could indicate that, having lost their official hats, the prisoners either made their own from straw or, if they had money, bought felt hats from their Brazilian guards. Albert Amerlan says that Paraguayan soldiers seen at San Fernando in 1868 'walked around almost naked. The skin of an animal, for the sake of decency slung around the hips, constituted the uniform. A belt with the cartridge box and the keen-edged macheta was buckled around the waist. Every Paraguayan, besides, carried two leather thongs around his neck. To one was fastened the picture of his patron Saint and the other a comb. A military regulation compelled every soldier to comb himself three times a day – a wise precaution under the circumstances, and the rule was rigorously enforced. A leather cap, the only piece of the uniform which the state was now able to provide, covered the head.'

241. ARTILLERYMAN 1866 *Morrion* as per Figure 225, although it has been noted that the artillery sometimes wore a fleur-de-lis in the national colours instead of the normal national cockade, with blue being on the right-hand side, then white, then red. The blouse is red with black collar, button fly, and cuffs, buttons brass. The *chiripá* is cream with blue stripes, and a brown leather apron is worn around the waist. Waistbelt and slings white leather.

A contemporary watercolour by José Ignacio Garmendia shows a garrison artillery unit in action at Humaitá. He depicts an officer wearing a red soft kepi with gold lace and black visor, a red blouse, and blue trousers tucked into black boots. The crew all wear high *morrions* with the national ribbon at the base, some without the national cockade. Blouses are either red or white. It would appear that one gunner is an NCO or junior officer, as he has a sword and is ranging the gun for the next shot, but wears a *morrion*, a red blouse, and blue trousers. Of the other three crew members, one wears white trousers as per Figure 224, another a multi-coloured *chiripá* which ends three inches above the ankles, and the last short grey trousers which either reach to the knees or are rolled up like those of Figure 229.

There were two types of artillery in the Paraguayan army, one for garrisons and the other for campaign service. The campaign artillery, comprising light horse-drawn guns, was made up of three regiments with four batteries in each, and six cannon in each battery. It was at the Battle of Riachuelo that the 2nd Horse Artillery Regiment under the command of Lieutenant-Colonel José Maria Bruguéz won the first Paraguayan commemorative medal of the war.

APPENDICES

A: THE USE OF CIVILIAN ATTIRE

Readers will have noticed that a number of the illustrations in this book include elements of civilian dress worn alongside official issue items. For instance, although the Paraguayan Army began the war with a uniform that relied basically on a red blouse and black *morrion*, trousers were often replaced by the more popular civilian *chiripá*. Whether this happened only after clothing supplies ran out, or occurred prior to this situation arising, I cannot say. It is equally hard to be sure if the men of a unit were all issued with trousers of the same colour after the first year of the war. Certainly after the second year it would appear that Paraguayan other ranks began to wear whatever items of clothing they could find, a red or white blouse becoming the most common upper body items to be seen on the battlefield, men of the same unit being illustrated wearing both. Later even shirts became hard to find. Thompson says that Argentine and Brazilian uniforms were taken off the dead after the Battle of Curupaytí and re-used by the Paraguayans.

As for the Allies, the issue of proper uniforms to their various battalions and regiments appears to have been maintained throughout the war, although from looking at the few campaign photographs it is clear that the cut and fit of their blouses left a lot to be desired. On the other hand, if we use photographs as a source it is clear that the officers of a unit might be seen in a variety of dress codes on the same day. A photograph of the Paraguayan Legion under Colonel Federico Báez, serving with the Allies, shows six officers all wearing kepis, whose jackets vary from the blue blouse type with chest pockets and no cuff lace, to blue jackets with pointed cuffs with rank lace. One wears a shell jacket with French-style arm rank lace and baggy trousers tucked into short boots, while another wears a full dress uniform with gold epaulettes, arm length rank lace, and trousers with side stripes that look white but could be gold. Others wear normal blue trousers with shoes or a baggy variety tucked into riding boots or high cavalry boots of soft leather. In other words, all six officers wear entirely different modes of uniform.

Another photograph of Brazilian officers in camp shows a variety of official uniforms worn with a selection of trouser colours, waistcoats, shirts, ties, and even a poncho. Although the majority wear kepis wide-brimmed felt hats are on show too. A photograph of the Conde d'Eu with his staff corps taken in 1869 shows them wearing a mixture of civilian and military-styled frock coats, with white, blue, and grey trousers worn either with shoes or tucked into riding boots. Their hats are either kepis with or without a white cloth cover, straw or felt civilian hats, and in one case a white Carlist-style beret. There are 13 men in this photograph, and all of them appear to be wearing different clothes. Seven look like army officers, one a naval officer, and the other five are dressed as civilians, including the Conde.

It is a pity that there are not as many photographs of men taken on campaign during this war as there are for other major conflicts of the mid-19th century, such as the Crimean War and the American Civil War. There are a number of studio photographs used as calling cards by officers, but these invariably depict the type of uniform worn in the city before going to war, and give no idea of how they would have looked in winter or after two years on campaign. I haven't seen a photograph of an officer in a civilian jacket, but everything else would have found its way to the front for the officer corps, so it seems likely that some did wear them. Even without them, the many different styles of official-issue jackets that were available gave a rather un-uniformed look to the officer corps as a whole.

Also strongly represented amongst troops from southern Brazil, Uruguay, or Argentina during this period was the dress of the gaucho. Often men accustomed to wearing this form of apparel when at work on the range or pampas could not adapt to the orthodox military dress codes that prevailed within the standing armies. This is why some units of volunteer cavalry wore a mixture of both, regulation boots and trousers being the items of official-issue clothing most often discarded. In addition, the gaucho's loose-fitting blouse was not only far more comfortable in the summer than a military tunic, but was cheaper to manufacture. Numerous examples of such mixed attire can be found amongst the figure drawings in

Argentine officers, unit unknown, photographed in 1867. The two men on the left are in civilian dress. (Courtesy of the Archivo General de la Nacion, Buenos Aires)

this book. Note too the use of ponchos amongst some officers and mounted troops in place of the more usual European-style riding overcoat.

Paraguayan troops likewise adopted many features of their own civilian dress, which, even though there were many similarities to gaucho costume – such as *calzoncillos* and *chiripá* – cannot be included under the same heading These latter items of dress were in use amongst all of the warring nations, but were of a noticeably different style in Paraguay – see Figures 227, 234, 236 and 237. The waistcloth worn by the soldiers depicted in Figures 231, 232, 238, and 241 actually resembles a kilt more than a *chiripá*.

B: NAVAL UNIFORMS

Information on the naval uniforms for all four countries mentioned in this work during the period 1826–70 is not as complete as I would wish it to be. I have seen only one set of regulations for this period, this, dated 1852, being for Brazilian officers. A few contemporary portraits exist of Brazilian and Argentine naval officers, but I have not seen any for Uruguay or Paraguay. Other than these, photographs provide a few uniforms, and some paintings of naval battles have proved helpful.

Sources for the drawings in this section are: *Soldados de la Memoria: Imágenes y Hombres de la Guerra del Paraguay*, by Miguel Angel Cuarterolo (2000); paintings by Candido López; *Riachuelo*, by Didio Costa (1952); *Relíquias Navais do Brasil*, published by the Ministerio da Marina (1983); 'River Passage Sought', by Ricardo Bonalume Neto, in *Military History Magazine* (March 2000); an Argentine magazine article by Juan Carlos Herken Krauer, entitled 'La Cobertura de la Guerra de la "Triple Alianza" por *The Times*'; Decreto N.1,829, de 4 de Outubro de 1856 (Rio de Janerio, 1856); *El Ejercito de la Epopeya, vol.1*, by Benigno Riquelme Garcia (1976); *História da Guerra entre a Tríplice Aliança e o Paraguai*, by General Augusto Tasso Fragoso (1934); the *Autobiography of Giuseppe Garibaldi* (1889); and *Los Corsarios de Artigas*, by Agustin Beraza (1978).

242. PARAGUAYAN NAVAL LIEUTENANT c.1860
From a photograph of Lieutenant H. Andrés. He is carrying a fore-and-aft bicorne with black lace edge, gilt button, and cockade holder of three cords. The jacket is in the style of a shell jacket with a rounded bottom, no turnbacks being visible. It is double-breasted, with nine gilt buttons on either side, a gold lace epaulette and contre-epaulette (the fine fringed, not bullion, epaulette on the left shoulder), gold lace epaulette straps, blue cuffs with two rank stripes, collar also blue with an embroidered fouled anchor on each side. The bottom of the jacket has a white lace edge, possibly in reality the edge of a waistcoat worn underneath it. The blue trousers are cut in the baggy French style. The waistbelt is gold lace with a round buckle, sword slings gold lace, scabbard black leather with gilt fittings, white grip to gilt hilt, and gold lace sword knot.

A photograph of Naval Captain Remigio Cabral shows him wearing the same uniform but with a black leather waistbelt and a peaked cap, while a photograph of Commodore Pedro Ignacio Meza shows him wearing a double-breasted frock coat with epaulettes, white shirt with black bow tie, a heavily laced kepi, a black leather

waistbelt, and blue trousers with a gold lace stripe. Luis Vittone, in *Las Fuerzas Armadas* (1969), mentions that the naval *petit uniforme* or everyday wear consisted of a black *camiseta* blouse with red *vivos* (piping).

Paintings of Paraguayan sailors invariably show them wearing the same clothing as their infantry comrades. One painting shows many sailors swimming ashore without shirts on; others are wearing red or white shirts, while one is shown wearing a light blue shirt. How much reliability can be placed on such paintings, produced after the war by artists who had not seen action, is open to question.

243. BRAZILIAN SAILOR At the beginning of the Paraguayan War the Brazilian Navy had 298 officers and 2,031 other ranks stationed in the River Plate area. By 10 April 1867 this figure stood at 551 officers and 2,367 other ranks, and during the period from April 1867 to April 1868 a further 20 officers and 2,358 other ranks were sent into the combat zone. The period April 1868 to April 1869 saw a further 117 officers and 1,063 other ranks despatched there. Brazilian naval casualties for the war were 52 officers and 208 other ranks killed in action, and 121 officers and 1,450 other ranks dead from other causes, making a total of 1,831 fatalities out of a total of 8,805 all ranks sent into the combat zone.

Contemporary photographs of Brazilian naval officers of the Paraguayan War era are few: I only have one, used by Admiral Francisco Manoel Barroso as a visiting card. In it, he is shown wearing a double-breasted dark blue frock coat with waistcoat, white shirt, black bow tie, and dark blue trousers with no side stripe. The cuffs of his coat show his rank. His cap, placed on the table next to him, is not a kepi but is more on the lines of a British naval peaked cap of this period. It is dark blue with a black silk band, black leather visor, gold lace chinstrap, and a naval badge within laurel leaves above the visor. Most other surviving illustrations dating to this war consist of engravings and photographs reproduced in contemporary newspapers. One, again of Admiral Barroso, shows him in the same cap, frock coat, shirt, and tie, but with the coat buttoned up and a waistbelt and sword, the belt having a round gilt buckle. Chest buttons are in five double rows, the fifth pair being under the waistbelt. Other illustrations show double-breasted frock coats being worn with or without epaulettes (full dress or undress).

The 1856 Naval Dress Regulations show a long tailed coat for use in No.1 and No.2 dress, while in No.3 dress a double-breasted frock coat was worn, with rank only on the cuffs. When fully buttoned up the frock coat had two rows of seven buttons. The cap illustrated with these regulations is not the one found in later photographs, being a soft-sided cap rather than the later stiff-sided type. Three portraits that show officers' uniforms are those of Admiral Luiz da Cunha Moreira, Viscount of Cabo Frio, painted 1860; Vice Admiral Joaquim José Ignácio, painted 1869; and First-Lieutenant Joaquim Antonio Cordovil Mauriti, painted 1873. Although depicted in the naval frock coat, the last is shown wearing epaulettes; this could be as a result of a new No.2 uniform regulation passed during the 1860s. All these paintings show that the cuff rank insignia had changed since the 1856 regulations.

Figure 243 comes from an illustration of Sailor

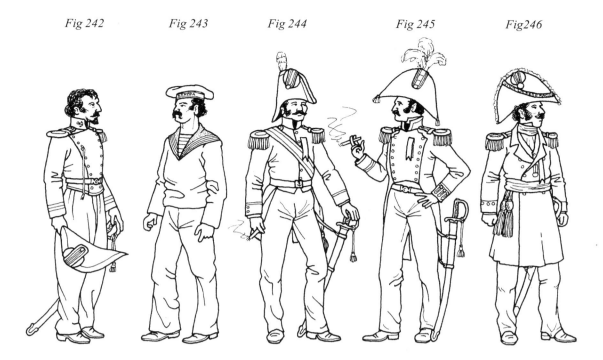

Fig 242   Fig 243   Fig 244   Fig 245   Fig246

First Class Marcílio Dias, which shows him wearing what must be parade dress. His blue sailors' cap has a white tally ribbon with the name 'PARNAHYBA' on it in black. His blouse and bib are also blue, the bib having a border of four white lines but no cords worn under it. A white vest with pale blue lines is worn under the blouse. Other sources for Brazilian sailors' dress are the paintings by Candido López, in which sailors are depicted in both summer and winter dress. They wear white trousers with either a white or blue shirt/blouse and brimmed black hats (possibly of blackened straw as in the British Royal Navy); sometimes no hat is worn. In another painting a naval officer is shown wearing an unbuttoned frock coat, white waistcoat, and white trousers. His cuff lace is of two gold rank bands. He has gold lace shoulder bars and a white cover to his peaked cap. In the painting of the ironclad *Rio de Janeiro* sinking, Brazilian sailors are shown wearing dark blue blouses with dark blue bibs, dark blue sailor hats with white tally ribbons, and light blue trousers. Another painting, of the Battle of Riachuelo, shows Brazilian sailors wearing dark blue trousers with a white blouse with blue cuffs, a blue bib with white piping, and a dark blue sailor hat.

Commander A.J. Kennedy wrote in his book *La Plata, Brazil and Paraguay during the Present War* (1869) that 'The Brazilian seaman appeared to be chiefly Negroes and Mulattos [i.e., of mixed race parentage]. The Marines were a fine looking body of men dressed in a tunic, shako and blue trousers, they were armed with smooth bored percussion muskets, but shortly afterwards received rifles.' When he saw the Brazilian Marines on parade at Corrientes in 1867 they were wearing 'brown overcoats, blue tunics with red facings, they were armed with musket, sword-bayonet etc.'

Shawn C. Smallman, in his *Fear and Memory in the Brazilian Army & Society* (2002), writes that racism was rife in the Brazilian armed services: 'The situation was far worse in the Navy, however, where many officers were descended from slaveholders ... Most sailors were ex-slaves, or the sons of slaves, who entered the navy against their will. Officers used leather whips tipped with metal balls to whip sailors for even minor infractions. Unable to leave the service until they completed 15 years in the ranks, sailors endured racial abuse and physical violence.' Although the time frame for this observation is 1888–1910, I am sure that the same comments are valid for the Paraguayan War period, when slavery still existed and blacks were used to compensate for losses suffered in the fighting.

244–252. ARGENTINE SAILORS Paintings of Admiral William Brown in his earliest uniform (1826–27) show him wearing a dark blue jacket with high collar, also dark blue, the collar having a wide gold lace edge and a gilt button, with folded lace along the collar of the same type as the edge. The bullion epaulettes have dark blue shoulders piped in gold lace, with a gilt button and gold lace holding strap, and a fouled anchor design on the half-moon. The jacket has straight, narrow, medium blue lapels edged in gold lace, with seven rows of double lace with a gilt button at each end, arranged as downward-pointing paired chevrons, the edge and button lace being the same pattern as the collar. Lining to the collar is the same as the lapel colour. He also wears a white shirt and black bow tie. In a later painting depicting the same uniform the cuffs are shown dark blue, possibly with three horizontal gilt buttons on the top cuff edge; in addition the Admiral wears a light blue waist-sash. Another portrait shows him in a black bicorne with gold lace laurel and oak leaf lace on its edge, gold bullion tassels on either end, and a national cockade held in place by a gold cord and gilt button. The tailcoat, collar, cuffs, turnbacks, and trousers are all dark blue, the collar, cuffs, and turnbacks with laurel and oak leaf gold lace embroidery, gold bullion epaulettes with dark blue boards edged in gold lace, and gold lace holding straps. The lapels have a thin gold lace edge with a single row of

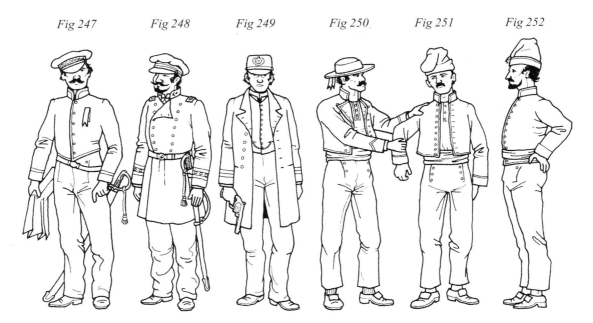

laurel and oak leaves embroidered within the border. The trousers have wide, gold lace side stripes. The gold lace waistbelt and sword slings have a laurel and oak leaf design and square gilt buckle. Scabbard is black leather with gilt fittings, and the waist-sash under his tailcoat is sky blue-white-sky blue with gold tassels.

By a decree of 5 August 1826 the facing colour for Naval officers became sky blue. An illustration by Fernandez Rivas shows a *sargento mayor de marina* (commander) wearing a black bicorne with gold lace tassels at either end and a gilt button with wide gold lace to keep the national cockade in place. His tailcoat is medium blue (possibly dark blue to begin with), with collar, cuffs, and lapels all sky blue edged with wide gold lace. The cuffs have three horizontal gilt buttons under lace, and six buttons per side are shown on the lapels. The black waistbelt with gilt 'S' buckle is worn over the seventh pair of lapel buttons. Rank insignia at this time was similar to that of the Army, the officer depicted by Rivas having a contre-epaulette on the right shoulder and a fringed epaulette on the left, the boards of the epaulettes being gilt metal in the style of scales. Turnbacks are white, trousers white for full and dark blue for service dress, and shoes black. The black leather scabbard has gilt fittings, and the gilt sword hilt has a gold lace knot.

In the 1830s the Navy's facing colour was changed to red, and officers' uniforms were in the style of the Army. The illustrations of officers from which Figures 244 (1833) and 245 (1836) are taken – depicted in, respectively, service and full dress – show both in black bicorne hats with a cockade and gold lace cord holder and button. Figure 245 also has gold lace tassels fore and aft of the hat plus three red feathers as a plume above the cockade. Figure 244's service tailcoat is a surtout style with red collar and cuffs, white turnbacks, and gold lace epaulettes. The collar is plain red, while the cuffs have a horizontal gold lace rank band with two gilt buttons on the back seam. Shirt, waistcoat, and trousers are white, cravat, shoes, waistbelt, and sword slings black. The scabbard is black leather with gilt fittings, the sword having a gilt single bar hilt and a red knot. A white-red-blue sash with gold lace tassels is worn over the right

shoulder. The full dress tailcoat is much the same, except that the collar has a wide gold lace edge, there are three horizontal buttons under the rank bands on the cuffs, and the lapels are red with two rows of seven gilt buttons. Both figures wear the mandatory red ribbon.

During the 1840s uniforms continued to resemble those of the Army, but with the Navy's red facings. A painting of Colonel of Navy (Captain) Joaquim Hidalgo dating to 1847, on which Figure 246 is based, shows his black bicorne with the normal national cockade and gold lace holding cord with button, but with red feather trim along its crest and a red ribbon from back to front bearing the inscription 'VIVA LA FEDERACION' in black. He wears an early style civilian frock coat in blue with gold lace epaulettes and gilt buttons. The cuffs have no lace, only a row of three buttons. He wears a white shirt with black cravat, a red waistcoat, a red waist-sash with gold lace toggles and red fringe, and white trousers and gloves. The scabbard is black leather with gilt fittings.

Another illustration (Figure 247) shows an officer in service dress in 1845. This has him wearing a soft, dark blue peaked cap with a gold lace sweatband. His dark blue shell jacket has red collar and cuffs with gold lace edging, red piping, and gilt buttons. Trousers are dark blue, waistbelt and sword slings white leather with gilt fittings, sword knot and chest ribbon red. Rank distinctions were worn on the cuffs, while epaulettes were used with full dress and by senior officers. It was during this decade that the latter began to wear just epaulette holding straps on their service uniform.

A new uniform regulation came into effect on 27 October 1853. The frock coat was now an official part of the uniform, to be used for service and parade dress. Junior officers wore rank lace on their cuffs and rank shoulder bars, while senior officers wore epaulettes on full uniforms. An illustration of an officer in service uniform in 1854 (see Figure 248) has him wearing a soft peaked cap in dark blue, with two rows of rank lace around the sweatband, and a black leather peak and chinstrap. His frock coat is dark blue with a double row of seven buttons. The shoulder bars are dark blue with a gold lace edge, the collar has a gold-embroidered anchor, and the cuffs have two bands of rank lace with three buttons between them. He also wears a white shirt and black tie, dark blue trousers with gold side lace, black shoes, waistbelt, and sword slings, and black leather scabbard with gilt fittings. These regulations were not changed until 1872.

A photograph used as a calling card in 1865, on which Figure 249 is based, shows a Naval officer in a dark blue frock coat with dark blue waistcoat and trousers, and a white shirt with a black tie. Buttons are gilt. His only rank insignia is the lace around his cuffs. His cap is dark blue with a gilt naval badge and a black leather visor and chinstrap, with gilt buckle and buttons. He wears a pocket watch in his waistcoat.

Naval other ranks dress followed European trends, when financial resources were sufficient to kit out the men. An illustration of a harbour crewman in 1830 (Figure 250) has him wearing a uniform not unlike that of a British sailor, with a black oilskin hat and a blue shell jacket with red half-lapels, white piping, and brass buttons, the red collar being a stand-up type three fingers high with a blue lining, the edges piped white. The blue pointed cuffs are also piped white. The vest or shirt and trousers are white, the waist-sash red. Shoes are black with a brass buckle. When carried, the sidearm was suspended from a white leather crossbelt.

Another sailor, this time dating to 1840 (Figure 251), is shown wearing a red knitted cap and a red shell jacket with red collar and cuffs, both piped white, the jacket also being piped white. Buttons are brass. A red vest is worn with a red woollen waist-sash. Trousers are white, shoes black. Once again, a white leather crossbelt was used for the sidearm. A sailor in 1844 (Figure 252) is depicted in a red cloth stable cap with a red tassel and

white piping. His shell jacket is dark blue with red collar and cuffs, the collar piped white, and brass buttons. Trousers are dark blue, waist-sash red, shoes and scabbard black, the latter with brass fittings.

The only illustrations of Argentine sailors during the Paraguayan War which I have seen are among the paintings of Candido López. In these they are depicted looking more like local fishermen and ferrymen than part of the official Argentine Navy, unlike the Brazilian sailors shown in other paintings by López. The Argentine Navy nevertheless had dress regulations for its other ranks along the same basic lines as prevailed in Europe during this period.

As regards the third navy of the Triple Alliance, it should be noted that no Uruguayan warships took part in any naval actions during the Paraguayan War, but a number of Uruguayan vessels served in the capacity of transports. The ships mentioned as transporting the troops for Flores' Army of the Vanguard were the transports *Roman* and *Uruguay*, both steamers, the transport *Emperatriz* (from its name probably a Brazilian vessel), and the gunboat *Curumania*, which I believe to have been Uruguayan. It would appear that some of the Uruguayan navy's transport steamers were subsequently utilised in the movement of supplies up and down the Rio de la Plata. Adrian English (1984) says that 'a total of 18 vessels of various sizes, most of them transports, were used in the Triple Alliance war.'

It is known that Artigas raised a naval force from privateers while in power, and later in the 1840s a naval force was also in existence. Garibaldi was initially given command of the Montevideo Squadron, which in 1842 consisted of the corvette *Constitución*, the brigantine *Pereira*, and the transport-schooner *Procida*.

BIBLIOGRAPHY

Academia Paraguaya de la Historia, *Historia Paraguaya* vols XI, XII, & XXI, Asunción 1966, 1967, & 1984.

Akers, Charles Edmond. *A History of South America* (3rd edition), London 1930.

Amerlan, Albert. *Nights on the River Paraguay: Scenes of War and Character Sketches*, London 1902.

Andrea, Julio. *A Marinha Brasileira*, Rio de Janeiro 1955.

Angel Scenna, Miguel. 'Origenes de la Guerra del Paraguay', *Todo es Historia* 136–137, 1978.

Araripe, General Alencar. 'Guerra do Paragua', *Revue International de Historie Militaire* 11, 1960.

La Armada en la Vida de los Argentinos: Evocacion Hacia el Futuro, Buenos Aires 1985.

Atlas Historico Militar Argentino, Buenos Aires 1970.

Aveiro, Colonel Silvestre. *Memorias Militares 1864–1870*, Asunción 1970.

Avenel, Jean-David. *L'Affaire du Rio de la Plata 1838–1852*, Paris 1998.

Bacchi, Reginaldo J. da Silva. Letter published in *Military History*, October 2002.

Baez, Adolfo I. *Yatayty-Cora*, Buenos Aires 1929.

— *Tuyuty*, Buenos Aires 1929.

Balaguer, José. 'La Legion Francesa en el Sitio de Montevideo 1843–1852', *El Dorado* IV, No.6, 1992.

Barroso, Gustavo, and Rodrigues, J. Washt. *Uniformes do Exercito Brasileiro*, Rio de Janeiro and Paris 1922.

Beattie, Peter M. 'The Paraguayan War Victory Parade', in Levine, R.M., and Crocitti, J.J. (eds.) *The Brazil Reader: History, Culture, Politics*, London 1999.

Beaufort, L. de, and Peyrot, Daniel. 'La Bataille d'Ituzaingo 1827', *Club Français de la Figurine Historique* 1, 2001.

Bejarano, Brigadier-General Ramon Cesar. *Panchito López*, Asunción 1970.

Beraza, Agustin. *Las Banderas de Artigas*, Montevideo 1957.

— *Los Corsarios de Artigas*, Montevideo 1978.

Beraza, Luis Fernando. 'Secuelas Diplomaticas de la Guerra de la Triple Alianza', *Todo es Historia*, April 1990.

Berra, F.A. *Bosquejo Historico de la Republica Oriental del Uruguay* (4th edition), Montevideo 1895.

Beverina, Colonel Juan. *La Guerra del Paraguay: Resumen Historico 1865–1870*, Biblioteca del Suboficial vol.118, Buenos Aires 1943.

— *Las Campañas de los Ejércitos Libertadores 1838–1852*, Buenos Aires 1974.

Biblioteca General Artigas, vol.48. *Major Romeo Zina Fernández de Potrero de Perez a Santos Lugares*, Montevideo 1959.

— vol.50. *Artigas Homenaje en el 150th Aniversario de las*

Piedras, Montevideo 1961.

— vol.56. *Ley Organica Militar No.10,757, Vol.I*, Montevideo 1972.

Bogart, Charles H. 'Confederate Sailor at War in South America', *Sea Combat* 2, No.6, December 1979.

Borges Fortes, C.M.G. Diogo. 'Passo da Patria, Uma Operacao Anfibia', *Revue International de Historie Militaire* 11, 1960.

Box, Pelham Horton. *The Origins of the Paraguayan War* (2 vols), Illinois 1927.

Bradford Burns, E. *A History of Brazil*, New York 1970.

Bray, Colonel Arturo. *Solano López: Soldado de la Gloria y del Infortunio* (3rd edition), Asunción 1984.

Brock, Darryl E. 'Naval Technology from Dixie: James Hamilton in the War of the Triple Alliance', *Américas*, July/August 1994.

Brodsky, Alyn. *Madame Lynch and Friend*, London 1975.

Burton, Captain Richard F. *Letters from the Battle-Fields of Paraguay*, Tonbridge 2001.

Campana de Cepeda, Anos 1858–59, Archivo del General Mitre, Buenos Aires 1912.

Canard, B.; Cascallar, J.; and Gallegos, M. *Cartas Sobre la Guerra del Paraguay*, Buenos Aires 1999.

Cancogni, Manlio, and Boris, Ivan. *El Napoleon del Plata: Historia de Una Heroica Guerra Sudamericana*, Barcelona 1972.

Cardozo, Efraim. *El Imperio del Brasil y el Rio de la Plata*, Buenos Aires 1961.

Carvalho, Affonso de. *Caxias*, Rio de Janeiro 1976.

Celesia, Ernesto. *Rosas: Aportes Para su Historia, vols.1–2*, Buenos Aires 1968.

El Centinela: April 25th 1867–Dec. 26th 1867, Buenos Aires 1964.

Centurión, Juan Crisostomo. *Mocedades: Los Sucesos de 'Puerto Pacheco'*, Asunción 1975.

Chaves, Julio Cesar. *El General Díaz*, Buenos Aires and Asunción 1957.

Chiavenatto, Julio José. *Genocidio Americano: A Guerra do Paraguay*, São Paulo 1987.

Circulo Militar. *Reseña Historica de la Infanteria Argentina*, Buenos Aires 1969.

— *Reseña Historica y Organica del Ejército Argentino* (3 vols), Buenos Aires 1971.

Colman, Major Saturnino. *Endayo de Historia Militar*, Montevideo 1930.

Cordeiro de Farias, General Gustavo. *Dicionario de Termos Militares: Portugues-Ingles*, Rio de Janeiro 1968.

Costa, Didio. *Riachuelo*, Rio de Janeiro 1952.

Cuarterolo, Miguel Angel. *Soldados de la Memoria: Imágenes y Hombres de la Guerra del Paraguay*, Buenos Aires 2000.

Cunninghame Graham, R.B. *Portrait of a Dictator*, London 1940.

Czech, K.P. 'Boys in Beards', *Military History*, August 1990.

Dallegri, Santiago. *El Paraguay y la Guerra de la Triple Alianza*, Buenos Aires 1964.

Damaria, Isidoro. *Anales de la Defensa de Montevideo 1842–1851, vols.1–4*, Montevideo 1887.

Davis, Arthur H. *Martin T. McMahon: Diplomatico*, Asunción 1985.

Díaz, Eduardo Acevedo. *Épocas Militares en los Paises del Plata*, Montevideo 1973.

Donato, Hernani. *Dicionario das Batalhas Brasileiras*, São Paulo 1987.

Dufort y Alvarez, A. *Invasion de Echague 'Batalla de Cagancha' 1839*, Montevideo 1894.

English, Adrian J. *Armed Forces of Latin America*, London 1984.

Escuela Naval. *Revista Militar y Naval* IV, Nos. 42, 43, and 44, 1924.

Ferrer Llul, Francisco. *Sinopsis Gráfica de la Historia Militar del Uruguay*, Montevideo 1975.

Franco, Victor I. *General Patricio Escobar*, Asunción 1974.

— *La Sanidad en la Guerra Contra la Triple Alianza*, Asunción 1976.

Ganson de Rivas, Barbara. *Los Consecuencias Demograficas y Sociales de la Guerra de la Triple Alianza*, Asunción 1985.

Garcia Mellid, Atilio. *Proceso a los Falsificadores de la Historia del Paraguay, vols.I–II*, Buenos Aires 1980.

Garibaldi, Giuseppe. *Autobiography of Giuseppe Garibaldi, vols.1–3*, London 1889.

Gill Aguinaga, Juan B. *La Asociacion Paraguaya en la Guerra de la Triple Alianza*, Asunción 1959.

Gillingham, Harrold E. *South American Decorations and War Medals*, New York 1932.

Graham-Yooll, Andrew. *Small Wars You May Have Missed*, London 1983.

Greene, Jack, and Massignani, Alessandro. *Ironclads at War: The Origin and Development of the Armored Warship, 1854–1891*, Pennsylvania 1998.

'La Guerra del Paraguay', *Mi Pais, Tu Pais* 95, 1970.

Guido, Horacio J. 'Triple Alianza: La Otra Guerra', *Todo es Historia* 288, June 1991.

Guido Spano, Carlos; Andrade, Olegario V.; Alberdi, Juan B.; and Seeber, Francisco. *Proceso a la Guerra del Paraguay*, Buenos Aires 1968.

Hooker, Terry D. 'Battle of Ituzaingo', *Military Modelling*, May 1990.

— 'The 1st Battle of Tuyuti', *Military Modelling*, September 1992.

Ireland, Gordon. *Boundaries, Possessions, and Conflicts in South America*, Harvard 1938.

Jefferson, Mark. *Peopling the Argentine Pampa*, American Geographical Society Research Series 16, New York 1926.

Jourdan, Emílio C. *História das Companhas do Uruguaï, Mato Grosso e Paraguaï* (3 vols), Rio de Janeiro 1893.

Kennedy, A.J. *La Plata, Brazil, and Paraguay during the Present War*, London 1869.

Kirkpatrick, F.A. *A History of the Argentine Republic*, Cambridge 1931.

Kolinski, Charles J. *Independence or Death!*, Miami 1965.

Kostianovsky, Olinda Massare de. *El Vice Presidente Domingo Francisco Sanchez*, Asunción 1972.

Kraay, Hendrik. '"The Shelter of the Uniform": The Brazilian Army and Runaway Slaves, 1800–1888', *Journal of Social History* 29, 1996.

— 'Slavery, Citizenship and Military Service in Brazil's Mobilization for the Paraguayan War', *Slavery and Abolition* 18, 1997.

Laing, E.A.M. 'Naval Operations in the War of the Triple Alliance 1864–70', *Mariners Mirror* 54, No.3, 1968.

Lello and Irmao (eds.). *A Guerra do Paraguai: Enciclopedia Pela Imagem*, Porto, 1970.

Levine, Robert M. *Historical Dictionary of Brazil*, New Jersey 1979.

Lopacher, Tobler. *Un Suizo en la Guerra del Paraguay*, Asunción 1969.

López, Candido. *Catalog of Paintings*, Buenos Aires 1998.

Luqui-Lagleyze, Julio Mario. *Los Cuerpos Militares en la Historia Argentina 1550–1950*, Buenos Aires 1995.

Lynch, John. *The Spanish American Revolutions 1808–1826*, London 1973.

— *Massacre in the Pampas, 1872: Britain and Argentina in the Age of Migration*, Oklahoma 1998.

Macaulay, Neil. *Dom Pedro: The Struggle for Liberty in Brazil & Portugal 1798–1834*, Durham, USA, 1986.

Machado, Carlos. *Historia de los Orientales*, Montevideo 1986.

MacDermont, B.C. 'Riachuelo 1865', *War Monthly* 57, October 1978.

McLynn, F.J. 'Consequences for Argentina of the War of Triple Alliance 1865–1870', *The Americas* XLI, No.1, July 1984.

Maia, Lieutenant-Colonel Jorge. *A Invasão de Mato Grosso*, Rio de Janeiro 1964.

Maiz, Fidel. *Etapas: De Mi Vida: Contestacion a las Imposturas de Juan Silvano Godoy*, Asunción 1919.

Majoribanks, Alexander. *Travels in South and North America*, London 1853.

Marti Garro, Colonel Pedro E. *Historia de la Artilleria Argentina*, Buenos Aires 1982.

Martin, D. Moyano. 'A Sanguinary Obsession', *Military History Quarterly* 4, No.4, 1992.

Masterman, George Frederick. *Seven Eventful Years in Paraguay*, London 1869.

Meister, Jurg. *Francisco Solano López 1864–70*, Osnabruck 1987.

'Memorias do Almirante Barao de Teffe: A Batalha Naval do Riachuelo' *História Marítima do Brasil* XXI, 1965.

'Memorias do Grande Exercito Aliado Liberador do Sul da America 1851–1852' *Biblioteca do Exercito* 151–152, 1950.

Ministério da Marinha. *Relíquias Navais do Brasil*, Rio de Janeiro 1983.

'Mitre: Quien Fue?', *Todo es Historia* 198, 1971.

Morin, C.J. 'La Legion Francesa en la Defensa de Montevideo 1843–52', *Le Briquet* 3, 1983.

Motta Teixeira, R. 'Brazilian and Paraguayan Uniforms of the 1865–70 War', *Tradition* 69, 1974.

Nabuco, Joaquin. *La Guerra del Paraguay*, Buenos Aires 1977.

Nalot, Colonel. 'Liasons Tactiques et Communications dans la Guerre de Triple Alliance', *Revue International de Historie Militaire* 11, 1960.

Natalicio González, J. *Solano López: Diplomatico*, Asunción 1948.

Neto, Ricardo Bonalume. 'River Passage Sought', *Military History Magazine*, March 2000.

Norman, C. A. Articles published in *El Dorado*, the Journal of the South and Central American Military Historians Society.

O'Leary, Juan E. *Lomas Valentinas*, conference booklet, Asunción 25 December 1915.

— *El Libro de los Heroes*, Asunción 1922.

— *El Heroe del Paraguay*, Montevideo 1930.

— *El Paraguay en la Unification Argentina: La Guerra de la Triple Alianza*, Asunción 1976.

Olmos Gaona, Alejandro. 'Alberdi y Dos Diplomaticos Paraguayos', *Todo es Historia* 209, 1984.

Otheguy, V.A. Rodriguez, and Dellepiane, N. *Cabalgando en la Frontera: Historia de los Blandengues Orientales*, Montevideo 1997.

Ouro Preto, Visconde de. *A Marinha d'Outr'ora*, Rio de Janerio 1895.

Page, Thomas J. *La Plata, the Argentine Confederation and Paraguay*, New York 1859.

Palleja, Leon de. *Diario de la Campaña de las Fuerzas Alliadas Contra el Paraguay*, Biblioteca Artigas vols.29–30, Montevideo 1960.

Palombo, Guillermo. *El Regimiento de Artilleria Ligera en la Guerra Con Brasil*, Buenos Aires 1995.

Paraguay and the Alliance Against the Tyrant F.S. López, New York 1869.

Partes Oficiales: Documentos Relativos a la Guerra del Paraguay, Buenos Aires c.1930.

Penalba, José Alfredo Fornos. 'Draft Dodgers, War Resisters and Turbulent Gauchos: The War of the Triple Alliance Against Paraguay', *The Americas* 38, 1982.

Pereira, Carlos. *Solano López y Su Drama*, Buenos Aires 1962.

Pereira de Sousa, Captain Octaviano. 'Historia da Guerra do Paraguai', *Rivista do Instituto Historico e Geographico Brasileiro*, 1930.

Perez Acosta, Juan F. *Carlos António López: 'Obrero Maximo'*, Asunción 1948.

Peterson, Harold F. 'Efforts of the United States to Mediate in the Paraguayan War', *Hispanic American Historical Studies* 12, 1932.

Pezzarini, Heriberto Maria. *Batalla de Arroyo Grande*, Santa Fe, Argentina, 1974.

Phelps, Gilbert. *Tragedy of Paraguay*, London 1975.

Pillar, General Olyntho. *Patronos das Forças Armadas*, Rio de Janeiro 1982.

Pino Menck, Alberto del. 'El Batallon "Florida" 1865–70: Brigada de Infanteria Oriental', *Master Magazine*, 1986.

— '1865: Serie 1a' eight coloured postcards showing various Uruguayan uniforms of the war, Asociacion do Uniformologia del Uruguay 1986.

— 'La Compagnie des Zouaves de Bahia 1865–6', *Le Bivouac* 3, 1988.

— 'Javier López, Fotografo de Bate & Cia en el Guerra del Paraguay', *Boletin Historico del Ejército* 68, 1997.

Pitaud, Henri. *El General Caballero*, Asunción 1976.

Plá, Josefina. *The British in Paraguay 1850–1870*, Richmond 1976.

Pomer, Leon. *La Guerra del Paraguay: Gran Negocio!*, Buenos Aires 1968.

Queirolo, Victor Ayala. 'Campaña de Mato Grosso', *Historia Paraguaya* 11, 1966.

Queiroz Duarte, General Paulo de. *Os Voluntários da Pátria na Guerra do Paraguai*, Rio de Janeiro 1983.

Quiroga, Carlos B. *Sarmiento: Hacia la Reconstruccion del Espiritu Argentino*, Buenos Aires 1961.

Ramirez Juarez, Lieutenant-Colonel Evaristo. *Las Banderas del Combate de la 'Vuelta de Obligado'*, Buenos Aires 1935.

Rebaudi, A. *Guerra del Paraguay: Un Episodio 'Vencer o Morir!'*, Tucuman 1918.

Rengger and Longchamps, M.M. *Essai Historique sur la Revolution du Paraguay et le Gouvernement Dictatorial du Docteur Francia*, Stuttgart 1829.

Reseña Historica de la Infanteria Argentina, Buenos Aires 1969.

Reseña Historica y Organica del Ejército Argentino, vols.1–3, Buenos Aires 1971.

Resquín, General Francisco Isidoro. *Datos Historicos de la Guerra del Paraguay Contra La Triple Alianza*, Asunción 1971.

Revista Militar, 'Uniformes Historicos', five plates of

Paraguayan uniforms, Asunción 1990.

Riquelme Garcia, Benigno. *El Ejército de la Epopeya, vols.1–2*, Asunción 1976.

Rivas, Jorge H. Fernández. 'Uniformes Navales, 1805–1854', set of 12 coloured plates showing Argentine Naval uniforms, Buenos Aires 1971.

Robertson, J.P. and W.P. *Letters on Paraguay, vols.1–2*, London 1839.

Rolon Medina, Anastasio. *El Lustro Terrible: Version Cronografica de la Guerra del Paraguay Contra La Triple Alianza*, Asunción 1964.

— *El General Bernardino Caballero*, Asunción 1965.

Ruas Santos, Francisco. *Osõrio*, Rio de Janeiro 1967.

Saldías, Adolfo. *Los Números de Línea del Ejército Argentino, vols.1–2*, Buenos Aires 1912.

Sanchez Quell, H. *Los 50,000 Documentos Paraguayos Llevados al Brasil*, Asunción 1976.

Sarmiento, D.F. *Life in the Argentine Republic in the Days of the Tyrants: Or Civilization and Barbarism*, New York 1868.

Scheina, Robert L. *Latin America: A Naval History, 1810–1987*, Annapolis 1987.

Schneider, L. *A Guerra da Tríplice Aliança* (3 vols), Rio de Janeiro 1925.

Sharples, John. 'The Great Paraguayan War 1864–70', *Wargames Illustrated* 43 and 45, 1991.

Silveira de Mello, General Raul. *Corumba, Albuquerque e Ladario*, Rio de Janeiro 1966.

Smallman, Shawn C. *Fear and Memory in the Brazilian Army & Society, 1889–1954*, North Carolina 2002.

Spence Robertson, William. *Rise of the Spanish-American Republics*, New York 1965.

Stanbury, H.F. 'Documents Relating to the First Military Balloon Corps Organized in South America: The Aeronautic Corps of the Brazilian Army 1867–68', *Hispanic American Historical Review* XIX, 1939.

Tasso Fragoso, General Augusto. *História da Guerra entre a Tríplice Aliança e o Paraguai, vols.1–5*, Rio de Janeiro 1934.

Tate, Edward Nicholas. 'Britain and Latin America in the Nineteenth Century: The Case of Paraguay, 1811–1870', *Ibero-Amerikanisches Archiv* 5, 1979.

Taunay, Visconde de. *A Retirada da Laguna*, São Paulo 1952.

Thompson, George. *The War in Paraguay*, Tonbridge 1996.

Tjarks, German O.E. 'Nueva Luz Sobre el Origen de la Triple Alianza', *Historia Paraguaya* 21, 1984.

Tobler, Alfred (ed.). *Ulrich Lopacher's Soldaten-Leben*, Heiden 1912.

Udaondo, Enrique. *Uniformes Militares Usados en la Argentina desde el Siglo XVI Hasta Nuestos Dias*, Buenos Aires 1922.

Vale, Brian. *Independence or Death: British Sailors and Brazilian Independence*, London 1996.

— *A War Betwixt Englishmen: Brazil Against Argentina on the River Plate 1825–1830*, London 2000.

Versen, Max von. *Historia da Guerra do Paraguai*, São Paulo 1976.

Vittone, Colonel Luis. *Tres Guerras, Dos Mariscales, Doce Batallas*, Asunción 1967.

— *Las Fuerzas Armadas (F.F.A.A.)*, Asunción 1969.

Walford, A. 'General Urquiza and the Battle of Pacon (1861)', *Hispanic American Historical Review* XIX, 1939.

Warship International XIV No.2, 1977, letters section (data on the Naval side of the Paraguayan War).

Washburn, Charles A. *The History of Paraguay* (2 vols), Boston 1871.

Whigham, Thomas Lyle. 'The Iron Works of Ybycue: Paraguayan Industrial Development in the Mid-Nineteenth Century', *The Americas* 35, 1978.

White, Dr Richard Alan. *Paraguay's Autonomous Revolution 1810–1840*, University of New Mexico 1978.

Wilgus, A. Curtis. *South American Dictators during the First Century of Independence*, New York 1963.

Williams, John Hoyt. 'Foreign Tecnicos and the Modernization of Paraguay 1840–1870', *Journal of Interamerican Studies and World Affairs* 19, 1977.

— *The Rise and Fall of the Paraguayan Republic 1800–1870*, University of Texas Press, Austin 1979.

— 'A Swamp of Blood: The Battle of Tuyuti', *Military History*, April 2000.

Williams, Mary Wilhelmine. *Don Pedro the Magnanimous: Second Emperor of Brazil*, New York 1978.

Winter, Frank H. *The First Golden Age of Rocketry: Congreve and Hale Rockets of the Nineteenth Century*, Washington DC 1990.

Young, H.L. *Eliza Lynch, Regent of Paraguay*, London 1966.

Zenequelli, Lilia. *Crónica de una Guerra la Triple Alianza, 1865–1870*, Buenos Aires 1997.

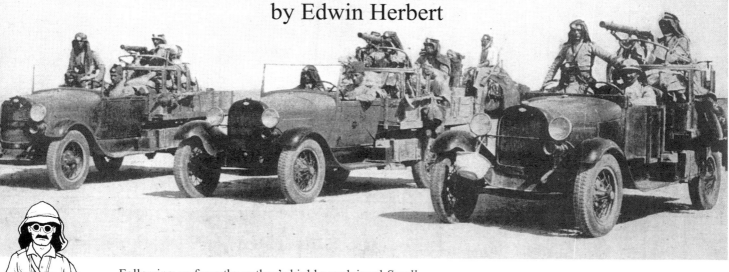

Interwar Colonial Campaigns in Africa, Asia, and the Americas

Risings and Rebellions 1919–39
by Edwin Herbert

Following on from the author's highly-acclaimed *Small Wars and Skirmishes*, this volume covers the most significant 'small wars' of the interwar period up to the Italian occupation of Abyssinia in 1935-36. Coverage is also extended to include the activities of 'social bandits' as exemplified by Lampião, the 'Bandit King of Brazil' since the tactics employed by both sides in such conflicts often mirrored those utilised in colonial warfare. It was during this period that the colonial powers embarked on a process of consolidation (often euphemistically referred to at the time as 'pacification') involving the controversial use of aerial policing and the deployment of large regular armies, supported by aircraft, armoured cars and tanks to counteract the increasing firepower, nationalistic fervour, and religious fanaticism of irregular forces and their increasingly successful guerrilla tactics. Its title *Risings and Rebellions* reflects this

change in emphasis compared with earlier colonial campaigns. Indeed, the sheer scale of such wars as the risings against the French and Spanish in Morocco and the Italian reconquest of Libya takes them out of the category of 'small wars' altogether. The author illustrates the

main types of campaign involved, the organisation of forces, the effects of new weaponry, and the tactics that the indigenous peoples adopted to counter the technology of the colonial invaders, particularly by applying their local knowledge of some of the most difficult terrain in the world. In most cases at least one battle or skirmish is described in some detail in order to give a flavour of the significant factors involved. Sketch maps are provided to indicate the main campaigns and illustrations show the uniforms or tribal dress of the combatants. There are also appendices on weaponry and equipment, mechanised vehicles, communications, and the use of aircraft, armoured cars and tanks. Political background and campaign narratives, organisation, tactics and terrain, dress and weapons, command and control, and historical effects. 137 figures, 36 illustrations, and 14 maps. 192 pages. ISBN-13: 978-1901543124.

FOUNDRY MINIATURES LTD. 24-34 St. Marks Street, Nottingham, NG3 1DE, United Kingdom Phone 0115 841 3000 Fax 0115 841 3250

FOUNDRY BOOKS

Colonial Armies

AFRICA 1850-1918

by Peter Abbott

In the second half of the 19th century, European-led columns began to fan out across the African continent from their coastal foothe smashing whatever forces could be brought against them, no matter how brave or determined the latter were. The process began at diffe

dates in different parts of the continent, but much of the main activity concentrated into the two decades between 1881 and 1902, subsequently accurately nicknamed the 'Scramble for Africa'. By 1914 the Europeans overrun the greater part of the continent, and, remarkably, had managed t so without clashing with each other in the process: conflict between them only occurred after 1914 because what was essentially a European power-struggle was inevitably projected on to the African landscape. The armies responsible for this extraordinary period of expansion have seldom been surveyed as a whole, and never in the organisational detail attempted here. As well as including an outline of the principal campaigns of the period, military historian Peter Abbott examines in detail the structure, dress and armament of the colonial armies fielded by the Congo Free State, the Belgian Congo, Great Britain, France, Germany, Italy, Portugal, and Spain, and includes in his text an unprecedented amount of order of battle material. Illustrations include 229 drawings of soldiers, 58 other illustrations, and two maps. 224 pages. ISBN 1-901543-07-2

FOUNDRY MINIATURES LTD. 24-34 St. Marks Street, Nottingham, NG3 1DE, United Kingdom Phone 0115 841 3000 Fax 0115 841

FOUNDRY BOOKS

Armies of the 19th Century

THE BRITISH IN INDIA 1826-59
by John French

all the military campaigns fought by the British during the 19th century, no area saw more conflict than the subcontinent of India. Dozens of counters, both great and small, involved many of its races as either friends or foes of Britain - indeed, it was not unusual for an area to furnish th ally and enemy at the same time! This volume covers the British, Indian and Anglo-Indian troops who fought for The Honourable East dia Company and Britain over the varied landscape of what is present day Afghanistan, India, Pakistan and Bangladesh, between the years 26 and 1859. The vast array of uniforms and dress worn by soldiers serving in India during this period is examined in detail, and extensive

information is also provided on regimental Colours. The book's nine chapters cover the campaign in Bhurtpore (1825-26); the Coorg campaign (1834); the First Afghan War (1839-42); the conquest of Sind (1843); the campaign against Gwalior (1843); the Sikh Wars (1845-46 and 1848-49); actions on the North-West Frontier (1849-58); the Santhal Rebellion (1855-56); and the Indian Mutiny (1857-59). Each of these chapters includes uniform information specific to the campaign covered, while that on the Indian Mutiny also includes details of Mutineer dress. Many orders of battle and battle-plans are also included. Illustrations comprise 199 drawings of troop types and flags, and 27 other illustrations and maps. 176 pages. ISBN 1-901543-11-0

UNDRY MINIATURES LTD. 24-34 St. Marks Street, Nottingham, NG3 1DE, United Kingdom Phone 0115 841 3000 Fax 0115 841 3250

FOUNDRY BOOKS

All the FOUNDRY books are A4 sized hardback with traditional linen and gilt binding. Each volume is the definitive work on its subject, fully illustrated comprehensively detailing organisation, tactics, dress, flags and weaponry.

SMALL WARS AND SKIRMISHES 1902-18:

Early Twentieth-Century Colonial Campaigns in Africa, Asia, and the Americas.

Written by Edwin Herbert, Illustrations by Ian Heath.
224 pages

Armies of the 19th Century
EAST AFRICA

by Chris Peers
Tribal and Imperial Armies in Uganda, Kenya, Tanzania and Zanzibar, 1800 to 1900—184 pages

Armies of the Nineteenth Century. The Armies of Asia:
BURMA AND INDO-CHINA

Written and Illustrated by Ian Heath
Burma; The Kingdom of Ava, The Kachins, The Karens, The Shan States, The Wa. Indo-China; Cambodia; The Lao States; Siam; Vietnam. 207 Pages

CENTRAL ASIA AND THE HIMALAYAN KINGDOMS
Written and Illustrated by Ian Heath
Bokhara, Chinese Turkestan, Kashgaria, Khiva, Khokand, Khotan, the Kirghiz, Kuldja, the Turcomans, Baltistan, Bhutan, Jammu and Kashmir, Ladakh, Nepal, Sikkim and Tibet, and details of their interaction with the British, Russian and Chinese Empires. This region was home to the celebrated "Great Game".
167 Pages

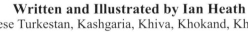

CHINA
Written and Illustrated by Ian Heath
Imperial China, the Boxer Rebellion, the Ever-Victorious Army, Formosa, the Mongols, the Miao Rebellion, Nien Rebellion, Panthay Rebellion, Taiping Rebellion and the Tungan Rebellions.
174 Pages

INDIA'S NORTH-EAST FRONTIER
Written and Illustrated by Ian Heath
The Abors, the Akas, Assam, Cachar, the Chin-Lushai, the Daflas, the Garos, the Khamtis, the Khasis, Manipur, the Mikirs, the Mishmis, the Nagas, the Singphos and Tripura. First ever in-depth study of a neglected theatre of British colonial conflict.
168 Pages

Armies of the Sixteenth Century
Written and Illustrated by Ian Heath:

THE ARMIES OF ENGLAND, SCOTLAND, IRELAND, THE UNITED PROVINCES, AND THE SPANISH NETHERLANDS 1487-1609
160 Pages

THE AZTEC & INCA EMPIRES, OTHER NATIVE PEOPLES OF THE AMERICAS, AND THE CONQUISTADORES 1450-1608
The Caribbean 1492-1603, Mesoamerica c.1450-1600, South America 1500-1600, North America 1497-1608 & Spanish America 1492-1600.
176 Pages

FOUNDRY MINIATURES LTD. 24-34 St. Marks Street, Nottingham, NG3 1DE, United Kingdom Phone 0115 841 3000 Fax 0115 841